RACE-ING JUSTICE,
EN-GENDERING POWER

RACE-ING JUSTICE, EN-GENDERING POWER

Essays on
Anita Hill,
Clarence Thomas,
and the
Construction
of Social Reality

Edited and with an Introduction by
TONI MORRISON

Pantheon Books, New York

Library of Congress Cataloging-in-Publication Data

Race-ing justice, en-gendering power : essays on Anita Hill, Clarence
    Thomas, and the construction of social reality / edited and with an
    introduction by Toni Morrison.
        p. cm.
     ISBN 0-679-74145-3
        1. Thomas, Clarence, 1948– . 2. Hill, Anita. 3. Judges—United
    States—Selection and appointment. 4. Afro-Americans—Social
    conditions. 5. Racism—United States. 6. Sexism—United States.
    I. Morrison, Toni. II. Title: Race-ing justice, en-gendering power.
    KF8745.T48R33 1992
    347.73'2634—dc20
    [347.3073534]   92-54119

Book design by Jo Anne Metsch
Manufactured in the United States of America
B98765432

CONTENTS

Introduction: Friday on the Potomac

I have never asked to be nominated. . . . Mr. Chairman, I am a victim of this process.

> —Clarence Thomas, Friday, October 11, 1991

It would have been more comfortable to remain silent. . . . I took no initiative to inform anyone. . . . I could not keep silent.

> —Anita Hill, Friday, October 11, 1991

At last he lays his head flat upon the ground, close to my foot, and sets my other foot upon his head, as he had done before; and after this, made all the signs to me of subjugation, servitude, and submission imaginable, to let me know how he would serve me as long as he lived.

> —Daniel Defoe, *Robinson Crusoe*

Clusters of black people pray in front of the White House for the Lord not to abandon them, to intervene and crush the forces that would prevent a black nominee to the Supreme Court from assuming the seat felt by them to be reserved for a member of the race. Other groups of blacks stare at the television set, revolted by the president's nomination of the one candidate they believed obviously unfit to adjudicate legal and policy matters concerning them. Everyone interested in the outcome of this nomination, regardless of race, class, gender, religion, or profession, turns to as many forms of media as are available. They read the *Washington Post* for verification of their dread or their hope, read the *New York Times* as though it were *Pravda,* searching between the lines of the official story for one that most nearly approximates what might really be happening. They read local papers to see if the reaction among their neighbors is similar to their own, or they try to figure out on what information their own response should be based. They have listened to newscasters and anchor people for the bits and bites that pointed to, or deflected attention from, the machinery of campaigns to reject or accept the nominee. They have watched television screens that seem to watch back, that dismiss viewers or call upon them for flavor, reinforcement, or routine dissent. Polls assure and shock, gratify and discredit those who took them into serious account.

But most of all, people talked to one another. There are passionate, sometimes acrimonious discussions between mothers and daughters, fathers and sons, husbands and wives, siblings, friends, acquaintances, colleagues with whom, now, there is reason to embrace or to expel from their close circle. Sophisticated legal debates merge with locker-room guffaws; poised exchanges about the ethics and moral responsibilities of governance are debased by cold indifference to individual claims and private vulnerabilities. Organizations and individuals call senators and urge friends to do the same—providing opinions and information, threatening, cajoling, explaining positions, or simply saying, Confirm! Reject! Vote yes. Vote no.

These were some of the scenes stirred up by the debates leading to the confirmation of Clarence Thomas, the revelations and evasions within the testimony, and by the irrevocable mark placed on those hearings by Anita Hill's accusations against the nominee. The points of the vector were all the plateaus of power and powerlessness: white men, black men, black women, white women, interracial couples; those with a traditionally conservative agenda, and those representing neoconservative conversions; citizens with radical and progressive programs; the full specter of the "pro" antagonists ("choice" and "life"); there were the publicly elected, the self-elected, the racial supremacists, the racial egalitarians, and nationalists of every stripe.

The intensity as well as the volume of these responses to the hearings were caused by more than the volatile content of the proceedings. The emptiness, the unforthcoming truths that lay at the center of the state's performance contributed much to the frenzy as people grappled for meaning, for substance unavailable through ordinary channels. Michael Rustin has described race as "both an empty category and one of the most destructive and powerful forms of social categorization." This paradox of a powerfully destructive emptiness can be used to illustrate the source of the confusion, the murk, the sense of helpless rage that accompanied the confirmation process.

It became clear, finally, what took place: a black male nominee to the Supreme Court was confirmed amid a controversy that raised and buried issues of profound social significance.

What is less clear is what happened, how it happened, why it happened; what implications may be drawn, what consequences may follow. For what was at stake during these hearings was history. In addition to what was taking place, something was happening. And as is almost always the case, the site of the exorcism of critical national issues was situated in the miasma of black life and inscribed on the bodies of black people.

It was to evaluate and analyze various aspects of what was and is happening that this collection suggested itself. The urgency of this project, an urgency that was overwhelming in November of 1991 when it began, is no less so now in 1992. For a number of reasons the consequences of *not* gathering the thoughts, the insights, the analyses of academics in a variety of disciplines would be too dire. The events surrounding the confirmation could be closed, left to the disappearing act that frequently follows the summing-up process typical of visual and print media. The seismic reactions of women and men in the workplace, in organizations and institutions, could be calmed and a return to "business as usual" made effortless. While the public, deeply concerned with the issues raised by the confirmation, waited for the ultimate historical account or some other text representing the "last word," there might not be available to it a more immediate aid to the reflective sorting out that subsequent and recent events would demand. Furthermore, the advancing siege upon American universities, launched by fears of "relevance" and change, has fostered an impression and atmosphere of scholarly paralysis, censorship, and intimidation. Yet residing in the academic institutions of the country are not only some of the most knowledgeable citizens, but also those most able to respond quickly with contextualized and intellectually focused insights. And insight—from a range of views and disciplines—seemed to us in low supply.

For insight into the complicated and complicating events that the confirmation of Clarence Thomas became, one needs perspective, not attitudes; context, not anecdotes; analyses, not postures. For any kind of lasting illumination the focus must be on the history routinely ignored or played down or unknown. For the kind of insight that invites reflection, language must be critiqued. Frustrating language, devious calls to arms, and ancient inflammatory codes deployed to do their weary work of obfuscation, short circuiting, evasion, and distortion. The timeless and timely narratives upon which expressive language rests, narratives so ingrained and pervasive they seem inextricable from "reality," require identification. To begin to comprehend exactly what happened, it is important to distinguish between the veneer of interrogatory discourse and its substance; to remain skeptical of topics (such as whether the "system" is "working") which pretend that the restoration of order lies in the question; to be wary of narrow discussions on the effectiveness or defect of the "process" because content, volatile and uncontextualized, cannot be approached, let alone adequately discussed, in sixteen minutes or five hundred words or less. To inaugurate any discovery of what happened is to be conscious of the smooth syruplike and glistening oil poured daily to keep the machine of state from screeching too loudly or breaking down entirely as it turns the earth of its own rut, digging itself deeper and deeper into the foundation of private life, burying itself for invisibility, for protection, for secrecy. To know what took place summary is enough. To learn what happened requires multiple points of address and analysis.

Nowhere, remarked an historian, nowhere in the debate before and during the confirmation hearings was there any mention, or even the implied idea, of the public good. How could there be, when the word "public" had itself become bankrupt, suffering guilt by association with the word "special," as the confusion of "public interest" with "special interest" proved. How could the notion of union, nation, or state surface when race, gender, and class, separately, paired, matched, and mismatched, collapsed in a heap or swinging a divisive sword, dominated every moment and word of the confirmation process?

For example, the nominee—chosen, the president said, without regard to race—was introduced by his sponsor with a reference to the nominee's laugh. It was, said Senator Danforth, second in his list of "the most fundamental points" about Clarence Thomas. "He is his own person. That is my first point. Second, he laughs. [Laughter] To some, this may seem a trivial matter. To me, it's important because laughter is the antidote to that dread disease, federalitis. The obvious strategy of interest groups trying to defeat a Supreme Court nominee is to suggest that there is something weird about the individual. I concede that there is something weird about Clarence Thomas. It's his laugh. It is the loudest laugh I have ever heard. It comes from deep inside, and it shakes his body. And here is something at least as weird in this most up-tight of cities: the object of his laughter is most often himself.''

Weird? Not at all. Neither the laugh nor Danforth's reference to it. Every black person who heard those words understood. How necessary, how reassuring were both the grin and its being summoned for display. It is the laughter, the chuckle, that invites and precedes any discussion of association with a black person. For whites who require it, it is the gesture of accommodation and obedience needed to open discussion with a black person and certainly to continue it. The ethnic joke is one formulation—the obligatory recognition of race and possible equanimity in the face of it. But in the more polite halls of the Senate, the laugh will do, the willingness to laugh; its power as a sign takes the place of the high sign of perfect understanding. It is difficult to imagine a sponsor introducing Robert Bork or William Gates (or that happy exception, Thurgood Marshall) with a call to this most clearly understood metonym for racial accommodation. Not simply because they may or may not have had a loud, infectious laugh, but because it would have been inappropriate, irrelevant, puzzling to do so.

But what was inappropriate, even startlingly salacious in other circumstances became the habitual text with this candidate. The *New York Times* found it interesting to include in that paper's initial story on the president's nominee a curious spotlight on his body. Weight lifting was among his accomplishments, said the *Times,* presciently, perhaps, since later on the candidate's body came violently into view. Of course, this may be simply a news account that aims to present an attractive image of a man about to step onto a national stage, yet a reference to a black person's body is de rigueur in white discourse. Like the unswerving focus on the female body (whether the woman is a judge, an actress, a scholar, or a waitress), the black man's body is voluptuously dwelled upon in biographies about them, journalism on them, remarks about them. "I wanted to find out," said Senator Pete Domenici, "as best I could what his life—from outhouse to the White House . . . has been like." With vulgar remarks like that in print, why wouldn't the public's initial view of this black nominee have an otherwise puzzling, even silly, reference to body-building? Other erstwhile oddities rippled through the media, glancing and stroking black flesh. President Bush probably felt he was being friendly, charmingly informal, when he invited this black man into his bedroom for the interview. "That is where Mr. Bush made the final offer and Judge Thomas accepted." To make Thomas feel at home was more important than to respect him, apparently, and the *Times* agreed, selecting this tidbit to report in an article that ended with a second tantalizing, not so veiled reference to the nominee's body. When asked by reporters whether he expected to play golf, "one of Mr. Bush's favorite sports," Thomas replied, "No. The ball's too small." Thomas's answer is familiar repartee; but the nuanced emphasis gained by the remark's position in the piece is familiar too. What would have been extraordinary would have been to ignore Thomas's body, for in ignoring it, the articles would have had to discuss in some detail that aspect of him more difficult to appraise—his mind.

In a society with a history of trying to accommodate both slavery and freedom, and a present that wishes both to exploit and deny the pervasiveness of racism, black people are rarely individualized. Even when his supporters were extolling the fierce independence and the "his own man" line about Clarence Thomas, their block and blocked thinking of racial stereotype prevailed. Without individuation, without nonracial perception, black people, as a group, are used to signify the polar opposites of love and repulsion. On the one hand, they signify benevolence, harmless and servile guardianship, and endless love. On the other hand, they have come to represent insanity, illicit sexuality, and chaos. In the confirmation hearings the two fictions were at war and on display. They are interchangeable fictions from a utilitarian menu and can be mixed and matched to suit any racial palette. Furthermore, they do not need logical transition from one set of associations to another. Like Captain Delano in *Benito Cereno,* the racist thinker can jump from the view of the slave, Babo, as "naturally docile, made for servitude" to "savage cannibal" without any gesture toward what may lie in between the two conclusions, or any explanation of the jump from puppy to monster, so the truth of Babo's situation—that he is leading a surreptitious rebellion aboard the slave ship, that he is a clever man who wants to be free—never enters the equation. The confirmation hearings, as it turned out, had two black persons to use to nourish these fictions. Thus, the candidate was cloaked in the garments of loyalty, guardianship, and (remember the laugh) limitless love. Love of God via his Catholic school, of servitude via a patriarchal disciplinarian grandfather, of loyalty to party via his accumulated speeches and the trophies of "America" on his office walls. The interrogator, therefore, the accusing witness Anita Hill, was dressed in the oppositional costume of madness, anarchic sexuality, and explosive verbal violence. There seemed to be no other explanation for her testimony. Even Clarence Thomas was at a loss to explain not her charges but why she would make them. All he could come up with is speculation on Professor Hill's dislike of "lighter-complexioned" women—meaning, one gathers, his marriage to a white woman. No other narrative context could be found for her charges, no motive except fantasy, wanton and destructive, or a jealousy that destabilized her. Since neither the press nor the Senate Judiciary Committee would entertain seriously or exhaustively the truth of her accusations, she could be called any number or pair of discrediting terms and the contradictions would never be called into question, because, as a black woman, she was contradiction itself, irrationality in the flesh. She was portrayed as a lesbian who hated men *and* a vamp who could be ensnared and painfully rejected by them. She was a mixture heretofore not recognized in the glossary of racial tropes: an *intellectual* daughter of black *farmers*; a *black female* taking *offense*; a black *lady* repeating *dirty words*. Anita Hill's description of Thomas's behavior toward her did not ignite a careful search for the truth; her testimony simply produced an exchange of racial tropes. Now it was he, the nominee, who was in danger of moving from "natural servant" to "savage demon," and the force of the balance of the confirmation process was to reorder these signifying fictions. Is he lying or is she? Is he the benevolent one and she the insane one? Or is he the date raper, sexual assaulter, the illicit sexual signal, and she the docile, loyal servant? Those two major fictions, either/or, were blasted and tilted by a factual thing masquerading as a true thing: lynching. Being a fact of both white history and black life, lynching is also the metaphor of itself. While the mythologies about black personae debauched the confirmation process for all time, the history of black life was appropriated to elevate it.

An accusation of such weight as sexual misconduct would probably have disqualified a white candidate on its face. Rather than any need for "proof," the slightest possibility that it was publicly verifiable would have nullified the candidacy, forced the committee members to insist on another nominee rather than entertain the necessity for public debate on so loathsome a charge. But in a racialized and race-conscious society, standards are changed, facts marginalized, repressed, and the willingness to air such charges, actually to debate them, outweighed the seemliness of a substantive hearing because the actors were black. Rather than claiming how certain feminist interests forced the confrontation, rather than editorializing about how reluctant the committee members were to investigate Anita Hill's charges publicly and how humiliated they were in doing so, it seems blazingly clear that with this unprecedented opportunity to hover over and to cluck at, to meditate and ponder the limits and excesses of black bodies, no other strategies were going to be entertained. There would be no recommendation of withdrawal by sponsor, president, senators, or anybody. No request for or insistence that the executive branch propose another name so that such volatile issues could be taken up in a forum more suitable to their airing, and possibly receive an open and just decision. No. The participants were black, so what could it matter? The participants were black and therefore "known," serviceable, expendable in the interests of limning out one or the other of two mutually antagonistic fabulations. Under the pressure of voyeuristic desire, fueled by mythologies that render blacks publicly serviceable instruments of private dread and longing, extraordinary behavior on the part of the state could take place. Anita Hill's witnesses, credible and persuasive as they were, could be dismissed, as one "reporter" said, apparently without shame, because they were too intellectual to be believed(!). Under the pressure of racist mythologies, loyal staff (all female) had more weight than disinterested observers or publicly available documentation. Under such pressure the chairman of the committee could apply criminal court procedure to a confirmation hearing and assure the candidate that the assumption of innocence lay with the nominee. As though innocence—rather than malfeasance or ethical character or fitness to serve—was the charge against which they struggled to judge the judge. As though a rhetorical "I am not a crook" had anything at all to do with the heavy responsibility the committee was under.

Would such accusations have elicited such outsize defense mechanisms if the candidate had been white? Would the committee and many interest groups have considered the suitability of a white candidate untainted by these accusations? Hardly, but with a black candidate, already stained by the figurations of blackness as sexual aggressiveness or rapaciousness or impotence, the stain need only be proved reasonably doubted, which is to say, if he is black, how can you tell if that really is a stain? Which is also to say, blackness is itself a stain, and therefore unstainable. Which is also to say, if he is black and about to ascend to the Supreme Court bench, if the bench is to become stain-free, this newest judge must be bleached, race-free, as his speeches and opinions illustrated. Allegations of sexual misconduct re-raced him, which, in this administration, meant, restained him, dirtied him. Therefore the "dirt" that clung to him following those allegations, "dirt" he spoke of repeatedly, must be shown to have originated elsewhere. In this case the search for the racial stain turned on Anita Hill. Her character. Her motives. Not his.

Clarence Thomas has gone through the nomination process before, and in that connection has been investigated by the FBI before. Nothing is not known about him. And the senators know that nothing about him is not known. But what is known and what is useful to be distributed as knowledge are different things. In these hearings data, not to mention knowledge, had no place. The deliberations became a contest and the point was to win. At stake always was a court: stacked or balanced; irreproachable in its ethical and judicial standards or malleable and compliant in its political agenda; alert to and mindful of the real lives most of us live, as these lives are measured by the good of the republic, or a court that is aloof, delusional, indifferent to any mandate, popular or unpopular, if it is not first vetted by the executive branch.

As in virtually all of this nation's great debates, nonwhites and women figure powerfully, although their presence may be disguised, denied, or obliterated. So it is perhaps predictable that this instance—where serious issues of male prerogative and sexual assault, the issues of racial justice and racial redress, the problematics of governing and controlling women's bodies, the alterations of work space into (sexually) domesticated space—be subsumed into the debate over the candidacy for the Supreme Court. That these issues be worked out, on, and inscribed upon the canvas/

flesh of black people should come as no surprise to anyone.

The contempt emanating from the White House was palpable—it was not necessary for the candidate to be a first-rate legal scholar (as it had not been necessary for other candidates). Nor was it necessary that he have demonstrated a particular sensitivity to the issues and concerns of a race he belonged to but which "had no bearing" on his selection to fill a seat vacated by the single Supreme Court Justice who both belonged to and did represent the interests of that race. The "race" that "had no bearing" on the president's choice could nevertheless be counted on to support the nominee, since "skin voting" would overwhelm every other consideration. This riskless gamble held almost perfect sway. Many blacks were struck mute by the embarrassing position of agreeing with Klansmen and their sympathizers; others leaped to the defense of the candidate on the grounds that he was "no worse than X," or that any white candidate would be a throwback, or that "who knows what he might do or become in those hallowed halls?" Who knows? Well, his nominators did know, and they were correct, as even the earliest action Clarence Thomas has taken in the cases coming before the court confirms.

Appropriate also was the small, secret swearing-in ceremony once the candidate was confirmed. For secrecy had operated from the beginning. Not only the dismissed and suppressed charges against the candidate, but also deeper, more ancient secrets of males bonding and the demonizing of females who contradict them.

In addition to race, class surfaced in both predictable and unexpected ways. Predictably, the nominee was required to shuck: to convince white men in power that operating a trucking business was lowly work in a Georgia where most blacks would have blessed dirt for such work. It wasn't a hard shuck. Because race and class—that is, black equals poor—is an equation that functions usefully if unexamined, it is possible to advance exclusionary and elitist programs by the careful use of race *as* class. It is still possible to cash in on black victimhood (the pain of being a poor innocent black boy), to claim victim status (Thomas called himself a victim of a process he of all people knew was designed to examine a candidate's worth), and to deplore the practice in others all at the same time. It is still possible to say "My father was a doorman" (meaning servant, meaning poor) and get the sympathy of whites who cannot or will not do the arithmetic needed to know the difference between the earnings of a Washington, D.C., doorman and those of a clerk at the census bureau.

In addition to class transformations, there was on display race transcendence. The nominee could be understood as having realized his yearning for and commitment to "racelessness" by having a white spouse at his side. At least their love, we are encouraged to conclude, had transcended race, and this matrimonial love had been more than ecstasy and companionship—it had been for Virginia Thomas an important education on how to feel and think about black people. The *People* magazine lead story, taken with a straight face, proved their devotion, their racelessness, which we already recognized because he shook her hand in public on three occasions. And it was envy of this racially ideal union that was one of the reasons Thomas came up with in trying to explain Anita Hill's charges. Professor Hill, he seemed to be suggesting, harbored reactionary, race-bound opinions about interracial love which, as everybody knows, can drive a black woman insane and cause her to say wild, incredible things. Expectedly, the nominee called for a transcendence of race, remarked repeatedly on its divisive nature, its costliness, its undeniable degradation of principles of freedom. Unexpectedly, however, race surfaced on the very site of its interment. And it was hard not to murmur "Freddy's back" as the specter of this living corpse broke free of its hastily dug grave. But this resurrection was buoyed and winged by the fact of its gender component. If the forward face of the not-dead was racism, its backward face was sexism. The confirmation procedure held my attention partly because the shape it took, in an effort to hold its explosive contents, was unique—the twists and turns of the public debate and its manipulation, the responses of the senators on the committee. Yet what riveted my attention most during the hearings was not its strangeness but rather its familiarity. The sense that underneath the acrylic in which the political discourse was painted were the outlines of figures so old and so stable as to appear natural, not drawn or man-made at all.

It was trying to penetrate the brilliant, distracting color in which the political argument was painted in order to locate the outlines that informed the argument that led me to focus on the day of the week that both Anita Hill's testimony and Clarence Thomas's response to that testimony were aired. And to select out of all that each said on that day the themes that to me appeared salient: Anita Hill's inability to remain silent; Clarence Thomas's claims to being victimized. Silence and victimization. Broken silence and built victimization. Speech and bondage.

Disobedient speech and the chosen association of bondage. On, and . . . Friday.

On a Friday, Anita Hill graphically articulated points in her accusation of sexual misconduct. On the same Friday Clarence Thomas answered, in a manner of speaking, those charges. And it was on a Friday in 1709 when Alexander Selkirk found an "almost drowned Indian" on the shore of an island upon which he had been shipwrecked. Ten years later Selkirk's story would be immortalized by Daniel Defoe in *Robinson Crusoe*. There the Indian becomes a "savage cannibal"—black, barbarous, stupid, servile, adoring—and although nothing is reported of his sexual behavior, he has an acquired taste for the flesh of his own species. Crusoe's narrative is a success story, one in which a socially, culturally, and biologically handicapped black man is civilized and Christianized—taught, in other words, to be like a white one. From Friday's point of view it is a success story as well. Not only is he alive; he is greatly enabled by his association with his savior. And it should not go unremarked that Crusoe is also greatly enabled—including having his own life saved—by Friday. Yet like all successes, what is earned is mitigated by what one has lost.

If we look at the story from Friday's point of view rather than Crusoe's, it becomes clear that Friday had a very complex problem. By sheer luck he had escaped death, annihilation, anonymity, and engulfment by enemies within his own culture. By great and astonishing good fortune he had been rescued. The gift of his own life was so unexpected, so welcome, he felt he could regulate the debt only by offering that life to his rescuer, by making the gift exchange literal. But he had a problem.

Before he appeared on the shore, his rescuer, Crusoe, had heard no other voice except a parrot's trained to say his owner's name—Robin, for short. Crusoe wanted to hear it again. For over twenty years he had had only himself for company, and although he has conquered nature and marked time, no human calls his name, acknowledges his presence or his authority. Lucky for him he discovers a refugee escaping certain slaughter. Once rescue has been effected, Crusoe is in a position to have more than unopposed dominion; now he is able to acquire status, to demonstrate and confirm his superiority. So important is status in Crusoe's self-regard he does not ask the refugee what his name is; instead, Crusoe names him. Nor does he tell the refugee his own name; instead, he teaches him the three words that for months will do just fine: "master," "yes," and "no."

Friday's real problem, however, was not to learn the language of repetition, easily, like the parrot, but to learn to internalize it. For longer than necessary the first words he is taught, first "master," then "yes" or "no," remain all he is permitted to say. During the time in which he knows no other English, one has to assume he thinks in his own language, cogitates in it, explains stimuli and phenomena in the language he was born to. But Crusoe's account suggests otherwise, suggests that before his rescue Friday had no language, and even if he did, there was nothing to say in it. After a year Friday is taught some English vocabulary and the grammar to hold it. "This was the pleasantest year of all the life I led in this place; Friday began to talk pretty well, and understand the names of almost everything

I had occasion to call for, and of every place I had to send him to, and talked a great deal to me. . . ."

Had he expected that the life he offered Crusoe would include not just his services, his loyalty, his devotion, but also his language as well? Did he ever wonder why Crusoe did not want to learn *his* language? Or why he could never speak his master's name? In the absence of his master's desire to speak his tongue, did Friday forget completely the language he dreamed in? Think no more of the home he fled before the weapons of those who had conquered and occupied it? On the two or three occasions when Crusoe is curious enough to ask Friday a question about the black man's feelings, the answers are surprising. Yes, he longs for his home. Yes, it is beautiful on his island. Yes, he will refrain from eating human flesh. Yes, if he has the opportunity, he will teach his tribe to eat bread, cattle, and milk instead. (If Crusoe's assumption that Friday's people eat only each other were true, the practice would have decimated them long ago, but no matter—the white man teaches food habits; the black man learns them.) But no, he will not return to his home alone; he will go only if Crusoe accompanies him. So far, Friday can be understood to engage in dialogue with his master, however limited. Eventually, he learns more: he moves from speaking *with* to thinking *as* Crusoe.

The problem of internalizing the master's tongue is the problem of the rescued. Unlike the problems of survivors who may be lucky, fated, etc., the rescued have the problem of debt. If the rescuer gives you back your life, he shares in that life. But, as in Friday's case, if the rescuer saves your life by taking you away from the dangers, the complications, the confusion of home, he may very well expect the debt to be paid in full. Not "Go your own way and sin no more." Not "Here, take this boat and find your own adventure, in or out of your own tribe." But full payment, forever. Because the rescuer wants to hear his name, not mimicked but adored. This is a serious problem for Friday and gets more complicated the more one thinks about it.

Friday has left and been rescued from not only the culture that threatened him, that wants to kill and engulf him, but also from the culture that loves him. That too he has left behind forever.

Even when he discovers his own father, half dead, in precisely the danger he himself had been in when Crusoe saved his life, his joy is not so reckless as to quarrel with the menial labor he and his father are directed to do, while an also-rescued Spaniard, who has lived among Friday's tribe for years, is given supervisory responsibilities. Nor is his joy so great that he speaks to his father in their mutual tongue for both their delight. Instead, he translates for Crusoe what his father says.

This loss of the mother tongue seems not to disturb Friday, even though he never completely learns the master's. He negotiates a space somewhere in between. He develops a serviceable grammar that will never be eloquent; he learns to shout warnings of advancing, also black, enemies, but he can never dare speak *to* these enemies as his master does. Without a mother tongue, without the language of his original culture, all he can do is recognize his old enemies and, when ordered, kill them. Finally, Friday no longer negotiates space between his own language and Crusoe's. Finally, the *uses* of Crusoe's language, if not its grammar, become his own. The internalization is complete.

In one of the incidents that occur on the island, a band of Spanish mutineers come ashore, holding their captain prisoner. Crusoe and Friday liberate the captain and consider how to dispose of the criminals. Some of the mutineers are singled out by their captain as villains; others are identified as being forced into mutiny. So some are spared, others slaughtered. This discrimination is never applied to Friday's people. With one exception, an old man tied and bound for execution, all of the blacks Friday and Crusoe see are killed or wounded (most of whom, in Crusoe's tallying of the dead, Friday kills). The exception, who turns out to be Friday's father, is not given a name nor, as with his son Friday, is one solicited from him. He becomes part of Crusoe's team, called upon and relied on for all kinds of service. He is sent back to his island on an errand with the Spaniard. The Spaniard returns, Friday's father does not, but most curiously, once his services are no longer needed, there is no mention of him again—by the master or the son. While he was among them, and after he has gone, he is called by Robinson Crusoe "the old savage." We still do not know his name.

Voluntary entrance into another culture, voluntary sharing of more than one culture, has certain satisfactions to mitigate the problems that may ensue. But being rescued into an adversarial culture can carry a huge debt. The debt one feels one owes to the rescuer can be paid, simply, honorably, in lifetime service. But if in that transaction the rescued loses his idiom, the language of his culture, there may be other debts outstanding. Leon Higginbotham has charted the debt Clarence Thomas owes the culture that fought for and protected him before he arrived out of a turbulent social sea onto the shore of political patronage. In that sea Thomas was teased and humiliated by his own people, called ABC, American's Blackest Child. He was chastened for wanting an education superior to theirs. He was also loved and nurtured by them. As in any and everybody's background, family, culture, race, and region, there are persecutors and providers, kindness and loathing. No culture ever quite measures up to our expectations of it without a generous dose of romanticism, self-delusion, or simple compassion. Sometimes it seems easier, emotionally and professionally, to deny it, ignore it, erase it, even destroy it. And if the language of one's culture is lost or surrendered, one may be forced to describe that culture in the language of the rescuing one. In that way one could feel compelled to dismiss African-American culture by substituting the phrase "culture of the victim" for the critique and redress of systemic racism. Minus one's own idiom it is possible to cry and decry victimization, loathing it when it appears in the discourses of one's own people, but summoning it up for one's expediently deracialized self. It becomes easy to confuse the metaphors embedded in the blood language of one's own culture with the objects they stand for and to call patronizing, coddling, undemanding, rescuing, complicitous white racists a lynch mob. Under such circumstances it is not just easy to speak the master's language, it is necessary. One is obliged to cooperate in the misuse of figurative language, in the reinforcement of cliché, the erasure of difference, the jargon of justice, the evasion of logic, the denial of history, the crowning of patriarchy, the inscription of hegemony; to be

complicit in the vandalizing, sentimentalizing, and triviali-
zation of the torture black people have suffered. Such
rhetorical strategies become necessary because, without
one's own idiom, there is no other language to speak.

Both Friday and Clarence Thomas accompany their res-
cuers into the world of power and salvation. But the problem
of rescue still exists: both men, black but unrecognizable at
home or away, are condemned first to mimic, then to
internalize and adore, but never to utter one single sentence
understood to be beneficial to their original culture,
whether the people of their culture are those who wanted to
hurt them or those who loved them to death.

Clarence Thomas once quoted someone who said that
dwelling on the horrors of racism invited one of two
choices: vengeance or prosperity. He argued for a third
choice: "to appeal to that which is good." He did not
elaborate on which he had chosen, finally, but the language
he speaks, the actions he takes, the Supreme Court decisions he has made or aligned himself with, the foot, as it
were, that he has picked up and placed on his head, give
us some indication of what his choice has been. The foot-
print in the sand that so worried Crusoe's nights, that
compelled him to build a fortress, and then another to
protect his new world order, disappears from his night-
mares once Friday embraces, then internalizes, his master's
voice and can follow the master's agenda with passion.

It is hard not to think of these events in any way but as
unfortunate. And it is difficult to convince anybody that

what happened is over—without serious consequences. For those who looked forward eagerly to Thomas's confirmation, the expectation of a reliably conservative court may be reassuring. Time will have the most to say about that. For those who believe the future of the nation as a democracy is imperiled by this most recent addition to the bench, again, time will speak rather definitively. Yet regardless of political alliances, something positive and liberating has already surfaced. In matters of race and gender, it is now possible and necessary, as it seemed never to have been before, to speak about these matters without the barriers, the silences, the embarrassing gaps in discourse. It is clear to the most reductionist intellect that black people think differently from one another; it is also clear that the time for undiscriminating racial unity has passed. A conversation, a serious exchange between black men and women, has begun in a new arena, and the contestants defy the mold. Nor is it as easy as it used to be to split along racial lines, as the alliances and coalitions between white and black women, and the conflicts among black women, and among black men, during the intense debates regarding Anita Hill's testimony against Clarence Thomas's appointment prove.

This volume is one of the several beginnings of these new conversations in which issues and arguments are taken as seriously as they are. Only through thoughtful, incisive, and far-ranging dialogue will all of us be able to appraise and benefit from Friday's dilemma.

RACE-ING JUSTICE, EN-GENDERING POWER

An Open Letter to Justice Clarence Thomas from a Federal Judicial Colleague

November 29, 1991

Dear Justice Thomas:

The President has signed your Commission and you have now become the 106th Justice of the United States Supreme Court. I congratulate you on this high honor!

It has been a long time since we talked. I believe it was in 1980 during your first year as a Trustee at Holy Cross

*Except for a few minor changes in the footnotes this article is a verbatim copy of the text of the letter sent to Justice Clarence Thomas on November 29, 1991. I would like to thank Judges Nathaniel Jones, Damon Keith, and Louis H. Pollak and Dr. Evelyn Brooks Higginbotham for their very helpful insights. I gratefully acknowledge the very substantial assistance of my law clerk Aderson Belgarde Francois, New York University School of Law, J.D. 1991. Some research assistance was provided by Nelson S. T. Thayer, Sonya Johnson, and Michael Tein from the University of Pennsylvania Law School. What errors remain are mine.

College. I was there to receive an honorary degree. You were thirty-one years old and on the staff of Senator John Danforth. You had not yet started your meteoric climb through the government and federal judicial hierarchy. Much has changed since then.

At first I thought that I should write you privately—the way one normally corresponds with a colleague or friend. I still feel ambivalent about making this letter public but I do so because your appointment is profoundly important to this country and the world, and because all Americans need to understand the issues you will face on the Supreme Court. In short, Justice Thomas, I write this letter as a public record so that this generation can understand the challenges you face as an Associate Justice to the Supreme Court, and the next can evaluate the choices you have made or will make.

The Supreme Court can be a lonely and insular environment. Eight of the present Justices' lives would not have been very different if the *Brown* case had never been decided as it was. Four attended Harvard Law School, which did not accept women law students until 1950.[1] Two attended Stanford Law School prior to the time when the first Black matriculated there.[2] None has been called a "nigger"[3] or suffered the acute deprivations of poverty.[4] Justice O'Connor is the only other Justice on the Court who at one time was adversely affected by a white-male dominated system that often excludes both women and minorities from equal access to the rewards of hard work and talent.

By elevating you to the Supreme Court, President Bush has suddenly vested in you the option to preserve or dilute the gains this country has made in the struggle for equality.

This is a grave responsibility indeed. In order to discharge it you will need to recognize what James Baldwin called the "force of history" within you.[5] You will need to recognize that both your public life and your private life reflect this country's history in the area of racial discrimination and civil rights. And, while much has been said about your admirable determination to overcome terrible obstacles, it is also important to remember how you arrived where you are now, because you did not get there by yourself.

When I think of your appointment to the Supreme Court, I see not only the result of your own ambition, but also the culmination of years of heartbreaking work by thousands who preceded you. I know you may not want to be burdened by the memory of their sacrifices. But I also know that you have no right to forget that history. Your life is very different from what it would have been had these men and women never lived. That is why today I write to you about this country's history of civil rights lawyers and civil rights organizations; its history of voting rights; and its history of housing and privacy rights. This history has affected your past and present life. And forty years from now, when your grandchildren and other Americans measure your performance on the Supreme Court, that same history will determine whether you fulfilled your responsibility with the vision and grace of the Justice whose seat you have been appointed to fill: Thurgood Marshall.

I. Measures of Greatness or Failure of Supreme Court Justices

In 1977 a group of one hundred scholars evaluated the first one hundred Justices on the Supreme Court.[6] Eight of the Justices were categorized as failures, six as below average, fifty-five as average, fifteen as near great and twelve as great.[7] Among those ranked as great were John Marshall, Joseph Story, John M. Harlan, Oliver Wendell Holmes, Jr., Charles E. Hughes, Louis D. Brandeis, Harlan F. Stone, Benjamin N. Cardozo, Hugo L. Black, and Felix Frank-furter.[8] Because you have often criticized the Warren Court,[9] you should be interested to know that the list of great jurists on the Supreme Court also included Earl Warren.[10]

Even long after the deaths of the Justices whom I have named, informed Americans are grateful for the extraordinary wisdom and compassion they brought to their judicial opinions. Each in his own way viewed the Constitution as an instrument for justice. They made us a far better people and this country a far better place. I think that Justices Thurgood Marshall, William J. Brennan, Harry Blackmun, Lewis Powell, and John Paul Stevens will come to be revered by future scholars and future generations with the same gratitude. Over the next four decades you will cast many historic votes on issues that will profoundly affect the quality of life for our citizens for generations to come. You can become an exemplar of fairness and the rational interpretation of the Constitution, or you can become an archetype of inequality and the retrogressive evaluation of human rights. The choice as to whether you will build a decisional record of true greatness or of mere mediocrity is yours.

II. *Our Major Similarity*

My more than twenty-seven years as a federal judge made me listen with intense interest to the many persons who testified both in favor of and against your nomination. I studied the hearings carefully and afterwards pondered your testimony and the comments others made about you. After reading almost every word of your testimony, I concluded that what you and I have most in common is that we are both graduates of Yale Law School. Though our graduation classes are twenty-two years apart, we have both benefitted from our old Eli connections.

If you had gone to one of the law schools in your home state, Georgia, you probably would not have met Senator John Danforth who, more than twenty years ago, served with me as a member of the Yale Corporation. Dean Guido Calabresi mentioned you to Senator Danforth, who hired you right after graduation from law school and became one of your primary sponsors. If I had not gone to Yale Law School, I would probably not have met Justice Curtis Bok, nor Yale Law School alumni such as Austin Norris, a distinguished black lawyer, and Richardson Dilworth, a distinguished white lawyer, who became my mentors and gave me my first jobs. Nevertheless, now that you sit on the Supreme Court, there are issues far more important to the welfare of our nation than our Ivy League connections. I trust that you will not be overly impressed with the fact that all of the other Justices are graduates of what laymen would call the nation's most prestigious law schools.

Black Ivy League alumni in particular should never be too impressed by the educational pedigree of Supreme Court Justices. The most wretched decision ever rendered against black people in the past century was *Plessy v. Ferguson.*[11] It was written in 1896 by Justice Henry Billings Brown, who had attended both Yale and Harvard Law Schools. The opinion was joined by Justice George Shiras, a graduate of Yale Law School, as well as by Chief Justice Melville Fuller and Justice Horace Gray, both alumni of Harvard Law School.

If those four Ivy League alumni on the Supreme Court in 1896 had been as faithful in their interpretation of the Constitution as Justice John Harlan, a graduate of Transylvania, a small law school in Kentucky, then the venal precedent of *Plessy v. Ferguson,* which established the federal "separate but equal" doctrine and legitimized the worst forms of race discrimination, would not have been the law of our nation for sixty years. The separate but equal doctrine, also known as Jim Crow, created the foundations of separate and unequal allocation of resources, and oppression of the human rights of Blacks.

During your confirmation hearing I heard you refer frequently to your grandparents and your experiences in Georgia. Perhaps now is the time to recognize that if the four Ivy League alumni—all northerners—of the *Plessy* majority had been as sensitive to the plight of black people as was Justice John Harlan, a former slave holder from Kentucky,[12] the American statutes that sanctioned racism might not have been on the books—and many of the racial injustices that your grandfather, Myers Anderson, and my grandfather, Moses Higginbotham, endured would never have occurred.

The tragedy with *Plessy v. Ferguson,* is not that the Justices had the "wrong" education, or that they attended the "wrong" law schools. The tragedy is that the Justices had the wrong *values,* and that these values poisoned this society for decades. Even worse, millions of Blacks today still suffer from the tragic sequelae of *Plessy*—a case which Chief Justice Rehnquist,[13] Justice Kennedy,[14] and most scholars now say was wrongly decided.[15]

As you sit on the Supreme Court confronting the profound issues that come before you, never be impressed with how bright your colleagues are. You must always focus on what *values* they bring to the task of interpreting the Constitution. Our Constitution has an unavoidable—though desirable—level of ambiguity, and there are many interstitial spaces which as a Justice of the Supreme Court you will have to fill in.[16] To borrow Justice Cardozo's elegant phrase: "We do not pick our rules of law full blossomed from the trees."[17] You and the other Justices cannot avoid putting your imprimatur on a set of values. The dilemma will always be which particular values you choose to sanction in law. You can be part of what Chief Justice Warren, Justice Brennan, Justice Blackmun, and Justice Marshall and others have called the evolutionary movement of the Constitution[18]—an evolutionary movement that has benefitted you greatly.

III. Your Critiques of Civil Rights Organizations and the Supreme Court During the Last Eight Years

I have read almost every article you have published, every speech you have given, and virtually every public comment you have made during the past decade. Until your confirmation hearing I could not find one shred of evidence suggesting an insightful understanding on your part on how the evolutionary movement of the Constitution and the work of civil rights organizations have benefitted you. Like Sharon McPhail, the President of the National Bar Association, I kept asking myself: Will the Real Clarence Thomas Stand Up?[19] Like her, I wondered: "Is Clarence Thomas a 'conservative with a common touch' as Ruth Marcus refers to him . . . or the 'counterfeit hero' he is accused of being by Haywood Burns . . . ?"[20]

While you were a presidential appointee for eight years, as Chairman of the Equal Opportunity Commission and as an Assistant Secretary at the Department of Education, you made what I would regard as unwarranted criticisms of civil rights organizations,[21] the Warren Court,[22] and even of Justice Thurgood Marshall.[23] Perhaps these criticisms were motivated by what you perceived to be your political duty to the Reagan and Bush Administrations. Now that you have assumed what should be the non-partisan role of a Supreme Court Justice, I hope you will take time out to carefully evaluate some of these unjustified attacks.

In October 1987, you wrote a letter to the *San Diego Union & Tribune* criticizing a speech given by Justice Marshall on the 200th anniversary celebration of the Constitution.[24] Justice Marshall had cautioned all Americans not to overlook the momentous events that followed the drafting of that document, and to "seek . . . a sensitive understanding of the Constitution's inherent defects, and its promising evolution through 200 years of history."[25]

Your response dismissed Justice Marshall's "sensitive understanding" as an "exasperating and incomprehensible . . . assault on the Bicentennial, the Founding, and the Constitution itself."[26] Yet, however high and noble the Founders' intentions may have been, Justice Marshall was correct in believing that the men who gathered in Philadelphia in 1787 "could not have imagined, nor would they have accepted, that the document they were drafting would one day be construed by a Supreme Court to which had been appointed a woman and the descendant of an African slave."[27] That, however, was neither an assault on the Constitution nor an indictment of the Founders. Instead, it was simply a recognition that in the midst of the Bicentennial celebration, "[s]ome may more quietly commemorate the suffering, the struggle and sacrifice that has triumphed over much of what was wrong with the original document, and observe the anniversary with hopes not realized and promises not fulfilled."[28]

Justice Marshall's comments, much like his judicial philosophy, were grounded in history and were driven by the knowledge that even today, for millions of Americans, there still remain "hopes not realized and promises not fulfilled." His reminder to the nation that patriotic feelings should not get in the way of thoughtful reflection on this country's continued struggle for equality was neither new nor misplaced.[29] Twenty-five years earlier, in December 1962, while this country was celebrating the 100th anniversary of the Emancipation Proclamation, James Baldwin had written to his young nephew:

This is your home, my friend, do not be driven from it; great men have done great things here, and will again, and we can make America what America must become. . . . [But y]ou know, and I know that the country is celebrating one hundred years of freedom one hundred years too soon.[30]

Your response to Justice Marshall's speech, as well as your criticisms of the Warren Court and civil rights organizations, may have been nothing more than your expression of allegiance to the conservatives who made you Chairman of the EEOC, and who have now elevated you to the Supreme Court. But your comments troubled me then and trouble me still because they convey a stunted knowledge of history and an unformed judicial philosophy. Now that you sit on the Supreme Court you must sort matters out for yourself and form your own judicial philosophy, and you must reflect more deeply on legal history than you ever have before. You are no longer privileged to offer flashy one-liners to delight the conservative establishment. Now what you write must inform, not entertain. Now your statements and your votes can shape the destiny of the entire nation.

Notwithstanding the role you have played in the past, I believe you have the intellectual depth to reflect upon and rethink the great issues the Court has confronted in the past and to become truly your own man. But to be your own man the first in the series of questions you must ask yourself is this: Beyond your own admirable personal drive, what were the primary forces or acts of good fortune that made your major achievements possible? This is a hard and difficult question. Let me suggest that you focus on at least four areas: (1) the impact of the work of civil rights lawyers and civil rights organizations on your life; (2) other than having picked a few individuals to be their favorite colored person, what it is that the conservatives of each generation have done that has been of significant benefit to African-Americans, women, or other minorities; (3) the impact of the eradication of racial barriers in the voting on your own confirmation; and (4) the impact of civil rights victories in the area of housing and privacy on your personal life.

IV. The Impact of the Work of Civil Rights Lawyers and Civil Rights Organizations on Your Life

During the time when civil rights organizations were challenging the Reagan Administration, I was frankly dismayed by some of your responses to and denigrations of these organizations. In 1984, the *Washington Post* reported that you had criticized traditional civil rights leaders because, instead of trying to reshape the Administration's policies, they had gone to the news media to "bitch, bitch, bitch, moan and moan, whine and whine."[31] If that is still your assessment of these civil rights organizations or their leaders, I suggest, Justice Thomas, that you should ask yourself every day what would have happened to you if there had never been a Charles Hamilton Houston, a William Henry Hastie, a Thurgood Marshall, and that small cadre of other lawyers associated with them, who laid the groundwork for success in the twentieth-century racial civil rights cases? Couldn't they have been similarly charged with, as you phrased it, bitching and moaning and whining when they challenged the racism in the administrations of prior presidents, governors, and public officials? If there had never been an effective NAACP, isn't it highly probable that you might still be in Pin Point, Georgia, working as a laborer as some of your relatives did for decades?

Even though you had the good fortune to move to Savannah, Georgia, in 1955, would you have been able to get out of Savannah and get a responsible job if decades earlier the NAACP had not been challenging racial injustice throughout America? If the NAACP had not been lobbying, picketing, protesting, and politicking for a 1964 Civil Rights Act, would Monsanto Chemical Company have opened their doors to you in 1977? If Title VII had not been enacted might not American companies still continue to discriminate on the basis of race, gender, and national origin?

The philosophy of civil rights protest evolved out of the fact that black people were forced to confront this country's racist institutions without the benefit of equal access to those institutions. For example, in January of 1941, A. Philip Randolph planned a march on Washington, D.C., to protest widespread employment discrimination in the defense industry.[32] In order to avoid the prospect of a demonstration by potentially tens of thousands of Blacks, President Franklin Delano Roosevelt issued Executive Order 8802 barring discrimination in defense industries or government. The order led to the inclusion of anti-discrimination clauses in all government defense contracts and the establishment of the Fair Employment Practices Committee.[33]

In 1940, President Roosevelt appointed William Henry Hastie as civilian aide to Secretary of War Henry L. Stimson. Hastie fought tirelessly against discrimination, but when confronted with an unabated program of segregation in all areas of the armed forces, he resigned on January 31, 1943. His visible and dramatic protest sparked the move towards integrating the armed forces, with immediate and far-reaching results in the army air corps.[34]

A. Philip Randolph and William Hastie understood—though I wonder if you do—what Frederick Douglass meant when he wrote:

The whole history of the progress of human liberty shows that all concessions yet made to her august claims, have

been born of earnest struggle. . . . If there is no struggle
there is no progress. . . .

This struggle may be a moral one, or it may be a physical
one, and it may be both moral and physical, but it must be
a struggle. Power concedes nothing without a demand. It
never did and it never will.[35]

The struggles of civil rights organizations and civil rights
lawyers have been both moral and physical, and their victories have been neither easy nor sudden. Though the
Brown decision was issued only six years after your birth,
the road to *Brown* started more than a century earlier. It
started when Prudence Crandall was arrested in Connecticut in 1833 for attempting to provide schooling for colored
girls.[36] It was continued in 1849 when Charles Sumner, a
white lawyer and abolitionist, and Benjamin Roberts, a
black lawyer,[37] challenged segregated schools in Boston.[38]
It was continued as the NAACP, starting with Charles
Hamilton Houston's suit, *Murray v. Pearson*,[39] in 1936,
challenged Maryland's policy of excluding Blacks from the
University of Maryland Law School. It was continued in
Gaines v. Missouri,[40] when Houston challenged a 1937
decision of the Missouri Supreme Court. The Missouri
courts had held that because law schools in the states of
Illinois, Iowa, Kansas, and Nebraska accepted Negroes, a
twenty-five-year-old black citizen of Missouri was not
being denied his constitutional right to equal protection
under the law when he was excluded from the only state
supported law school in Missouri. It was continued in
Sweatt v. Painter[41] in 1946, when Heman Marion Sweatt
filed suit for admission to the Law School of the University

of Texas after his application was rejected solely because he was black. Rather than admit him, the University postponed the matter for years and put up a separate and unaccredited law school for Blacks. It was continued in a series of cases against the University of Oklahoma, when, in 1950, in *McLaurin v. Oklahoma*,[42] G. W. McLaurin, a sixty-eight-year-old man, applied to the University of Oklahoma to obtain a Doctorate in education. He had earned his Master's degree in 1948, and had been teaching at Langston University, the state's college for Negroes.[43] Yet he was "required to sit apart at . . . designated desk[s] in an anteroom adjoining the classroom . . . [and] on the mezzanine floor of the library, . . . and to sit at a designated table and to eat at a different time from the other students in the school cafeteria."[44]

The significance of the victory in the *Brown* case cannot be overstated. *Brown* changed the moral tone of America; by eliminating the legitimization of state-imposed racism it implicitly questioned racism wherever it was used. It created a milieu in which private colleges were forced to recognize their failures in excluding or not welcoming minority students. I submit that even your distinguished undergraduate college, Holy Cross, and Yale University were influenced by the milieu created by *Brown* and thus became more sensitive to the need to create programs for the recruitment of competent minority students. In short, isn't it possible that you might not have gone to Holy Cross if the NAACP and other civil rights organizations, Martin Luther King and the Supreme Court, had not recast the racial mores of America? And if you had not gone to Holy Cross, and instead had gone to some underfunded state college for Negroes in Georgia, would you have been admitted to Yale Law School, and would you have met the alumni who played such a prominent role in maximizing your professional options?

I have cited this litany of NAACP[45] cases because I don't understand why you appeared so eager to criticize civil rights organizations or their leaders. In the 1980s, Benjamin Hooks and John Jacobs worked just as tirelessly in the cause of civil rights as did their predecessors Walter White, Roy Wilkins, Whitney Young, and Vernon Jordan in the 1950s and '60s. As you now start to adjudicate cases involving civil rights, I hope you will have more judicial integrity than to demean those advocates of the disadvantaged who appear before you. If you and I had not gotten many of the positive reinforcements that these organizations fought for and that the post-*Brown* era made possible, probably neither you nor I would be federal judges today.

V. What Have the Conservatives Ever Contributed to African-Americans?

During the last ten years, you have often described yourself as a black conservative. I must confess that, other than their own self-advancement, I am at a loss to understand what it is that the so-called black conservatives are so anxious to conserve. Now that you no longer have to be outspoken on their behalf, perhaps you will recognize that in the past it was the white "conservatives" who screamed "segregation now, segregation forever!" It was primarily the conservatives who attacked the Warren Court relentlessly because of *Brown v. Board of Education* and who stood in the way of almost every measure to ensure gender and racial advancement.

For example, on March 11, 1956, ninety-six members

of Congress, representing eleven southern states, issued the "Southern Manifesto," in which they declared that the *Brown* decision was an "unwarranted exercise of power by the Court, contrary to the Constitution."[46] Ironically, those members of Congress reasoned that the *Brown* decision was "destroying the amicable relations between the white and negro races,"[47] and that "it had planted hatred and suspicion where there had been heretofore friendship and understanding."[48] They then pledged to use all lawful means to bring about the reversal of the decision, and praised those states which had declared the intention to resist its implementation.[49] The Southern Manifesto was more than mere political posturing by Southern Democrats. It was a thinly disguised racist attack on the constitutional and moral foundations of *Brown*. Where were the conservatives in the 1950s when the cause of equal rights needed every fair-minded voice it could find?

At every turn, the conservatives, either by tacit approbation or by active complicity, tried to derail the struggle for equal rights in this country. In the 1960s, it was the conservatives, including the then-senatorial candidate from Texas, George Bush,[50] the then-Governor from California, Ronald Reagan,[51] and the omnipresent Senator Strom Thurmond,[52] who argued that the 1964 Civil Rights Act was unconstitutional. In fact Senator Thurmond's 24 hour 18 minute filibuster during Senate deliberations on the 1957 Civil Rights Act set an all-time record.[53] He argued on the floor of the Senate that the provisions of the Act guaranteeing equal access to public accommodations amounted to an enslavement of white people.[54] If twenty-seven years ago George Bush, Ronald Reagan, and Strom Thurmond had succeeded, there would have been no position for you to fill as Assistant Secretary for Civil Rights in the Department of Education. There would have been no such agency as the Equal Employment Commission for you to chair.

Thus, I think now is the time for you to reflect on the evolution of American constitutional and statutory law, as it has affected your personal options and improved the options for so many Americans, particularly non-whites, women, and the poor. If the conservative agenda of the 1950s, '60s, and '70s had been implemented, what would have been the results of the important Supreme Court cases that now protect your rights and the rights of millions of other Americans who can now no longer be discriminated against because of their race, religion, national origin, or physical disabilities? If, in 1954, the United States Supreme Court had accepted the traditional rationale that so many conservatives then espoused, would the 1896 *Plessy v. Ferguson* case, which announced the nefarious doctrine of "separate but equal," and which allowed massive inequalities, still be the law of the land? In short, if the conservatives of the 1950s had had their way, would there ever have been a *Brown v. Board of Education* to prohibit state-imposed racial segregation?

VI. The Impact of Eradicating Racial Barriers to Voting

Of the fifty-two senators who voted in favor of your confirmation, some thirteen hailed from nine southern states. Some may have voted for you because they agreed with President Bush's assessment that you were " 'the best person for the position.' "[55] But, candidly, Justice Thomas, I do not believe that you were indeed the most competent person to be on the Supreme Court. Charles Bowser, a distinguished African-American Philadelphia lawyer, said, " 'I'd be willing to bet . . . that not one of the senators who voted to confirm Clarence Thomas would hire him as their lawyer.' "[56]

Thus, realistically, many senators probably did not think that you were the most qualified person available. Rather, they were acting solely as politicians, weighing the potential backlash in their states of the black vote that favored you for emotional reasons and the conservative white vote that favored you for ideological reasons. The black voting constituency is important in many states, and today it could make a difference as to whether many senators are or are not re-elected. So here, too, you benefitted from civil rights progress.

No longer could a United States Senator say what Senator Benjamin Tillman of South Carolina said in anger when President Theodore Roosevelt invited a moderate Negro, Booker T. Washington, to lunch at the White House: " 'Now that Roosevelt has eaten with that nigger Washington, we shall have to kill a thousand niggers to get them back to their place.' "[57] Senator Tillman did not have to fear any retaliation by Blacks because South Carolina and most southern states kept Blacks "in their place" by manipulating the ballot box. For example, because they did not have to confront the restraints and prohibitions of later Supreme Court cases, the manipulated "white" primary allowed Tillman and other racist senators to profit from the threat of violence to Blacks who voted, and from the disproportionate electoral power given to rural whites. For years, the NAACP litigated some of the most significant cases attacking racism at the ballot box. That organization almost singlehandedly created the foundation for black political power that led in part to the 1965 Civil Rights Act.

Moreover, if it had not been for the Supreme Court's opinion in *Smith v. Allright*,[58] a case which Thurgood Marshall argued, almost all the southern senators who voted for you would have been elected in what was once called a "white primary"—a process which precluded Blacks from effective voting in the southern primary election, where the real decisions were made on who would run every hamlet, township, city, county and state. The seminal case of *Baker v. Carr*,[59] which articulated the concept of one man-one vote, was part of a series of Supreme Court precedents that caused southern senators to recognize that patently racist diatribes could cost them an election. Thus your success even in your several confirmation votes is directly attributable to the efforts that the "activist" Warren Court and civil rights organizations have made over the decades.

VII. Housing and Privacy

If you are willing, Justice Thomas, to consider how the history of civil rights in this country has shaped your public life, then imagine for a moment how it has affected your private life. With some reluctance, I make the following comments about housing and marriage because I hope that reflecting on their constitutional implications may raise your consciousness and level of insight about the dangers of excessive intrusion by the state in personal and family relations.

From what I have seen of your house on television scans and in newspaper photos, it is apparent that you live in a comfortable Virginia neighborhood. Thus I start with Holmes's view that "a page of history is worth a volume of logic."[60] The history of Virginia's legislatively and judicially imposed racism should be particularly significant to you now that as a Supreme Court Justice you must determine the limits of a state's intrusion on family and other matters of privacy.

It is worthwhile pondering what the impact on you would have been if Virginia's legalized racism had been allowed to continue as a viable constitutional doctrine. In 1912, Virginia enacted a statute giving cities and towns the right to pass ordinances which would divide the city into segregated districts for black and white residents.[61] Segregated districts were designated white or black depending on the race of the majority of the residents.[62] It became a crime for any black person to move into and occupy a residence in an area known as a white district.[63] Similarly, it was a crime for any white person to move into a black district.[64]

Even prior to the Virginia statute of 1912, the cities of Ashland and Richmond had enacted such segregationist statutes.[65] The ordinances also imposed the same segregationist policies on any "place of public assembly."[66] Apparently schools, churches, and meeting places were defined by the color of their members. Thus, white Christian Virginia wanted to make sure that no black Christian churches were in their white Christian neighborhoods.

The impact of these statutes can be assessed by reviewing the experiences of two African-Americans, John Coleman and Mary Hopkins. Coleman purchased property in Ashland, Virginia in 1911.[67] In many ways he symbolized the American dream of achieving some modest upward mobility by being able to purchase a home earned through initiative and hard work. But shortly after moving to his home, he was arrested for violating Ashland's segregation ordinance because a majority of the residents in the block were white. Also, in 1911, the City of Richmond prosecuted and convicted a black woman, Mary S. Hopkins, for moving into a predominantly white block.[68]

Coleman and Hopkins appealed their convictions to the Supreme Court of Virginia which held that the ordinances of Ashland and Richmond did not violate the United States Constitution and that the fines and convictions were valid.[69]

If Virginia's law of 1912 still prevailed, and if your community passed laws like the ordinances of Richmond and Ashland, you would not be able to live in your own house. Fortunately, the Virginia ordinances and statutes were in effect nullified by a case brought by the NAACP in 1915, where a similar statute of the City of Louisville was declared unconstitutional.[70] But even if your town council had not passed such an ordinance, the developers would in all probability have incorporated racially restrictive covenants in the title deeds to the individual homes. Thus, had it not been for the vigor of the NAACP's litigation efforts in a series of persistent attacks against racial covenants you would have been excluded from your own home. Fortunately, in 1948, in *Shelley v. Kraemer*,[71] a case argued by Thurgood Marshall, the NAACP succeeded in having such racially restrictive covenants declared unconstitutional.

Yet with all of those litigation victories, you still might not have been able to live in your present house because a private developer might have refused to sell you a home solely because you are an African-American. Again you would be saved because in 1968 the Supreme Court, in

Jones v. Alfred H. Mayer Co., in an opinion by Justice Stewart, held that the 1866 Civil Rights Act precluded such private racial discrimination.[72] It was a relatively close case; the two dissenting Justices said that the majority opinion was "ill-considered and ill-advised."[73] It was the values of the majority which made the difference. And it is your values that will determine the vitality of other civil rights acts for decades to come.

Had you overcome all of those barriers to housing and if you and your present wife decided that you wanted to reside in Virginia, you would nonetheless have been violating the Racial Integrity Act of 1924,[74] which the Virginia Supreme Court as late as 1966 said was consistent with the federal Constitution because of the overriding state interest in the institution of marriage.[75] Although it was four years after the *Brown* case, Richard Perry Loving and his wife, Mildred Jeter Loving, were convicted in 1958 and originally sentenced to one year in jail because of their interracial marriage. As an act of magnanimity the trial court later suspended the sentences, " 'for a period of 25 years upon the provision that both accused leave Caroline County and the state of Virginia at once and do not return together or at the same time to said county and state for a period of 25 years.' "[76]

The conviction was affirmed by a unanimous Supreme Court of Virginia, though they remanded the case back as to the re-sentencing phase. Incidentally, the Virginia trial judge justified the constitutionality of the prohibition against interracial marriages as follows:

"Almighty God created the races white, black, yellow, Malay and red, and he placed them on separate continents.

And but for the interference with his arrangement there would be no cause for such marriages. The fact that he separated the races shows that he did not intend for the races to mix."[77]

If the Virginia courts had been sustained by the United States Supreme Court in 1966, and if, after your marriage, you and your wife had, like the Lovings, defied the Virginia statute by continuing to live in your present residence, you could have been in the penitentiary today rather than serving as an Associate Justice of the United States Supreme Court.

I note these pages of record from American legal history because they exemplify the tragedy of excessive intrusion on individual and family rights. The only persistent protector of privacy and family rights has been the United States Supreme Court, and such protection has occurred only when a majority of the Justices has possessed a broad vision of human rights. Will you, in your moment of truth, take for granted that the Constitution protects you and your wife against all forms of deliberate state intrusion into family and privacy matters, and protects you even against some forms of discrimination by other private parties such as the real estate developer, but nevertheless find that it does not protect the privacy rights of others, and particularly women, to make similarly highly personal and private decisions?

Conclusion

This letter may imply that I am somewhat skeptical as to what your performance will be as a Supreme Court Justice. Candidly, I and many other thoughtful Americans are very concerned about your appointment to the Supreme Court. But I am also sufficiently familiar with the history of the Supreme Court to know that a few of its members (not many) about whom there was substantial skepticism at the time of their appointment became truly outstanding Justices. In that context I think of Justice Hugo Black. I am impressed by the fact that at the very beginning of his illustrious career he articulated his vision of the responsibility of the Supreme Court. In one of his early major opinions he wrote, "courts stand . . . as havens of refuge for those who might otherwise suffer because they are helpless, weak, out-numbered, or . . . are non-conforming victims of prejudice and public excitement."[78]

While there are many other equally important issues that you must consider and on which I have not commented, none will determine your place in history as much as your defense of the weak, the poor, minorities, women, the disabled and the powerless. I trust that you will ponder often the significance of the statement of Justice Blackmun, in a vigorous dissent of two years ago, when he said: "[S]adly . . . one wonders whether the majority [of the Court] still believes that . . . race discrimination—or more accurately, race discrimination against nonwhites—is a problem in our society, or even remembers that it ever was."[79]

You, however, must try to remember that the fundamental problems of the disadvantaged, women, minorities, and the powerless have not all been solved simply because you have "moved on up" from Pin Point, Georgia, to the Supreme Court. In your opening remarks to the Judiciary Committee, you described your life in Pin Point, Georgia, as " 'far removed in space and time from this room, this day and this moment.' "[80] I have written to tell you that your life today, however, should be not far removed from the visions and struggles of Frederick Douglass, Sojourner Truth, Harriet Tubman, Charles Hamilton Houston, A. Philip Randolph, Mary McLeod Bethune, W. E. B. Dubois, Roy Wilkins, Whitney Young, Martin Luther King, Judge William Henry Hastie, Justices Thurgood Marshall, Earl Warren, and William Brennan, as well as the thousands of others who dedicated much of their lives to create the America that made your opportunities possible.[81] I hope you have the strength of character to exemplify those values so that the sacrifices of all these men and women will not have been in vain.

I am sixty-three years old. In my lifetime I have seen African-Americans denied the right to vote, the opportunities to a proper education, to work, and to live where they choose.[82] I have seen and *known* racial segregation and discrimination.[83] But I have also seen the decision in *Brown* rendered. I have seen the first African-American sit on the Supreme Court. And I have seen brave and courageous people, black and white, give their lives for the civil rights cause. My memory of them has always been without bitterness or nostalgia. But today it is sometimes without hope; for I wonder whether their magnificent achievements are in jeopardy. I wonder whether (and how far) the majority of the Supreme Court will continue to retreat from protecting the rights of the poor, women, the disadvantaged, minorities, and the powerless.[84] And if, tragically, a majority of the Court continues to retreat, I wonder whether you, Justice Thomas, an African-American, will be part of that majority.

No one would be happier than I if the record you will

establish on the Supreme Court in years to come demonstrates that my apprehensions were unfounded.[85] You were born into injustice, tempered by the hard reality of what it means to be poor and black in America, and especially to be poor because you are black. You have found a door newly cracked open and you have escaped. I trust you shall not forget that many who preceded you and many who follow you have found, and will find, the door of equal opportunity slammed in their faces through no fault of their own. And I also know that time and the tides of history often call out of men and women qualities that even they did not know lay within them. And so, with hope to balance my apprehensions, I wish you well as a thoughtful and worthy successor to Justice Marshall in the ever ongoing struggle to assure equal justice under law for all persons.

Sincerely,
A. Leon Higginbotham, Jr.

NOTES

1. Justices Blackmun, Scalia, Kennedy, and Souter were members of the Harvard Law School Classes of 1932, 1960, 1961, and 1966 respectively. *See* THE AMERICAN BENCH 16, 46, 72, 1566 (Marie T. Hough ed., 1989). The first woman to graduate from Harvard Law School was a member of the Class of 1953. Telephone interview with Emily Farnam, Alumni Affairs Office, Harvard University (Aug. 8, 1991).

2. Chief Justice Rehnquist and Justice O'Connor were members of the Stanford Law School Class of 1952. *See* THE AMERICAN BENCH, *supra* note 1, at 63, 69. Stanford did not graduate its first black law student until 1968. Telephone interview with Shirley Wedlake, Assistant to the Dean of Student Affairs, Stanford University Law School (Dec. 10, 1991).

3. Even courts have at times tolerated the use of the term "nigger" in one or another of its variations. In the not too distant past, appellate courts have upheld convictions despite prosecutors' references to black defendants and witnesses in such racist terms as "black rascal," "burr-headed nigger," "mean negro," "big nigger," "pickaninny," "mean nigger," "three nigger men," "niggers," and "nothing but just a common Negro, [a] black whore." *See* A. Leon Higginbotham, Jr., *Racism in American and South African Courts: Similarities and Differences,* 65 N.Y.U.L. REV. 479, 542–43 (1990).

   In addition, at least one Justice of the Supreme Court, James McReynolds, was a "white supremacist" who referred to Blacks as "niggers." *See* RANDALL KENNEDY, *Race Relations Law and the Tradition of Celebration: The Case of Professor Schmidt,* 86 COLUM. L. REV. 1622, 1641 (1986); *see also* David Burner, *James McReynolds, in 3* THE JUSTICES OF THE UNITED STATES SUPREME COURT 1789–1969, at 2023, 2024 (Leon Friedman & Fred L. Israel eds., 1969) (reviewing Justice McReynolds's numerous lone dissents as evidence of blatant racism). In 1938, a landmark desegregation case was argued before the Supreme Court by Charles Hamilton Houston, the brilliant black lawyer who laid the foundation for *Brown v. Board of Education*. During Houston's oral argument, McReynolds turned his back on the attorney and stared at the wall of the courtroom. Videotaped Statement of Judge Robert Carter to Judge Higginbotham (August 1987) (reviewing his observation of the argument in Missouri ex rel. Gaines v. Canada, 305 U.S. 337 (1938)). In his autobiography, Justice William O. Douglas described how McReynolds received a rare, but well deserved comeuppance when he made a disparaging comment about Howard University.

> One day McReynolds went to the barbershop in the Court. Gates, the black barber, put the sheet around his neck and over his lap, and as he was pinning it behind him McReynolds said, "Gates, tell me, where is this nigger university in Washington, D.C.?" Gates removed the white cloth from McReynolds, walked around and faced him, and said in a very calm and dignified manner, "Mr. Justice, I am shocked that any Justice would call a Negro a nigger. There is a Negro college in Washington, D.C. Its name is Howard University and we are very proud of it." McReynolds muttered some kind of apology and Gates resumed his work in silence.

WILLIAM O. DOUGLAS, THE COURT YEARS: 1939–1975, at 14–15 (1980).

4. By contrast, according to the Census Bureau's definition of poverty, in 1991, one in five American children (and one in four preschoolers) is poor. *See* CLIFFORD M. JOHNSON ET AL., CHILD POVERTY IN AMERICA 1 (Children's Defense Fund report, 1991).

5. JAMES BALDWIN, *White Man's Guilt, in* THE PRICE OF THE TICKET 409, 410 (1985).

6. *See* ALBERT P. BLAUSTEIN & ROY M. MERSKY, THE FIRST ONE HUNDRED JUSTICES (1978). The published survey included ratings of only the first ninety-six Justices, because the four Nixon appointees (Burger, Blackmun, Powell, and Rehnquist) had then been on the Court too short a time for an accurate evaluation to be made. *See id.* at 35–36.

7. *Id.* at 37–40.
8. *Id.* at 37.
9. You have been particularly critical of its decision in *Brown v. Board of Education. See, e.g.,* Clarence Thomas, *Toward a "Plain Reading" of the Constitution—The Declaration of Independence in Constitutional Interpretation,* 30 How. L.J. 983, 990–92 (1987) (criticizing the emphasis on social stigma in the *Brown* opinion, which left the Court's decision resting on "feelings" rather than "reason and moral and political principles"); Clarence Thomas, Civil Rights as a Principle Versus Civil Rights as an Interest, Speech to the Cato Institute (Oct. 2, 1987), *in* Assessing the Reagan Years 391, 392–93 (David Boaz ed., 1988) (arguing that the Court's opinion in *Brown* failed to articulate a clear principle to guide later decisions, leading to opinions in the area of race that overemphasized groups at the expense of individuals, and "argue[d] *against* what was best in the American political tradition"); Clarence Thomas, The Higher Law Background of the Privileges and Immunities Clause of the Fourteenth Amendment, Speech to the Federalist Society for Law and Policy Studies, University of Virginia School of Law (Mar. 5, 1988), *in* 12 Harv. J.L. & Pub. Pol'y 63, 68 (1989) (asserting that adoption of Justice Harlan's view that the Constitution is "color-blind" would have provided the Court's civil rights opinions with the higher-law foundation necessary for a "just, wise, and *constitutional* decision").
10. *See* Blaustein & Mersky, *supra* note 6, at 37.
11. 163 U.S. 537 (1896).
12. *See* Alan F. Westin, *John Marshall Harlan and the Constitutional Rights of Negroes: The Transformation of a Southerner,* 66 Yale L.J. 637, 638 (1957).
13. Fullilove v. Klutznick, 448 U.S. 448, 522 (1980) (Stewart, J., joined by Rehnquist, J., dissenting).
14. Metro Broadcasting, Inc. v. FCC, 110 S. Ct. 2997, 3044 (1990) (Kennedy, J., dissenting).
15. For a thorough review of the background of *Plessy v. Ferguson,* and a particularly sharp criticism of the majority opinion, see Loren Miller, The Petitioners: The Story of the Supreme

COURT OF THE UNITED STATES AND THE NEGRO 165–82 (1966). As an example of scholars who have criticized the opinion and the result in *Plessy,* see LAURENCE H. TRIBE, AMERICAN CONSTITUTIONAL LAW 1474–75 (2d ed., 1988).

16. *See, e.g.,* BENJAMIN CARDOZO, THE NATURE OF THE JUDICIAL PROCESS 10 (1921) (noting that "judge-made law [is] one of the existing realities of life").

17. *Id.* at 103.

18. The concept of the "evolutionary movement" of the Constitution has been expressed by Justice Brennan in Regents of the University of California v. Bakke, 438 U.S. 312 (1978), and by Justice Marshall in his speech given on the occasion of the bicentennial of the Constitution. In *Bakke,* in a partial dissent joined by Justices White, Marshall, and Blackmun, Justice Brennan discussed how Congress had "eschewed any static definition of discrimination [in Title VI of the 1964 Civil Rights Act] in favor of broad language that could be shaped by experience, administrative necessity and *evolving judicial doctrine.*" *Id.* at 337 (Brennan, J., dissenting in part) (emphasis added). In Justice Brennan's view, Congress was aware of the "*evolutionary change* that constitutional law in the area of racial discrimination was undergoing in 1964." *Id.* at 340. Congress, thus, equated Title VI's prohibition against discrimination with the commands of the Fifth and Fourteenth Amendments to the Constitution so that the meaning of the statute's prohibition would evolve with the interpretations of the command of the Constitution. *See id.* at 340. In another context, during his speech given on the occasion of the bicentennial of the Constitution, Justice Marshall commented that he did "not believe that the meaning of the Constitution was forever 'fixed' at the Philadelphia Convention." Thurgood Marshall, *Reflections on the Bicentennial of the United States Constitution,* 101 HARV. L. REV. 1, 2 (1987). In Justice Marshall's view, the Constitution had been made far more meaningful through its "*promising evolution* through 200 years of history." *Id.* at 5 (emphasis added).

19. Sharon McPhail, *Will The Real Clarence Thomas Stand Up?,*

NAT'L B. ASS'N MAG., Oct. 1991, at 1.

20. *Id.; see* Ruth Marcus, *Self-Made Conservative; Nominee Insists He Be Judged on Merits,* WASH. POST, July 2, 1991, at A1; Haywood Burns, *Clarence Thomas, A Counterfeit Hero,* N.Y. TIMES, July 9, 1991, at A19.

21. *See, e.g.,* Clarence Thomas, *The Equal Employment Opportunity Commission: Reflections on a New Philosophy,* 15 STETSON L. REV. 29, 35 (1985) (asserting that the civil rights community is "wallowing in self-delusion and pulling the public with it"); Juan Williams, *EEOC Chairman Blasts Black Leaders,* WASH. POST, Oct. 25, 1984, at A7 ("These guys [black leaders] are sitting there watching the destruction of our race. . . . Ronald Reagan isn't the problem. Former President Jimmy Carter was not the problem. The lack of black leadership is the problem.").

22. *See supra* note 9.

23. *See* Clarence Thomas, *Black Americans Based Claim for Freedom on Constitution,* SAN DIEGO UNION & TRIB., Oct. 6, 1987, at B7 (claiming that Marshall's observation of the deficiencies in some respects of the Framers' constitutional vision "alienates all Americans, and not just black Americans, from their high and noble intention").

24. *See id.*

25. Marshall, *supra* note 18, at 5.

26. Thomas, *supra* note 23, at B7. In the same diatribe, you also quoted out of context excerpts from the works of Frederick Douglass, Martin Luther King, Jr., and John Hope Franklin. *See id.* Their works, however, provide no support for what amounted to a scurrilous attack on Justice Marshall. In fact, John Hope Franklin wrote the epilogue to a report by the NAACP opposing your nomination to the Supreme Court. *See* John Hope Franklin, *Booker T. Washington, Revisited,* N.Y. TIMES, Aug. 1, 1991, at A21. There he quite properly observed that, by adopting a philosophy of alleged self-help without seeking to assure equal opportunities to all persons, you "placed [yourself] in the unseemly position of denying to others the very opportunities and the kind of assistance from public and private quarters that have placed [you] where you are today."

Id.

27. Marshall, *supra* note 18, at 5.

28. *Id.*

29. On April 1, 1987, some weeks before Justice Marshall's speech, I gave the Herman Phleger Lecture at Stanford University. I stated in my presentation:

    > In this year of the Bicentennial you will hear a great deal that is laudatory about our nation's Constitution and legal heritage. Much of this praise will be justified. The danger is that the current oratory and scholarship may lapse into mere self-congratulatory back-patting, suggesting that everything in America has been, or is, near perfect.
    >
    > We must not allow our euphoria to cause us to focus solely on our strengths. Somewhat like physicians examining a mighty patient, we also must diagnose and evaluate the pathologies that have disabled our otherwise healthy institutions.
    >
    > I trust that you will understand that my critiques of our nation's past and present shortcomings do not imply that I am oblivious to its many exceptional virtues. I freely acknowledge the importance of two centuries of our enduring and evolving Constitution, the subsequently enacted Bill of Rights, the Thirteenth, Fourteenth, Fifteenth and Nineteenth Amendments, and the protections of these rights, more often than not, by federal courts.
    >
    > Passion for freedom and commitment to liberty are important values in American society. If we can retain this passion and commitment and direct it towards eradicating the remaining significant areas of social injustice on our nation's unfinished agenda, our pride should persist—despite the daily tragic reminders that there are far too many homeless, far too many hungry, and far too many victims of racism, sexism, and pernicious biases against those of different religions and national origins. The truth is that, even with these faults, we have been building a society with increasing levels of social justice embracing more and more Americans each decade.

    A. Leon Higginbotham, Jr., *The Bicentennial of the Constitution: A Racial Perspective,* STAN. LAW., Fall 1987, at 8.

30. JAMES BALDWIN, *The Fire Next Time, in* THE PRICE OF THE TICKET 336 (1985). In a similar vein, on April 5, 1976, at the dedication of Independence Hall in Philadelphia on the anniversary of the Declaration of Independence, Judge William Hastie told the celebrants that, although there was reason to

salute the nation on its bicentennial, "a nation's beginning is a proper source of reflective pride only to the extent that the subsequent and continuing process of its becoming deserves celebration." GILBERT WARE, WILLIAM HASTIE: GRACE UNDER PRESSURE 242 (1984).

31. *See* Williams, *supra* note 21, at A7 (quoting Clarence Thomas).

32. *See* JOHN HOPE FRANKLIN & ALFRED A. MOSS, JR., FROM SLAVERY TO FREEDOM: A HISTORY OF NEGRO AMERICANS 388–89 (1988); *see also* RICHARD KLUGER, SIMPLE JUSTICE: THE HISTORY OF *BROWN V. BOARD OF EDUCATION* AND BLACK AMERICA'S STRUGGLE FOR EQUALITY 219 (1975).

33. *See* FRANKLIN & MOSS, *supra* note 32, at 388–89; KLUGER, *supra* note 32, at 219.

34. *See* WARE, *supra* note 30, at 95–98, 124–33.

35. Frederick Douglass, Speech Before The West Indian Emancipation Society (Aug. 4, 1857), *in* 2 PHILIP S. FONER, THE LIFE AND WRITINGS OF FREDERICK DOUGLASS 437 (1950).

36. *See* Crandall v. State, 10 Conn. 339 (1834).

37. *See* LEON F. LITWACK, NORTH OF SLAVERY: THE NEGRO IN THE FREE STATES, 1790–1860, at 147 (1961).

38. *See* Roberts v. City of Boston, 59 Mass. (5 Cush.) 198 (1850).

39. 182 A. 590 (1936).

40. 305 U.S. 337 (1938).

41. 339 U.S. 629 (1950).

42. 339 U.S. 637 (1950).

43. *See* MILLER, *supra* note 15, at 336.

44. *McLaurin,* 339 U.S. at 640.

45. I have used the term NAACP to include both the NAACP and the NAACP Legal Defense Fund. For examples of civil rights cases, see DERRICK A. BELL, JR., RACE, RACISM AND AMERICAN LAW 57–59, 157–62, 186–92, 250–58, 287–300, 477–99 (2d ed. 1980); JACK GREENBERG, RACE RELATIONS AND AMERICAN LAW 32–61 (1959).

46. 102 CONG. REC. 4255, 4515 (1956).

47. *Id.* at 4516.

48. *Id.*

49. *See id.*

50. *See* Doug Freelander, *The Senate-Bush: The Polls Give Him 'Excellent Chance,'* HOUSTON POST, Oct. 11, 1964, § 17, at 8.

51. *See* David S. Broder, *Reagan Attacks the Great Society,* N.Y. TIMES, June 17, 1966, at 41.

52. *See* CHARLES WHALEN & BARBARA WHALEN, THE LONGEST DEBATE: A LEGISLATIVE HISTORY OF THE 1964 CIVIL RIGHTS ACT 143 (1967).

53. *Id*.

54. SENATE COMMERCE COMM., CIVIL RIGHTS—PUBLIC ACCOMMODATIONS, S. REP. NO. 872, 88th Cong., 2d Sess. 62–63, 73–76 (1964) (Individual Views of Senator Strom Thurmond).

55. *The Supreme Court; Excerpts From News Conference Announcing Court Nominee,* N.Y. TIMES, July 2, 1991, at A14 (statement of President Bush).

56. Peter Binzer, *Bowser Is an Old Hand at Playing the Political Game in Philadelphia,* PHILA. INQUIRER, Nov. 13, 1991, at A11 (quoting Charles Bowser).

57. WILLIAM A. SINCLAIR, THE AFTERMATH OF SLAVERY: A STUDY OF THE CONDITION AND ENVIRONMENT OF THE AMERICAN NEGRO 187 (Afro-Am Press 1969) (1905) (quoting Senator Benjamin Tillman).

58. 321 U.S. 649 (1944).

59. 369 U.S. 186 (1962).

60. New York Trust Company v. Eisner, 256 U.S. 345, 349 (1921).

61. Act of Mar. 12, 1912, ch. 157, § 1, 1912 Va. Acts 330, 330.

62. *Id*. § 3, at 330–31.

63. *Id*. § 4, at 331.

64. *Id*. There were a few statutory exceptions, the most important being that the servants of "the other race" could reside upon the premises that his or her employer owned or occupied. *Id*. § 9, at 332.

65. *See* Ashland, Va., Ordinance (Sept. 12, 1911) [hereinafter, *Ashland Ordinance*]; Richmond, Va., Ordinance (Dec. 5, 1911) [hereinafter, *Richmond Ordinance*].

66. *Ashland Ordinance, supra* note 65, §§ 1–3; *Richmond Ordinance, supra* note 65, §§ 1, 2.

67. *See* Hopkins v. City of Richmond, 86 S.E. 139, 142 (Va. 1915). At the time of the purchase, the house was occupied by a black tenant who had lived there prior to the enactment of the ordinance, so the purchase precipitated no change in the color composition or racial density of the neighborhood or block.

68. *Id*. at 141.

69. *Id*.

70. *See* Buchanan v. Warley, 245 U.S. 60 (1917).

71. 334 U.S. 1 (1948).

72. 392 U.S. 409 (1968).

73. *Id*. at 449 (Harlan, J., dissenting).

74. *See* Loving v. Virginia, 388 U.S. 1, 4–6 (1967).

75. *See* Loving v. Virginia, 147 S.E.2d 78 (Va. 1966), *rev'd,* 388 U.S. 1 (1967).

76. *Id*. at 79 (quoting the trial court).

77. *Loving,* 388 U.S. at 3 (quoting the trial judge).

78. Chambers v. Florida, 309 U.S. 227, 241 (1940).

79. Wards Cove Packing Co. v. Antonio, 490 U.S. 642, 662 (1989) (Blackmun, J., dissenting).

80. *The Thomas Hearings; Excerpts from Senate Session on the Thomas Nomination,* N.Y. TIMES, Sept. 11, 1991, at A1 (opening statement of Clarence Thomas).

81. It is hardly possible to name all the individuals who fought to bring equal rights to all Americans. Some are gone. Others are fighting still. They include Prudence Crandall, Charles Sumner, Robert Morris, William Lloyd Garrison, William T. Coleman, Jr., Jack Greenberg, Judges Louis Pollak, Constance Baker Motley, Robert Carter, Collins Seitz, Justices Hugo Black, Lewis Powell, Harry Blackmun and John Paul Stevens. For those whom I have not named, their contribution to the cause of civil rights may be all the more heroic for at times being unsung. But, to paraphrase Yale Professor Owen Fiss's tribute to Justice Marshall: "As long as there is law, their names should be remembered, and when their stories are told, all the world should listen." Owen Fiss, *A Tribute to Justice Marshall,* 105 HARV. L. REV. 49, 55 (1991).

82. For an analysis of discrimination faced by Blacks in the areas of

voting, education, employment, and housing, see GUNNAR MYRDAL, AN AMERICAN DILEMMA: THE NEGRO PROBLEM AND MODERN DEMOCRACY 479–86 (9th ed. 1944) (voting); JOHN HOPE FRANKLIN & ALFRED A. MOSS, JR., FROM SLAVERY TO FREEDOM: A HISTORY OF NEGRO AMERICANS 360–69 (6th ed. 1988) (education); COMMITTEE ON THE STATUS OF BLACK AMERICANS, NATIONAL RESEARCH COUNCIL, A COMMON DESTINY: BLACKS AND AMERICAN SOCIETY 88–91, 315–23 (Gerald D. Jaynes & Robin M. Williams, Jr. eds., 1989) (housing and employment); *see also* MARY FRANCES BERRY & JOHN W. BLASSINGAME, LONG MEMORY: THE BLACK EXPERIENCE IN AMERICA (1982).

83. *See* A. LEON HIGGINBOTHAM, JR., IN THE MATTER OF COLOR at vii–ix (1978); A. Leon Higginbotham, Jr., *The Dream with Its Back Against the Wall,* YALE L. REP., Spring 1990, at 34; A. Leon Higginbotham, Jr., *A Tribute to Justice Thurgood Marshall,* 105 HARV. L. REV. 55, 61 (1991).

84. As I wrote in a recent tribute to Justice Marshall:

> There appears to be a deliberate retrenchment by a majority of the current Supreme Court on many basic issues of human rights that Thurgood Marshall advocated and that the Warren and Burger Courts vindicated. This retrenchment . . . caused Justice Marshall's dissents to escalate from a total of 19 in his first five years while Earl Warren was Chief Justice, to a total of 225 in the five years since William Rehnquist became Chief Justice.

Higginbotham, *supra* note 83, at 65 n.55 (1991) (citation omitted); *see also* Higginbotham, *supra* note 3, at 587 & n.526 (citing Justice Marshall's warning that "[i]t is difficult to characterize last term's decisions [of the Supreme Court] as the product of anything other than a deliberate retrenchment of the civil rights agenda"); A. Leon Higginbotham, Jr., F. Michael Higginbotham & Sandile Ngcobo, *De Jure Housing Segregation in the United States and South Africa: The Difficult Pursuit for Racial Justice,* 4 U. ILL. L. REV. 763, 874 n.612 (1990) (noting the recent tendency of the Supreme Court to ignore race discrimination).

85. In his recent tribute to Justice Marshall, Justice Brennan wrote: "In his twenty-four Terms on the Supreme Court, Justice

Marshall played a crucial role in enforcing the constitutional protections that distinguish our democracy. Indeed, he leaves behind an enviable record of opinions supporting the rights of the less powerful and less fortunate." William J. Brennan, Jr., *A Tribute to Justice Marshall,* 105 HARV. L. REV. 23 (1991). You may serve on the Supreme Court twenty years longer than Justice Marshall. At the end of your career, I hope that thoughtful Americans may be able to speak similarly of you.

ANDREW ROSS

The Private
Parts of
Justice

Before the Thomas-Hill hearings came to a close, the
Cable News Network ran a feature on how the spectacle
had been playing in other countries. Two British citizens,
both white, were interviewed on London streets. The first,
a rather proper, middle-aged woman of means, walking
her dog in a Belgravia-type square, told the interviewer
that she just couldn't see what all the fuss was about. The
second, a younger, more bohemian man, standing on a less
posh street, said that the hearings demonstrated that the
British had a good deal of catching up to do in the area of
women's rights. The CNN double play reinforced some
obvious British stereotypes. But its real purpose was to
reinforce the perception of U.S. culture as both democratic
in its public exposure of political corruption (no doubt
quite "vulgar" from the perspective of the classy English-
woman) and pioneering in the advancements of its civil

society ("progressive" from the perspective of the male feminist). Among other things, this dual perception of the national culture is the primary shaping principle behind CNN's own house style for editing and broadcasting world news across the major league of nations. Performing the global function once served by the BBC in the age of radio, CNN's decentered corporate populism has effectively replaced the voice of paternal imperialism that used to issue from Europe's metropolitan centers.

To underline the contrast, consider the other sex-and-power scandals that were in the news that week. The British public was still ritually recovering from the latest scandal in the grand national tradition of "kinky barrister sex." Sir Allan Green, the Director of Public Prosecutions no less, resigned after his detainment for "kerb crawling" under the Sexual Offences Act (a bill that criminalizes the persistent male solicitation of women for sex, and had been widely used by police on the street to harass immigrant men on a range of unrelated issues). The class dimensions of the barrister sex scandal are such an integral part of the national culture that such instances function discreetly in the manner of a familiar institutional farce with Pythonesque overtones. Every so often a case like Green's is thrown up to resolve the otherwise persistent contradiction perceived by the general public that the upper class can have its own separate morality while at the same time enjoying the authority to police and judge the morality of all other classes.

In the States the revelations of that week were less discreet and more, as it were, republican. The Kennedy-dynasty saga was loudly spinning its umpteenth true-life yarn, televangelist Jimmy Swaggart's tryst with yet another prostitute was being rudely exposed on national TV, a whole slew of celebrities like LaToya Jackson, Roseanne (Barr) Arnold (and her husband), Brian Wilson, and Sinead O'Connor were confessing in the national press to having been abused as children, and, in a small Texas grill, George Hennard, Jr., was blowing a fuse while watching Anita Hill's first televised press conference: screaming at the TV screen, "You dumb bitch! You bastards opened the door for all the women," this was the man who would slaughter twenty-three people the very next day, ostensibly as an act of revenge against women—"those mostly white tremendously female vipers," as he put it—who had wronged him in his life.

These were the bizarre ingredients of a media celebrity culture, where the express elevator from obscurity to fame, wealth, and power is often shared by the most unlikely occupants. On Capitol Hill another episode of the great exceptionalist national soap opera called "Only in America" was being telecast, and if at times it resembled what Senator Charles Grassley (R-Iowa) called "a soap opera about the elite, and aspiring power brokers here in Washington, D.C. [where] there was plenty of talk about Yale law school, establishment law firms, and moving up the political ladder," no one involved needed a populist cue card to know when to evoke the lowly social origins of the chief witnesses or when to address the people of America as a jury in attendance. As a media event, the hearings, to use Marshall McLuhan terms, were both "hot" and "cool" by turns, stage-managed to quench the mini prairie fire, in the spontaneous form of women's anger, that had precipitated the need for this gathering. In the course of the hearings, women's anger was redefined as a shadowy conspiratorial impulse, ruthlessly conjured up in the form of the slick legal tactics of equally shadowy fifth-column interest groups; the "real women of America," the female equivalents of John Q. Public, were ventriloquized as speaking out against a star witness who had been cast as delusional and repressed; and the sentiments of African Americans, whom none of the white senators felt comfortable about ventriloquizing, were represented by the anemic statistic of a poll percentile.

So much for the populist elements. As for the elite soap opera, the glamour had been written out of the script, revealing an awkward and pathetic underside—a full ethnographic exposure of the style and manners of powerful white males stretched out, for three days, on the prime-time rack, and exhibiting classic confessional types, from the shambling, guilt-tripped liberal on the left to the unregenerate misogynist pit bull on the right. It is difficult to imagine a more effective way of dramatizing the crisis in legitimacy of the country's ruling elite than this pitiful comedy of manners in which distinctions between sexual harassment, date rape, seduction tactics, flirting, and erotic fantasy (not to mention the distinction between public questioning and lynching) were all quite deliriously jumbled up in the minds of the nation's lawmakers. It wasn't just one bad guy being exposed, as had been the case, say, with the televised Army-McCarthy hearings forty years earlier; what was on trial here was a whole class. All that was salvaged on the elite side was the reputation of the TV network news division, for whom the hearings were a no-lose option offered on a plate, guaranteed to wash away the stain of warmongering left over from the Gulf War, and to win back some of the news clout lost to CNN during that war.

In the print media, voices partial to Anita Hill's claims were also hoisted on the populist petard. In its Monday edition, the *Wall Street Journal* rolled up its sleeves and set about disparaging "the state of political correctness in the nation's elite newsrooms." Rich as it was to hear the editors of this people's organ proclaim that "the media live in a different reality plane from the people who do things like believing Clarence Thomas and giving landslide victories to a Ronald Reagan," their anti-intellectual line reappeared in many other forms in the wake of polls depicting widespread support for Thomas (three out of five) and not least in the suggestion that feminists were also hopelessly out of touch with the real women of America. Polled public opinion, that old ghost in the machine of statistical surveillance, was wheeled out to stick it to the nattering nabobs and the protesting prudes. Worse yet, the polls, like those conducted during the Gulf War, were given widespread credence as indicators of popular conviction, and provoked much soul-searching, especially among feminists and the African-American left. If nothing else, this response proved that, in the lack of anything remotely close to a majority of voters at election time, the capacity of the selectively polled to say yes or no to a set of bluntly diagnostic questions increasingly serves as one of the primary institutions for manufacturing and regulating consent in the modern American technocracy. As a medium, polling tells us no more about what and how people think about politics than does the TV news convention of sound-biting moving bodies on a street. As a medium, polls rarely carry a message; they *are* the message, to cite McLuhan's consistently misunderstood dictum.

To further illustrate this point, consider that the conduct of the politicians and witnesses involved in the Thomas-Hill hearings was widely interpreted at the time as yet another example of how successful the right wing has been in winning the war of images over the last decade. Conservatives, it is often argued, have come to understand the media better than liberals. This argument, which is by now a commonplace, assumes that the language of images is a neutral medium that is simply maximized by those who have the best command of the language. It ignores the fact that the media industries are owned by certain corporate interests, and that they are structurally organized in such a way as to generate consent for the political and economic interests of business and government elites. To put it more bluntly, the spin doctors get it the wrong way round when they say that conservatives understand media better. It's much more accurate to say that currently existing media, both popular and elite, understand conservatives and conservatism better, and that they work to preserve established interests, their own included. This was all too apparent during the Gulf War, when the phrase "military-industrial-media complex" took on a highly visible dimension on nightly TV.

The Thomas-Hill hearings bore out this point in a number of ways. Above all, the hearings were not broadcast, C-Span style, as an unedited event. The sessions were surrounded with, and were stitched together by, commentary from a small battalion of anchorpeople, reporters, lawyers, media managers, and expert opinion-makers. It was in the recaps, updates, and summarized reports that a narrative plot was created out of the story's raw materials, accompanied by selected footage to illustrate the plot. Much of this commentary turned on speculation about the apparently absent role of Thomas's White House handlers. By way of compensation, the commentary of the network news teams was habitually framed to fit the perspective of the White House trying to make profitable sense out of the proceedings. While the White House worked around the clock to contain and limit the agenda of the hearings, the editing job performed by the network news teams anticipated, if it did not entirely mimic, the administration's concerns. In addressing the problem of how to manage such an "unregulated" media event, a shared logic prevailed—the preservation of authority and privilege on the part of news commentators as well as the senatorial oligarchy and the Bush administration. When the rules of the game are so widely agreed upon and so faithfully observed by the major players, then the populist wild card— throw 'em all out—turns out to be one of the safest cards in the pack.

On the face of it, however, there weren't supposed to be any rules. From the very beginning no one on the hearings committee seemed to be able to agree about the rules, except to pay lip service to the bromide that legal rules of evidence did not apply. As for the rules of broadcast TV, it took only a few minutes of Anita Hill's testimony to breach network "family standards" (George Bush averred that her revelations were "deeply offensive to American families") and to open up a floodgate of speech that was all too free by anyone's standards. The result had little to do with the drama of the *personal* that is telejournalism's stock-in-trade. Instead, we saw a hypervisible account of experiences customarily sealed off within the genre of the private, things not seen even in the land of tabloid TV. This is why TV viewers sat openmouthed all weekend; the prosaic shock effect of Hill's plain-style description of everyday sexist behavior broke the viewer's first law of mainstream news reporting—your own politics, if they return, always return to you in an alienated form. That was how it felt, at least until the spin people broke the trance at the end of each session of the hearings. Without their contextualizing, the feel of the testimony announced that the rules were being challenged, especially the separation between private and public that is as rigorously observed in TV land as it is regulated in the law of the land.

The Thomas-Hill hearings were nothing if not a media event, a milestone in TV history, as they say. More important, however, they were also a legal event. The letter of the law may have been absent, but the spirit of the law, with all of its ideological trappings, was all too present. Although the analogy was often made, the hearings felt nothing like TV courtroom drama, a genre punctuated by a series of tried and true emotional hooks. Nor was there much in common with the new *vérité* courtroom shows, although, throughout the hearings that weekend, the advertising moment was seized in a timely fashion by Court TV, a new cable channel wholly devoted to "live" trial coverage, and which subsequently scored its first big scoop with the William Kennedy Smith trial. On the networks' programming schedule, liberally stuffed with law-enforcement shows and yuppie-lawyer-lifestyle dramas, the Thomas-Hill show could have been just another popular genre segment to add to the vastly disproportionate attention that broadcast TV devotes to legal culture (dispropor-

tionate, that is, in relation to the infrequency of legal interventions in most of our daily lives).

But the hearings were also telling another story about
the nation founded on law, and Clarence Thomas, ironically, was the first to sound the alarm, in a prepared statement that lashed out against the "invasion" of his privacy:
"This is not America. This is Kafkaesque. It has got to stop.
It must stop for the benefit of future nominees and our
country. Enough is enough. . . . This is not what America
is all about." Notwithstanding that his own conception of
"natural law" sounded Kafkaesque to almost everyone to
whom it was explained, Thomas was appealing here to the
popular ideology of constitutionalism. America, unlike
other, more Kafkaesque countries, is supposed to be the
place where the legal process is not an instrument of state
repression, where it makes sense to its citizens, where
everyone is entitled to a fair shake, and where there is no
contradiction between the fact that the country's laws are
constantly in a state of redefinition and the perception that
the legal rights of its citizens were already fully formed in
the mind's eye of its constitutional framers, whose intentions fully reflected the common sense or natural reason of
the people. "What America is all about" has more to do
with the law than is the case in any other national culture.
This is why Thomas's complaint carried the rhetorical
weight that it did. It is also why his appeal for privacy,
served up with lashings of corny pathos, nauseated those
who knew that, as a Supreme Court judge, he was likely
to legislate against the protection of their own "private"
rights.

Aside from Thomas's mock self-presentation as a victim,
there were other reasons why the hearings questioned

"what America is all about." More than any other political event since Watergate, the televised hearings overtly challenged the legitimacy of government by law in a nation which, according to a recent Harper's Index, produces fifty law-school graduates for every engineering graduate (as against Japan's ten-to-one ratio of engineers to lawyers, a figure that explains, among other things, the rank, unchecked corruption of Japanese politicians). In a society where a great majority of problems and decisions are turned over to the law without any semblance of a prior public debate, how is popular consent obtained for non-democratic government by law, as interpreted by *unelected* officials in the judiciary, rather than by democratic government by the people, as interpreted by *elected* officials in the legislature? It would be too facile to reply that much of this consent is obtained through TV and filmic representations of the law, and yet without today's barrage of cop shows and courtroom docudramas, people would be less willing to grant officers of the law the kind of powers that they exercise in civil and juridical life. In recent years the need to obtain consent has required the television industry to become a junior partner in the business of law. In a 1981 case, *Chandler* v. *Florida,* the Supreme Court recognized that states may need to grant direct media access to their courts in order to affirm the legitimacy of their judicial systems. It therefore upheld the Florida court's view that "because of the significant effects of the courts on the day-to-day lives of the citizenry, it was essential that the people have confidence in the process. . . . broadcast coverage of trials would contribute to wider public acceptance and understanding of decisions." Most states today utilize this practice, and Florida itself went to town with the

Kennedy trial, the first to be broadcast nationally in its entirety. While Thomas and his senatorial supporters objected histrionically to the close scrutiny of the hearings, it is nonetheless true that the legitimacy of the legal system today is increasingly dependent upon some such media scrutiny. Indeed, it is precisely through the integral assistance of a media presence that the legal system is able to continue performing "high-tech lynchings" of the sort that Thomas so dishonestly evoked at the hearings.

No matter how shamelessly professional lawyers and politicians play their cases to the fourth estate, the official presumption is that ultimately the rules of law, being rational, are immune to everything that the media represents, as an arena of social and political opinion. Consider the following remarks made by Senator Alan Simpson (R-Wyoming), who distinguished himself by the most Neanderthal performance of all the committee's members. In his infamous McCarthyist attack on Hill—"Now I really am getting stuff over the transom about Professor Hill. I've got letters hanging out my pockets, I've got faxes, letters from her former law professors, statements from Tulsa, saying 'Watch out for this woman' "—Simpson unleashed his impatience with "this sexual harassment crap" by reminding us that the truth, in the case of hearings such as these, would always be elusive. The question of "who ate the cabbage, as we say out in the wild west," could not be determined outside of a court of law: "I'll tell you how you find the truth. You get into an adversarial courtroom, and everybody raises their hand once more, and you go at it with the rules of evidence, and you really punch around in it, and we can't do that. It's impossible to do that in this place." Simpson may have been presenting a cowboy version of legal process (among the good, the bad, and the ugly on TV that weekend, he was surely the ugliest, in all senses), but his version was nonetheless an orthodox statement of the liberal view of the rules of law shared by all the lawyers on the committee, regardless of their positions on the political spectrum. According to this view, the rules of law alone can determine the rectitude of judgments because these rules are founded on neutral and objective legal reasoning, rather than upon social and political reasoning. The authority of the law rests entirely upon the supposition that legal and evidentiary reasoning is a higher realm of scientific logic. The "correct" judgment will be reached, inevitably, if only sufficiently qualified people—technical experts who alone understand the obfuscatory rhetoric of legal language and culture—have the opportunity to "punch around" in the rule-ordered system of an "adversarial court." Subservience to precedents and prior decisions—*stare decisis*—reinforces the perception that legal reasoning is subject to its own history of rulings, and is no way bound to political pressures of the moment.

While the senators were not structurally empowered to ascertain who "ate the cabbage," their loud disagreements over the conduct of the hearings fully dramatized, for every viewer, the political significance of the rules of order that were established at the rocky outset and subsequently wrangled over throughout the proceedings. What this debate exposed to view were the actual political decisions that go into creating a consensus about internal rules. As a result, the crucial distinction between internally accepted rules—formally neutral—and externally imposed rules—politically motivated—was inoperative from the get-go.

Nor were matters helped by the committee members' repeated caveat that "this is not a trial," and that "this is not
a courtroom." Such warnings cast as much dizzying doubt
upon the procedural logic of the hearings as Magritte's
painting *This Is Not a Pipe* had cast upon the rules for
representing a pipe.

Of course, it will be said that there is a difference between the rules of order in hearings of this sort and rules
of law in a courtroom. It will be said that the political
disputes only arose because the rationally proven rules of
law were not, and could not be, observed. But this response only begs the question of the social and political
underpinnings of all such "neutral" rules. In the course of
the hearings what we saw was a dress rehearsal (finally, very
little was improvised) of the conditions of expediency
under which rules for any such legal proceeding would be
debated and agreed upon. Deprived of an authentic context for the corrosionproof discourse of legal reasoning, the
senators constructed a makeshift setting from as much of
the legal furniture as could be permitted. The architecture
of this setting was governed by the rhetoric of disavowal:
"although this is not a trial . . ." or "we know this is not
a trial, but nonetheless. . . ." On the one hand, this could
include the familiar methodological structure of
prosecutorial questioning employed by Arlen Specter
(R-Pennsylvania) during Anita Hill's testimony, or Joseph
Biden's (D-Delaware) reminder to Thomas that, just as in
a court of law, "the presumption is with you" (a presumption that happened to be at odds with the sexual harassment
policy drawn up at Thomas's own Equal Employment
Opportunity Commission (EEOC), which allowed for the
charging party to prevail in cases that lacked third-party

evidence). On the other hand, it could also include confessional reminders that the nation's lawmakers are not in the Senate to judge people but to make policy in the name of the people. The combined result looked something like the Janus face of the state, exercising power in a way that is usually not exposed to public view, because the state is supposed to be composed of separated powers, just as the legitimacy of the law depends upon its claim to be independent of state power. The effect of this exposé was to trigger a wave of public disgust with the committee, feeding off the kind of social disrespect that habitually makes lawyers and politicians the most frequent butts of anti-professional humor in our society.

But it would be all too easy to conclude that the hearings vividly demonstrated how law, and everything pertaining to the law, is simply politics by other means. Those devoted to demystifying the authority of the law might well have applauded the whole farce as a job well done: the emperor's clothes were undone, revealing long dong and all. To my mind, this would be a dangerous conclusion. First of all, the decade-long movement for judicial restraint, which is only now beginning to exert its pervasive influence on the entire system, has rested its claims precisely on the argument that the law has been used too expediently for activist purposes in creating new rights and freedoms in the postwar period. It is the conservatives who are now on the Supreme Court who have argued that law should not be in the business of politics. It is in their interests that the law, as we have understood it until recently, should be delegitimized, thereby reining in the power of the courts. Clarence Thomas himself was practicing this philosophy during the hearings when he questioned the legitimacy of the entire process. Playing the Black Panther card—I will not recognize the "white justice" of this "court"—he culled a good deal of sympathy, and helped to save his nomination, by assailing the authority of his questioning posse of white patrician lawmakers. Over a decade earlier he (along with Hill, another career Reaganite) had been appointed at the EEOC, like most of Reagan's wrecker appointees at similar agencies, explicitly to gut the agency and to trash its laws and guidelines.

It may not be enough to say, then, that the Court today has lost its legitimacy, and is operating as a kind of rogue agency for right-wing opinion. This argument makes little headway against conservative claims that the authority of the current Rehnquist court has been earned by a movement righteously aimed at purging politics from the law. That judicial restraint is now defined as apolitical, at least in relation to judicial activism, is a sign of the times, reflecting current conservative power to rule definitions. In the earlier part of the century it was judicial restraint as preached and practiced by liberals that was seen as the political option. So, too, in the early days of the republic, theories of natural law (even of the sort espoused, however nebulously, by Clarence Thomas) could be invoked on the one hand as a Lockean guarantee of the sanctity of private property and on the other as a populist hedge against the elitist expertise of a lawyer class hired to protect the property interests of the aristocracy. My point here, in appealing to legal history, however briefly, is not to demonstrate the utter relativism of claims made by legal theory, but rather to suggest that arguments made about the legitimacy of the law are only as strong as the political forces mobilized behind them. There may be little to be gained, and much to be lost, by analytically reducing the law to a realm of barely tenable language propositions, sustained only by the myth of legal reasoning, on the one hand, and the need to maintain a hierarchical social order, on the other. However alienating its form as an institutional system, the medium of the law also remains of paramount importance to those who have used it as a means of achieving democratic freedoms and rights, and who need it today to preserve and extend those freedoms and rights. Unlike almost anything else, only the law can change itself.

Consequently, what was striking about the Thomas-Hill hearings was not simply their merciless exposé of the political chicanery underlying every aspect of the nomination and confirmation process. What was also on dramatic display was the crucial process by which the law is called upon to distinguish between public and private spheres, a distinction between virtually separated spheres that is indeed fundamental to the business of modern law. The law itself may have been on trial during these hearings, but the hearings themselves were only important because it was the law's definition of public and private spheres, challenged at every level by the charge of sexual harassment, that was at stake and under scrutiny.

Anita Hill may have put it best when in the course of intense questioning about details of her statement by Arlen Specter she suggested that this seasoned trial lawyer from Pennsylvania could not see the wood for the trees:

If you start to look at each individual problem with this statement, then you are not going to be satisfied that it is true, but I think that the statement needs to be taken as a whole . . . there is nothing in my background, no motivation that would show I would make up something like this. I guess one does really have to understand something about the nature of sexual harassment, it is very difficult for people to come forward with these kinds of things. It wasn't as if I rushed forward with this information. I can only tell you what happened, and, to the best of my recollection, what occurred, and ask you to take that into account. Now, you have to make your own judgment about it from there on, but I do want you to take into account the whole thing.

In drawing everyone's attention to the big picture ("the whole thing"), Hill delivered a blow to the fetishizing of detail that was Specter's first-strike weapon in the stockpile of legal reasoning. To dwell, she was suggesting, with hairsplitting precision on specific details would be to miss the much wider social significance of her statement. This wider significance included not only the nature of sexual harassment but also the state of gender relations and race relations in society at the present time. From an evidentiary perspective, legal reasoning has a prior obligation to attend to the logical consistency of claims, statements, and arguments, often at the cost of disregarding the social implications of the law. The spirit of Hill's entreaty was one in which the law does have an obligation, as a socially attuned body of interpretive codes and enabling powers, "to take into account the whole thing." Indeed, it is only from the latter perspective that issues related to gender and race make any sense at all. It would not otherwise be possible to see how, in the course of the hearings, the public import of sexual harassment was consistently privatized, in Hill's case, or, by contrast, to see how Thomas's attempt to protect his privacy was consistently respected.

This contrast was, perhaps, most evident in the attention focused on private bodily parts during the hearings. Here surely was a very literal (even anatomical) example of how the sphere of privacy relates to boundary definitions of the public sphere. As the questioning of senator after senator homed in on discussion of genitalia and other discrete bodily parts, it also provided a dramatic illustration of the methodology of "male" fetishism. Again Hill countered this follow-the-parts strategy by insisting that it was the context of her unequal relations with Thomas in the workplace that gave significance to what would have been otherwise inconsequential to her—the isolated description by Thomas of sexual acts and sexual parts. In other words, it was the relationship of the private part to the public whole that made these descriptions objectionable to her. Arguably, the Republicans' fetishist strategy of isolating the parts won the day, because they succeeded, partly through their own mock embarrassment, and partly through the systematic character destruction of Hill, to define her as an essentially private individual, with private motives. As remote as could be from the stereotype of the public actor who may desire to be "a hero in the Civil Rights Movement," she was portrayed as either overtaken by private erotomaniac fantasies or as prudishly incapable of decoding boisterous male social intercourse. Hill was defined by a private characterology that determined all of her responses, rather than as someone whose public identities as a professional, a government employee, a lawyer, an African American, a woman, a Republican, among others, all had a heavy sociohistorical bearing upon her treatment in the workplace. In contrast to the kind of private person who might have been influenced by *The Exorcist,* Thomas was allowed to cast himself as the kind of private person who might have read Kafka's *Trial* and understood the Kafkaesque significance of his being the accused in a pseudotrial. In contrast to Hill's fantasy-filled mind, Thomas was accused only of having a "closed mind," a public deficiency in his capacity as a judge that could be easily construed as a virtue when it came to protecting his own privacy, as any self-respecting man would want to do, and would be expected to do, in a context such as these hearings.

The contrast in treatment of privacy in the case of Hill and Thomas was also marked by racial elements. This was particularly evident in the discussion by Senator Orrin Hatch (R-Utah) of the significance of the size of Thomas's penis, a discussion that centered upon the public mythologies historically associated with the penis size of black men. In this instance the distinction between the stereotypical phallus and the anatomical penis more or less corresponded to the division between public and private spheres. In the course of the discussions, it was established that the size of Thomas's penis was not, and perhaps could not ever be, a private affair. Thomas's supporters, like Hatch, were trying to show that his privacy in this matter was being violated, and that this was a consequence of racist history. But no one who watched the interchange between Hatch and Thomas could avoid the impression that here was a white man publicly taunting a black man about his sexuality. By suspiciously prolonging the discussion through simulating his own sexual innocence, Hatch was also demonstrating how he still had the authority, as a powerful white man, to exploit Thomas's discomfort. At that moment in the hearings Thomas was being refused his privacy in ways he could not control. If Anita Hill's sexual characterology was defined as nothing but private, Clarence Thomas's sexual profile was defined as anything but private, as equally unreal because it belonged to the realm of racist mythology. This protected his nomination, but it also exploited his identity as a black man, leaving the Republicans laughing all the way to the electoral-race bank. In Hill's case the injustices of race and gender were served up in double helpings (triple, if you count Simpson's homophobic innuendo about her "proclivities"). The message, as they say, was clear enough. How it was received remains to be seen.

TV Watchers' Postscript

Two weeks after the Senate vote on Thomas, CBS's "Designing Women" aired a hastily produced episode called "The Strange Case of Clarence and Anita," which included, in twenty minutes of tight sitcom polemics, some of the most direct critiques of the hearings I saw on TV ("Murphy Brown" pitched in when it aired an episode in February that featured Murphy's appearance before a ruthlessly caricatured Senate subcommittee composed of Hatch, Kennedy, et al.). Playing to wild applause from the studio audience, Mary Jo and Julia, in full Bette and Joan drag from an amateur production of *Whatever Happened to Baby Jane?*, channeled their anger through a series of hilarious set-piece dismissals of the hearings' male protagonists: in turn, casting Danforth as delusional, Thomas as a ham actor, Doggett as a dog, Simpson as a pig, Kennedy as another dog ("putting Ted Kennedy in charge of sexual harassment is like asking Dom DeLuise to guard the dessert bar"), and Specter as a perjurer. As for Bush, the show ended with the president's words at Thomas's nomination ceremony—"America is the first nation in history founded on an idea, on the unshakable certainty, that all men are created equal"—being played over a poignant shot of Anita Hill, looking weary and defeated, at the end of her testimony. But the most telling moment lay in Mary Jo's dismissal of polls suggesting that most women had believed Thomas. Noting that polls also suggest that most women aren't feminists, she took the opportunity to point out that most women who don't want to call themselves feminists nonetheless agree on all the individual feminist issues: "I am a single parent, and a working mother, and if believing in things like equal pay and mandated child care makes me a feminist, then I'm proud to be one."

This was populism, going out on a corporate medium, but it wasn't the voice of corporate populism speaking.

As for the Supreme Court, let's be mischievous and leave the last word to Charles Manson, who had granted a TV interview with CBS's "Hard Copy" a couple of months earlier, and who, in a choice moment of hillbilly rage, had this to say about the legal system:

> Wake up, [bleep]! dammit, ain't you got enough sense to look at it? The Supreme Court was started when there was 13 million people in this country. You had nine judges with 13 million people. You got 250 million people now. How the hell you gonna take a Supreme Court with nine [bleeps] and make a court out of it for 250 million people? It's impossible, man. Your government's a shell of madness that you're preachin' off in schools. It's not real, guy, it's a game.

MANNING MARABLE

Clarence Thomas and the Crisis of Black Political Culture

The controversy surrounding Clarence Thomas's nomination and confirmation as an associate justice of the Supreme Court represents the first decisive national debate in the post-civil-rights era. The Second Reconstruction, the great historical epoch characterized by the democratic upsurgence of African Americans against the structures of racial discrimination and social inequality, effectively ended with the Reagan administration. Although much of the commentary on Thomas focused largely on the sexual-harassment charges against him by former aide Anita Hill, the case must be seen against even larger political currents that symbolize the contemporary crisis within the African-American political culture. This crisis is represented by the overlapping contradictions of gender, race, and the flawed ideology of liberalism. Each of these elements simultaneously illuminates and obscures the actual character of

American politics and the status of African Americans within the apparatus of state power. Beyond the dimensions of personality, they alone explain how and why Clarence Thomas succeeded in being appointed to the Supreme Court and why the majority of African Americans were persuaded to support his nomination.

Clarence Thomas's climb to power is directly related to his abandonment of the principles of the black-freedom struggle. A quarter century ago, as a college student in the late 1960s, Thomas proclaimed himself a devoted disciple of Malcolm X. Thomas wore the black beret of the Black Panther Party and signed his letters "Power to the People." He secured a position at Yale Law School because of its aggressive affirmative-action program, which had set aside roughly 10 percent of all places in each class to racial minorities. Yet less than a decade later Thomas would condemn affirmative action as being destructive to blacks' interests. When initially appointed head of the Equal Employment Opportunity Commission, Thomas embraced for a time the use of numerical hiring goals and timetables as a means to increase the employment of blacks. Yet following Reagan's landslide electoral victory in 1984, he reversed himself and strongly attacked affirmative-action goals and timetables. Two years later, when seeking reappointment to the EEOC from a Democratic-controlled Congress, Thomas solemnly promised that he would reinstate affirmative-action measures inside his office.

In dozens of published articles and in more than one hundred public speeches, Thomas repeatedly attacked the entire civil rights agenda as hopelessly anachronistic and irrelevant to the more conservative political environment of the 1980s. Thomas denounced welfare and other liberal reforms of the Great Society as a form of government-sponsored paternalism that reinforced dependency and undermined self-help and practical initiative within the black community. Thomas even went so far as to criticize the famous 1954 Supreme Court decision *Brown* v. *Board of Education of Topeka, Kansas,* which abolished racially segregated schools, as being based on "dubious social science" evidence. Thomas's subsequent appointment to a federal judgeship in Washington, D.C., was due less to his reputation as a legal scholar and for his judicial temperament, which was nonexistent, but for his noteworthy service as a partisan ideologue for conservative Republicanism.

Moreover, Thomas was one of the few people of color elevated by both former President Reagan and President Bush to federal judgeships. During Bush's first two years as president, he appointed seventy federal judges, nearly all of whom were white, affluent males. Less than 12 percent of Bush's federal judges were women; only 6.5 percent were from racial minority groups. Virtually all of his selections were deeply hostile to civil rights, affirmative-action enforcement, civil liberties for those charged with criminal offenses, environmental-protection laws, and the freedom of choice for women on the issue of abortion. Thus, the reality of Thomas's racial identity, and any personal or political connections he might have had with the African-American community, were secondary to his role as legal apologist for reactionary politics. Indeed, during these years Thomas attempted to "transcend" his blackness and condemned those who argued that his race necessarily imposed an obligation to conform to certain progressive political attitudes or policies.

From the moment of Bush's nomination of Thomas to

replace liberal Associate Justice Thurgood Marshall on the Supreme Court, the president's justification and defense of the black conservative was essentially a series of unambiguous lies. No one in Congress or the legal profession seriously believed Bush's assertion that Thomas was nominated because he was "the best-qualified" jurist in the nation. No one was convinced by Bush's initial claims that Thomas's race had "nothing" to do with the decision to advance his candidacy. At best, Thomas's published writings revealed the working of a mediocre mind. If Bush had genuinely desired to nominate a black Republican judge with outstanding legal credentials, he would have ignored Thomas entirely and selected Amalya Kearse, an African American currently serving on the federal appeals court in New York. But Kearse's legal reputation as a moderate, despite her Republican Party affiliation, made her unacceptable to the extreme right wing. Bush's objective in selecting Thomas was, in part, to gain political capital at the expense of the core constituencies within the Democratic Party, astutely pitting feminists against civil rights activists.

By contrast, other Republican presidents when considering Supreme Court appointments frequently have chosen quality over narrow partisanship. Dwight Eisenhower appointed two of the most liberal Supreme Court justices in American history—Chief Justice Earl Warren and Associate Justice William Brennan. Gerald Ford appointed Justice John Paul Stevens to the court, who is viewed today as a moderate. Even Reagan nominated Sandra Day O'-Connor, who is essentially a moderate conservative. Bush's goal clearly was not judicial excellence. He wanted a nominee who was opposed to a woman's freedom of choice on abortion, an ideologue with slim intellectual qualifications who would attack the liberal political agenda from the protected confines of the court for the next thirty years.

Even before Professor Anita Hill's charges of sexual misconduct began to circulate, thoughtful observers noted in Thomas's record a disturbing characteristic of contempt for African-American women. This perception was not directly linked to his divorce from his first wife, an African American, and his remarriage in 1987 to Virginia Bess Lamp, a white Republican attorney. Thomas had first come to the attention of white conservatives nationally at a San Francisco conference sponsored by black Reaganites in the late 1980s. In his remarks before the conference, Thomas attacked welfare programs for perpetuating dependent behavior among blacks by focusing his negative remarks on his own sister, Emma Mae Martin. "She gets mad when the mailman is late with her welfare check," Thomas announced, as other black conservatives laughed aloud. "That's how dependent she is," Thomas affirmed.

Years later, journalists investigated Thomas's statements and discovered that they were false, because his sister was not on welfare at the time of his speech. Thomas didn't mention that his sister had received none of the educational advantages and affirmative-action benefits that he had taken for granted. It was also Thomas's sister who had assumed the responsibility of caring for their mother, and had taken two part-time jobs to get off welfare. As economist Julianne Malveaux critically observed: "For providing that kind of support in her family, Emma Mae Martin earned her brother's public scorn. What can the rest of us women expect from Supreme Court Justice Clarence Thomas as issues of pay equity and family policy come before this court?"

As Hill's charges of sexual harassment by Thomas reached the headlines, other disturbing evidence surfaced. Classmates of Thomas during his years at Yale Law School had already informed members of the Senate Judiciary Committee that he had displayed a strong "interest in pornographical films" at that time. Most damaging was Hill's testimony before the committee, which was detailed, credible, and persuasive. Witnesses also corroborated her testimony. Hill's charges of sexual misconduct echoed sharply across the country and transcended the specific case of Thomas, largely because the experience of sexual harassment was so common to millions of working women, regardless of their race, ethnicity, education, or class background. According to an October 1991 *New York Times/CBS News* poll, about four out of ten women across the country have been the "object of sexual advances, propositions, or unwanted sexual discussions from men" in supervisory positions at their places of employment. Only one out of eight women who had been sexually harassed actually reported the incident. Like Hill, they knew that without hard evidence their assertions were unlikely to be believed. Their professional careers would suffer. Interestingly, even one-half of all men polled admitted that they have "said or done something which could have been construed by a female colleague as harassment."

The Senate and the Bush administration were first inclined to ignore the gravity of Hill's charges, which had originally been made in private, and to rush a confirmation vote on Thomas. But the public outcry, particularly from women's groups, was so profound that the leaders of both parties were forced to retreat. Part of the dilemma for the White House was the collapse of its basic strategy, which had avoided any analysis of Thomas's meager record as a legal scholar or federal judge, and had concentrated totally on his Horatio Alger, "Up from Slavery" saga. Now it was exactly Thomas's personality, character, and private morals that were seriously open to question.

But as the Senate committee was forced to reopen the hearings to evaluate Hill's testimony, the scales were tipped decisively in Thomas's favor. First, both the White House and the Senate were determined to keep the hearings from becoming, as Bush lieutenants put it, a "referendum on sexual harassment." Thomas should not be the "victim of two thousand years of male dominance." None of the senators had any familiarity with the legal requirements for sexual harassment, and had no knowledge of the massive body of scholarship and legal decisions on the issue. Second, a strategic error was committed by Senate Judiciary Committee Chairman Joseph Biden. Biden perceived Hill's accusations in the context of a criminal trial, with the presumption of innocence resting with Thomas. But this was completely erroneous; no one had filed criminal charges against Thomas. The process should not have been seen as a trial, with the issue of establishing witness credibility, but as a political hearing to determine the qualifications and fitness of Thomas to serve on the Supreme Court. The point should have been made repeatedly that even if Hill did not exist, or even if grave doubts could be established concerning her testimony, there was already more than sufficient evidence to reject Thomas's nomination to the court.

Thomas helped his own case by taking the offensive. "If someone wanted to block me from the Supreme Court of the United States because of my views on the Constitution, that's fine," he declared before the committee. "But to destroy me? . . . I would have preferred an assassin's bullet to this kind of living hell that they have put me and my family through." Thomas proclaimed himself a martyr of an elaborate smear campaign inspired by racism. Without even listening to Hill's testimony or specific charges, Thomas declared that he was the victim of a "high-tech lynching." This was, of course, the most supreme irony: the black conservative who had done so much to destroy affirmative-action and civil rights programs designed to attack racial discrimination now sought refuge on the grounds of racism. As Janelle Byrd, a lawyer with the NAACP Legal Defense Fund, observed: "Thomas has run from his blackness, and now that he is backed into a corner, all of a sudden, Judge Thomas is black. He has used race in the most manipulative way." Nevertheless, Thomas's strategy was effective. The white liberal Democratic senators did not wish to be accused of racism, and they deliberately permitted Thomas to dictate the terms of the discourse. They were so effectively cowed that they neglected even to ask Thomas about the evidence of his long-time interest in pornographic films.

As the Democrats equivocated, the Reaganite Republicans smelled blood and circled for the political kill. The Senate's leading demagogue, Alan Simpson of Wyoming, vowed that Hill would be "destroyed, belittled, hounded, and harassed." With sinister innuendoes, he claimed to have faxes and letters attacking Hill's credibility "hanging out of my pockets," which warned him to "watch out for this woman." Senator Strom Thurmond of South Carolina declared Hill's allegations to be "totally without merit," even *before* listening to her testimony!

In a racist, sexist society, it is relatively easy for white men with power to discredit and to dismiss a black woman. The media contributed to the political assassination of Hill by projecting the controversy as part soap opera, part public trial, and by accepting the interpretation that Thomas merited the presumption of innocence. In this context it was not terribly surprising that the majority of Americans witnessing the spectacle concluded that Thomas was telling the truth and that Hill was lying. But in response those who smeared Anita Hill for possessing the courage and dignity to step forward, one should ask: Why would she lie? What did she actually gain from her actions? Politically a conservative and identified with her tenure in the Reagan administration, she clearly was not a liberal. Conservative politicans, ideologues, and sexists may attack her personal integrity and professionalism for decades to come. Her probable goal of one day becoming a federal judge is lost forever. As University of Maryland law professor Tanya Banks observed, Hill certainly "would not have taken this step without full consideration of consequences."

But at the moment of truth the liberals lacked the courage of their convictions. They sacrificed their principles before the volatile politics of gender and race. They physically recoiled when Thomas, in a moment of desperation, cynically charged "racism." They refused to acknowledge the reality that Anita Hill, not Thomas, was the real victim of "lynching"—not once but twice: the first time a decade ago, when she was sexually humiliated and harassed in private, and the second time on Capital Hill before the eyes of the world.

From the vantage point of African-American politics,

the most crucial factor that contributed to Thomas's narrow confirmation by the Senate was the obvious support he had received from the majority of blacks. In several polls about 60 percent of all African Americans expressed support for Thomas's confirmation, even after Hill's charges were widely circulated. The Southern Christian Leadership Conference, established in 1957 by Martin Luther King, Jr., announced its endorsement of Thomas. The National Urban League took no official position against Thomas's nomination. The reality of black support for Thomas was a major reason that several southern Democrats who faced reelection in 1992 gave their votes to the black nominee. These senators included Wyche Fowler, Jr., of Georgia, Richard Shelby of Alabama, and John B. Breaux of Louisiana. Several other southern Democrats who had voted against Robert Bork's nomination to the Supreme Court four years before, Senators J. Bennett Johnston of Louisiana and Sam Nunn of Georgia, also cast their votes for Thomas. Black southern votes were absolutely essential for these white Democrats to survive politically.

When Bush first selected Thomas to replace Marshall, most African-American leaders and national organizations expressed strong opposition. The Congressional Black Caucus, with few exceptions, condemned Thomas as unfit to serve in Marshall's place. After some initial hesitancy, the NAACP came out against the black Reaganite on the grounds of his bitter hostility to civil rights and affirmative action. Many powerful black religious and trade-union leaders also issued similar condemnations of Thomas's nomination.

But the initial opinion polls of African Americans clearly

indicated a willingness to support Thomas's appointment. There were at least three reasons for this curious response. The first factor was due to the growth of black "neoaccommodation." Since the rise of Reaganism within national politics more than a decade ago, white conservatives have made an effort to establish a base of political support within the African-American community. One primary reason for this can be attributed to racial patterns in national presidential and congressional politics. Since 1948 the majority of white voters have given a Democratic presidential candidate their support only once—Lyndon Johnson in 1964. Neither John F. Kennedy nor Jimmy Carter received a majority of whites' votes in their successful presidential elections. White middle-class voters, especially males, consistently support Republican candidates. Conversely, since 1964 an average of 88 percent of all African Americans have supported Democratic presidential candidates. Black support for Democratic senatorial candidates usually exceeds 90 percent. Republicans recognized that they would only need to increase their electoral support among blacks to roughly 20 to 25 percent—a realistic figure, given that Dwight Eisenhower had received over 40 percent of blacks' votes in 1956. With this increased black support, the Republicans would regain control over Congress, and would be virtually unbeatable in presidential contests, regardless of the Democratic candidate.

Thus, despite Reagan's vicious posturing and rhetoric against the civil rights community and most black officials, the Republicans began to fashion a "black-middle-class agenda": federal governmental support for black-owned banks and entrepreneurship, criticism of social welfare programs, endorsement of all-black male public schools, em-

bracing the discourse of "self-reliance" historically associated with Booker T. Washington and Elijah Muhammad. A series of neoaccommodationist-conservative black
spokespersons were promoted in the national media:
economists Thomas Sowell and Walter Williams; journalist
Tony Brown; Glenn C. Loury, professor at Harvard University's Kennedy School of Government; Robert Wood-
son, president of the National Center for Neighborhood
Enterprises; J. A. Y. Parker, president of the Lincoln Institute for Research and Education; and of course Thomas.

The collaboration between black Democrats and conservative Republicans began to grow in statewide and congressional elections throughout the 1980s. In a
half-million-dollar project, Benjamin L. Ginsberg, the
chief counsel of the Republican National Committee, assisted civil rights organizations in their legal challenges to
redraft congressional district boundaries, which might increase the number of African-American and Latino representatives. Republicans frequently observed that about
eighty white Democrats represented congressional districts
that were at least 30 percent black; for blacks to gain greater
political power, they would have to do so at the expense
of the Democratic Party's white establishment. Republicans began to provide Chicano and African-American
groups free computer time, legal assistance, and political
support. In several statewide races blacks began to support
"moderate" Republicans. In 1986, 60 percent of all blacks
voted for Republican incumbent Thomas Kean in New
Jersey's gubernatorial race. In 1990, in Illinois, Republican
gubernatorial candidate James Edgar received more than
one-fifth of the black vote, and with this slender percent-
age was elected. Many black Chicagoans who had sup-

ported progressive mayor Harold Washington announced their support for Edgar.

Bush was well aware of these trends, and he sought to advance some public-policy positions that would appeal to the black middle class. One central example is provided by the Bush administration's inconsistent position on the desegregation of historically black state colleges. In July 1991, U.S. Solicitor General Kenneth Starr was ordered to file an initial brief with the Supreme Court on a major school desegregation case, taking the position that states did not have to increase funds to black public colleges. The initial brief stated that there was no "independent obligation" for states "to correct disparities" between white and black public institutions. In protest, Bush's board of advisors on historically black colleges, chaired by former Howard University President James Cheek, demanded a meeting with the president. On September 9, 1991, Bush was told by his black advisors that Starr's brief had created a "crisis" among African-American educators. Partially due to the pressures of the Thomas nomination, Bush totally repudiated his earlier position, ordering Starr to issue a new brief stating that it was "incumbent" for states to "eradicate discrimination" by implementing "equitable and fair funding to historically black institutions." Just in case the Supreme Court overlooked the significance of Bush's new position, the revised brief added: "Suggestions to the contrary in our opening brief no longer reflect the position of the United States."

The second factor contributing to black support for Thomas was the ideology of "liberal integrationism" that permeated the strategic and tactical vision of the entire black middle class. For nearly a century, since the founding of the NAACP, most middle-class blacks have espoused a political ideology of integrationism, a commitment to the eradication of racial barriers within government, business, and society. In its simplest terms, "liberal integrationism" argues that if *individual* African Americans are advanced to positions of political, cultural, or corporate prominence, then the entire black community will benefit. This concept is essentially "symbolic representation": the conviction that the individual accomplishments of a Bill Cosby, Michael Jordan, Douglas Wilder, or Oprah Winfrey trickle down to empower millions of less fortunate African Americans. In municipal politics liberal integrationism's "symbolic representation" means that if the number of African Americans appointed to the police department increases, or if a black professional becomes police commissioner, working-class black neighborhoods will eventually become safer, or police brutality gradually will be reduced. The 1989 mayoral victory of David Dinkins in New York, for example, is broadly interpreted in the black media as yet another "gain" for the entire race.

The fundamental contradiction inherent in the notion of integrationist "symbolic representation" is that it presumes a degree of structural accountability and racial solidarity that binds the black public figure with the larger masses of African Americans. During the period of Jim Crow, the oppressive external constraints of legal discrimination imposed norms of racial conformity and solidarity. Despite an individual's educational attainments, capital formation, or excellence on the athletic field, for example, a person could never entirely escape the oppressive reality of segregation. The very definition of "race" was a social category defined by the presumed and very real hierarchies within the socioeconomic and political system, preserving and perpetuating black subordination. Black conservatives in an earlier era, such as George Schuyler, felt an obligation to their "race" that was imposed by the burden of exploitation, commonly experienced by all. But in the post-civil-rights period, in the absence of the legal structures of formal discrimination, the bonds of cultural kinship, social familiarity, and human responsibility that had once linked the most affluent and upwardly mobile African Americans with their economically marginalized sisters and brothers were severely weakened. It is now possible for a member of the present-day Negro elite to live in the white suburbs, work in a white professional office, attend religious services in an all-white church or synagogue, belong to a white country club, and never come into intimate contact with the most oppressed segments of the black community. Moreover, for those privileged blacks within the expanding elite, the benefits of betraying the commonly-held perceptions of the liberal politics and social democratic assumptions deeply entrenched within the black working class are greater than ever. So the argument that, regardless of individual personal histories, class affinities, and cultural identities, the professional successes of individuals within the African-American elite benefit the entire black community is no longer valid.

But old beliefs die hard. A number of black liberal intellectuals, whose worldviews and political perceptions were hardened by the turmoil of the sixties and the heroic struggles against legal segregation, implicitly accept the notion of symbolic representation, and the totality of the ideological baggage of liberal integration. Noted author Maya Angelou expressed her support for Thomas in a *New York*

Times editorial. Stephen Carter of Yale University, author of the controversial book *Reflections of an Affirmative Action Baby,* termed many of the charges leveled against Thomas by blacks irrelevant and "ridiculous." Carter declared that he "admire[d] much of what [Thomas] stands for," and that the black conservative who had done so much to undermine the black struggle for equality nevertheless represented "an important voice in the black community and in national affairs. His ostracism as a traitor, an enemy, an Uncle Tom, reflects no credit on those who have sought to cast him out." Carter's effort to salvage a degree of credibility from Thomas's shabby and shameful record was based on a faulty set of political assumptions. Carter never questioned the belief that a Thomas victory in the Senate would translate into a type of political advancement for other African Americans.

Other liberal integrationists in the media admitted having second thoughts about Thomas, but gradually voiced approval for his nomination to the Supreme Court. Columnist William Raspberry expressed his willingness to accommodate to the dominant conservative realities of the Reagan-Bush era. "I never thought of Thomas as some sort of judicial Tonto, willing to betray his people for his own selfish interests," Raspberry observed. Raspberry's principal "disappointment" with Bush's selection was not ideological, but was based on the grounds that Thomas was "too inexperienced and untested for so important a post." But with the startling revelations of Hill, Raspberry's hostility shifted easily from right to left. The idea that such a gentleman as Thomas might actually engage in vulgar sexist intimidation was inconceivable. Without a shred of evidence, Raspberry declared that the "sexual harassment allegations" were nothing less than "cheap shots, eleventh hour flimflammery and character assassination." He also condemned that Congressional Black Caucus's opposition to Thomas, which was deplored for having been determined "with no debate" and with "no witnesses." Raspberry's stuffy rhetoric might make sense if Thomas had no decade-long track record as an opponent of civil rights and affirmative action, or if Hill's politics had been identified with feminism or the left. But within its immediate context Raspberry's argument represented a restatement of old dogmas and tired integrationist formulas, a faith in the bourgeois respectability of the Negro elite.

Liberal journalist Juan Williams, author of the documentary history of the Civil Rights Movement, *Eyes on the Prize,* also rushed to Thomas's defense. The liberals' criticism of Thomas, Williams worried, had gone too far. "[Thomas] has been conveniently transformed into a monster about whom it is fair to say anything," Williams charged. "In pursuit of abuses by a conservative president, the liberals have become the abusive monsters." Williams's assertions helped to justify Thomas's hypocritical claim that he was the victim of a political "lynching" because of his racial identity. By equating Hill's plausible charges with the bloody record of terror by the Klan, Thomas was able to swing millions of undecided blacks behind his cynical campaign to obtain a lifetime appointment.

However, the most articulate defense of Thomas from liberal black quarters was offered by Harvard sociologist Orlando Patterson. Thomas was probably guilty of violating the cultural norms of "his white, upper-middle-class work world," Patterson suggested. But he had only offered sexual advances "to an aloof woman who is esthetically and socially very similar to himself, who had made no secret of her own deep admiration for him." In short, Thomas was guilty of bad judgment and poor office manners. If anyone was to blame, it was Hill. Patterson argues: "Raising the issue ten years later was unfair and disingenuous: unfair because, while she may well have been offended by his coarseness, there is no evidence that she suffered any emotional or career damage, and the punishment she belatedly sought was in no way commensurate with the offense; and disingenuous because she has lifted a verbal style that carries only minor sanction in one subcultural context and thrown it in the overheated cultural arena of mainstream, neo-Puritan America, where it incurs professional extinction." The approach to redeem Thomas taken by Patterson is familiar to any African Americans schooled in cultural norms of their own people. How can any man be blamed for expressing his sexual interest in an available, attractive black woman? Doesn't the punishment for these sweet words uttered in the executive suite so many years ago far exceed the crime? Patterson goes so far as to defend Thomas's falsehoods given under oath because the black conservative's behavior did not merit censure. "Judge Thomas was justified in denying making the remarks, even if he had in fact made them," Patterson concluded, "not only because the deliberate displacement of his remarks made them something else but on the utilitarian moral grounds that any admission would have immediately incurred a self-destructive and grossly unfair punishment."

Patterson's thesis is grounded in several contradictory falsehoods. There is certainly a deep tradition of sexism within the black community, a pattern of denying human rights and leadership for women within our own institu-

tions. In both black nationalist and integrationist forma-
tions, practices and policies of gender discrimination are
apparent. But to dismiss the brutal language and offensive
actions of Thomas by recalling similar behavior by other
black men makes absolutely no sense. Shouldn't it matter
that when this incident occurred, Thomas was the head of
the Equal Employment Opportunity Commission, the
agency responsible for outlawing sexual harassment in the
workplace? Patterson's query concerning the number of
years that had transpired between the alleged act of harassment and its public revelation blatantly ignores the legal
evolution that has occurred in the past decade in such cases.
The EEOC did not issue guidelines concerning sexual
harassment, which was defined as any behavior that has the
"purpose of unreasonably interfering with an individual's
work performance or creating an intimidating or hostile or
offensive environment," until 1980. It was not until 1986,
in *Meritor Savings Bank* v. *Vinson,* that the Supreme Court
actually ruled that sexual harassment in the workplace was
a form of sex discrimination covered under Title VII of the
1964 Civil Rights Act. At the time of her harassment in the
early 1980s, Hill would have had few legal avenues for
redress. If she had filed a grievance, she would not have had
a federal case, because judges viewed sexist intimidation as
merely "bad manners." Even as late as 1991, Hill would
not have been able to recover damages from such a suit.
Most professional women in this situation would have
done what Hill did: stay with the position, hoping that her
supervisor would change, or seek employment elsewhere
without alienating her boss. But to claim as Patterson does
that Thomas's obnoxious behavior was just a "down-home
style of courting" is dishonest and disturbing.

A third factor that explains African-American support for Thomas can be attributed to the quasi-black-nationalist sentiment among millions of African-American working-class people and elements of the black middle class that were radicalized during the 1960s. A distinguishing feature of black nationalism is the belief that "race" is more important than other factors, such as gender or class, in determining social and political outcomes. Given the reality of Thomas's racial background, some black nationalists could support him on the grounds that Bush would simply appoint a white reactionary to the court if he was rejected by the Senate. Some even argued that any black person, regardless of his or her public record as a reactionary, nevertheless had experienced daily life as a black person. The factor of race was inescapable, and certainly this meant that Thomas ought to be given the benefit of the doubt. With the security of a permanent judicial appointment, he might eventually come to embrace the progressive perspectives of other African Americans.

The most articulate neoaccommodationist of Thomas from a "black-nationalist" perspective was Dr. Niara Sudarkasa, noted anthropologist and president of Lincoln University in Pennsylvania. Sudarkasa has previously identified herself as a black nationalist, and has claimed that one of the most influential African Americans in her own political development was Malcolm X. She has informed Lincoln University students and alumni that the *n* in the university's name stands for "nation-building," a phrase taken directly from the black-nationalist cultural upsurgence of two decades ago. Nevertheless, Sudarkasa went before the Senate Judiciary Committee to praise Thomas's conservative credentials. She insisted that Thomas was "an openminded and independent thinker" who should not be attacked for holding views in opposition to liberal integrationists in the civil rights establishment. African Americans "have been fortunate in having a long line of leaders who, in retrospect, seem right for their times," she argued. "These leaders did not always have the same ideology or agree on strategies, but they all agreed that the goal was to secure freedom and justice for our people. . . . Who can say that we are not better off for having the benefit of their separate and distinct voices?" Invoking black history, Sudarkasa perceived Thomas in the "nation-building" tradition of Frederick Douglass, Marcus Garvey, and Martin Luther King, Jr.

Sudarkasa's thesis is only partially true. Throughout African-American history the political ideology of black people has been characterized by a struggle for both human equality and political democracy. Different leaders have approached these goals with different strategies. Black nationalists such as Malcolm X and Marcus Garvey have sought to build strong, black-controlled economic, political, and social institutions that could empower the black community from within. They have linked our struggles for freedom with the larger currents of political protest in Africa and the Caribbean. Other black leaders, such as Frederick Douglass and Martin Luther King, Jr., have emphasized the necessity of achieving full integration and the eradication of all barriers to equality within this country.

Sudarkasa's analysis presumes that Thomas and other upper-middle-class blacks who favor the repressive policies of the Reagan-Bush agenda are consciously working on behalf of other African Americans as an oppressed national minority. Actually, they are working fundamentally to promote their own careers, manipulating the mantle of blackness to cloak political perfidy. No doubt Thomas feels some ambiguous connections with the historical achievements of previous African-American leaders, who sacrificed to advance the boundaries of freedom for their people. The critical difference that separates him from this earlier leadership is a rupture between "race" and "ethnicity." Racially, Thomas remains "black": both by governmental definition and societal recognition, he belongs to a specific racial group characterized in part by physical appearance and political condition. Racial identity is essentially passive, a reality of being within a social formation stratified by the oppressive concept of race. Yet ethnically Thomas has ceased to be an African American, in the context of political culture, social values and ideals, and commitment to collective interests. Thomas feels absolutely no active ideological or cultural obligations to the dispossessed, the hungry and homeless who share the ethnic rituals, customs, and traditions of blackness. Thomas's accomplishment is a logical product not simply of personal cynicism but of the flawed perspective of liberal integrationism, which all too frequently made no distinction between race and ethnicity in black life. This is the reason that Louisiana racist politician and former neo-Nazi David Duke had little difficulty endorsing Thomas for appointment to the Supreme Court. Thomas was racially black, but in most other respects stood in bitter opposition to the resistance traditions in the culture of African-American people.

The great danger of Thomas's appointment will be measured in the political outlook and ideological attitudes of a new generation of African Americans, who were born after the period of Jim Crow and have no personal memories or involvement in civil rights demonstrations, protest marches, and Black Power activism. Like Thomas, they stand outside a period of history that binds them to a political culture of resistance and social transformation. Many seek not to challenge the established structures of power but to prepare themselves to assimilate within these systems. This tremendous sense of impending crisis for the future of young African Americans was reinforced for me during a visit to Lincoln University, in the midst of the national debate over Thomas-Hill. One of Lincoln's most articulate young male students argued passionately after I presented several critical comments on the Thomas nomination. The student did not deny that the evidence in the case weighed heavily against Thomas. Nevertheless, he insisted that African Americans had no choice except to applaud this appointment to the Supreme Court. After all, Thomas claimed to be opposed to welfare and the white liberal policies of dependency; didn't this place Thomas in harmony with black activists such as Malcolm X and black nationalists like Elijah Muhammad, who advocated "self-help"? In brief, he forcefully presented Sudarkasa's thesis of neo-accommodationism. I was deeply impressed with the student's seriousness, and tried to raise every counterargument conceivable. I argued just as passionately that Thomas's opposition to a woman's freedom of choice on abortion would mean that thousands of pregnant black women annually would be subjected to back-alley butchers. Thomas's hatred of affirmative action meant a monolithically conservative Supreme Court that would reduce blacks' opportunities in education and the job market.

The Lincoln University student replied: "That's the

problem with black people today. We aren't willing to settle for half a loaf. Sometimes less than half a loaf is all we can expect, and we should be happy to get even that." This is not the political perspective of resistance, the enthusiastic defiance of youth that characterized the Student Nonviolent Coordinating Committee and the cadre of the Black Panther Party. This is not the aggressive posture of young people who oppose oppression and who are unwilling to accept anything less than freedom. The central tragedy of Thomas for black America is his powerful image as a negative role model for millions of young people who have never walked a picket line or occupied a public building in protest. Thomas's victory reinforces the tendencies toward compromise, accommodation, and pessimism. His elevation to the court illustrates to our next generation that any instincts toward the political culture of resistance must be forgotten, that the way forward is by accepting the "less than half a loaf" offered to us by our oppressors.

The price of Thomas's personal advancement into the corridors of national power thus has been achieved at an unprecedented price. Our young people have witnessed an unprincipled individual who possesses a deep hostility toward African-American women, possibly commiting acts of sexual harassment, who is nevertheless rewarded and praised at the highest levels of government. Seldom has the black intelligentsia and political leadership been in such disarray, debating the merits of supporting an obvious opportunist. Seldom has the black middle class so confused its actual material interests with the symbolic satisfaction of seeing one of its own being appointed to high judicial office. The Thomas case is one of the rare instances in which the majority of the African-American community has supported the wrong person for the wrong position for the wrong reasons. Unfortunately, given the profound level of confusion in both the strategic and ideological perspectives of the African-American middle class, its present inability to transcend the bankrupt politics of liberal integrationism, it is probable that we will witness more Clarence Thomases in the near future.

MICHAEL THELWELL

False, Fleeting, Perjured Clarence:
Yale's Brightest and Blackest Go to Washington

. . . "What scourge for perjury
Can this dark monarchy afford false Clarence?" . . .
. . . Then came wandering by
A shadow like an angel, with bright hair
Dappled in blood; and [s]he shrieked out aloud,
"Clarence is come,—false, fleeting, perjured Clarence . . .
Seize on him, Furies! Take him unto torment."
> —Shakespeare, *King Richard III,* act 1,
> scene 4, lines 50–58

Poor George Bush got the wrong Thomas! He went looking for "Uncle" but came back with "Bigger."
> —Prof. John H. Bracey, Jr.

Chillun, ah tell yo', black people ought to quarantine that Yale Law School. It sholy done ruint mo' good niggers than whiskey.
> —June Bug Jabbo Jones, "On the
> Education of Young Blacks," Pin Point,
> Georgia, October 15, 1991

It have fe Bu'n.
　　　　　　—Bob Marley

Twenty-three years ago I had, as I can now see, a most portentous conversation with a prominent Yale professor. Although he was one of the bright stars in the Yale firmament, I found him intelligent. And though this might sound perverse, I even liked him a great deal and still do, for he is a humane and compassionate man. At the time, and largely as a consequence of other young blacks' dying in the burning cities of this nation, black students were, for the first time, being admitted to Ivy League universities in something slightly better than token numbers.

I berated my colleague for the abysmally condescending and paternalistic behavior of the Yale faculty and administration as expressed in their dogged resistance to every serious effort to establish a substantive program of study of the black American social and cultural experience.

"But, Michael, my dear fellow, you do not understand," he protested. "You do not understand at all. Our president, noble fellow that he is, has a vision. A vision, Michael! It is his intention to integrate—fully and completely—this nation's establishment. And"—here his voice grew hushed with awe—"he means to do so within a single generation."

He went on to describe the considerable effort and resources being deployed in an ongoing, nationwide talent search for the purpose of identifying and bringing to Yale "the brightest young black students this nation has," as instruments for the execution of that vision. This being 1968, I did not share his enthusiasm. Kingman Brewster's vision of integrating an otherwise unchanged American establishment impressed me as being neither as desirable, progressive, nor benign as my friend's tone suggested.

I remember giving my Yale colleague an essay I had just written on the need for black studies in white institutions that ended with the following:

> The present generation [Thomas's age set] of black college students is perhaps the most important generation of black students ever to live in the United States. They stand poised between two cultures. Their loyalties are being besieged. They must choose between a culture and a heritage they are being taught to despise, and a social establishment which, having rejected and oppressed their parents, is now making a determined bid to dissolve history and obscure reality. The vision that this generation leaves college with, the commitments they espouse, the decisions they take, will determine not only the future of the black community, but will affect the nature of the struggle in the motherland and other areas of the Third World.

And in fact, even as I write, considerable sections of that establishment have indeed been integrated. There are, for example, General Colin Powell and our new associate justice of the Supreme Court; the governor of the Old Dominion; the head of the Ford Foundation; the chairman of the New York Bar Association; many heads of public universities; the chief executive officer of the Dime Savings Bank; a number of division chiefs at Fortune 500 corporations, i.e., American Express, John Hancock; partners in prestigious law firms; and so on. Despite this conspicuous expansion of black influence and affluence, diffused and apparently unconnected at the top, our national community has never in its history been so confused and divided, or so alienated from itself, our working people at greater economic risk, or our inner-city youth in such great jeopardy, mired in such hopelessness, violence, and despair.

In October of 1991, at the tawdry dog and pony show cum Restoration comedy staged by the Senate Judiciary Committee, we caught a glimpse of the real effect—and underlying bankruptcy—of that well-intentioned vision. Judge Clarence *"I would have preferred an assassin's bullet, Senator"* Thomas and Professor Anita *"I was humiliated and embarrassed"* Hill, the protagonists, and the aptly named comic relief John *"Oh, she remembers me, Senator"* Doggett, all being prime products of the Brewster vision.

And what a piece of work that Doggett was! Even the name suggests one of Shakespeare's comic bumpkins, except that not even the Bard could possibly have imagined this Doggett. A living, unanswerable indictment of American higher education, Mr. Doggett was proof that a young black could successfully attend the University of Michigan and the Yale Law and Harvard Business schools and end up a monument to stupidity and insensitivity. His chief concern, apart from his own irresistible memorableness, was an absurd obsession with *demonstrating to white folk* that blacks can indeed, in his word, excel.

In any event, there they were in full display, Yale Law's blackest and brightest, in all their tunnel-visioned, expedient, careerist splendor. Young black conservatives on the make, evincing not a scintilla of obligation to anything save naked self-advancement unmediated by any principle— moral, political, or intellectual—that was visible to the naked eye. Thank you, Kingman Brewster, wherever you are.

Indeed, "false, fleeting, perjured Clarence!" What can it be about that name, apparent even from the War of the Roses? Perhaps black people ought to give serious thought to retiring Clarence from general use as a name in our communities. Henceforth and in perpetuity, black mothers, under penalty of law and draconian sanction, should be prohibited from encumbering male issue with the burden of that name. And those already so burdened ought to consider a legal change at the first onset of symptoms, say the beginning of a warm feeling toward the politics of Strom Thurmond or Jesse Helms.

For, as students at Howard University in the early sixties, we knew another Clarence. This 'un was the "not-right-bright"—our word was "doofus"—son of a much-admired and respected senior faculty member in the Athletic Department. Which was, so we speculated, the only reason the younger Clarence was given a position as an assistant baseball coach, the uppermost level of his incompetence, so to say, from whence it was expected he could do no real harm. Upon graduation, we had no reason to think of the young man for many years.

Then who should surface in the early years of the Reagan administration? Coach Doofus, not one whit wiser, but reincarnated as Clarence Pendleton, Jr., conservative Republican and chairman of the U.S. Civil Rights Commission.

Sure, you remember Clarence Jr., a stubby, energetic, pit bull of a man, enthusiastically demolishing the English language and any target to which he was pointed by his radical right-wing handlers. At their behest he deliberately trashed the commission he was named to head, and began the crude public attack on affirmative action, legal aid, and the Voting Rights Act by which southern blacks gained their first measure of the political rights supposedly guaranteed all citizens of this republic. But one could understand, if not forgive, that Clarence. Intelligence and restraint was never the Reagan administration's strong suit, so our Clarence must have, for the first time in his life, felt himself among intellectual equals there, and probably, with reason, grateful not to be on welfare or in prison.

Then sadly Clarence Jr. went to his reward, and a replacement was needed. Another man of sufficiently dark pigment to pass—for as Jimmy Baldwin once told a class, "You can't tell a black man by the color of his skin, either"—and who was willing to be the Reaganites' point man in their assault on the grudging and belated concessions that, during the sixties, a reluctant Congress had made to a century of black struggle and disappointment.

Enter Clarence of Pin Point *(solus,* very *solus).* He is somewhat better trained than the departed Coach Doofus, just as cynical, infinitely more cunning, and a little smoother, though as we will see, not by much. The former chairman, judge and now justice is but one particularly gaudy gander in a gaggle of self-proclaimed black conservatives battening on the crumbs from their master's table, or the Republican trough—to recall David Stockman's memorable characterization of supply-side economics in practice as "feeding time at the trough."

These born-again, porkchop conservatives fairly gleaming with cupidity and expedience make—and an obligingly ignorant media circulates—a series of self-serving and irresolvably contradictory claims for their political parentage and legitimacy.

On the one hand, they claim association with an "honorable" tradition of black conservatism tracing its ancestry—they say—to Booker T. Washington. In almost the same breath they proclaim themselves *sui generis,* a quite unprecedented political phenomenon, representing not just progress but total innovation in black political thought and courage. Indeed, according to them, they are the powerful intellectual wedge breaking the lockstep and logjam of an "imposed liberal orthodoxy" that has paralyzed a black leadership hopelessly mired in the past and unable to apprehend the changed realities of a kinder, gentler America in which race is of "declining significance."

Let us take first the Booker T. Washington canard, for nothing could be a more meretricious distortion of Mr. Washington's legacy than to associate his name and work with these operators. While one might well disagree with Mr. Washington's analysis and strategies—the direction of his leadership—there was never any doubt about his selfless dedication to his people's advancement. Mr. Washington's leadership coincided with one of the darkest of many dark hours in African Americans' history in this country. Seeing the rancor and bigotry of the Confederate resurgency expressed daily, and ruthlessly enforced by the violence of the mob and the state, Mr. Washington publicly counseled compromise. For his generation the word "lynching" was not a cheap rhetorical ploy to prey on white guilt. Do not provoke the primitive passions of these people with talk of political rights or social equality at this time, he counseled. Rather let us hold our peace and quietly seek to acquire land, to found institutions and develop among ourselves those industrial and agrarian skills that lead to economic independence, and which will render our labor and presence indispensable to the south. *Then* we shall see about the rest. While publicly disavowing any interest in political rights, Mr. Washington secretly contributed significant financing to the NAACP's voting rights campaigns. Sure, he bowed and scraped, "Tommed" if you will, to white philanthropists and politicians, but he usually returned from these journeys into self-abasement with another classroom, science lab, dormitory, or teacher to place in service to our youth.

The vision may have been limited, and the character even flawed, but Mr. Washington's was a pragmatism founded on an earned awareness of the potential violence of the racial resentments that surrounded his people. Even as he advocated restraint, he proclaimed self-reliance and organized our people along principles of mutual aid, *"lifting as ye climb."*

I challenge Justice Thomas, his supporters, and fellow black conservatives, to point to a single initiative (much less institution) that they have launched to benefit the black struggle, or to advance anything more meaningful than their own petty careers. Judging from the eagerness and fulsome sentimentality with which the Senate Republicans seized on the "car-sold-to-pay-son's-school-fees" motif, there cannot be many such, or we should certainly have heard of them. These men are not in the responsible tradition of Booker T. Washington. Quite the opposite, they are disconnected to an amazing degree from the higher values of the black tradition. They have been quite willing to lead the attack on programs and policies, to disembowel agencies, however imperfect, that better people have literally died to put in place in order to help correct social injustice in this country.

The only smattering of hope for the race in this regard came, improbably enough, in the testimony of John Doggett, when he revealed that according to Thomas, William Bradford Reynolds became assistant attorney general for civil rights because no black Republican lawyer approached would accept the assignment from President Bush. At least those black Republicans had more shame or principle than to associate themselves publicly with the Bush civil rights agenda.

Other conservatives though, associated with Justice Thomas, are men of black pigment who are willing, for a fee, to undertake the representation of South African apartheid. Having with great fanfare "climbed" out of poverty, they have not been inhibited by conscience or shame from burning behind them the very ladders—created by others' struggle—upon which they ascended. This false association between present-day conservatives and Booker T. Washington does as much violence to Mr. Washington's memory as it does to our intelligence.

The other silly claim made by these greasy-chinned black mercenaries of the right is that they represent a new and refreshing intellectual force destroying forever "the myth of a monolithic black community" and opening up "new vistas of political possibility," which in the words of a fellow traveler named Glenn Loury "is a good thing for all Americans."

This is utter nonsense, for there has never been a monolithic black community or even a myth of one—ask Elijah

Muhammad and Martin Luther King, Jr., or Dr. Du Bois, Booker T. Washington, and Marcus Garvey.

But what there has been is massive and close agreement *at the center*. The vast majority of black people have had no difficulty at all in agreeing almost completely on what our interests are; who our friends are and, conversely, our enemies; and about the real nature of our relationship to white America at any given time. What these born-again converts to the right conveniently ignore is that this "unanimity" is dearly bought, compelled by the incontrovertible logic of America's racial history and the bitter evidence of our daily experience. It is not, as they would glibly have it, the consequence of knee-jerk liberalism or our genetic predisposition to the herd mentality. Because, sadly enough, for the great majority of us, very little of substance has changed in that historical relationship, so our interests are still very clear and our real enemies not easily disguised.

But even this particular brand of porkchop conservatism is not entirely without precedent—as so very little ever really is. Because these historical precedents add a measure of perspective on the present, a couple of them merit examination in some detail.

In 1855, Uncle Julius Loury and Deacon Shelby Sowell, two thoughtful slaves on the Atwater plantation in South Carolina, jumped, or were pushed prominently, into the heated debate over the future of slavery. This came about by means of a slender pamphlet, *Colored People Be Not Fooled!*, printed and widely circulated by the generosity of their master, Colonel Herbert Walker Atwater. In a series of skillful and complex arguments, Loury and Sowell inveighed against the idea of any sweeping and total abolition of slavery by unilateral imposition of the federal government. They argued—in constitutional, psychological, and economic terms—that the swift and total abolition of slavery as advocated by the free black leadership, befuddled and misled by a manipulative and misguided white-abolitionist orthodoxy, would be constitutionally illegal, psychologically impossible, and economically disastrous.

For one thing, slaves were property, and valuable property to boot. A citizen's right to property was inviolate, enshrined at the very center of the Constitution, protected particularly against encroachment by big government bureaucracies. Did this mean that slavery as currently practiced was therefore eternal? By no means, but simply that any changes, or even its eventual termination, should come gradually as a matter of local initiative, and then, only on an individual, *case-by-case* basis. Where there were proven instances of gross cruelty—as opposed to a necessary and beneficent paternal discipline—it was the responsibility of government to intervene, to give relief to the victims, but only on the principle of "abuse of property." The pamphlet mentions physical brutality, mutilation, starvation, and the like. (There is pointedly no mention of sexual exploitation or harassment—a concession, one speculates, to the sensibilities of their sponsor, the notoriously libidinous Colonel Atwater.)

Their economic argument was equally persuasive and farseeing. Any blanket abolition of slavery would create hardship for black and white alike, the real burden, however, accruing to the innocent whites. The dismal truth, they wrote, was that too many slaves had become "lazy, improvident, shiftless and dependent on the institution." If, by some thoughtless bleeding-heart impulse, they were removed from its protection, the cost of supporting them and their indigent progeny would pass to the public treasury, possibly in perpetuity. The attendant higher taxation would impoverish the nation, creating a justifiable white resentment. Therefore, keeping the dependent majority in slavery, and thus the financial responsibility of their owners, was good sense, simple justice, and sound fiscal policy, a kind of preemptive privatization of public assistance.

At the same time, Uncle Julius and Deacon Shelby argued, the notion that *all* blacks were worthy only of perpetual servitude was both wrong and racist, in fact, the first use of the term "un-American" appears in their pamphlet in this context. Character and individual initiative, they argued, had to be taken into account, nurtured and encouraged by incentives, public or private. Where slaves demonstrated the initiative and business acumen to accumulate 95 percent of their market value, by their owner's estimate, the government—or better yet the abolitionists—would have to contribute the balance, whereupon the master would have to acquiesce to those slaves' manumission.

In this way the clearly deserving elements of the slave community would be free, but at a natural and organic pace dictated only by their own initiative, self-reliance, and the strength of their proverbial bootstraps. The improvident and undeserving rest would, in the meantime, be maintained and *worked* totally at private expense with no burden to the already distressed American taxpayer, an early form of workfare.

The two men were given passes enabling them to travel to neighboring plantations to rally support for the program among the slaves, who were inexplicably unenthusiastic. A disappointed Uncle Julius attributed this to their "lock-step" rigidity and dependence on abolitionist orthodoxy. "All they do," he said of the slave leadership, "is moan, moan, moan, bitch and bitch and whine."*

Our brothers Julius and Shelby passed from the pages of history, clearly having been before their time. In our kinder, gentler, certainly stupider America there is no telling how far they might have risen—as constitutional scholars, social analysts, or generic experts on black folk—under the benevolent sponsorship of George Herbert Walker Bush et al.

But there is an interesting footnote. Scholars have unearthed a much later letter from Jefferson Davis to the president of Yale College. Davis inquired whether "these two unusual darkies, might not by *special dispensation* be given instruction in the legal profession at your fine institution." For, Davis explained, he could "well envision a time when one or the other (but not both), when properly trained, might serve on the Supreme Judicial Court of the Confederated States." The advantages of such an appointment were many, Davis wrote: "They could make not only a legal contribution, but also by becoming a role model for our young darkies, as well as giving the lie to all those scurrilous slanders against us on the matter of race." There is no record of the Yale president's response and no record of either man having attended that institution. But

---

*An elegant formulation picked up by Chairman, now Justice, Thomas to describe the current generation of black leadership.

the Davis letter was found, heavily annotated, among the papers of Kingman Brewster on the occasion of his retirement.

Another interesting precedent emerged in late 1909, at a time when the black community's leaders and many white Americans of conscience were pressing Congress for legislation to outlaw lynching. This impulse was stimulated by the fact that at this time, somewhere in the country, and by no means limited to the old Confederacy, a Negro, and not necessarily a man, or an adult, was done to death by groups of public-spirited whites on an average of once every three days.

On this question there was again a suspicious and clearly unhealthy degree of unanimity among black folk. This attracted the attention and concern of a civic-minded, intellectually independent black journalist, one Stanly "The Jedge" Steele, of Pin Head, Alabama.

"Jedge" Steele won himself a transitory celebrity with a series of highly praised columns in Pin Head's weekly *Cotton Picker's Voice*. In coming out against "any ill-considered, generalized prohibition of this venerable American cultural practice by the federal bureaucracy," Steele's arguments were also constitutional, social, and economic. "While it is true," he wrote, "that the Constitution does not *explicitly* affirm the practice, the right was clearly *implicit* in its language and intent. For what other possible purpose did that prescient document unequivocally and specifically affirm the right of citizens to bear arms?"

The clear intent had to be that they use those arms to enforce community standards of decency and to dispense justice. "Or," he jeered, "was it for the purpose of making revolution?" "Some will deny it," he wrote, "but it is the sad truth that a few renegade blacks—to the enduring mortification of the law-abiding majority—routinely violate these standards so dear to the moral majority of God-fearing, Christian Americans."

That being the case, "Jedge" Steele argued, it was only natural, appropriate, and inevitable that responsible and courageous citizens would live up to their hard responsibilities to administer swift and punitive justice. "Justice delayed," he warned, "is justice denied."

Besides, without such salutary and *public* citizen's vigilance, "Jedge" Steele wrote, other criminally inclined miscreants would take license to run amok, eroding not just the standards but the *safety* of the community. For, he said pithily, "while there are no horses in Alabama that need stealing, there certainly—and unfortunately—are a few buck Negroes who would benefit unmeasurably from the firm application of rope to neck."

To summarily ban this time-honored practice, the argument went, would have the opposite effect from that envisioned by its misguided opponents, black and white. A sweeping ban would "send the wrong signal" and without the calming, regulatory effect of lynching on race relations, would inevitably result in exacerbated community hostilities, a white backlash, and possibly even a race war. "It is best," he advised, "for the good of both races, to leave well enough alone."

Besides, there were the serious economic implications of such a move. If the government is foolish enough to stifle private initiative in administering rough justice, what will be the consequences? An inevitable growth of the sprawling octopus of judicial bureaucracy at great and unnecessary cost to the taxpayer. Equally certain, a clogging of the judicial process with the proliferation of bleeding-heart pettifoggers pontificating about "civil liberties" and the "rights" of criminals, while disparaging the civil rights of innocent victims and the right of retaliation of the community's defenders.

Also, he fussed, there has been a cynical exaggeration of the alleged cases where the lynchee was innocent, or at least proclaimed so by "special interests" such as godless Bolsheviks* and the NAACP.

"It is sad, but true," he conceded honestly, "that there is the *occasional* case where a quite understandable community eagerness to see justice done *may* have miscarried." However, in most cases where the lynchee was not guilty of the crime alleged, he was almost certainly guilty of something else as gross. Why else would he have drawn the citizens' attention? It was a matter of character and reputation.

But since mistakes could happen, the government should proceed not with a sweeping prohibition but on a case-by-case basis. Not abolition but *regulation*. From this perspective a useful law might well be entertained. A law, for example, decreeing that in any county where, within a calendar year, more than three lynchings occurred in which it was *proved* that the lynchee was innocent, then, and only then, would government intervention be swift and automatic.

In such cases the right to lynch will be withdrawn. It would be suspended for three years, after which a chastened community would have the right to apply for resto-

---

*In 1909 this reference generated a certain confusion, which was happily resolved in 1917.

ration of the privilege. (Where it could be proved that community standards were being adversely affected by the suspension, the right to lynch could be restored in as little as eighteen months.)

However, without such proof, and upon presentation of a court-approved plan detailing safeguards against future abuse, the right to lynch would be restored in three years. This would be for a probationary period of a year during which time federal observers would have to be present at any lynching undertaken there.

The wisdom and courage of "Jedge" Steele was widely praised in the American media, and Woodrow Wilson is said to have mentioned him in a speech. But black America, benighted by "liberal orthodoxy," remained stubbornly opposed to the practice, and to Steele himself, so that his plan never enjoyed the popular black support it otherwise so richly merited. There is, however, one point of light. There is a persistent rumor, denied by the White House, that the Steele columns were retrieved and carefully studied by the architects of the president's omnibus anticrime bill now making its way through the Congress as I write.

Here also there is a footnote; one hopes it is apocryphal. There is a legend that some years later the "Jedge" himself fell victim to community standards. It is alleged that he unwisely proposed marriage (or worse) to a Reubenesque white widder lady of Pin Head. He could not have known, as he described his priapic powers and epic endowments, that the lady in question was the inamorata of one Billy Dave Duke, local imperial Klaxon of the Klan. Just before the fire was set, "Jedge" Steele made one last plaintive, unavailing plea. "White folk, white folk," he cried, "tain't

my fault, I'm jes' a nachual man, an' all the colored wom-
ens done stopped talking to me. What else could I do?"
Again, the tragedy of a man born out of his time. In our
kinder, gentler, color-blind America, who knows where
this promising conservative career might not have ended?

The point is that the Sowells, Thomases, Crouches, and
Steeles of the world do indeed have progenitors. But as
Langston Hughes affirmed, "black folks are not all second
class fools," and will accept neither the historical nor the
contemporary versions of "intellectual" leaders nominated, anointed, and imposed on us by the most arrogantly
ignorant elements of white American society. It is no accident that these "leaders" speak most loudly and most often
only to white folk.

There is a conservative streak in traditional black American culture, but the current crop of "conservative" charla-
tans stand from that stream "as far as the east is from the
west." Black core culture is conservative on questions of
religion, patriotism in time of war, in its unshakable faith
in the moral and democratic vision and promise of the
Constitution, in its reverence for education, hard work,
self-uplift, and an abiding faith in collective social struggle
and the progress of the group. "The arc of the universe
curve toward freedom. It do, *it do.*" But blacks are also
very clear on the national responsibility; that blacks have
only been able to lighten the oppressiveness of localized
white racism with the intervention, however reluctant, of
the federal government. And that whenever the national
government has been in retreat, or, as it has been doing
under Reagan and Bush, refused its clear responsibility to
lead on the question of racial justice—and indeed, becomes
the agent of reaction—we have all suffered.

But for the historical present, it is discomfiting the extent to which Essex's heated question applies to George Bush's Washington. Indeed, "What scourge for perjury doth this dark monarchy afford false Clarence?" That dark monarchy seems to have had a cruder, but clearer, sense of justice. Richard drowned his Clarence in a butt of malmsey. George Bush contrived—with the complicity of a gutless Senate—to elevate his to this nation's highest court. A rather sobering comment on the evolution, over the centuries, of the political culture, behavior, and moral sensibilities of the Anglo-Saxon race.

On one crucial point, however, Mr. Bush is absolutely right—the sexual-harassment hearings were disgraceful and should never have taken place. That disgrace, began, though, with his politically cynical and thoroughly irresponsible nomination of a distressingly healthy forty-three-year-old who had never practiced law, had no record whatsoever—distinguished or pedestrian—of legal scholarship,* with less than two years' experience on the federal bench, and who would subsequently be pronounced barely qualified by the American Bar Association. A nominee recommended only by a "distinguished" record of public service, which turns out under examination to be some fifteen years of hack political appointments for which his chief qualification appears to have been a shameless availability and expedience in service to whatever right-wing political agenda and mythology he was trotted out to espouse.

---

*Unless one counts a number of speeches before admiring conservative audiences that sniped at the Warren court, the Brown decision, and the legal philosophy and scholarship of the justice he was nominated to replace.

. . .

When Mr. Bush saw fit to introduce his nominee to the American people, with the words "Clarence Thomas is, on the merits, the best man for the job" and "this appointment has nothing to do with race," he was not guilty of perjury only because he was not under oath. One supposes also that the Willie Horton ads were not about "race," but "liberal" permissiveness in penal policy. Those two statements were either shameless, transparent lies from the president of the United States, indicating his deep-seated contempt for the intelligence of the nation, or in the event he believed them, an indication of very troubling intellectual deficiencies of his own.

It is at that point that a responsible, self-respecting bipartisan Senate leadership should have sent the nomination back with a note saying, "Surely you gotta be kidding, Mr. President!" and very bluntly—as a matter of principle and their own and the Court's integrity—refused to entertain that latest presidential hoax in the matter of Supreme Court nominations.

And if the above-mentioned points were not sufficiently disqualifying, Judge Thomas's performance during the first set of hearings should certainly have settled the question. Judge Thomas's bland, unblinking denial of *ever* having discussed *Roe* v. *Wade,* along with his claim to have evolved no position, or even thoughts he was prepared to share with the Senate, on the most troubling and contentious moral and legal question of the day, should have done it. That had to be either outright perjury or else admission of an intellectual torpor so profound as to constitute in itself grounds for disqualification.

As was his casual, unembarrassed admission to having affixed his signature to public documents *that he had not read,* and for whose callous and punitive language regarding the nation's homeless he could therefore not be held accountable.

Or, what has to be the most novel and capricious gambit in recent political discourse, the Thomas defense-by-way-of-expedience, which distressingly enough seemed persuasive to that particular audience, since no senator picked up on it. But, after all, the Senate is a club governed by the aphorism "You gotta go along to git along."

"Well, Senator, you must remember that when I said that, I was working for the Reagan administration." Or, *"On that occasion, Senator,* [put yourself in my place] *I was talking to an audience of convinced conservatives."*

The implication being a creative rewriting of St. Paul: "When I was a political flack, I saw as a toady, I understood as a toady, I spake as a toady. But now only make me a justice, and I shall put away toadyish things." Let the church say, Amen!

And unbelievably, it got worse. What appeared a transparently cynical effort to distance a born-again judge from the absurd and extreme positions taken in his earlier incarnation as Reagan's most visible and vocal black ideological foot soldier may *not* always have been the barefaced dissembling it appeared at all. For in one exchange, it became clear—abundantly and incontrovertibly—that the man actually had no notion at all of the real constitutional or political implications of a speech he had himself delivered. *"Oh, Senator, I did not know there was another agenda."* It is regrettable that the senator did not have a biblical turn of mind, for at this juncture St. Paul's rather condescending question to the gospel-reading Ethiopian Eunuch, *"Understandeth thou what thou readest?"* would in the circumstances have resonated with at least three levels of irony.

Shades of foolish, feckless Ronald Reagan! But then he was only a president. This was a Supreme Court nominee, who presumably needs a sophisticated legal and moral intelligence, sitting in front of the nation and revealing himself fully content to utter, apparently without comprehension, any language put in his mouth by his ideological masters.

Actually, I must confess that had the stakes not been so great, I might have taken a certain pleasure—albeit a perverse one—in the style of his performance. After all, here was a black man facing twelve of the most complacent, orotund, self-important—as only a U.S. senator can be—white men under creation. And there he was, bold-faced as you please, telling them in effect, *"Yo' ain't shit."*

"In yo' face, Senators! Most potent, grave and reverend Segneurs, Ima tell you only as much as I want you to know. I shall from time to time utter statements that strain human credulity. More than that, I shall look you dead in the eye, grin and lie. And you gonna know I'm lying, and I and the world will know I'm doing it. And I dare you sorry mothers to do diddly-shit about it. I dare y'awl. In your face, you sorry mothers."

In other circumstances, were the consequences less grave, or had the judge been defending honorable principles or the clear interests of his people, I might well have, as a black man, cheered him on, enjoying the sheer audacity of his performance and his thinly veiled contempt for his interlocutors. But, of course, had the judge been defending legitimate black interests, that posture would scarcely have been tolerated by the likes of Strom Thurmond and the rest.

In any event, from the Senate's point of view that performance cobbled in equal parts out of arrogance and servility, ignorance and mendacity, should have ended the whole travesty. But whether out of timidity or partisan excess, the Senate leadership failed to act in a forthright way, leaving time and space for the almost irrelevant character issue, represented by the sexual-harassment charge, to emerge.

I say "almost irrelevant" because there is a prior issue of character and perhaps of fundamental intelligence to which the black people that I know—male and female—are much more sensitive and unforgiving. This involves issues exploited and completely distorted by Thomas's White House handlers, and about which I have seen no informed or intelligent discussion in the superficial and often ignorant coverage offered by the white media.

I give one example, and in this case a few white journalists did pick up on the revealing gap between the language in which the White House handlers referred to this nominee and the way they referred to previous ones. For these White House aides it had been "Judge Ginsburg will" or "Judge Bork won't," but in this case, at least in the beginning, it was "Clarence will," "Clarence thinks," etc. Black people, being cursed with oversensitivity, notice such things, as someone else must have, for it abruptly ceased.

In the absence of persuasive intellectual or scholarly support, the decision was made to "foreground" the life, to

exploit the sentimental, prototypically American story of
one man's "rise" out of the "stark" and numbing poverty
and racial oppression represented by Pin Point, Georgia,
under Jim Crow.

Early on in that text, the figure of Mr. Myers Anderson,
the entirely admirable grandfather who saw to young Clarence's education, loomed very large indeed. (Subsequently, and for cause, we heard less and less of Mr.
Anderson in the press.) Which is kind of a shame for he
may well be the only entirely admirable figure in this sorry
mess.

Born one generation out of slavery, Mr. Anderson had
little formal education. He seems the kind of man to which
the community would direct student organizers of the
sixties with the locution, "Son, go talk to Mr. Anderson.
He a good man; doan have much education, but he got
good mother wit."

In this, Mr. Anderson reminds me of a host of heroic
southern black men of his generation we met in the Civil
Rights Movement. Simple men, uneducated but very able,
dignified, with a strong sense of independence and what
Jesse Jackson calls "personhood." Men like the heroic E.
D. Nixon of Montgomery, Amsie Moore, Hartman Turn-
bow, or E. W. Steptoe of Mississippi. Brave, hardworking,
self-employed men, wresting a relatively secure livelihood
for their families from a hostile environment, educating
their children, and always in the forefront of community
efforts toward struggle and progress. Men whose home-
spun, southern appearance concealed deep centers of vision, fortitude, and indeed, wisdom, and who were present
in the black South in far greater numbers and effect than
white America generally understands. I urge you to read a

book called *All God's Dangers;* in its narrator, Nate Shaw, you will understand what I mean.

How do I know that Mr. Anderson, whom I have never met, is in that tradition? From nuggets almost lost in the media blitz that opened the political campaign for his grandson's confirmation.

Early on, I read that "the grandfather had little education but was able to build up a modest business distributing fuel oil." So we know that he was independent, scorning both public assistance and employment—as a sharecropper, field hand, handyman, or family retainer—by white folks in apartheid Georgia. His independence of spirit is reinforced by the grandson's recollection (apparently with no sense of irony) that his grandfather frequently urged him to get all the education he was able "so you won't have to depend on the white folk for anything."

In another story, or it could have been the same one, my attention was held by this account: the nominee remembered being presented by an education-proud grandfather at community meetings where the academically bright boy would start before the gathering to read the grades on his latest report card. That is a scene I had no difficulty visualizing. During the sixties in rural Mississippi, just about every "mass" meeting began with the community's children. Usually presented by their proud grandparents, the kids would perform—sing songs, recite poems, make orations (speeches by Frederick Douglass and Dr. King were big), or otherwise display the progress they were making in school.

In the case of the young Clarence it was indiscreetly let slip that these meetings of youthful recollection were, lo and behold, of the local branch of the NAACP! From

7

which we know that the barely educated Myers Anderson
was also a courageous, self- and people-respecting black
man. For in that time and place simply to attend NAACP
meetings was an expression of commitment to struggle and
a faith in your people's progress that placed both life and
livelihood at serious risk. Only the bravest and most independent of our people did so openly.

So—a proud, brave, enterprising grandfather enjoining
the youth to "get as much education as you can, son, so
you won't be dependent on the white folks for anything."
I would almost bet that that injunction was accompanied
by another very common southern homily as he departed
for college. "Boy, you going off to that white college. Git
your books, son, but *don't you grow away from your raising,*
hear. Get knowledge, son, but with thy knowledge get
understanding." And the inevitable, *"Boy, your character will
be judged by the company you keep, so avoid low-lifeted companions."*

One piece I read bemoaned Mr. Anderson's passing
before seeing the extraordinary fruition of his hopes for his
grandson. That may be a trifle facile. One wonders if his
undoubted joy and pride might not be mediated by some
slight misgivings and a measure of confusion over the path
traveled and the associations cultivated en route to that
lofty eminence.

Two bit players in the drama—Justice Marshall and Senator Thurmond—can serve to illustrate the ambiguity for
such a man as Mr. Anderson. To committed and politically
active black people of Mr. Anderson's generation, Justice
Thurgood Marshall was Moses. His elevation to the high
court was considered an achievement of the race, not
merely because he was the "first Negro" but because of the

manner of his achieving it, a life effectively and productively in service to his people and the advancement of social justice in the nation. Justice Marshall was to that southern generation a towering black colossus, of a stature equaled only by Martin Luther King, Jr.

Similarly, to that generation, the very embodiment of mean-spirited southern bigotry in high places, after the passing of Theodore Bilbo, was the senior senator, the gentleman from South Carolina, Mr. Thurmond. They remember Thurmond as the racist demagogue who was the acknowledged leader—and whose language never strayed far from "mongrelization and race mixing"—of every Dixiecrat filibuster intended to defeat any piece of national legislation with even a suggestion of lifting the institutionalized oppression of black people in the South.*

How then would Mr. Anderson take Justice Marshall's unambiguous reference to the bite of a "black snake." (In which Justice Marshall's uncanny prescience emerges, since that was weeks before the nomination and a month before Professor Hill's evocation of the chairman's alleged descriptions of his epic phallic endowment.)

How would Mr. Anderson have understood the reluctant, unprecedented, and pained decision by his beloved NAACP, against their every instinct, history, and their deepest disposition, to oppose the appointment of a black man to the Supreme Court? Conversely, what would he have made of Strom Thurmond's fervent, paternal embrace of his grandson now? Gratifying evidence of the old

---

*Thurmond's twenty-four-hour eighteen-minute harangue during the debate on the 1964 Civil Rights Act remains the Senate record. Among other things, Thurmond argued that extending blacks equal access to public accommodations bordered on the "enslavement" of white people.

racist's moral improvement and intellectual evolution, or something less benign?

If he had seen Senator Thurmond almost foaming at the mouth, and sawing the air, on the Senate floor fulminating (with a grandiloquent passion and indignation every bit as great as that he had brought to the filibusters) against "this scu'lous attack on this good man's character by special interests," what would he have thought?

Would Mr. Anderson have fantasized, as I did, that this nomination were twenty-five years earlier? That the president was not Bush but Johnson. That the nominee had served as head of the War on Poverty, from which position he had militated for equal access, affirmative action, and social activism by the government. Now nominated to the court, the candidate and (the same) loyal wife were now present before the committee and a younger, unreconstructed Strom Thurmond? But to even imagine that scenario, one needs more of a sense of history than seems present in the society. But a Mr. Anderson might well have thought it, even as I did. What also would he have made of Klansman-turned-Republican David Duke's warm endorsement of his grandson's elevation? *"Son, your character will be judged by the company you keep. Avoid low-lifeted companions, hear me!."*

Closer to the bone, what would Mr. Anderson have made of the manner—humiliating and apparently very unfair—in which the grandson had introduced another family member into right-wing political discourse to win himself a few more points as a true believer?

During the Reagan administration, then–Chairman

Thomas had complained bitterly about the suspicion in which black appointees were held by the fundamentalist zealots who had captured the party. They believe that all blacks are closet liberals, he complained. Why are we always called upon to prove our conservative good faith? One can certainly sympathize, but he should remember that even a conservative icon like Barry Goldwater was not pure enough for these hardscrabble zealots.

In his own—an American far-right—version of the Soviet kids who became heroes of the revolution by denouncing their parents' deviationism, the chairman offered up his own kin in the person of his sister. In fairness, it should be recorded that this has since been denied by Mr. Thomas, as he has denied so much else. But the report is that, in a speech to black "conservatives" in which he deplored the dependency syndrome that public assistance is said to engender among blacks, he used the example of his sister, at one time a welfare recipient.

"Why, she even gets mad whenever the check is late," he is reported to have complained piously.

For his sake one hopes he didn't say it, or, if he did, that his conservative stocks rose gratifyingly. I hope he didn't, because I saw a recent interview with his sister that tells a much different story. For one thing, she is no long-term welfare addict but was on public assistance for a specific period during a family emergency. Presently, she works not one, but two minimum-wage-level jobs. She also pointed out that she did not have her brother's education because she elected to stay home to take care of the old folks who were in failing health.

But even were his characterization accurate, I know no black person who does not hold in contempt what can only appear to be a callous, self-serving, low-down exploitation of family, which, quite possibly, is what led to his denial of the statements attributed to him.

But this begs the issue. It misses the real irony of the story, which exposes not only a failure of character but the shallowness of his public rhetoric about traditional family values.

At the time of his sister's misfortune Mr. Thomas was star ascendant in the conservative galaxy, where his stock-in-trade was invocations of black self-help and bootstrap responsibility for self and family. Forget for the moment his government salary as a highly placed bureaucrat. As a leading black dispenser of comforting conservative clichés to the faithful, he was much in demand as a speaker, and must have commanded handsome speaking fees. The laborer is, after all, worthy of his hire.

What can a monthly welfare check amount to in Pin Point, Georgia? Couldn't it be expected that the chairman, acting on the values he so piously preached, would put his money where his mouth was? Couldn't he, by the obvious and painless expedient of scheduling just one more speaking engagement per month, have kept his sister from the disgrace of public assistance?

There are many blacks, without the chairman's high visibility or access to the endowments of wealthy conservative think tanks, who have done as much. It is, of course, possible that he made such a gesture. If so, was it a sudden, uncharacteristic, and entirely admirable rush of delicacy that inhibited him and his advocates from broadcasting that to the world?

To the people with whom I spoke, the foregoing was already ample enough grounds to compromise the nomination, so—in an elegant Bushian usage—the "sexual-harassment thing" was almost superfluous. And the reasons for that were interesting.

In the first place, the committee's decision to shelve the FBI report on Professor Hill's allegations was shameful and irresponsible, grossly insensitive, but typical. So was the pious handwringing and the blustery denunciation of the leaker of the FBI report, typical of the colossal inversion of values that informed the entire farce. In light of the committee's clubby decision to ignore the issue, whoever made the report available to the press, and therefore the American people, was a whistle-blower performing a public service. I am by no means persuaded that the Democrats necessarily did it. It seems entirely possible that some anonymous Republican staffer, trying to negotiate between an unyielding party line and his or her own patriotic conscience, might well have done so.

The committee then reversed itself and went to the other equally foolish extreme—the decision to televise the sentimental melodrama. That was a public service only to the extent that it exposed first the hypocrisy of those camera-struck windbags, then later the win-at-all-costs-and-the-truth-be-damned viciousness and desperation of the White House attack dogs on the committee. And this came only after two days of demonstrated outrage by the nation's women had compelled the committee's attention to the issue's seriousness.

Among the people I have spoken with, only one black woman did not believe in the literal and unvarnished truthfulness of Professor Hill's account. It was patently not delusion, fantasy, or a coldly manufactured series of lies designed to bring the nominee down. Just about everyone was convinced by the detail, the consistency, and to an extent, the evident reluctance of the witness. Most liars do not, after all, volunteer to submit themselves to polygraph examinations.

Most folk simply shook their head in wonderment, grinned ruefully, and said, "Hell, yes! He did it, man, that Clarence, he a big dowg."

Much more interesting and surprising was the fact that none of the people watching the squalid revelations, this ultimately demeaning spectacle unfolding in the full view of white America, admitted to any feeling of embarrassment for the race. Surprising because these are conscious black people normally very sensitive to our greater need for a dignified public image—folks, for example, who gloried in the *gravitas,* charisma, and strength of character in the persona of Nelson Mandela, and who are equally quick to be offended by the occasional charlatan and demagogue being presented as our spokesmen by a very willing media.

But in this instance they watched the drama that catered to the lurid interest, bordering on the prurient, of both senators and media, with a singular detachment and very little sympathy for either protagonist. A typical response.

"Embarrassed. But why? These two have nothing at all to do with us. They seem some kind of mutant . . . something from another planet. Where do these young people come from. Who dey folk? They got any?"*

I know only one black person over ten years old who

---

*What *was* deeply offensive was the suggestion by a number of conservative columnists that the hearings represented a media triumph for the race. This because the "audience" saw for the first time a succession of articulate, accomplished, well-dressed blacks rather than the crack-dealing, violent criminals or homeless derelicts common to the six o'clock news!

was not convinced that Professor Hill was speaking the truth. Not so for our elected representatives, however. The senators postured into the cameras in pious public torment, totally, earnestly, anxiously, and somewhat too obviously involved in the "difficult task" of deciding just who was telling the truth. Oh, how they rolled their eyes and grimaced, virginal ears literally burning, with each new sexually explicit revelation. They emoted big-time into the cameras with all the innocence of so many superannuated Cub Scouts traumatized by their first exposure to the grosser facts of life. Get a life, Senators; which town do you work in? One hopes the folks back home in Middle America for whom the charade was so clearly intended bought the sanctimony, for no one else did.

How could these men even think they could successfully affect such pristine naïveté on the sleazy convergence of sex, power, and the machismo of male politicians in the political culture and social exchange of the nation's capital? To his credit, the senior senator from Massachusetts had the grace to sit stone-faced and not debase himself with these theatrical expressions of outraged surprise.

We are talking about a culture in which the peddling of "influence" is an honorable way of life; where which "high" officials will accept or return your call is an index of status and often income; where who you know can be money in your purse; where "favors" are a political currency to be carefully calculated, invested, and repaid on demand, and with interest. In a culture where access is confused with influence, and influence with power, there are sexual protocols of an astounding crudeness and exploitativeness. And until an unconscionable press broke ranks and began reporting it, it was remarkably overt, so that unless you were brain-dead on the Hill you knew this. And you also know that while this culture is generally and crassly exploitative of women, there are said to be a few ladies who are among the very best players, and too many who seem quite happy to cooperate with it.

Among the men, politicians and powerful bureaucrats alike, there is a syndrome of the phallic mystique of candidacy and power. In this atmosphere of competition and the victor mentality, the adolescent egotism and status anxiety endemic to the profession combines with the hunger for, and the illusion of power, usually well lubricated by alcohol, to create in these politicians an erotic compulsion that invariably seems to settle right in their respective groins.

In this ambience women become the legitimate spoils of victory and office and, where the woman is malleable enough, sometimes the small change of political favors. Their faceless but complaisant bodies become the arena in which the virility and eroticism of male power find expression. This is not a new phenomenon in human history, but I have never seen it as intense and as visible in any other American city, except perhaps, one might hazard, Las Vegas. In all candor, it must be said that there is a type of Washington woman—the Beltway Bimbo of song and legend—who is complicit in her own oppression, if that is indeed what it is, and who trades on this complex protocol of power, money, sex, and access. These women seem to derive status from Monday morning one-upwomanship, as in:

"How was your weekend, dear?"

"Fabulous, I went on a cruise on Lobbyist X's yacht with Senator A or Secretary B. Yours?"

"Oh, how nice for you! Ginny and I went on Chairman X's junket to Hawaii. It was *wonderful.*"

The syndrome I have been trying to describe is clearly true not only of elected but also of appointed officials.

"Power," gloated the rotund, avuncular Henry Kissinger—though the young ladies on his arm were rarely the nieces they so resembled—"is the ultimate aphrodisiac." How would he possibly know? I would have thought that for him bombing, not ladies, would have had that effect. Better men, even my old Movement colleague Marion Barry, also proved vulnerable. A number of presidential candidates have fallen victim to it, and in a more impartially just world, many more would have, and probably will. Surely you recall House Ways and Means Committee Chairman Wilbur Mills, his stripper, and their *danse macabre* in the reflecting pool? Or the other committee chairman's nubile ex-beauty-queen staffer, capable of neither typing nor *answering the phone*? The freshman congressman from the South so intoxicated by the emanations of erotic power on his first visit to the Capitol that he could not make it back to his hotel and had to have sexual congress with his wife on the Capitol lawn?

So if Professor Hill was lying, she was not only a consummate actress and confinably psychopathic, but must have gathered, during her D.C. sojourn, an impeccable command of the vocabulary, style, and dynamic of the dominant male, power-resides-in-my-phallus syndrome so much a part of the subterranean social discourse in Capitol Hill culture.

What undermined her credibility in the eyes of black folk was not the truthfulness of her account, but its *meaning,* the implications of her *behavior.* Were she as humiliated and embarrassed as she avers, why on earth would she follow in the chairman's orbit as he rose to new bureaucratic heights, and why did she, once having escaped, maintain such cordial contact? Besides, there was never a claim that he had ever used his position to damage or impede her career ambitions; he had seemed to foster them. Could the chairman have been so egomaniacal and insensitive—not only to her reactions, but more pointedly to his all-important career—as not to see that his rough courtship was causing her distress and him potential embarrassment? And why would he have continued such an ill-advised offensive?

"Look, man, after my dad died, my mother, who was a young, very attractive woman, had to go work in various jobs to support us—in the South, in the fifties. Almost every other month she had to cuss out some cracker and risk losing the job. And she had two children to support and nothing like the qualifications of Professor Hill. This girl is a Yale-trained lawyer. I have no sympathy for that story." This response from my friend Benjamin is more or less typical.

That is what cost Professor Hill a measure of the sympathy that otherwise would have been her due among black folk: her apparent inability, at that time, to resist the careerist impulse to follow the rising star, and later to use the association to score points and win status with her new dean and faculty colleagues.

"Oh, Dean, you want to invite the chairman, but you can't get through? Let me, I *know* he'll return *my* call. We're good friends. . . ." (*In D.C., who returns your call . . . ?*)

· · ·

One suspects that the most popular and successful course at Yale Law must have a title something like Career-Building and Expedience 101, most appropriately offered by Professor Bork, he of the ready availability, demonstrated by his eagerness to do Richard Nixon's dirty work in the Saturday Night Massacre.

Even so, the Republicans' indecorous, thoroughly despicable, and cowardly assault, totally without evidential basis, on Professor Hill's motives, character, and psychological health was the most chilling and self-revealing exhibition of primitive political thuggery since George Bush got on national television—exactly like a movie-version *capo mafioso* putting out a contract hit—and offered with a revealing edge of hysteria in his voice $1 million, no questions asked, for the delivery of his former CIA "asset" Noriega—*"dead or alive."* Acceptable as spook-craft perhaps, but as public behavior from an American president?

So it came as small surprise to learn that this shameless public savaging of a black woman had been approved by the patrician in the White House. (Where, if he went at all, did Bush go to school?) Nor was there much surprise in learning that his chief agent, Arlen Specter, was also an alumnus of Yale Law. What do you think was the *"gentleman"* from Pennsylvania's grade in Expedience 101? Judge Thomas was, as usual, a little excessive in his rhetoric. No "lynching," high-tech or otherwise, took place in that committee room. But something uncomfortably close to a gang rape certainly did. Perhaps though, as usual, "She asked for it"?

• • •

The patent absurdity and desperation of their charges demonstrated only that the Republicans' decency was at one with their intelligence. It is with amazement and despair that one had to remind oneself exactly to what goal this paroxysm of win-at-all-costs, knee-to-the-groin political hardball was in service: the salvaging of a mortally tainted nomination to the Supreme Court which, in an even minimally responsible administration, would never even have been contemplated.

The most mindless and transparent of their irresponsible maneuvers was the allegation that Professor Hill was an agent of sinister "special interests" intent on making of Thomas a Bork. Unfortunately, for that theory, Professor Hill, bless her ahistorical technocrat's heart, holds (or held) nothing but an appropriate Republican contempt for those "special interests," which she is reported to feel very strongly had so unfairly politicized and derailed the appointment of her mentor and friend Professor Bork. It is hard, therefore, to now see her as their willing agent.

But she could benefit from an excursion into recent history. Maybe a reminder or clarification of the meaning and context of her respected professor's celebrated reference to a "principle of unsurpassed ugliness."

This characterization arose when the good professor was affirming the inviolability of property rights by attacking the equal-accommodation clause of the 1964 Civil Rights Act. Professor Bork held that the notion that privately owned businesses serving the public were, because licensed and inspected by the state, obliged to serve *all* members of the public without reference to race, was a "principle of unsurpassed ugliness."

A large number of Professor Hill's relatives supported her at the hearing. Had they driven from Oklahoma, and had Professor Bork's opinion prevailed, here is what they would have been subjected to. They might have had to drive through the night, or to catch a few hours' sleep in a locked car. Her mother, sisters, and aunt might have had to squat behind bushes to relieve themselves, and without a hamper of fried chicken, endured either humiliation or hunger. *"Daughter, your character will be judged by the company you keep."*

Perhaps if President Brewster had it to do over he might well have diverted a fraction of those resources to some politically informed black faculty and a few meaningful courses in black history. Who knows?*

But now the thing is done, our 106th justice now sits on the high bench. What does it portend? Some desperate souls like Maya Angelou, seeking a ray of hope or a point of light, pray that as with Saul on the road to Damascus, lightning will strike again. Others speculate that maybe, just perhaps, the man from Pin Point, the grandson of Myers Anderson, the avowed admirer of Malcolm X, is indeed really, at heart, a conscious and responsible black man who was only playing the cards dealt him by a bitter history. His rabid conservatism merely a convenience, for as the Russians say, "When you run with the wolves, you must howl like a wolf." Our Akan ancestors also said, "A

---

*I am pleased to report that the current generation of black Yale undergraduates seem more informed, clear-eyed, and historically conscious than the Thomas-Hill-Doggett group.

log may lie in the river for ten years, but it will never become a crocodile." The extreme right having dominated the executive all his professional life, the brother merely did what he had to. Now unfettered, he will, in Senator Danforth's refrain, "surprise a lot of people." Not unlike Justice Hugo Black, a Klansman in his early life, of whom it was said, "In his youth he wore white robes and terrified Black people, and in maturity he wore black robes and terrified whites." Bro Clarence's true colors will emerge, he will do right.

Either scenario seems unlikely, with Bro Justice Clarence, I fear that what you see is exactly what you get.

One last piece of white presumption and arrogance cannot be allowed to pass unremarked. In militating for the appointee, both Mr. Bush and Mr. Danforth have justified the confirmation so as to give the nation's black youth a much-needed new role model. I very much doubt that our youth will allow these gentlemen to select their role models, any more than blacks let J. Edgar Hoover anoint his choice of leader to be projected in place of Dr. King. Hoover's candidate was none other than the same Samuel Pierce who presided over the Republican apparatchiks' looting of the Department of Housing and Urban Development at a time when homelessness was growing in the nation.

One of the senators on the committee—who, of course, voted apparently without reflection or reservation for Thomas—expressed a most interesting concern about the Gates nomination to be head of the CIA. He said, without visible irony, *"I think we should examine this nomination some more. It may send the wrong message to the intelligence community about just what it takes to get to the top in this town."* What message does Justice Thomas's elevation send to black youth on that or any subject? Messrs. Bush and Danforth should be required to explain to our youth exactly what the moral superiority of their "model" might be over, say, the local big-hatted hustler down the block.

There used to be a professional football team which had their training camp at the university where I teach. A veteran lineman was forced into retirement by injuries. The departed had not been the most physically or athletically talented, but before his physical capital had been completely expended, he had toughed out an honorable career in the trenches. I overheard a group of his peers paying tribute to that career.

"The Bear's gone, man."

"Gon' miss him, man. Ol' Bear always came to play."

"Yeah, Bro. Every game, every series . . . every damn *down,* man."

"Hell, yes . . . even in *practice,* man."

"Wasn't y'know, no superstar. . . . *But y'know that Bear didn't have no whore in him.*"

Can that simple tribute be given to our new associate justice? It may be too early to say. But what about the fifty-two members of the U.S. Senate who voted to confirm?* The voters of this nation, men and women alike, will certainly have their work cut out for them.

---

*"I'd be willing to bet," said an accomplished black attorney, "that not one of the senators that voted to confirm Clarence Thomas would hire him as their lawyer."

CLAUDIA BRODSKY LACOUR

Doing Things with Words:
"Racism" as Speech Act and the Undoing of Justice

It was understood during the Thomas proceedings, while never directly stated, that the process of questioning Clarence Thomas would be shaped—curtailed and attenuated—by potential ascriptions of "racism." It was, of course, precisely this understanding that enabled George Bush to nominate Thomas in the first place, and, in so doing, to call him "the best-qualified man for the job." By tacit convention the president could use blunt hyperbole to describe as uniquely well qualified to sit on the Supreme Court a nominee whose record showed no demonstrable qualifications for that office but, instead, many demonstrably disqualifying actions:* no body of legal writing, but a

*It should be noted that Thomas is, of course, not the only recently confirmed Justice to lack demonstrable qualifications for one of the most

collection of inflammatory speeches attacking already-
instituted legal rights and liberties, the constitutional powers of the Congress, and even those of the Court; no
courtroom experience, but a brief tenure in a stepping-
stone judgeship; indeed, no direct legal experience to speak
of and no other form of constructive public work, but
stints stewarding federal agencies with the purpose of rendering ineffectual, reducing, or terminating the activity of
those same agencies; no evidence of confidence earned and
bestowed either by the professional and academic legal
community or the public at the ballot box, but a career
fueled entirely by patronage; no indication of superior legal
knowledge, of any degree of judicial prowess or analytic
independence of mind, but a consistent history of political

---

vital offices in the land. Asked to comment on the consensus of the American Bar Association that Thomas was "qualified," but not "highly" or
"very qualified," to sit on the highest court, Guido Calabresi, dean of the
Yale Law School, responded that if a Souter or a Kennedy might be called
"highly qualified," then so could Thomas. Calabresi's comments (made
well before any public report of Anita Hill's statements) pointedly deflated
a certain self-serving use of the now largely rhetorical notion of "standards." Although Calabresi was testifying for Thomas at that early stage,
attributing his endorsement to pragmatic calculations (the certainty that the
next nominee would be no better versus the slightest uncertainty as to how
a Justice Thomas would vote), the candor and courage of his remarks,
coming from a sitting law-school dean, came not a minute too soon. Yet
while an equally rigorous assessment would find that none of these former
nominees possessed the demonstrable juridical qualifications for the position he subsequently attained, Thomas alone possessed a public record of
disqualifying actions.
Since his confirmation to the Court, Thomas's votes in all cases and the
minority opinion (concerning the beating of prisoners) he wrote in one
case—an opinion so far to the right of the Bill of Rights that it provoked
the ire of Justice Sandra Day O'Connor—have proven Dean Calabresi's
pragmatism overly optimistic, his calculations, most unfortunately, wrong.

appointments to posts of bureaucratic oversight whose exercise was, at the very least, controversial, and about whose documented negligence, if not thwarting of the law, much could have been said.

In brief, in Clarence Thomas the anti-"quota" president found his quota of one. Performing an act of "affirmative action" dramatically surpassing any against which he vigorously protests, George Bush found the opponent of affirmative-action programs he had been looking for, an opponent who had also been the beneficiary of such programs. For without the decision of the Yale Law School to take affirmative action in the face of de facto segregation in higher education and the white-collar professions—to break the spiral of segregation, which tightens as it rises in society, by taking into consideration each applicant's race—Clarence Thomas would in all likelihood never have appeared before the Senate Judiciary Committee as a nominee to the Supreme Court. Yet the nominee who justly benefited from affirmative action was never compelled by that committee to account in any coherent fashion for the glaring conflict between that fact of his personal history and his publicly professed political beliefs, to speak to the blindness, bad faith, or, to put the matter less delicately, selfish ambition and opportunism that such a denial of history by ideology bespeaks. If an affirmative-action policy clearly aided Thomas in the past, supporting and aiding antiaffirmative-action policies was just as clearly helping him in the present, and the only witness called upon to resolve this salient contradiction in "character" was Thomas's grandfather, surely the William Casey of these

particular hearings, the presiding absence whose narrative
presence served to deflect any present interrogation at
all.*

With rare exceptions which, for their part, always took
the guarded path of indirection, members of both parties in
the Senate, of the press and editorial corps, of the American
Bar Association, and of every ethnic group composing the
American public agreed implicitly to the convention that
rendered intelligible the president's hyperbole. According
to that convention, the race of a nominee could be used for
political leverage while the word "race" remained unmen-
tioned. A demonstrably unqualified nominee could be
called "qualified" (the ABA), or, for that matter, "best-
qualified," because any findings to the contrary could
themselves be disqualified by verbal attributions of "racism," the word that silently generated and determined the
rhetorical logic of this exclusively verbal political process.

The word "racism" and not the thing, the potential

*Apparently incredulous that one's deceased grandfather could be used
in a public hearing of the federal government in the place of relevant
testimony—and in so obviously self-serving a fashion—Chairman Biden
began his questioning of Thomas by remarking that, of course, we all had
grandfathers, some of us tough, hardworking grandfathers (and even some
of us Catholic sisters as teachers), but that now it was time to talk about
Thomas himself, his writings, employment history, and qualifications.
Thomas, however, knew better than to relinquish his one line of defense,
and Biden, not realizing that his "now-let's-get-serious" tone would never
be taken seriously, failed to insist that it be so taken and that Thomas speak
instead to the issues. Under the influence of the unspoken word "racism,"
Biden allowed Thomas to invoke his grandfather whenever Republican
senators invited him to, or whenever questions from the Democratic side
became slightly more difficult to side-step. In the unstated contest for
authority over the Thomas proceedings, Thomas's absent grandfather, or
rather, the narrated story in which the words "my grandfather" figured,
usurped Biden's official authority early on, winning presiding power over
the hearings hands down.

verbal weapon and not the actual injustice it signifies, was the object of concern that defined the way the Thomas hearings proceeded; the distinction between that word and its objective meaning, their bifurcation and intersection, are the focus of the present analysis of the proceedings. For it is also the place at which Anita Hill enters the verbal process, the context in which her testimony recounting sexual harassment comes into question and is effectively silenced, raising the larger question of whether any such testimony can ever be heard, in the conventional sense of receiving a just "hearing." Witnesses for Anita Hill stated that, like her, they too would have kept quiet—one witness stating that she had already done so in her own life and would do so again. Recalling the explicit sexual discrimination that two decades ago had blocked her professional advancement, a lawyer commenting on the hearings in the *New York Times* observes that she now knows she "did the right thing" in doing nothing to identify and redress that discrimination; her commentary concludes, stunningly, "that in declining to invoke the legal process," Anita Hill's "judgment was dead on."[1] Stated flatly by a member of the legal profession, these words startle with a hard, diamond-like glint. The timeworn view they articulate, shared to some degree by every woman, is less fatalistic than pragmatic—it faces squarely the facts of how things work—and one would have to think at least twice before presuming to criticize it from a higher moral ground, although every senator (whether voting for or against Thomas) who felt compelled to pass additional judgment on Anita Hill also found himself ascending effortlessly to just such condescending heights.

Rather than judge an earlier and infinitely explicable

silence, we would do better to consider Anita Hill's actual testimony, and the fact of verbal sexual harassment in general, with regard to the specific verbal action by which *it* was silenced. For Anita Hill's words were silenced not by any conflicting testimony, nor certainly by anything that could be passed off as evidence, but by a word, the very word that, unspoken, had previously safeguarded Clarence Thomas from rigorous interrogation. It was in "response" to Anita Hill's testimony that Thomas said the word "racism," and in proclaiming himself a "victim" of "racism" an apparently enraged Thomas disarmed his interrogators even more thoroughly than had the story, told in apparent docility, of his humble origins and modest ambitions, the story of "my grandfather." In saying the word "racism" Thomas could be taken to have meant on a literal level that he wanted to indicate the existence of the thing. But it was "racism" the word, not the thing, that rendered Anita Hill's words effectively meaningless by rendering deaf those for whom those words were intended. From the Senate hearing room, to the press room, to the living room, the word "racism" cut off a mental channel of communication.

Now what Anita Hill had to say was not "racism," nor for that matter was it "sexism," nor even "sexual harassment": it was a literal citation of words previously said—common nouns, proper nouns, adjectives, verbs, etc.—and of the physical circumstances in which their utterance occurred. The very spareness of her testimony—words, dates, and details shorn of any embellishment or conceptualization—made it meaningful in the way that things are experienced as meaningful: the way four walls, for example, are meaningful when one does not wish to be overheard; or a table behind which one sits, or a closed or an open door. The words and details recited in Anita Hill's testimony went straight to the brain—a simple way as good as any other of describing the unfathomable effect of literality—and it is unlikely that they will be forgotten by anyone who heard them anytime soon. Yet for all their literality, or precisely because of their literality, Anita Hill's words will endure the terrible status of being at once unforgettable and insignificant. "Racism," the word that followed her words, drove a wedge between their literal or objective meaning and what those literal meanings were meant to mean in context, their sense or significance—the sense or significance conveyed in this instance, for example, by the customarily literal "Coke can." "Racism," the word, separated the literal words said by Anita Hill from their powerful and unseemly significance; it made that significance vanish in the minds of all those listeners to whom their meaning was addressed. From the Senate hearing room, to the press room, to the living room, those words echoed, but echoed now as purely literal, stuck in the mind, impossible to make sense of, impossible to forget, gibberish—a "Coke can" is a "Coke can" is a "Coke can" is a "Coke can."

What matters is not only that "racism" did this but, most importantly, how it did it. What happened to the word "racism," the unspoken master of the proceedings, once it was said? How did it mean and what, literally, could it have meant? But here the rule of literal meaning is reversed: what goes straight to the brain is literally, objectively, unthinkable. "Racism," the word, rendered the literality of

Anita Hill's unforgettable testimony affectively meaning-less precisely because as used by Clarence Thomas it was and *could only have been* literally meaningless itself.

As used by Clarence Thomas, the word "racism" was a "speech act." J. L. Austin defined a "speech act" as that kind of speech that, rather than *state* something, actually *does* something. This distinction, if not immediately obvi-ous, is fundamental to how language works. We tend natu-rally to view language as a means for describing or reporting the world, for making statements about things and states of affairs that exist independently of the words used to relate them. But Austin noted that language can also make things happen, bring previously nonexistent states of affairs into being. Such uses of language "do not 'describe' or 'report' or constate anything at all"; they are, instead, "the performing of an action."[2] In a speech act, or "performance utterance," "to *say* something is to *do* some-thing";[3] to judge a speech act " 'true or false,' " as one instinctively judges any descriptive or constative statement, is, then, as inappropriate as ascribing truth or falsity to the act of closing a door, or getting up from the table.

The kind of speech act Austin first has in mind are those linguistic formulations conventionally endowed with legal or some other binding power—"I name," "I bequeath," "I promise," "I pronounce you," "I bet you," "I swear," "I do"—examples of utterances in which saying *is* doing, and the doing could not get done otherwise. The power of these speech acts to do what they do, to affect human relations, is understood by all who share the same language; indeed, one can hardly imagine any society that could function without them. But another kind of speech act takes a more devious route to do what it does, masquerading as something else. It uses the language of a constative statement *in order to* effect an action without explicitly saying so; in these speech acts, *"by* saying or *in* saying something we are doing something."[4] If you say, for example, "It's hot in here," your interlocutor may respond that it is or it is not, but more likely he will offer to open a window, or simply get up and proceed to do so; if he says, "I can't concentrate with all that noise outside," you may say that's not true, you certainly can, but more likely you will offer to close the window. These are speech acts in which *"in* saying" one thing—in the form of a straightforward report, or "constative utterance"—we are actually doing something else, something which in this trivial example concerns the position of panes in a window.

But it may be the case that, even in such a trivial situation, things are cloudier still. Perhaps there *is* no "noise outside," and perhaps it never *was* "hot in here." Perhaps these absolutely banal speech acts are tokens of yet something else again, a dispute or ongoing state of tension in which windowpanes are brokering chips, and the act of getting them moved in any direction expresses not any objective and immediate desire to affect the state of a room, but a more insidious desire, the desire to exercise power. If this suggestion seems a dramatic exaggeration, it is also the stuff of daily life, the scenario of innumerable quotidian dramas in which the importance of the props employed often stands in direct inverse proportion to the significance of the relation of power in question.[5] As personal stakes rise, the inherent value of the chips may fall: for what other reason could one person possibly feel compelled to remind another person which one of them it was who last took out the garbage. The sense of relational disequilibrium gets expressed in countless, often exponentially petty ways, just as the feeling of power exercised comes in all sizes and psychological varieties, including, along with the straightforward desire to dominate, the desire to give or to withhold the respect another desires.

Austin named "perlocutionary acts" those speech acts that masquerade as constative, "locutionary acts," using sentences in the form of reports in order to achieve performative ends. These speech acts "do" something "*by* saying something," rather than "in" asking, urging or ordering directly that that thing in fact be done ("illocutionary acts"): "We must distinguish 'in saying it I was warning him' from 'by saying it I convinced him, or surprised him, or got him to stop.'"[6] Speech acts that warn "*in* saying something" (say, the words "watch out") work because they "have a certain (conventional) force;" speech acts that get someone to stop "*by* saying something" work because, even if that something is a "conventional act" or "a straightforward constative utterance," their use of it in context is "*not* conventional."[7] This explanation of speech acts, and of indirect or perlocutionary speech acts in particular, does much to explain in practical terms how the verbal tables were turned on Anita Hill. For if the threat of the use of the word "racism" kept even the mention of Professor Hill out of the proceedings to begin with, the actual use of the word made her eventual testimony insignificant. By saying "racism," Thomas, in Austin's words, "got" Anita Hill's listeners "to stop" (listening); Austin's explanations gives us some idea of how, defying any conventional logic, he did this. In defining himself as a "victim" of "racism," Thomas "did something" "*by* saying something." That something—*what* he said—was a straightforward constative utterance; yet its overriding effect on the proceedings was assured exactly to the extent that it could not be processed as a straightforward constative utterance. Thomas's utterance of the word "racism" was not only "not conventional" in context; it depended directly for its active, rhetorical effect on the absence of any literal or identifiable object to which it could refer. Locutionary, constative speech is understood to refer to such objects; Thomas's perlocutionary speech act exercised decisive influence because it was understood to make no such reference; in short, as not meaning what it said.

The word "racism" was introduced into the proceedings following the testimony of a black woman. What could it have meant? The clear implication, that Anita Hill is racist, immediately makes no sense. This does not mean that black racism against blacks does not or could not exist. Like Jewish anti-Semitism, it most surely does exist: knowing oneself to be existentially hated or held in contempt has the doubly damning effect of causing one, at some more or less conscious level, to hate oneself. But if some form of self-hatred is the deformed and inevitable fruit of being hated, it is also the mirror image of the aggressively inverted act of self-denial that is already at work in all racism, bigotry, or imperious nationalism. Still, of all the actors in the proceedings to whom the role of "racist" could be ascribed, Anita Hill does not come to mind; not only her race, but, just as significantly, her own history, her words, and unmistakable self-respect quite ruled her out for the part. The only serious contenders for that role were to be found among Thomas's histrionic supporters; Anita Hill could not have been the object of Thomas's complaint. Yet that complaint was made in "response" to her testimony, or rather took the place of any response or responsibility in its regard. It aimed blame in melodramatic gestures at no one in particular and at everyone: the mysterious Senate staffer or senator, the member or members of the press, "special interest groups"—meaning anyone against Thomas's nomination, including civil rights activists, national associations of black clergymen, prominent black legal scholars, and congressmen—and of course the Congress itself, whose democratic leadership had written and passed every piece of civil rights legislation the nation had ever known. With a calculated ripple effect the word "racism" took everyone supposedly surrounding Anita Hill into its scope, even after another law professor testified under oath that Professor Hill had supported the nomination of Robert Bork. In spite of, or, again, precisely because of the evident indefensibility of this line of attack, the attack worked; Thomas drew sympathy from blacks and whites alike and "racism" was universally deplored. By the strange bedfellowship of a racialist politics that wedded Strom Thurmond to Clarence Thomas, the issue of "racism" could only be raised in the hearings in the context of testimony to which it could not refer. "Racism," the word that acted decisively upon the proceedings, was said in "response" to the testimony of a black woman because only within that context could it lack all constative dimension, refer to no identifiable object, literally mean nothing. In order for Thomas to utter the speech act "racism," it had to be understood in purely performative terms, as doing something *by* saying something, something which would only gain admittance into the process if said in a context in which it could have no objective meaning.

If this bifurcation of "racism" from the realm of literal

referents does not at first appear the necessary condition for its performative success (the "nonconventional" condition of any successful perlocutionary speech act), the necessity of that bifurcation, by which claims of "racism" are made by a black man in "response" to a black woman, can be shown by way of a simple test. Let anyone now imagine that Anita Hill was white. Against a white Anita Hill the word "racism" could have meant something, and precisely for that reason could never have been said. Claims by white women to have been violated by black men are legion in history; their threatened or actual outcome in this country was often in fact a lynching.[8] Because a white Anita Hill would have spoken within this all-too-real, referential context, a Clarence Thomas speaking after her would have been the last man to have said "racism"—or "lynching," or "assassin's bullet," or even "victim." To say in "response" to the testimony of a white woman that "racism" motivates her allegations is to say something that could be true, having been true all too often. Such an utterance would indeed be taken as constative, as describing or reporting reality directly, and for that very reason would have destroyed the nomination, turning Thomas's supporters against him. For "racism" in such an utterance would have meant racism, the thing literally meant by the word, and, in pointing to the fact of racism, would have been—on the part of a black man—an inadmissible defense. This logic, while paradoxical, is also the logic of racism itself, whose pervasive existence depends on its tenacious nonadmission and complicitous nonrecognition. In order to implement itself in action racism must deny that it is what it is: such is the understanding, and explicit strategy not only of a "born-again" David Duke (who, not coincidentally, supported Clarence Thomas); it is also the logic implicit in calling Thomas "the best-qualified man for the job."

By contrast, "racism," the literally meaningless speech act aimed at a black woman, freed white (and many black) Americans from thinking about racism. Small wonder so many Americans rallied with doubled fervor to Thomas's support: his performative use of "racism" told them racism did not really exist, that they themselves were not racist, that the "racism" they now deplored was not a real thing, not a real problem after all. "Racism," the word or reference, evacuated the possibility of recognizing and criticizing racism, the object or referent, and it was just because "racism" thoroughly obfuscated racism that it could be said, quoted, and, as a verbal act without a referent, loudly denounced, everywhere abhorred.

Used as a speech act, "racism" in the Thomas–Hill hearings effected a double action: that of justifying and solidifying identifiable racism (the literal object to which "racism" did *not* refer), and that of disguising and displacing another object whose overt identification it silenced—misogyny. "Racism" said in defense against a black woman emptied racism of its reality and real power; but it also shunted aside the object described by that black woman, actions by which men show their existential contempt for women, and whose power is unchecked. In this respect "racism" as speech act resembled the verbal object described in the testimony of Anita Hill: the act of using words as unanswerable actions, sexual harassment. If Thomas's use of "racism" was unconventional, sexual harassment may well be defined as the unconventional become a convention—a *classic* speech act—the example that defines the rule: a mode of dominating social exchanges, and of silencing its own criticism, whose admittance into and influence upon such exchanges owe directly to its verbal, rather than physical, nature. For, while the word "lynching" is not the thing it may be used rhetorically to usurp, verbal sexual harassment *is* a mental violation, a form of rape without traces of semen to identify, the imposition of one's will upon another whose untraceable means to that end are the indomitable combination of superior position and privately spoken words. A speech act standing in for the act of rape that is its nonverbal model, sexual harassment performs. It *does* something in *saying* something, and in the process enforces and augments the imbalance of power that makes such actions not only possible, but probable, a social norm.

The argument that all language in society inevitably works along these divisive lines was made by the first modern theorist of democracy, Jean-Jacques Rousseau. According to Rousseau, the performative use of language promoted rather than redressed the development of injustice and inequality: "The first man who, having enclosed a piece of ground, to whom it occurred to say *this is mine* and found people sufficiently simple to believe him, was the true founder of civil society. How many crimes, wars, murders, how many miseries and horrors Mankind would have been spared by him who, pulling up the stakes or filling in the ditch, had cried out to his kind: Beware of listening to this imposter; you are lost if you forget that the fruits are everyone's and the Earth no one's."[9] At this imagined moment of the original institution of property, and, with property, accumulated wealth, social power, and inequality, the words *"this is mine"* actually create the state of affairs they appear to constate. Places and objects once confined to the immediate reach of their overseer became "property," kept by language rather than physical effort, and so expandable without limit. Extensive property bred wealth and power, which in turn bred more property, all the while increasing the inequality that the first act of appropriation imposed.

That first act was a speech act: in saying something that was not so much true or false as objectively meaningless, it did something to human relations that can only be called unjust, creating inequality where none naturally existed before. Rousseau, of course, recognized that all men are not created "equal" in any quantitative sense; he carefully distinguished verbally imposed inequality from differences in strength, for example, or size, or agility, proving in this respect an early Darwinian. But he viewed the fact of such "natural or physical" inequalities among individuals much as he viewed geography and weather, as arbitrary in origin and either empirically favorable to survival or not. "Moral or political inequality," on the other hand, was another matter entirely, a social condition of strength and weakness instituted by linguistic "convention"; made by man, it increased with every iniquitous action.[10] That such escalating inequality could never be redressed naturally was the revolutionary thesis of Rousseau's *Social Contract*, the idea that artifically instituted social inequity, maintained and protected by law, could only be combatted in kind: with artificially instituted equal rights, a republic formed by legal convention. Yet Rousseau also argued that even before the speech act that invented property, an experience of inequality colored the very invention of language itself.

The example Rousseau gives of such a moment of origin is the sighting by one man of other men whom he had never seen before. Since language "is the first social institution," Rousseau reasons, it must "owe its form to natural causes."[11] Like animals who share a form of language, man begins to speak while living in a state of nature (the condition of Rousseau's "savage" or natural man), but unlike animals, man makes the transition from nature to society in the very act of speaking. While animals remain, so to speak, animals, communicating by means of "some natural language" that does not change, man becomes man, a social being, in perfecting the language he had invented naturally, rendering it conventional rather than natural and, at the same time, more precise, a sharper tool for living in society and affecting social life: "Conventional language belongs to man alone. That is why man makes progress in good as well as in evil, and why animals do not."[12]

The scenario Rousseau offers of this natural invention, which leads to convention, is the following:

A savage, upon meeting others, will at first have been frightened. His fright will have made him see these men as larger and stronger than himself; he will have called them *Giants*. After much experience, he will have recognized that, since these supposed Giants are neither bigger nor stronger than he, their stature did not fit the idea he had initially attached to the word Giant. He will therefore invent another name common both to them and to himself, for example the name *man,* and he will restrict the name *Giant* to the false object that had struck him during his illusion. This is how the figurative word arises before the proper [or literal] word does, when passion holds our eyes spellbound and the first idea which it presents to us is not that of the truth.[13]

In seeing other men, Rousseau theorizes, man invents not only language but himself. The invention of a word based on a natural passion, fear, leads to its intellectual correction by way of further comparison: "after much experience" natural man recognizes other men to be like him and invents "man," a "name common to both of them" that then takes the place of "Giant." "Giant," the "figurative" and false name for figures whose first sighting caused fear, acquires as its literal definition the meaning fear had personalized: larger and stronger than me becomes "Giant," larger and stronger than "man." But "Giant" was not a literal misnomer by accident; its reference to men *had* to be improper because it was in fact a metaphor for something else. In saying "Giant" natural man *literally* named no one and nothing outside him but, rather, *figuratively* or *rhetorically,* gave voice to his own fear, the fear that made the unknown look as threatening as it did. Fear, unrecognized, was transferred to an external object; like any transfer of sense, this false objectification of fear resulted in a metaphor, "Giant." Fear, rather than reality, prescribed to the eyes what they saw, and what they saw was not fear itself, that invisible passion, but "Giant," fear falsely objectified in the person of others, a mentally invented, physical threat.

Rousseau does not say how the change from spontaneous figurative meaning to eventual literal meaning takes place, "after" what and how "much experience" "Giant" becomes "man." Nor does he ever say that the real and immediate cause of the metaphor is ultimately recognized as a result of this process of literalization. Rather, fear seems to stay underground, unknown for its distortive power, even after "man" is invented and the name "Giant" comes to mean "giant," or what the word literally says. That fear itself can ever be named literally is an idea left out of Rousseau's analysis, and this omission implies that fear remains active, producing further "Giants" right and left. (We may even surmise that any attempt to refer to fear would similarly produce metaphors in its stead, words like "honor" and "national pride," falsely attributed not to a stranger but to one's unknown, fearful self.) Keeping that fear in mind, however, we can well imagine how Rousseau's "savage" would have responded to his misperceived object. Before replacing "Giant" with the comparative concept "man," it seems likely that he would conduct his comparison at close quarters, by going on the attack. Attack, in any of its myriad forms, is the mode of action that would have followed the metaphor, attacks of "self-defense" against the distorted object of one's own fearful creation, attacks which, if they do defend the self, also further delude the self, conceal and misconceive it unutterably.

"After much experience," in other words, might as well mean war, or murder, or pickaxes held in front of high schools, or houses set on fire. It could also, of course, mean retreat, to some place of fantasized safety and inaction, desertions of entire neighborhoods or even of the larger human society, a move to the suburbs, or a cult community, or a "return to nature," as if at the mall, or in the exhaustively structured enclave, or in the thoroughly unstructured mountains there would never be anything or anyone, never be "reason" to fear, as if fear itself were reasonable and removable, rather than a human passion kindled by a lack of knowledge, the natural baggage every deserter takes with him, remaining wherever he goes a "savage."

Rousseau's "natural man" or "savage," then, may wear blue jeans, a suit, or a uniform, work at the 7-Eleven, the post office, or the Pentagon, feel safely in his element charming birds off the trees or an audience from a podium. Indeed, as long as he feels no fear, never faces anything or anyone with a will or powers of its own that all his previous experience could not have prepared him to know, he may well be taken for that other man, the one Rousseau specifically called a "citizen," and whose "true meaning" he described as the essential basis for a contractual republic— that of possessing and granting to all others in the republic equal "rights," the revolutionary notion that we now sum up in the unconsciously Rousseauian term "law-abiding citizen."[14] According to the "social contract," we are all citizens under the law, but, as we all say, while that may look easy on paper, in practice—which is also the realm of the passions—it's often quite another story. The "citizen" in us can get canceled, annihiliated, wholly forgotten: as the attacked or as the attacker, we may lose or destroy the concept of "citizen," which, in a republic, boils down to the concept of "man." It is in this sense that the generic use of the word "man," consciously adhered to in the present analysis, takes on a surprising and revelatory meaning. For to deny man his rights as a citizen is, historically and actually, to treat him as "woman," that genre of "man" whose rights are forgotten instantly without that oversight even being noticed, without a first, let alone a second, thought on the part of the man who does the forgetting. If "woman" literally meant "citizen" in the minds of most male citizens, there would be no such classic speech act as that ubiquitous performative, sexual harassment. There would be, unimaginably, no discrimination against women, no treatment of any woman as if the fact of her sex placed her in a category existentially separate from that of the generic "man" or "citizen." There would be no objective meaning to the word "misogyny," the actual practice of which spans a gamut of discrimination extending from highly publicized to lesser-known professions, to virtually unregarded labor, to perceptual and conceptual prejudice, to threats of violence, to violence, to repeated violence, to rape, and to death.

If women were perceived as citizens, the act of denying them their equal rights would not be the normal course of events. Loved, liked, or disliked as individuals, appreciated, admired, or not admired as individuals, they would be treated, in short, the way most men and women treat most men. Instead, the experience of most women is the omitted experience of Rousseau's "Giant," that of being perceived as a subspecies apart. The consequence of this perception is "much experience" to come, acts of assault or of exclusion committed with a sense of self-righteous justification. Should that justice be questioned, attacks will only intensify.

Clarence Thomas went on the attack, not against a "Giant" of his own making—Anita Hill was already clearly defined as his dependent subordinate—but against a woman whose perceived equality he had felt compelled to destabilize. Whatever fears or desires the presence of Anita Hill inspired in Thomas, he transferred to her, attacking not her body, but her mind with language. And this is what many men, but no woman I know, cannot perceive clearly. In recounting details of pornographic films, in describing himself as an unsung star of the genre, and in insisting over and over that Hill would want to see such films, would want to "see" him, he was attacking her psyche, forcing her to see him as "Giant." Without attacking, even touching her body, he was murdering with words, killing whatever was free in her, free to believe she had the liberty to do and imagine what she wanted, including that she could work for Thomas but not under him, as one labors under the weight of hopelessness that such injustice would or ever could be redressed. With words and words alone Thomas compelled Hill, whether or not she ever "saw" him, to "see" him as "Giant"—the mode of the obscene phone caller but with an additionally repugnant and demoralizing twist: she knew who was doing the speaking, the recounting, the describing; she knew the reference of her suffering, he was before her eyes, and, wherever she or he went, he would not go away. For even if the two never met again, there would always be memory and the threat: I know you know what I did, so you had better prove the opposite—that you don't know, that you have forgotten, that nothing did happen. This thoroughly common phenomenon, never mentioned by any questioner or witness during the proceedings, permeates all our lives as surely as do inequalities of power. Its structure is the very structure of racialist politics, which, on the one hand, uses race as a threat without saying the word, and, on the other, threatens those who say the word with accusations of "racism." It is the act of telling someone over whom you have power, I can do this, I can do what I want. I did it, I can still do it, and you must show me it never happened. Show me, reassure me, that you have not only accepted this but are continuing to do so; give no sign, no matter how subtle, of any injury done. Prove you have accepted my power when people speak about me, for I will be listening; prove it *by* speaking, for to say nothing is to say too much: no silence is innocent when two people are known to know each other. Prove it to me directly by being solicitous, friendly, courteous. Stop proving it to me and I will assume you have stopped proving it to them.

If this routine experience of unequal power went un-recognized and unremarked in the proceedings—if, in Austin's terms, it was never uttered constatively, reported, described, or stated—one of the remarks made most fre-quently was a speech act *disguised* as a constative—repeated references to the fact that Anita Hill "followed" Thomas. Posed as a simple matter of fact, this observation pro-claimed its willful ignorance of the no-win decision innu-merable women make, or try to make, or try to put off making daily: whether to give up the job, the place, the people, the future one holds dear, denying one's own mental capacities, independence, and desires (what are left of them, what one remembers of them) just to get away. As long as women have any self-respect, they will bridle at that action. They will find themselves disgusting if they let their tormentor get his way, not—once again—by touch-ing their body (never forget the obscene caller), but by forcing them to flee, to change anything they would not have changed if they were free to keep it: their white-collar career or their cash register at the supermarket, it doesn't matter in the slightest; their phone number, or their apart-ment, their patterns of movement, or of speech, of dress, or of personality, of temperament, or of friendship, of intellect or just plain expectation or belief—the list is the list of the forms of living and it is endless.

We say, I can handle this, this won't destroy me; this won't force me to give up what I hold dear, what I take to define, to be me in the world. The world does not, cannot, belong to my tormentor; if he oppressed me, I can repress me—a depressing alternative, and practically, the only alternative. I can conquer my own disgust and go on until I can no longer go on, and I'll know when that day comes. For Anita Hill it seems to have come in a hospital bed. With her head and heart working at overcoming themselves, her stomach gave way, telling her as only the nonlinguistic body can, that she could indeed stand it no longer. Truth was out of the question, justice was never a possibility, and like the ways of power here at the very federal commission charged to protect the powerless, this was the American way as American women have known it.

Anita Hill, forced to see her employer as "Giant," was never seen in kind by Clarence Thomas, the self-proclaimed "victim" of the "process." In this web of metaphorical transferrals, only Judge Susan Hoerchner dared say the obvious: that if he chose to see himself, or, more accurately, name himself "the victim" (so as to be so seen by others), Thomas had no one, no unknown staffer or faceless process, but himself to blame. If he was suffering now, she added, someone else had been suffering longer.

Rather than address what Anita Hill said about him—going so far as to say he hadn't bothered to hear it—Thomas refocused all attention on him by recreating himself as "victim." The rhetoric of victimization he em-

ployed bears a powerful and perverse relation to the function of victimization in narrative fiction, and in Judeo-
Christian society historically, as described by the literary
theorist René Girard. According to Girard, victimization
or scapegoating arises when members of a society engage
in escalating acts of "mimetic" violence, a volley of attacks
in which, in the very act of attempting to distinguish itself
from its perceived adversary, each group actually imitates
that adversary, causing the violence to spiral, with no
group the victor. The only way for the society as a whole
to avoid annihilation from within is to perform an act of
victimization to which both adversaries unconsciously
agree; by a sort of mutual convention, the "sacrificing" of
a scapegoat "miraculously" or incomprehensibly brings
peace, all violence ceasing as if by magic (for the time
being).[15] Thomas, by contrast, donned the mask of a scapegoat; his violently mimetic act was that of imitating the
victim. Speaking in the voice of the victim, he masked not
only himself, but the actual process and violence of victimization.[16]

That process and that violence require the victim's silence—the silence of a sexually harassed Anita Hill, and for
which Hill, now speaking as a witness, was held in suspicion. More, perhaps, than any other characteristic, that of
suffering without speaking, of not naming the violence one
experiences and certainly not oneself as its victim, is what
makes a victim a victim, the nonact that defines the term.
The cliché "silent victims" is not only a redundancy but
also a demonstration that we habitually and profoundly
misunderstand victimization, the act and the word. The
success of Thomas's speech act, his emotional claim to
having been the "victim" of "racism," demonstrates that

misunderstanding in truly dramatic terms. For what could less bespeak a victim than this grandiloquent performance of being a "victim"; and what points more conspicuously to the rhetorical use of the mask of the sacrificial lamb than the language of martyrdom with which Thomas described his affliction. "Dying," "lynching," "an assassin's bullet," "wounds" from which "I can never recover," "killing"— these were words with which, in his lengthy monologues, Thomas referred to himself, as if indeed he *could* be killed and still speak from the dead. The death and the resurrection was the tale this speaking "victim" dramatically told; resurrection indeed, for when asked if, after all the horrors inflicted on him, the crimes of which he had been the "victim," he could possibly go on to judge anything dispassionately—in short, to sit on the Court—the voice and mask of the indignant "victim" transformed themselves instantly into those of the humble and unbegrudging nominee, the voice answering without hesitating, the face without blinking, yes.

This, then, was a nominee who, in the process of getting named "Justice Thomas," acted verbally on the proceedings by which he was judged, managing to conceal misogyny with claims of "racism," to unspeak the reality of racism by using the word, and, finally, to unspeak his own reality by referring exclusively to himself while acting or impersonating different parts, even the part of the existential nonactor, the "victim." The naming of "Justice Thomas" and the undoing of justice were televised lessons in the incompatibility of rhetoric and justice, and here one is reminded ultimately of that most ancient theory of justice, Plato's *Republic*. For *The Republic* is an "answer" in dialogue to an "enquiry into the nature of justice"; the

vision of a republic for which the dialogue is named arises
only indirectly within it, as a means of imagining, "on a
larger scale and on a larger object," "the justice of one
man."[17] But even when projected onto the big screen of
the state, the concept of justice proves extremely difficult
to define; dependent upon the kind of wisdom that Socrates denied he possessed, it is finally described in mechanical
rather than moral terms as a balanced coordination of individual "tasks" or interacting "parts"—less like "justice" as
we normally think of it than what in French is called
justesse, the quality of being "fitted" for or appropriate to
one's specific function.[18] And this is where Socrates' scandalous exclusion of poets from his "just" republic fits in,
for a poet has the verbal power to play any part, to throw
the "justly" functioning machine of the republic into chaos
by making us believe a function is being fulfilled—a part
played rather than play-acted—when it is not. A poet has
the capacity "to make [himself] like somebody else in voice
or form," to "impersonate" anyone and anything, and so
spells disaster in a republic whose justice depends on everyone doing *his or her* part.[19] For Socrates puts men and
women on absolutely equal footing in this regard, specify-
ing that no function should be granted or denied to any
member of the republic on the basis of gender. Like Rousseau's "citizen," every member of Socrates' republic must
have the same rights and obligations if the machine of the
state is to function.[20] Only the poet-impersonator is to be
censored, or better, praised and gotten out of town:

> It seems then that if a man who in his cleverness can
> become many persons and imitate all things should arrive
> in our city and want to give a performance of his poems,

we should bow down before him as being holy, wondrous, and sweet, but we should tell him that there is no such man in our city and that it is not lawful that there should be. We would pour myrrh on his head and crown him with wreaths, and send him away to another city.[21]

Socrates invented the model of the republic in order to define justice; the notion that the model would have to judge what it stood for, would itself have to judge what it believed to be justice, certainly surpasses the relationship of model to concept on which *The Republic* is built—but then again, Socrates had very little good to say about democracy, preferring the rule of a philosopher, no matter how unwilling, to "an emporium of constitutions" in which the freedom of individual desire is king.[22] As a result of the Thomas proceedings, a "Justice" was named, and during those proceedings the meaning of justice was lost. Thomas was not sent, crowned with wreaths, to another city, but neither had he performed poems. Clarence Thomas used words to say what they could not have meant literally, not in order to imitate but to mask reality, and for this he was kept, clothed in robes, in the heart of the city. Neither a poet who impersonates all men indiscriminately nor a man justly performing his part, Thomas was given the role of impersonating "Justice" for life. Because the republic is a verbal construct and *not* a smoothly running machine, *not* the fitted coordination of so many functional parts, one need not be a poet to throw it out of sync; one need only be a speaker of language against whose speech acts no republic, not ours and not Plato's, stands up. Language that distorts the identification of its referents is indeed threatening to just government—not, however, because it may disrupt the machinery of justice (as Plato feared), but rather, and more injuriously to justice, because it may be absorbed and exploited by the machine. This machine is verbal, which means that it is artificial, conventional, political. This means also that it can do or undo justice to the extent that our understanding of language fits the fact that language acts, and that for every speech act there is a literal victim. No republic can stand up to this, for even the laws and rules by which it functions must be made. For the same reason, however, no "law-abiding citizen" of any description will ever be only literal, silenced.

NOTES

1. See Laura Mansnerus, "Don't Talk," *New York Times Magazine,* December 1, 1991, pp. 42–44.

2. J. L. Austin, *How to Do Things with Words,* 2nd ed. (Cambridge: Harvard University Press, 1975), pp. 5–6.

3. Ibid., pp. 6, 12.

4. Ibid., p. 12.

5. Cf. Erving Goffman, *Behavior in Public Places* (New York: Free Press, 1963); *Strategic Interaction* (Philadelphia: University of Pennsylvania Press, 1969); *The Presentation of Self in Everyday Life* (Woodstock, N.Y.: Overlook Press, 1973); *Forms of Talk* (Philadelphia: University of Pennsylvania Press, 1981).

6. Austin, "How to Do Things," pp. 121, 110.

7. Ibid., pp. 110, 120–21.

8. On the little-publicized frequency of lynchings, see Paula Giddings, *When and Where I Enter: The Impact of Black Women on Race and Sex in America* (New York: Morrow, 1984), pp. 17–31; and John d'Emilio and Estelle B. Freedman, *Intimate Matters: A History of Sexuality in America* (New York: Harper & Row, 1988), esp. pp. 216–21. D'Emilio and Freedman put the number of lynchings of black men and women "in the former Confederacy" at "at least thirty-eight hundred" between 1889 and 1940 (p. 216).

9. Rousseau, *Discourse on the Origin and the Foundations of Inequality Among Men,* in *The First and Second Discourses, Together with the Replies to Critics, and Essay on the Origin of Languages,* trans. Victor Gourevitch (New York: Harper & Row, 1986), p. 138.

10. "I conceive of two sorts of inequality in the human Species: one, which I call natural or Physical, because it is established by Nature, and which consists in differences of age, health, strengths of Body, and qualities of Mind or of Soul; the other, which may be called moral, or political inequality because it

depends on a sort of convention and is established, or at least authorized by Men's consent. It consists in the different Privileges which some enjoy to the prejudice of the others, such as to be more wealthy, more honored, more Powerful than they, or even to get themselves obeyed by them.

"It makes no sense to ask what the source of Natural inequality is, because the answer would be given by the simple definition of the word: Still less does it make sense to inquire whether there might not be some essential connection between the two inequalities; for that would be to ask in different terms whether those who command are necessarily better than those who obey, and whether individuals always possess strength of Body or of Mind, wisdom, or virtue, in proportion to their Power or their Wealth: A question which it may perhaps be good for Slaves to debate within hearing of their Master, but not befitting rational and free Men who seek the truth" (Rousseau, p. 138).

11. Rousseau, *Essay on the Origin of Languages,* p. 240.

12. Ibid., p. 244.

13. Ibid., pp. 246–47.

14. Rousseau, *On the Social Contract,* in Rousseau, *The Basic Political Writings,* trans. Donald A. Cress (Indianapolis: Hackett, 1987), pp. 148–49n.: "The true meaning of this word is almost entirely lost on modern men. Most of them mistake a town for a city and a townsman for a citizen. They do not know that houses make a town but citizens make a city. . . . Only the French adopt this name *citizen* with complete familiarity, since they have no true idea of its meaning, as can be seen from their dictionaries. If this were not the case, they would become guilty of treason for using it. For them, this name expresses a virtue and not a right."

15. See René Girard, *Violence and the Sacred* (Baltimore: Johns Hopkins University Press, 1977 [Paris, 1972]); *"To Double Business Bound": Essays on Literature, Mimesis, and Anthropology* (Baltimore: Johns Hopkins University Press, 1978); *Deceit, Desire, and the Novel: Self and Other in Literary Structure* (Baltimore: Johns Hopkins University Press, 1966 [Paris, 1961]); *Things*

Hidden Since the Foundation of the World (Baltimore: Johns Hopkins University Press, 1987 [Paris, 1978]).

16. I am indebted for this observation to Pierre Lacour.

17. *Plato's Republic,* trans. G. M. A. Grube (Indianapolis: Hackett, 1974), pp. 27, 39.

18. "I think that justice is the very thing, or some form of the thing which, when we were beginning to found our city, we said had to be established throughout. We stated . . . that everyone must pursue one occupation of those in the city, that for which his nature best fitted him. . . . Further, . . . that justice is to perform one's own task and not to meddle with that of another"; "And justice was in truth, it appears, something like this. It does not lie in a man's external actions, but in the way he acts within himself, really concerned with himself and his inner parts. He does not allow each part of himself to perform the work of another, or the sections of his soul to meddle with one another" (Ibid., pp. 97–97, 107).

19. Ibid., p. 64.

20. "[As] there has been no kind of proof that a woman is different from a man as regards the duties we are talking about . . . [t]here is therefore no pursuit connected with city management which belongs to a woman because she is a woman, or to a man because he is a man, but various natures are scattered in the same way among both kinds of persons. Woman by nature shares all pursuits, and so does man" (Ibid., p. 117).

21. Ibid., p. 68.

22. Ibid., pp. 206–7.

PATRICIA J. WILLIAMS

*(with apologies to Zora Neale Hurston,[1]
Charlotte Perkins Gilman,[2]
and Mary Shelley[3])*

A Rare Case Study of Muleheadedness and Men

or How to Try an Unruly Black Witch, with Excerpts from the Heretical Testimony of Four Women, Known to Be Hysterics, Speaking in Their Own Voices, as Translated for This Publication by Brothers Hatch, Simpson, DeConcini, and Specter

Exhibit A. Final Field Notes of a Fanatical Female Anthropologist Who Could Not Tell the Difference Between Being Spurned and Being Burned

I was glad when the prayerwoman told me, "You should go among the Menfolk and share with them Our-story, so that this knowledge may hasten their civilization, and so that they may yet be saved from themselves."

In a way, I had always sensed that this would be a part of my destiny. I had grown up knowing men, and be-friending them. From my earliest days, I remembered having a father. I had played in the fields and worked in the groves among men and once when confronted by a war-rior with his sword unsheathed, had skillfully avoided being drawn into battle. I had even learned a few words of their language. So it would not be an altogether new experience for me, and it might be interesting to learn more about their mannish folkways.

Thus it was that when the moon was full and the river calm, I set out in a small craft for Hisland, the adventures hereinafter recounted being absolutely true.

Day One. My arrival naturally having created quite a stir, I was nevertheless greeted with as much cordiality as curiosity and was pressed to tell, in every detail, of my long journey to this place. Although it was impossible to understand everything of their strange and rambling dialect, they smiled at me with simple pleasure and made much of the exotic cut of the clothing that I wore.

Day Two. When I awoke to the dawn of the new day, the chieftains of the Menfolk appeared agitated. They spoke in loud voices and waved their arms and gesticulated in my direction. I thought I could hear my name oft repeated in the savage din: "Anitawana! Anitawana!" (This word, which dates back more than a thousand years in their lore, is their name for us, the tribe of Black Witches; it seems the clumsiness of their tongues and the natural limitation of their memories, far shorter than our own, prevent their ever coming close to being able to pronounce our real names.) After much difficult translation, I came to understand that a man had alleged that he had been killed during the night. And only with the utmost patience did I come to understand further that he was accusing me of his murder.

Alas! How little I knew then of the anguish that would shortly befall me! How confident I was that my innocence should manifest itself in the midst of this impossible circumstance!

Day Three. But where is the body, I asked repeatedly and in some confusion. Of what body do you speak? the Men asked. There is no body among us, they said to me with great disdain for all I did not know. And despite my poor amazement, my accuser then rose up again to insist that he had died, and was Not the Same Person he had been before my arrival on Hisland.

Day Four. I was given to understand that one of the Menfolk elders would act as my counsel. "Dearest one," he said. "Dry your tears. If you are, as you believe, innocent, rely on the justice of our laws, and the activity with which I shall prevent the slightest shadow of partiality."[4]

Day Five. I have been most brutally betrayed. I am to be burned at the stake in the morning, along with those few brave souls who dared speak sympathetically of my unfortunate plight. Farewell, farewell.

Exhibit B. Questions, Drafted by a Cynical Saboteur of the Holy Canon While in the Employ of the National Association for the Advancement of Western Civilization, to Which All Answers Are Correct

1. Who spoke these immortal words? "How fetching you look, my dear. Bosom heaving and eyes wide with innocence. The pity of it is that you probably are innocent, by your warped definition. Never mind the pain you've caused a harmless woman by casting your net over her witless husband."[5] (a) Alan Simpson, in the *Congressional Record;* (b) Virginia Lamp Thomas, in *People* magazine; (c) Rhett Butler, in *Scarlett: The Sequel.*

2. "By campaigning against the thing called 'date rape,' the feminist creates immense hatred and suspicion between men and women, so the feminist advice to any woman going out on a date is to establish a virtual contract governing what will happen in the course of an evening. This is to destroy the free and easy relations between men and women which have long characterized the Western world—and only the Western world. . . . But anyone contemplating this remarkable situation is likely to have a further thought. Political doctrines always invite the question: Cui bono? Who is it, one might ask, that would benefit from dormitories filled with attractive young women who have been worked up into a state of hysterical mistrust of men? One of the most influential fragments of feminism has been its lesbian wing."⁶ This classic jeremiad is taken from which great text of Western Civilization: (a) *The Holy Bible;* (b) William Shakespeare's *As You Like It;* (c) William Buckley's *National Review*.

3. "[L]usty female professors seem to be quite common on campus, to judge from the tales of our male correspondents."⁷ This is: (a) gossip; (b) fantasy; (c) documented anthropological fact, as reported by Professor David Danziger in *Penthouse Hot Talk: The Voice of America*.

4. "Modern psychiatrists have amply studied the behavior of errant young girls and women coming before the courts in all sorts of cases. Their psychic complexes are multifarious, distorted partly by inherent defects, partly by diseased derangement or abnormal instincts, partly by bad social environment, partly by temporary physical or emotional conditions. One form taken by these complexes is that of contriving false charges of sexual offenses by men. The unchaste (let us call it) mentality finds incidental but

direct expression in the narration of imaginary sex incidents of which the narrator is the heroine or victim. On the surface the narration is straightforward and convincing. The real victim, however, too often in such cases is the innocent man; for the respect and sympathy naturally felt by any tribunal for a wronged female helps to give easy credit to such a plausible tale."[8] This is: (a) news; (b) Wigmore, *A Treatise on the Anglo-American System of Evidence . . . ,* pp. 459–60.

5. "Moreover, the standards that the courts have been adopting—that the conduct be viewed from the perspective of a 'reasonable woman' and that the unwelcomeness of the speech or behavior has to be communicated—provide little guidance on what behavior or speech to avoid. It may be that someone who engages in what might be considered harassing conduct is therefore entitled to a 'free bite' before liability can attach."[9] This is: (a) more from the pages of *Hot Talk;* (b) *Labor Relations Reporter,* October 28, 1991, p. 268.

6. "If Clarence Thomas had been a woman, he might have been Anita Hill. . . ."[10] This statement presupposes that: (a) Paris is burning; (b) Mississippi is burning; (c) if Long Dong Silver had wheels, he'd be a bus; (d) if a bus could write, there would be a job waiting for him at *Time* magazine.

7. "To let John the Conqueror win your case; take one-half pint whiskey, nine pieces of John the Conqueror root one inch long. Let it soak thirty-eight hours till all the strength is out. (Gather all roots before September 21.) Shake up good and drain off roots in another perfume bottle. Get one ounce of White Rose or Jockey Club perfume and pour into the mixture. Dress your client with

this before going to court."[11] Identify John the Conqueror; he is: (a) a prophet; (b) a pimp; (c) a pope; (d) the secret of John Doggett's repeated success.

8. "Later, after two hours' sleep, we walked into the . . . room, and people were lining the hallways, urging him on. 'Who are these people?' [he] asked me, and I said, 'I think they are angels.' "[12] What character in which, famous passion play utters these lines? (a) David Duke, in *Born Again, The Sequel;* (b) the ghost of Christmas future, in his debut appearance on "Arsenio Hall"; (c) Virginia Lamp Thomas, at the portals of the Senate.

9. "In a righteous fury, he told his judges that their hearing was a 'national disgrace. . . . You are ruining the country.' He had been a victim, he said, of the vitriol of the left. His message: 'Unless you kowtow to an old order . . . you will be lynched, destroyed, caricatured by a committee of the Senate rather than hung from a tree.' "[13] Who delivered this famous soliloquy? (a) Julius Caesar; (b) Hamlet; (c) Othello; (d) Richard Nixon; (e) G. Harrold Carswell; (f) John Tower; (g) Oliver North; (h) John Sununu; (i) Robert Gates; (j) Clarence Thomas; (k) etc., etc., etc.

10. True or False:

She said: "Objection to sexual harassment is not a neo-puritan protest."[14]
She said: "This psychodrama is puritanism reborn."[15]

Exhibit C. Secretly Transcribed Speech of a Professional Witch and Principle Agitator, Who Regretfully Was Drowned in the First Round of That Ordeal Which She Had Brought Upon Herself

I can't remember if I put this on my résumé or not, but given the promised kindness of our gentler times, I guess it's safe to come out and say it: I'm a witch. Now I know this may be a little hard to comprehend, but I can prove it.

First of all, I'm a black female law professor, a status so miraculous that that alone should convince you of my powers. The statistical probability of such a creature existing is about the same as that for mermaids and the Loch Ness monster, with the Loch Ness monster having a slight edge. To those who have never seen me and the monster in action, the rumors of our existence are scoffed at as a lot of supersititious nonsense. But I am a witch. And not the good, wimpy variety with the squeaking voices and wands; I'm of the potent black witchcraft breed, with tar and owl feathers and howling winds. Now I know witchcraft is unpopular these days, but it is after all a strong female tradition, internationally revered, and something that bonds women across the boundaries of the universe. And in this day and age, absolutely nothing else I know of works, so I highly recommend it.

This is how you do it: for example, when I thought about what I was going to say today, I started off by drawing a medicine wheel of my life, a circle of north, south, east, and west, with my life's forces positioned at each of the four winds. It was a wheel of exceptionally stormy stresses: I placed my inner self, my soul, my spirit to the south. South is the direction of purity and innocence, youth and fragility, and my self still feels itself to be all those things. I placed my external, physical manifestations to the other three winds; I put my professional, law-professor, self to the north, for that is the direction of strength and bullishness. I put my blackness to the west, for that is the color of the west, the color of the earth, and the color of deep and dark introspection. And I put my femaleness to the east, which is fiery and full of light, the giver of life.

And I analyzed the magic associated with each of these directions:

To the south, I visualized myself associated with the magic of strength. I am descended matrilineally from strong African root magicians and Cherokee medicine women, whose power was passed over the generations through a long line of refined boogie practitioners of voodoo. So I grew up knowing the secrets of blackberry paste and saltpeter pudding and inversion chants and magic stones taped to the brow. A diet of frogwart and bee pollen made me strong, and my power, the power of belief in myself and my own magic, developed.

Next was the power of the north, of my professional self. I found that if I rub a little pennyroyal oil on my brow, right around the temples, wear pinstripes with a little silk bow at the throat, and go to corporate business meetings, I can invoke the powers of Medusa; and strong men who look at me will turn to stone.

I found that I could break that spell with the magic of the east, my female self. I found that if I wear patchouli oil at the wrists and the downy feathers of a parrot on my bosom, men melt at that. Except for some who are warlocks with magic of their own; they use talismanic words to ward off my magic. They call me "girl" and my magic "girlish" and that has the effect of making me diminish; I grow small.

In the ritual of the west, the magic of my blackness, my black mask, first I rub olive oil and ashes all over my body, hang an amulet around my neck, say "Black is beautiful" three times before an altar with white candles on it, put on my happiest black face; then I go out into the street of any public forum. If I do all that, I can turn myself invisible; I can render myself completely undetectable to most eyes even if I jump up and down and wave and shout. I can't tell you how many eyeballs I've burned out just by walking into places with the wrong chemistry. Places flammable, I guess, to olive oil and ashes. And that's magic I feel bad about. Because once my blackness puts scales on their eyes, I don't know how to undo it very well. I haven't found the potions or whatever it takes to make them see again. I can do a partial restoration though, where the magic strikes only partial blindness. The partially blind see part, but not all of me. They say, "I like you. I don't even see you as black." I just use the following magic words: "You don't see me as black because I'm not black," and in a sulfurous flash, they see me as black again. (This also works well when someone says I'm one of the boys. I say, "Oh, I am indeed," and suddenly their vision is restored.)

But even then I have trouble getting them to see just one of me. For example, if I spill soup in a restaurant, they tend to see hundreds of me; if I have a baby, I tend to have a population explosion; if I move into a neighborhood, I come as the forward phalanx of an invading army; if I have an opinion, it is attributed to "you people."

So you can see I have powers. I recommend these powers because they impart control. But they can also drive you insane. It is imperative to remember that the power lies in the words, the symbols, and not in the self. Show your subjects the symbol of blackness and you will be protected by your invisibility. Show them the symbol of your femaleness and you will be able to diminish in size and escape through a crack in the wall. Show them the symbol of professionalism and you will be able to stop strong rampaging armies by turning them into brick walls.

But don't forget that it is magic, and a tool separate from yourself. If you begin to see yourself as the source of the magic—as invisible, as shrinking, as Medusa—you will lose the power. You will be powerless, scattered, invisible, small. All will be well if you simply honor self and others first, the simple, unmagic spirit and soul, the kernel of life, solid, visible, and precious. . . .

Exhibit D. Heretofore Unrevealed Pages from the Explosive Diary of an Incurably Mad Law Professor, Which Blasphemy Was Found Scribbled in the Margins of the Uniform Commercial Code

Watching the Clarence Thomas/Anita Hill hearings, I was reminded of something I once read in Hans Peter Duerr's book *Dreamtime:* "In archaic times, a person who stood outside the law of a culture was considered dead by ordinary people." On the heels of Clarence Thomas's self-proclaimed death and rebirth by religious, "faith"-based senatorial confirmation, I found it riveting, this idea of illegitimacy as a form of death, of legality as its own life force. It seemed to me to be an intriguing paradigm from which to consider our profane national passion play, this Not-Truly-a-Trial, this bodily Ordeal. What is the "law of our culture," I have been asking myself. Who are the "ordinary," real-life people in our society who hold this power of "considered" death? Who are the unreal nonpersons who ghost-walk through the underworld of the illegitimate?

Now as everyone knows, it is settled law in our land that witches are those who fly upside down. Thus it is that Anita Hill is dispositively a witch. Everything she touched inverted itself. She was relentlessly ambitious yet "clinically" reserved, consciously lying while fantasizing truth. Lie detectors broke down and the ashes of "impossible truth" spewed forth from her mouth. She was controlled yet irrational, naïve yet knowing, prim but vengeful, a cool, hotheaded, rational hysteric.

It is also a tenet of our legal system that when an ordinary man is "tortured," "crucified," and then rises again after only 106 days of "scurrilous" "inquisition," he may take his rightful place in the pantheon of apostolic prophets. Thus it is that Clarence Thomas, man of the People, was able to invoke "God as my judge" rather than Congress, and thus it was that the entire Senate of the United States of America fell back in reverential awe.

I get into lots of trouble with lawyers, to say nothing of my psychiatrists, for my frequent assertion that the boundary between the legal and the illegitimate is just a metaphysical scripting of negotiated power. But after the calculated masquerade of the Thomas hearings, how could anyone doubt the Essential Truth of that? Perhaps what connects the distraction of these glittering fan-dancing stories is, as a friend of mine writes, that "there are no bodies (nobodies?)—only ciphers for the will of other entities. They do not exist except as markers of narrative transactions."[16]

Just think: we live in a culture in which Scarlett O'Hara and *The Scarlet Letter* compete with the Bible and *The Exorcist* for popularity. Where what took place in the boardroom of the EEOC is walled off from questions in deference to Clarence Thomas's "most private sanctum, the bedroom." Where the Lady in the Red Dress (or the yellow or the purple or the turquoise, with a double row of buttons down the front) is all danger and unresolvable mystery; where the Mystery Man is strong-jawed, silent, and cuts a figure of quiet integrity. Where Hester Prynne has the uppity self-promoting audacity to try to recast herself as "the Rosa Parks of sexual harassment," and where Reverend Dimmesdale breaks with his faith and martyrs himself, giving birth to the world's first case of "reverse sexual harassment." Where "witch-hunt" is used to mean not a posse for but by; where "high-tech lynching" means a Broad with a Bullhorn.

Where kinder and gentler feels terribly cruel and ironic.

What account, in the name of law, are we to make of all this? What accountability, in the face of chaos, are we to take from all this? Where's the truth? Where's the falsity? Where's Waldo? And where, by the way, is Robert Gates?

In the rotunda just inside the CIA building, the largest covert intelligence operation on the planet earth, there is an engraving of the words from the Gospel According to John: "Ye shall know the truth, and the truth shall set you free."

So perhaps it is *truth* that any woman who is not a witch shall simply refuse to burn when tied to the stake. And perhaps it is *truth,* after all is said and done, that masturbation really does make men go blind.

NOTES

1. Zora Neale Hurston, *Mules and Men* (New York: Harper & Row, 1990).
2. Charlotte Perkins Gilman, *Herland* (New York: Pantheon Books, 1979).
3. Mary Shelley, *Frankenstein* (New York: Pyramid Books, 1957).
4. With more apologies to Mary Shelley, *Frankenstein*, p. 69.
5. Alexandra Ripley, *Scarlett: The Sequel to Margaret Mitchell's Gone with the Wind* (New York: Warner Books, 1991), p. 277.
6. Kenneth Minogue, "The Goddess That Failed," *National Review*, November 18, 1991, p. 48.
7. David Danziger, "Vox Pop Sexualis," *Penthouse Hot Talk: The Voice of America*, November–December 1991, p. 12.
8. John Henry Wigmore, *A Treatise on the Anglo-American System of Evidence . . . ,* 3rd ed., vol. 3 (1924), pp. 459–60.
9. *Labor Relations Reporter* (Bureau of National Affairs), vol. 138, no. 9 (October 28, 1991), p. 268.
10. John Hull, "A Real Straight Arrow," *Time,* October 21, 1991, p. 44.
11. Zora Neale Hurston, "Court Scrapes," in *Mules and Men* (New York: Harper & Row, 1990), p. 275.
12. Virginia Lamp Thomas, "Breaking Silence," *People Weekly,* November 11, 1991, p. 112.
13. "Judging Thomas," *U.S. News & World Report,* October 21, 1991, p. 33.
14. Catharine MacKinnon, as quoted in "Harassment: Men on Trial," *U.S. News & World Report,* October 21, 1991, p. 40.
15. Camille Paglia, as quoted in "Harassment: Men on Trial," *U.S. News & World Report,* October 21, 1991, p. 40.
16. Letter of March 26, 1991, from Professor Wahneema Lubiano, Department of English, Princeton University, to Patricia Williams, Professor of the Uniform Commercial Code, University of Wisconsin School of Law.

GAYLE PEMBERTON

A Sentimental Journey:
James Baldwin and the Thomas—Hill Hearings

If they hear not Moses and the prophets,
neither will they be persuaded, though
one rose from the dead.

—Luke 16:31

"Many of us looked at each other and sighed, saying, *Lord, we really need Malcolm now.*"[1] This is James Baldwin in *No Name in the Street,* expressing a sentiment held by quite a few black Americans in the late 1960s and early '70s. It was a voice of frustration, perhaps even despair, brought on by yet another decade's worth of escalating violence against blacks through assassination and police bullet. It was the recognition that the Vietnam War was an avoidable, abominable tragedy that was being borne primarily by the poor and the lower middle class, black and otherwise. Everything smacked of racism, and Malcolm or Martin—

or *somebody*—was needed to put it, at least, in perspective, since no sense could be made of it. But Malcolm and Martin were dead.

After the Senate Judiciary Committee hearings on Clarence Thomas's nomination to the Supreme Court, I said, "Lord, we really need James Baldwin now." But after the sensory nightmare of the second set of hearings, held on October 11 and 12—after Clarence Thomas's denials that he sexually harassed Anita Hill; after Hill's composed assertions that he did; after the disingenuous surprise and mock innocence in the questions of a jury's worth of white, male Senators; after the improvisations of newscasters astounded by what they perceived as the articulateness of both Thomas and Hill—there was greater urgency. *Lord, Lord, we really need James Baldwin now.* He would have put it all into perspective; of that I was sure. He might have even made sense of it.

Why I would have wished on Baldwin (or anyone I do not hate) this "fresh hell," to use Dorothy Parker's words, was a question I did not raise. It was unnecessary to worry about it. After all, James Baldwin had been dead for just over four years, and dead men don't talk. Everyone knows that. He was spared this particular spectacle—which in reality was anything but fresh, but which was all the hell I or any other black person needed to know—when he died on November 30, 1987.

I was not acquainted with Baldwin the man. I had met him once when I was one of many graduate students standing reverently around him as he kindly answered our youthful, urgent questions about art, life, the United States, France, and color. But I never had an opportunity to converse with him or to look, without the self-consciousness of a tourist, on a face I thought fascinating, lovely, and almost too sensitive for words—a face very different from the unflattering descriptions of it that some of Baldwin's critics, and Baldwin himself, gave for forty years. No, it was Baldwin the artist—the essayist, novelist, and playwright— that I prized, that made me feel as if I did know him. I wanted some words from him this past October because for so many years he had taken upon himself, with full responsibility and precious little thanks, the unenviable role of "witness"—not spokesman, but "public witness to the situation of black people."[2] It was obvious from his writing that he truly loved black people and his country. He made a good witness because he cared enough to scrutinize both. He spoke of this role many times, clarify- ing it for new generations of readers and different critics. When asked by Julius Lester in 1984 what he was a witness *to,* Baldwin replied, "Witness to whence I came, where I am. Witness to what I've seen and the possibilities that I think I see."[3] He saw the distant past as clearly as he recalled the days of his youth in Harlem and Greenwich Village, and the years of his "commuter" adulthood spent between Paris and the United States. He saw into the future and frequently shuddered because he knew what people are capable of doing to each other. His beautiful prose was influenced by centuries of the best writing in English, the Bible, and the cadences of heartbreak, joy, and hope of urban black Americans. He was not given to euphemism. He detested sentimentality. He was con- cerned with evoking the truth. Answering Lester further about his witnessing, he said, "I don't think I ever resented it, but it exhausted me."[4]

Baldwin's witnessing was religious at its core. His stepfather was a preacher; at age fourteen Baldwin himself was a preacher in a Harlem storefront. At seventeen he left the church, but as one of his biographers has noted, "while he was not a believer in the sense of subscribing to a particular faith, or belonging to a specific church, his life was based on a faith that can only be called religious, just as his thought was infused with religious belief."[5] Every Baldwin text is a meditation, and most of them have as their subject the meaning of black life in America and the world. He saw the huge chasm that lay between illusion and reality in this country—it was a distance as great as that from heaven to hell. And like a prophet, he warned us that our illusions were blinding us and destroying all of our other senses as well. "Where there is no vision, the people perish," he said, quoting the book of Proverbs.[6] All of the essays, the novels, the plays, give us the wisdom of those large eyes that saw so much.

Neither do I want anyone to suppose that I think that the gem of the ocean has kept any of its promises, but my ancestors counseled me to *keep the faith;* and I promised, I vowed that I would. If I am a part of the American house, and I am, it is because my ancestors paid—*striving to make it my home*—so unimaginable a price: and I have seen some of the effects of that passion everywhere I have been, all over this world.[7]

The purpose here is not to guess what James Baldwin's reactions to the hearings would be, to put words in a dead man's mouth. That is unnecessary: his writing offers an exegesis of the hearings. He once said, "Only poets, since they must excavate and recreate history, have ever learned anything from it."[8] This poet was our teacher—our Virgil through this inferno—and we would be wise to remember precisely what it was that he started telling us over forty years ago. James Baldwin, the dead man, may not be able to speak to us, but James Baldwin, the poet and prophet, is yelling.

For millions of Americans the hearings were quite simply unbearable. A common refrain heard around the country was "Don't get me started." But people did get started, and testimonies in newspapers and magazines, in hallways, supermarkets, barbershops and beauty salons, at water coolers, and on the telephone—doubtless to the delight of all long-distance and local carriers—revealed the extent to which blacks and whites, women and men, had been transfixed by the whole scene—the bright lights, the senators, and the stars: Anita Hill and Clarence Thomas.

Baldwin, in essay after essay, provided a historical context for his commentaries on the customs of the country. "History," he said, "as nearly no one seems to know, is not merely something to be read. And it does not refer merely, or even principally, to the past. On the contrary, the great force of history comes from the fact that we carry it within us, are unconsciously controlled by it in many ways, and history is literally *present* in all that we do."[9] American history, warts and all, sat in that committee room. It was packed with people and symbols; unpacking either would not be easy.

Here in one room, under the lights, the cameras, the murmur of the crowd—certainly there was no air in the room—here was played out the tragedy of several centuries of illusion, a masque of the failure, not the success, of the American dream. All of the historic emblems of utopia and dystopia were colliding in that room. And time boomeranged from the centuries of legal slavery to the present and back again. The senators were illustrative of the high ideals of the republic, found in its Constitution and Bill of Rights, yet their partisan sniping recalled the long history of legislative failure in enacting laws to provide and protect the rights of all Americans, particularly black Americans. There were a multitude of representatives of the national press, historically the ready hand of white supremacy—yet, at least once, the press played a significant, vigilant role, reporting the Civil Rights Movement to a general population that might easily have believed, and preferred to believe, that the struggle and the violent resistance to it were isolated, local incidents in a benighted South.

Clarence Thomas and Anita Hill provided a set of contradictions as great as those manifested by the Senate and the press. Both were described as conservatives, which means they aligned themselves with a political tradition that has been expressly antiblack. Thomas had the backing of this political right—senators such as Strom Thurmond of South Carolina, who ran for president in 1948 on the white-supremacist States' Rights Party ticket, and the sympathy of white-supremacist politician David Duke. Hill, though less interested in partisan politics—to judge from her voting habits in Oklahoma—had been a staunch supporter of Robert Bork. Bork's 1987 nomination to the Court had been blocked by Senate liberals, who contended that his reading of the Constitution was so radical that it could practically justify a return to a slave society. Those are the easy contradictions. The more difficult ones—the absurd, numbing ones about race and sex and cultural lies that set heads to shaking, nervous systems to near chaos, and voices to high G—those were the ones Baldwin, brilliantly, succinctly, and boldly had identified, decoded, and translated.

In 1987 when blacks protested the draconian de facto segregation of Forsyth County, Georgia, a placard held by a white supremacist read, WE DON'T WANT NO NIGGERS, NO DRUGS AND NO AIDS. There was something anachronistic about the march—no white northern sensibilities to be shocked by the expression of racism; no proto–freedom riders, galvanized for action. However, the white protesters were familiar; nothing appeared to have changed in several decades. As one would expect, David Duke was there, among the Klansmen and just plain folk, jeering at the marchers. The placard conveyed a proud racist, xenophobic, antiurban sentiment not confined to the rural South. It was particularly revealing in what it said about identity formation in this country. Baldwin (reworking Ralph Ellison's notion of invisibility) spoke of this to Studs Terkel in 1961: "What white people see when they look at you is not visible. What they do see when they do look at you is what they have invested you with . . . all the agony, and pain, and the danger, and the passion, and the torment—you know, sin, death, and hell—of which everyone in this country is terrified."[10] The ultimate in sin, death, and hell right now is AIDS. Baldwin put it more poetically in "Many Thousands Gone" when he said, "One may say that the Negro in America does not really exist except in the darkness of our minds."[11] Ignoring the barefaced racists, Baldwin contended that even liberals failed to recognize black humanity: "They could deal with the Negro as a symbol or victim but had no sense of him as a man."[12]

The placard tells more. It suggests that whites would inevitably become quite intimate with these blacks should Forsyth County become integrated. This is akin to Baldwin's insight on *the* question: "Would you let your sister marry one?" He said, "The question, by the way, depends on several extraordinary assumptions. First of all it assumes . . . that I *want* to marry your sister and it also assumes that if I asked your sister to marry me, she would immediately say yes. There is no reason to make either of these assumptions, which are clearly irrational."[13] The third assumption even Baldwin missed: that your sister would ask your permission in the first place.

On some level, of course, the sentiment conveyed by the placard is primordial, standard fare, the basis of all group exclusivity. But no one has said it any better than Baldwin: "We would never, never allow Negroes to starve, to grow bitter, and to die in ghettos all over the country if we were not driven by some nameless fear that has nothing to do with Negroes. We would never victimize, as we do, children whose only crime is color and keep them, as we put it, in their place."[14] These words were spoken to a college audience in 1960—an audience not at all used to thinking about race and racism. That the words are as accurate now as they were then is not surprising; it is both unpardonable and frightening.

The relationship between the placard and what went on in the Senate hearing room is quite close. Clarence Thomas and Anita Hill were symbolic presences, symbolic *sexual* presences, and nothing either could say would alter that. Indeed, it was absolutely essential to the identity of white Americans to keep the symbolic black identities inviolate. In 1961 Baldwin had lamented, "It is still true, alas, that to be an American Negro male is also to be a kind of walking phallic symbol: which means that one pays, in one's own personality, for the sexual insecurity of others."[15] Thirty years later it is nearly impossible for a black male to be anything else.

The symbol of the black woman, manifested as Anita Hill, is no less complex. Given the nature of her questioning by Senators Arlen Specter, Alan Simpson, and Orrin Hatch, she was not far from Baldwin's rendering of the Aunt Jemima myth: "There was no one more forbearing . . . no one stronger or more pious or more loyal or more wise; there was, at the same time, no one weaker or more faithless or more vicious and certainly no one more immoral."[16] Hill's depiction of the language Thomas allegedly used to sexually harass her—which the senators insisted that she repeat *ad nauseam*—reinforced notions of black vulgarity and inferiority. Senators from both parties insisted on repeating the crassest parts of her testimony themselves, giving new meaning to the word "prurient." What was reinforced through all this repetition, then, was not just a notion of black as base, but white, by contrast, as exalted and pure. Baldwin's experiences taught him that the thing that "most white people imagine that they can salvage from the storm of life is really, in sum, their innocence."[17] Beyond the hearings, the vagaries of such a longing for innocence form the unstated message of David Duke to his followers: once the nation is rid of "others," the all-white United States will bask in its natural and innocent grace. In the storm of the hearing room this shelter emerged. Senator Hatch portrayed himself as an innocent, ostensibly bewildered by the description of the harasser described by Hill: "That person, it seems to me, would not be a normal person. That person, it seems to me, would be a psychopathic sex fiend or a pervert."[18] In the most bizarre and downright eerie moment of the entire proceedings, Hatch said that it seemed to him that Hill borrowed some of her accusations from *The Exorcist*. The specter of McCarthyism arose. There being no available Communists to blame, Anita Hill became the dupe of the Democrats. Thus, Hatch—who had referred to the nominee as Clarence and not Judge Thomas soon after the nomination was announced—in disbelieving Hill even denied her a smutty imagination. She must have been given her lines to speak.

In *The Man Who Mistook His Wife for a Hat,* Oliver Sacks writes about a ward filled with patients suffering from global aphasia who were hysterically laughing at a speech given by Ronald Reagan during his presidency. According to Sacks, global or receptive aphasics know that "speech—natural speech—does *not* consist of words alone. . . . It consists of *utterance*—an uttering-forth of one's whole meaning with one's whole being—the understanding of which involves infinitely more than mere word-recognition."[19] A global aphasic "cannot grasp your words, and so cannot be deceived by them; but what he grasps he grasps with infallible precision, namely the *expression* that goes with the words, that total, spontaneous, involuntary expressiveness which can never be simulated or faked, as words alone can, all too easily."[20] By seeing *expression* and hearing the tones of *utterance,* these patients, according to Sacks, could not be deceived. "This is why they laughed at the President's speech."[21]

Few nonglobal aphasics have the ability to spot such inauthenticity or duplicity. To have seen Clarence Thomas, Anita Hill, and the senators through a global aphasic's senses might have helped uncover the mendacious ones. But that still would not have answered the real questions—those that have to do with hopes, dreams, self-identification, loyalty, and history—that so contortedly emerged that October weekend. Perhaps not even aphasics would have understood the historic significance behind every word and gesture of these two black lawyers. As Baldwin once mused, "[James] Joyce is right about history being a nightmare—but it may be the nightmare from which no one *can* awaken. People are trapped in history and history is trapped in them."[22]

Clarence Thomas's testimony to the Senate committee revealed much about history as nightmare. His statements and answers to the senators' questions were roundly held by the media to be "powerful"—"equally powerful" as Hill's, said the *New York Times*.[23] He was also called "convincing," "eloquent," and "articulate"—that favorite of reporters and pundits after any encounter with a fluent "standard"-English-speaking black person. Thomas was nothing if not emphatic. Answering a lob from Senator Hatch about what it felt like to be accused of sexual harassment, Thomas replied:

Senator, as I have said throughout these hearings, the last two and a half weeks have been a living hell. I think I've died a thousand deaths. What it means is living on one hour a night's sleep; it means losing 15 pounds in two weeks; it means being unable to eat, unable to drink, unable to think about anything but this and wondering why, how. It means wanting to give up. It means losing the belief in our system, in this system, in this process, losing a belief in a sense of fairness and honesty and decency. That's what it meant to me.

When I appeared before this committee for my real confirmation hearings, it was hard. I would have preferred it to be better. I would have preferred more members to vote for me. But I had a faith that at least the system was working in some fashion, though imperfectly.[24]

Thomas suggests that the real problem of the hearings was the confirmation process: a process can be a villain; no one has to point fingers at living individuals. It is not clear from Thomas's "articulation" whether the system failed because he had so much opposition or for other reasons. In any case, to Thomas the process failed and this failure challenged long-held beliefs.

He went further, declaring:

Senator, as I've indicated before—and I will continue to say this and believe this—I have been harmed. I have been harmed. My family has been harmed. I've been harmed worst [sic] than I've ever been harmed in my life. I wasn't harmed by the Klan. I wasn't harmed by the Knights of Camelia. I wasn't harmed by the Aryan Race. I wasn't harmed by a racist group. I was harmed by this process—this process—which accommodated these attacks on me.[25]

This was not unlike Booker T. Washington, who spoke of the ills of the *institution* of slavery but resisted castigating slave owners.

In the first set of hearings Thomas had spoken about his humble birth in Georgia, of his sharecropper grandfather, of the nuns who educated him. He had wept publicly when his nomination was announced, saying that only in America could something like this happen.

That may be true. And there can be no challenge to the veracity of Thomas's statements about his past. But the manner in which he spoke of both that past and the confirmation process was quite revealing. Baldwin once said, "I think it's a great mistake to be sentimental about human beings, and to be sentimental about oneself."[26] To some viewers Thomas's testimony was petulant and maudlin by turns; to others he was stalwart and proud. How such divergent opinions could refer to the same evidence further illuminates the confoundedness of race, sex, and symbol in our culture. Reactions are tied to that history that each of us carries throughout life. Many a black man felt that Thomas was collectively defending black manhood as he resolutely answered senators' questions. But Thomas came to the hearing table with a version of American history produced by few blacks since Washington. For example, if the greatest harm to Thomas has not come from white supremacists, then there are three Georgias and he is referring to one not on this planet. It is a place, perhaps, only for Thomas Nelson Page stories. Thomas's American history has no villains, only bad processes and systems. His rise from the isolation, extreme poverty, and cultural inertia of rural Georgia to Holy Cross, to Yale Law School, and then to state and federal government was effected and maintained by programs designed to aid people just such as him. There is no need to elaborate on Thomas's opinions about affirmative action, for example, that seem so inconsistent and at variance with the facts of his own good fortune. Others have clearly noted that particular problem. More disturbing than any inconsistency, or even the "I've got mine, you get yours" mentality, was Thomas's use of history. As Baldwin so masterfully put it,

Now, if I as a black man profoundly believe that I deserve my history and deserve to be treated as I am, then I must also, fatally, believe that white people deserve their history and deserve the power and the glory which their testimony and the evidence of my own senses assure me that they have. And if black people fall into this trap, the trap of believing that they deserve their fate, white people fall into the yet more stunning and intricate trap of believing that they deserve *their* fate and their comparative safety and that black people, therefore, need only do as white people have done to rise to where white people now are.[27]

Baldwin put it another way when he said, "Whoever cannot tell himself the truth about his past is trapped in it, is immobilized in the prison of his undiscovered self. This is also true of nations."[28]

Responding to Senator Hatch on black male stereotypes, Thomas said:

Senator, in the 1970s, I became very interested in the issue of lynching. And if you want to track through this country in the 19th and 20th century the lynchings of black men, you will see that there is invariably, or in many instances, a relationship with sex, and an accusation that person cannot shake off. That is the point that I'm trying to make, and that is the point that I was making last night, that this is high tech lynching. I cannot shake off these accusations, because they play to the worst stereotypes we have about black men in this country.[29]

Most black children from any region of this country, born in 1948, as Thomas was—especially in the South—knew about lynching and its pathology. Yet Thomas appears unable to articulate what the "invariable, or in many instances" relationship is between sex and lynching. Instead of depicting the lynchers as evil incarnate—which they were and which, if this is a high-tech lynching, the Senators are too—Thomas concentrates on the question of the guilt of the victims, which in any case of real lynching is irrelevant. Thomas may have believed he was a victim of a "high-tech lynching," but he miraculously found himself a week later—through a high-tech confirmation—very much alive and ready to serve on the Court. To the many thousands gone, truly lynched, killed by the poison of white supremacy, Thomas's historical revisionism is disgraceful.

One of the most popular media clips from the hearings showed Thomas determinedly refusing to step down. He said:

I'd rather die than withdraw from the process. Not for the purpose of serving on the Supreme Court, but for the purpose of not being driven out by this process. I will not be scared. I don't like bullies. I've never run from bullies. I never cry uncle, and I'm not going to cry uncle today, whether I want to be on the Supreme Court or not.[30]

In no other statement during the hearings was his resolve
to be on the Court more plain. Global aphasics are not the
only ones who could discern that message. The passwords
were in place; Thomas's uses of history corroborated many
a master text. By attacking the system and the process,
Thomas even deflected his outrage from Anita Hill. His
advocates on the Senate committee would take care of her.

At the news conference in Oklahoma prior to her departure for Washington, Anita Hill said:

> I resent the idea that people would blame the messenger
> for the message rather than looking at the content of the
> message itself and taking a careful look at it, and fully
> investigating it. And I would hope that the official process
> will continue, and that careful investigation of this infor-
> mation will be done.[31]

Hill would have done well to remember Cassandra or
those unfortunate women in Salem, Massachusetts, in the
seventeenth century. The message she brought exposed
hypocrisy and delusion at the heart of American sexual
mores and rituals. Men commonly sexually harass women;
it is a daily occurrence everywhere and everybody knows
it. Like its furthest conclusion—rape—it has little to do
with sex and everything to do with power. It has nothing
to do with love, and ours is a loveless society. As Baldwin
noted, "When the loveless come to power, or when sexual
despair comes to power, the sexuality of the object is either
a threat or a fantasy."[32] Two days before the hearings
began, a thirty-five-year-old Texas man had murdered

twenty-two people before committing suicide, laying the blame for his actions on "mostly white treacherous female vipers."[33] The vicious game is power and society accepts it because it says boys will be boys, and these are immutable facts of nature. Baldwin also noted, "It is one of the greatest impulses of mankind to arrive at something higher than a natural state. How to be natural does not seem to me to be a problem—quite the contrary. The great problem is how to be—in the best sense of that kaleidoscopic word—a man."[34] What Anita Hill was to discover was that in a room where blacks were symbols, her accusations of sexual harassment would come to mean far less than she anticipated.

Like Thomas, Hill was aware that a symbolic dimension to her accusations and even to her presence did exist. She was dressed very conservatively—her habit, we were told. At her side were members of her very large family, all hardworking, pious Christians who had pulled themselves up from rural poverty in Oklahoma. She told the senators:

> My childhood was one of a lot of hard work and not much money, but it was one of solid family affection as represented by my parents. I was reared in a religious atmosphere in the Baptist faith, and I have been a member of the Antioch Baptist Church in Tulsa, Okla., since 1983. It is a very warm part of my life at the present time.[35]

She was a vision of decorum, telling the senators, "It would have been more comfortable to remain silent. . . . I took no initiative to inform anyone." But once she was asked to testify, she said, "I could not keep silent."[36]

"Every society is really governed by hidden laws, by

unspoken profound assumptions on the part of the people, and ours is no exception."[37] Baldwin is stating an obvious truth. Hill, by virtue of her race, is the focus of two sets of unspoken assumptions. White America has never paid much attention to the injustices blacks inflict upon each other, as these merely reinforce stereotypes of blacks as base and violent, and those injustices are rarely a threat to the stability of the state. There is not an available statistic, for example, that establishes how many black men were lynched for allegedly raping black women. Moreover, American society makes distinctions between black and white women. All we need to do is recall the language of the signs of segregation: WHITE LADIES and COLORED WOMEN.[38] There are no BLACK LADIES deserving our protection; they are not valuable. There was much speculation among black women how the hearings might have been transformed had Anita Hill been white.

There are many hidden laws governing intraracial black behavior. One of the most important is the cardinal rule that says one simply does not complain about another black person to a white one, particularly a white person in a supervising position. A black woman *absolutely* does not indict a black man in front of a white one, as this act is hopelessly entangled within a welter of images and symbols from slavery. The structure of the hearings alone was unbearable for many black Americans; there could be no black victor under such circumstances.

Anita Hill remained unflappable throughout the long day of her testimony. She remained so in spite of questions that were designed to undermine her credibility as a law professor and as a balanced human being. Senator Howell Heflin, a Democrat of Alabama, and one of the few southerners who voted against Thomas, asked Hill (not without some measure of humor): "Are you a scorned woman? . . . Are you a zealot civil rights believer that progress will be turned back if Clarence Thomas goes on the court? . . . Do you have a militant attitude relative to the area of civil rights? . . . Do you have a martyr complex. . . . Are you interested in writing a book?"[39]

The senators did not know what to do with Hill or her charges. She did not live up to the stereotype. There was no way to sentimentalize her. According to Baldwin, white Americans do not know what to do with a black who falls outside of their expectations:

> If he breaks our sociological and sentimental image of him we are panic-stricken and we feel ourselves betrayed. When he violates this image, therefore, he stands in the greatest danger (sensing which, we uneasily suspect that he is very often playing a part for our benefit); and, what is not always so apparent but is equally true, we are then in some danger ourselves—hence our retreat or our blind and immediate retaliation.[40]

The spirit and intent of the immediate retaliation was that no lady would have either put up with or been able to repeat the things Hill alleged Thomas said. And not one Democrat defended her honor in the face of such implications.

Like Thomas, Hill took her law degree from Yale. The path from rural Oklahoma to New Haven and beyond was made easier because of initiatives taken by government and private institutions to open doors formerly closed to young black Americans. Like Thomas and the senators, and all of us, Hill was trapped in history and history was trapped in her. The senators had no more idea of her as a woman than they did of Thomas as a man. That she appeared to understand the symbolism—to know how dangerous and complex it is—could not protect her from being further victimized. She could not manipulate time and history any better than Thomas could.

When all was said and done, the polls said most Americans did not believe Hill. No person would have stayed on the job after having been so harassed, the public said. They also did not think that race had anything to do with the nature of the questioning from the Senate. Thomas's haughtiness did not appear to be in conflict with his future role as Supreme Court justice. Baldwin said, "White America remains unable to believe that black America's grievances are real; they are unable to believe this because they cannot face what this fact says about themselves and their country."[41] That may well be true; it keeps white America from changing. And Baldwin certainly was correct when he said that

> it is exceedingly difficult for most of us to discard the assumptions of the society in which we were born, in which we live, to which we owe our identities; very difficult to defeat the trap of circumstance, which is also the web of safety; virtually impossible . . . to envision the future, except in those terms which we think we already know."[42]

Black Americans are not immune to this either. They either accept what the world makes of them and act accordingly, or because of that, they create a self that transcends the contradictions.

. . .

There is a chilling moment at the very end of the acclaimed *Civil War* documentary by Ken Burns. The pictures show reunions of Union and Confederate soldiers that were held until the last of the veterans were dead. The voice-overs talk of the respect and affection these men grew to have for each other—many of them survivors of the terrible battle of Gettysburg. Notably absent are black veterans or any remembrance of the black Americans whose enslavement had been the basis of it all. Like their descendants in twentieth-century world wars and police actions, once black soldiers were allowed to fight for the ideas of freedom, they did so with great intensity and pride. But in the final analysis they were forgotten at the end of *The Civil War* just as their free labor in building the nation went unrewarded.

Anita Hill went back to Oklahoma. Among other things, she said, "I am hopeful that others who have suffered sexual harassment will not become discouraged by my experience, but instead will find the strength to speak out about this serious problem."[43] The big nasty secret was exposed to light. *New York Times* headlines read, "Sexual Harassment at Work Is Pervasive, Survey Suggests" and "Facing Issue of Harassment, Capital Gets Bath in the Mud."[44] Op-ed pages became filled with essays and recollections of women harassed by bosses, family members, teachers, and friends. One pundit said the nation was going through some bloodletting. But really it was just another moment when the country's image of itself was held up to reality and found to be illusory. The socialization of men and women in this country makes any other outcome unlikely. And because sexual harassment is about power, it is ridiculous to assume that those who have wielded it in such a fashion would either admit it or want to stop. Baldwin might suggest that anyone believing this does not know "how ruthless and powerful is the evil that lives in the world."[45] One of the meanings of the hearings was not unlike the final scenes from *The Civil War*. Thomas and Hill were two more black Americans who facilitated new communication between warring whites. Hill's courage could be appropriated by white ladies to challenge the status quo of the workplace, without their having the slightest idea what Hill may have sacrificed in the process. More likely, as Baldwin noted, white middle-class women—who will be the beneficiaries, if any, of Hill's courage—are not likely "to embrace my mother and my sister, unless my mother and my sister happen to work in the same office and are as bored as most white middle-class women are."[46]

No, the hearings were tragic in a way that most white Americans middle-class or otherwise, could not comprehend. In picking Thomas, the president said he had chosen the best nominee for the Court. As Thomas functions as a symbol, the president was correct. There simply was no basis for his ascendancy to the Supreme Court given his credentials, save one: his color. From his performance during both sets of hearings, it is clear that Thomas acquiesced to a sentimentalized portrait of himself and his history that satisfies white power. The Bush administration can point with pride to Thomas, whose career record and whose answers to the senators at the hearings did imply obedience, if nothing else.

Thomas delivered testimony his supporters wanted to

hear. He fortified a favorite Reagan administration picture of a welfare mother, using his sister—who had been given none of his advantages and whom he had not chosen to help—as object lesson. And in response to Senator Specter's hypothesis that the brown Anita Hill had a color-linked, ulterior and jealous motive, Thomas assented, saying, "There seemed to be some tension as a result of the lighter complexion of the women I dated and the woman I chose to be my chief executive, my preferring individuals of the lighter complexion."[47] That broke hearts across black America, because it proclaimed the stereotype to be true: Thomas, sitting next to his white wife, with those lines became, incarnate, the black man white America imagines. Anita Hill would never be able to shatter that image.

As Baldwin so compellingly once said, "In the lives of black people—everyone overlooks this and it's a very simple fact—love has been so terribly menaced."[48] The American dream manifested in Thomas and Hill was a failure, because the price had been too high—and this is what many, many black people knew as they watched and listened. Newspapers and television recorded black men *and* women saying that here was yet another example of a woman "bringing a good man down." Others, men and women, affirmed what Hill had alleged, calling it standard. As Hill herself noted, "I had a call from a male who identified himself by name, and also identified himself as associated with a national organization, a civil rights organization, and he said to me that Clarence Thomas was only acting the way any man would act with a woman"[49]— which proclaims sex as power, power as sex, and nothing else.

Baldwin knew what love was, how desperately we all need it and how thoroughly loveless our society is. Without love, without vision, we would perish. He saw black people as a kind of family. He came from a large one, was the oldest child, helped raise the younger children, became, in effect, both brother and father to his siblings. Invoking his role as witness, he once said, "We cannot afford despair. We have too many children. Despair is a luxury only white men can afford."[50] What he meant was that there was a great amount of business to be done, and black people had great responsibilities toward each other. There is a crisis between black men and women and the hearings disclosed just how deep and resistant to change it is. The quality of the discourse on the subject is not very good, and in the meantime people literally are dying in the streets. It is as if black America, transformed into an airplane, has crashed in the Andes and the survivors argue with each other about who to eat first instead of blazing a trail through the mountains toward safety. Baldwin would tell us that we have to redeem the hearings, to disengage ourselves from their careless and ruinous conclusions. He was unequivocal about what black people had to do: "Love each other and raise our children. We have to do that!" he said. "The alternative, for me, would be suicide."[51] The tragedy of the hearings, then, shows us where we must go if we are to find a way to redeem both the hearings and ourselves. Baldwin tells us about the nature of that redemption, if we will only hear him:

For nothing is fixed, forever and forever and forever, it is not fixed; the earth is always shifting, the light is always changing, the sea does not cease to grind down rock.

Generations do not cease to be born, and we are responsible to them because we are the only witnesses they have. The sea rises, the light fails, lovers cling to each other, and children cling to us. The moment we cease to hold each other, the moment we break faith with one another, the sea engulfs us and the light goes out.[52]

NOTES

1. James Baldwin, *No Name in the Street*, in *The Price of the Ticket* (New York: St. Martin's, 1985), p. 519.

2. Ibid., p. 513.

3. Baldwin, "Reflections of a Maverick: Interview with Julius Lester/1984," in *Conversations with James Baldwin*, ed. Fred L. Standley and Louis H. Pratt (Jackson: University of Mississippi Press, 1989), p. 225.

4. Ibid.

5. James Campbell, *Talking at the Gates: A Life of James Baldwin* (New York: Viking, 1991), p. 281.

6. Baldwin, "The Black Boy Looks at the White Boy," in *The Price of the Ticket*, p. 303.

7. Baldwin, "Every Good-Bye Ain't Gone," in *The Price of the Ticket*, p. 647.

8. Baldwin, *No Name in the Street*, p. 464.

9. Baldwin, "White Man's Guilt," in *The Price of the Ticket*, p. 410.

10. Baldwin, "An Interview with James Baldwin," in *Conversations with James Baldwin*, p. 6.

11. Baldwin, "Many Thousands Gone," in *The Price of the Ticket*, p. 66.

12. Baldwin, *The Fire Next Time*, in *The Price of the Ticket*, p. 357.

13. Baldwin, "In Search of a Majority," in *The Price of the Ticket*, p. 233.

14. Ibid.

15. Baldwin, "The Black Boy Looks at the White Boy," p. 290.

16. Baldwin, "Many Thousands Gone," p. 68.

17. Baldwin, "The Black Boy Looks at the White Boy," p. 290.

18. Orrin Hatch, quoted in "Excerpts from Senate's Hearings on the Thomas Nomination," *New York Times*, October 13, 1991.

19. Oliver Sacks, *The Man Who Mistook His Wife for a Hat* (New

York: Summit Books, 1985), p. 77.

20. Ibid., p. 78.
21. Ibid., p. 79.
22. Baldwin, "Stranger in the Village," in *The Price of the Ticket*, p. 81.
23. R. W. Apple, Jr., "On Thomas: More Questions, Not Fewer," *New York Times*, October 12, 1991.
24. Clarence Thomas, quoted in "Excerpts from Senate's Hearings," p. 33.
25. Ibid., p. 31.
26. Baldwin, "James Baldwin Interviewed, John Hall/1970," in *Conversations with James Baldwin*, p. 105.
27. Baldwin, "White Man's Guilt," in *The Price of the Ticket*, p. 411.
28. Baldwin, "The Creative Process," in *The Price of the Ticket*, p. 318.
29. Thomas, quoted in "Excerpts from Senate's Hearings," p. 31.
30. Ibid., p. 33.
31. Anita Hill, quoted in "Excerpts from News Conference on Harassment Accusations Against Thomas," *New York Times*, October 8, 1991, p. 20.
32. Baldwin, *No Name in the Street*, p. 482.
33. "Gunman Kills 22 and Himself in Texas Cafeteria," *New York Times*, October 17, 1991.
34. Baldwin, "The Male Prison," in *The Price of the Ticket*, p. 102–3.
35. Hill, quoted in "Prof. Anita F. Hill: 'I Felt That I Had to Tell the Truth,'" *New York Times*, October 12, 1991, p. 11.
36. Ibid.
37. Baldwin, "The Discovery of What It Means to Be an American," in *The Price of the Ticket*, p. 175.
38. See Baldwin, *The Fire Next Time*, in *The Price of the Ticket*, p. 356.
39. Senator Howell Heflin, quoted in "Excerpts from the Senate's Hearings," p. 14.
40. Baldwin, "Many Thousands Gone," p. 66.
41. Baldwin, *No Name in the Street*, p. 536.

42. Baldwin, "Every Good-Bye Ain't Gone," p. 643.
43. "Excerpts from Statement by Anita Hill in Oklahoma," *New York Times,* October 15, 1991.
44. *New York Times,* October 11, 1991, p. 1; October 9, 1991, p. A1.
45. Baldwin, *No Name in the Street,* p. 520.
46. Baldwin, quoted in "James Baldwin, an Interview: Wolfgang Binder/1980," in *Conversations with James Baldwin,* p. 197.
47. Thomas, quoted in "Excerpts from the Senate's Hearings," p. 29.
48. Baldwin, quoted in "James Baldwin: Looking Towards the Eighties: Kalamu ya Salaam/1979," in *Conversations with James Baldwin,* pp. 183–184.
49. Hill, quoted in "Stress That Follows Filing of a Complaint," *New York Times,* October 8, 1991.
50. Baldwin, quoted in "James Baldwin: Looking Towards the Eighties," p. 182.
51. Baldwin, quoted in "James Baldwin: Reflections of a Maverick," p. 226.
52. Baldwin, "Nothing Personal," in *The Price of the Ticket,* p. 393.

NELL IRVIN PAINTER

Hill, Thomas, and the Use of Racial Stereotype

Just now I have had a teaching experience with Princeton graduate students, who were reading a lot and thinking hard, that reminds me of the formidability of seeing class and gender, as well as race, in matters African-American. The assignment challenged even thoughtful young people, who had an entire semester in which to work things out. But the Thomas-Hill hearings were entirely different, for few in the audience were graduate students dedicated to making sense of complicated issues. This time the scenario played itself out in the fast-paced medium of television before an audience unaccustomed to thinking about gender and race simultaneously. Because the protagonists of this American theatrical production were black, race stayed in the forefront nearly all the time. Even so, viewers realized, however fuzzily, that something else was going on. The unusual cast of characters made the viewers' task novel and hard: to weigh the significance of race in an intraracial drama. But the exercise proved too daunting, and stereotype, almost inevitably, became the medium of exchange. Even before the second part of the televised hearings began, Clarence Thomas had shown me that he would portray issues of gender as racial cliché.

As troubled as I was by what happened to the person and the persona of Anita Hill in the hearings, I had begun to have doubts about Clarence Thomas's manipulation of gender issues well before she entered the scene. My own difficulties with Thomas regarding women began when I learned that he had portrayed his sister, Emma Mae Martin, as a deadbeat on welfare. In a speech to Republicans (who practically invented the role of welfare queen), he had made Martin into a stock character in the Republican scenario of racial economics. His point was to contrast her laziness with his hard work and high achievement to prove, I suppose, that any black American with gumption and a willingness to work could succeed. Thus, a woman whom he had presumably known and loved for a lifetime emerged as a one-dimensional welfare cheat, one of the figures whom black women cite as an example of the pernicious power of negative stereotype. For Thomas, it seemed, all the information that needed to be known of his sister compared her to him: she was a failure on welfare and he was a high-ranking official. He left it to others—who were his critics—to describe his sister more completely.

Other people, like Lisa Jones in the *Village Voice,* had more to say about Emma Mae Martin. It turns out that she was only on welfare temporarily and that she was usually a two-job-holding, minimum-wage-earning mother of four. Unable to afford professional help, she had gone on welfare while she nursed the aunt who had suffered a stroke but who normally kept her children when Martin was at work. Feminists noted that Martin belonged to a mass of American women who were caregivers to the young, the old, and the infirm. She had followed a trajectory common in the experience of poor women, regardless of race; this pattern Clarence Thomas did not acknowledge.

That his life and the life of his sister had differed by virtue of their gender was not included in Clarence Thomas's rendition of contrasting destinies. He seemed not to have appreciated that he was the favored boy-child who was protected and sent to private schools and that she was the girl who stayed behind, married early, and cared for a relative who had fallen ill. If he realized how common his family's decisions had been, he gave no indication of seeing those choices as gendered. His equation balanced one thing only, and that was individual enterprise. Even though as a hospital worker his sister was a symbol of Jesse Jackson's masses of black folk who work every day, her life as a worker counted for naught in Thomas's story. His eagerness to shine on a conservative stage allowed him to obscure the actual circumstances of her life and her finances and to disregard her vulnerabilities as a poor, black woman. If he were ignorant of how very characteristic of poor women's her life's course had been, he would seem to have performed his job heading the Equal Employment Opportunity Commission in a perfunctory manner; if he were aware of how often families in need engage in such triage and distorted her situation to satisfy a Republican audience, he is guilty of outright cruelty.

. . .

Clarence Thomas's wielding of stereotype against his sister—a woman whose identity was already overburdened by stereotype—foreshadowed his strategy in the hearings that pitted him against another black woman, both in its heartlessness and its exploitation of racial imagery. Both times he distorted his relative position vis-à-vis a specific black woman, as though lacking a sense of social perspective.

Comparing his sister's failings to his own achievements, he spoke as though the two of them had played with the same advantages and handicaps, as though he had seized his chances while she had unaccountably kicked her own equal opportunities aside. Later, as he confronted Anita Hill, his translation of the power relations of gender were similarly skewed. This time he ultimately portrayed himself as the person at the bottom facing terrible odds. His older adversaries were his favorite cardboard-cutout bogey-people: the (black, male) civil rights establishment and organized (white) feminists who persecuted him for being of independent mind. Squared off against his bogey-people, he saw himself as a symbol of integrity and as an underdog.

Thomas's version of American power dynamics reversed a decade's worth of his own rhetoric, in which he had castigated black civil rights advocates for whining about racist oppression. The haughty dismissal of claims that racism persisted had previously been his stock-in-trade. But once a black woman accused him of abusing his power as a man and as an employer, he quickly slipped into the most familiar role in the American iconography of race: that of the victim. Accused of misuse of power, he presented himself as a person with no power at all. It mattered not that the characterization was totally inappropriate, in terms of gender and of race.

In a struggle between himself and a woman of his same race, Thomas executed a deft strategy. He erected a tableau of white-black racism that allowed him to occupy the position of "the race." By reintroducing concepts of white power, Thomas made himself into "the black person" in his story. Then, in the first move of a two-step strategy, he cast Anita Hill into the role of "black-woman-as-traitor-to-the-race."

The black-woman-as-traitor-to-the-race is at least as old as *David Walker's Appeal* of 1829, and the figure has served as a convenient explanation for racial conflict since that time. Although Thomas did not flesh out his accusation, which served his purposes only briefly, it should be remembered that in the tale of the subversion of the interests of the race, the black female traitor—as mother to whites or lover of whites—connives with the white man against the black man. Such themes reappear in *Black Skin, White Masks,* by Frantz Fanon; in *Black Rage,* by William Grier and Price Cobbs; and in *Madheart,* by LeRoi Jones, in which the figure of "the black woman," as "mammy" or as "Jezebel," is subject to loyalties to whites that conflict with her allegiance to the black man. Unable to extricate herself from whites, the black-woman-as-traitor misconstrues her racial interests and betrays black men's aspirations to freedom. Freedom, in this particular instance, meant a seat on the United States Supreme Court.

Although she is well known among African Americans, the black-woman-as-traitor-to-the-race is less familiar to white Americans and thus is not a useful trope in the television shorthand of race through which Clarence Thomas communicated. Having made Anita Hill into a villain, he proceeded—wittingly or not—to erase her and return to a simpler and more conventional cast. By the end of his story Anita Hill had lost the only role, that of villain, that his use of stereotype had allowed her. She finally disappeared, as he spun out a drama pitting the lone and persecuted figure of Clarence Thomas, the black man, against an army of powerful white assailants. Democratic senators became the lynch mob; Thomas became the innocent lynch victim. As symbol and as actual person, Anita Hill was no longer to be found.

Hill's strategy was different from Thomas's. But had she not stood on the ground of personal integrity and the truth of her own individual experiences, she might have sought to work within the framework of racial typecasting. To do so would have tested the limits of the genres of senatorial testimony and televised hearings, for she would have needed at least a semester to reveal, analyze, and destroy the commonplaces of American racism that Thomas manipulated so effectively. Her task could neither be undertaken, nor completed in sound bites and within a matter of days. Simply to comprehend Hill's identity as a highly educated, ambitious, black female Republican imposed a burden on American audiences, black and white, that they were unable—at least at that very moment—to shoulder. With breathtaking cynicism, Thomas evoked the pitiable image of the victimized black man, and his exploitation of the imagery of race succeeded. Such images, such stereotypes, of black women as well as of black men, bear closer inspection.

. . .

Black people of both sexes have represented the American id for a very long time, a phenomenon rooted in our cultural identities of race and class. The stereotypes are centuries old and have their origins in European typecasting of both the poor and the black, for sex is the main theme associated with poverty and with blackness. Even where race is not at issue, the presence of the poor introduces the subject of sex. William Shakespeare's characters provide a handy reminder across spectra of race, class, and ethnicity: the nurse in *Romeo and Juliet* speaks of sex purposefully and unintentionally, so that her every other utterance is characterized as bawdy; Caliban, in *The Tempest,* is a playfully uninhibited savage; and of course, there is Othello the Moor in a tortured saga of desire.

Sexuality, in the sense of the heightened desirability of working-class characters, figures centrally in the diaries of Arthur J. Munby and Hannah Cullwick, in *My Secret Life,* in D. H. Lawrence's *Lady Chatterley's Lover,* and, homoerotically, in Hermann Hesse's *Demian*. In each case, members of the middle and upper classes seek sexual titillation or fulfillment with lovers of a lower class. Sigmund Freud, describing the complex family dynamics of bourgeois households, spoke of women in domestic service as people of low morals, because they were so likely to become entangled sexually with the men of the families that employed them. More recently, Susan Brownmiller has noted that women who are particularly vulnerable to sexual violence by token of their ethnicity or race—Jews in Europe, Negroes in the United States—are viewed as especially provocative by potential assailants.

Over and over in European imaginations, the poor epit-
omize unfettered sexuality, and this convention has come
to serve in the United States as well. American writing not
only echoes the sexualization of the poor (Stephen Crane's
Maggie, A Girl of the Streets, Wilbur Cash's *Mind of the
South*), but, reflecting a history in which masses of workers
were enslaved, also adds the ingredient of race. In American iconography the sexually promiscuous black girl—or
more precisely, the yellow girl—represents the mirror
image of the white woman on the pedestal. Together,
white and black women stand for woman as madonna and
as whore.

Today, as in the past, race and class are hopelessly intertwined in the United States. This is so even a generation after
the end of legal segregation and the confusion of usages
related to race and usages related to class. In eighteenth- and
nineteenth-century England, it was the lower classes who
were expected to show deference toward the aristocracy by
bowing their heads, doffing their hats, tolerating the use of
their first names, entering by the service entrance, and,
above all, revealing no sign of independent thought. In the
era of American segregation these habits became the patterns
of racial subordination that all black people, no matter what
their class standing, were expected to observe. For most
Americans race became and remains the idiom of expression
of differences and characteristics of class. Just as slaves were
the most exploited of workers, so blacks in the United States
have become the sexiest of the American poor.

The imagery of sex in race has not and does not work in
identical ways for black women and men, even though

figures of educated black people, whether male or female, are not well enough established for quick recognition on TV, where the Thomas-Hill saga played and where so many American stereotypes are reinforced. Aside from Bill Cosby, there is no handy black character in our national imagination, male or female, who has strayed very far from the working class. And Cosby constitutes less a symbol than an individual phenomenon. If Clarence Thomas could not reach for a stereotypical black man who would be educated and respectable, Anita Hill (had she succumbed to the temptation) could not have done so either. To silence his questioners quickly, Clarence Thomas had to draw on older, better-known formulations of racial victimization, and he had to reach across lines of class and privilege to do so.

Thomas appropriated the figure of the lynch victim despite glaring dissimilarities between himself and the thousands of poor unfortunates who, unprotected by white patrons in the White House or the United States Senate or by the law, perished at the hands of white southern mobs. As though education, status, and connections counted for nothing, Thomas grasped a chain of reference that begins with the stereotypical black-beast-rapist, as depicted in D. W. Griffith's *Birth of a Nation*. As Thomas knew well, however, those associations do not end with the rapist; they extend into meanings that subvert Griffith's brutalized invention.

The black-beast-rapist connects to the black man accused of rape, who, in turn, is only one link in a chain that also casts doubt on the validity of the charge of rape when leveled against black men. Ida B. Wells began to undermine the credibility of the accusation in the 1890s, and the

NAACP and the Communist Party helped to discredit lynching even after trials, as in the case of the eight young black men summarily sentenced to hang in Scottsboro, Alabama, in 1931. Since that time the presumption (among non–Ku Klux Klansmen, at least) has been that the quintessential lynch victim was, like the Scottsboro boys, a casualty of the miscarriage of justice. To mention the figure of the southern black lynch victim is to cite a man unjustly accused, and this was the meaning that Clarence Thomas summoned. Had the sexualized figure of the black man not evolved past *Birth of a Nation,* he could not have served Thomas's purpose.

Anita Hill, on the other hand, had no comparable tradition of a stereotype that had been recognized, analyzed, and subverted to draw upon. The mammy image is in the process of being reworked, while the welfare queen and the oversexed-black-Jezebel are still unreconstructed. Considering that Hill is a beautiful young woman who was leveling a charge of sexual harassment, adapting herself to stereotype and then reworking the stereotype would not have been a simple matter. (No odder, perhaps, than assimilating the figure of a lynch victim to the person of a nominee for the United States Supreme Court.) Stereotypes of black women remain fairly securely in place, and the public discussion that would examine and dislodge them has only begun to occur around the mammy image. The oversexed-black-Jezebel is more likely than not still taken at face value.

The depiction of the oversexed-black-Jezebel is not so salient in American culture as that of the black-beast-rapist/

lynch victim, but she has sufficient visibility to haunt black women to this day. This stereotypical black woman not only connotes sex, like the working-class white woman, but unlike the latter, is assumed to be the instigator of sex. Theodore Dreiser's Sister Carrie may have been seduced by a fast-talking city slicker she met on a train, but Rose Johnson, in Gertrude Stein's *As Fine as Melanctha,* positively revels in sexual promiscuity.

Overdetermined by class and by race, the black-woman-as-whore appears nearly as often as black women are to be found in representations of American culture. Mary Chesnut, in her Civil War diary, pities the virtuous plantation mistress surrounded by black prostitutes anxious to seduce white men and boys. The stereotype that averred there were no virginal black women over the age of fourteen was prevalent enough in the 1890s to mobilize black clubwomen nationally against it. The figure of the oversexed-black-Jezebel has had amazing longevity. She is to be found in movies made in the 1980s and 1990s—*She's Gotta Have It, Jungle Fever, City of Hope*—in which black female characters are still likely to be shown unclothed, in bed, and in the midst of coitus.

Mammy, welfare cheat, Jezebel, period. These were the roles available to Anita Hill. Hill chose not to make herself into a symbol Americans could recognize, and as a result she seemed to disappear, a fate reserved for black women who are well educated and are thus doubly hard to see. Mammy and Jezebel and the welfare queen may be the most prominent roles for black women in American culture, but even these figures, as limited as is their range, inhabit the shadows of American imagination.

As commentators like Darlene Clark Hine and Patricia

Hill Collins have noted, silence and invisibility are the hallmarks of black women in the imagery of American life. The most common formula for expressing minority status, in the nineteenth century as in the twentieth, is "women and blacks." As the emblematic woman is white and the emblematic black is male, black women generally are not as easy to comprehend symbolically. Barbara Smith, Gloria Hull, and Patricia Bell Scott noted in 1982 that while all the women seem to be white and all the blacks seem to be men, some of us are brave.

Because black women have been harder than men to fit into clichés of race, we often disappear. Few recall that after Bigger Thomas, in Richard Wright's *Native Son,* accidentally killed rich, white Mary Dalton, he committed the brutal, premeditated murder of his girlfriend, the innocent black Bessie. *Native Son* is generally summed up as the story of a racial crime in which a white woman dies and a black man emerges as the victim of society. Two generations later Eldridge Cleaver said in *Soul on Ice* that he raped black women for practice; he was honing his skills before attacking white women, who were for him real women. The poet Audre Lorde remembered and grieved for the twelve black women who were murdered in Boston in the spring of 1979, but their remembrance grows shadowy beside the figure of the Central Park jogger. Who recalls that Joan Little had been sexually assaulted by the man she killed?

Disregarded or forgotten or, when remembered, misconstrued, the symbolic history of black women has not functioned in the same way as the symbolic history of black men. If the reality of the Scottsboro boys and other black men accused of rape showed that the charge was liable to be false and thereby tempered the stereotype, the meaning of the history of black women as victims of rape has not yet penetrated the American mind. In the absence of an image equivalent to that of the Scottsboro boys, black women's reputed hypersexuality has not been reappraised. It is as though silence and invisibility had entirely frozen the image of black men at the black-beast-rapist stage. Lacking access to the means of mass communication, black women have not been able to use our history of abuse as a corrective to stereotypes of rampant sexuality.

Since the seventeenth-century beginnings of their forcible importation into what would become the United States, black women have been triply vulnerable to rape and other kinds of violence: as members of a stigmatized race, the subordinate sex, and people who work for others. The history of sexual violence against black women is rooted in slavery, but as bell hooks points out, it did not end there. Despite two centuries' worth of black women's testimony, as exemplified in Harriet Jacobs's *Incidents in the Life of a Slave Girl,* Alice Walker's *The Color Purple,* and the St. John's University rape case of 1991, our vulnerability to rape has not become a standard item in the list of crimes against the race. When the existence of rape is acknowledged, it is, as often as not, to name a crime of which the black man, rather than she who was raped, is the victim. Unable to protect "his" woman, the black man suffers the loss of his manhood when a female family member is assaulted. The belief persists that black women are always ready for sex and, as a consequence, cannot be raped. Introducing the specter of sex, Hill made herself vulnerable to Virginia Thomas's doubly stereotypical retort: Hill—as both the oversexed black Jezebel anxious for sex and as the rejected, vindictive woman who trumps up a charge of sexual harassment—really wanted to sleep with Clarence Thomas. The injury, then, is to him, not to her.

More, finally, is at stake here than winning a competition between black men and black women for the title of ultimate victim as reckoned in the terms of white racism, as tempting as the scenario of black-versus-white tends to be. Anita Hill found no shelter in stereotypes of race not merely because they are too potent and too negative to serve her ends. There was no way for Hill to emerge a hero of the race, because she would not deal in black and white. By indicting the conduct of a black man, Hill revealed the existence of intraracial conflict, which white Americans find incomprehensible and many black Americans guard as a closely held secret of the race. Keeping that secret in the interest of racial unity has silenced black women on the issue of sexual abuse, for our attackers have been black men as well as white, as *The Black Women's Health Book* poignantly reveals. Because discussions of the abuse of black women would not merely implicate whites, black women have been reluctant to press the point. Our silence, in turn, has tended to preserve intact the image of oversexed black Jezebel. Who knows how long Anita Hill would have held her tongue had not circumstances forced her to go public?

As things turned out, in the short run at least, Clarence Thomas and his allies managed once again to "disappear" the black woman and to stage a drama of race. But the gender issue that Anita Hill raised, despite its potential for deep divisiveness, looks toward the future of racial politics in the United States (unless the David Dukes of the world force us back into a terrorized, defensive, androcentric unity). Ironically, black conservatism, which is not very hospitable to feminism, initially staked the claim for diversity within the race. Black feminists are enlarging this claim in the name of our history as black women.

Black women, who have traditionally been discounted within the race and degraded in American society, are becoming increasingly impatient with our devaluation. Breaking the silence and testifying about the abuse, black feminists are publishing our history and dissecting the stereotypes that have been used against us. So far, the discussion has not engaged large numbers of Americans, but I trust that Anita Hill will have helped us reach many more. If my experience with earnest and hardworking Princeton graduate students offers any guidance, the process, though ultimately liberating, will prove to be intellectually demanding. We will know we have succeeded in taking a first step when Americans greet the images of the mammy, the welfare queen, and the oversexed-black-Jezebel with the skepticism they turn toward the figure of the lynch victim accused of raping a white woman. Our work, however, cannot end there, for both the black-beast-rapist and the oversexed-black-Jezebel would still survive with enough vigor to dog both our tracks. The next step, which is just as necessary, will free African Americans from sexualized stereotypes that tyrannize us as black men and black women, for black men as well as black women feel their lives are circumscribed by just such stereotypes.

CAROL M. SWAIN

Double Standard, Double Bind:
African-American Leadership After the Thomas Debacle

Whatever the Clarence Thomas confirmation hearings did for the U.S. Supreme Court, they were a disaster for those who purport to speak for African Americans. During the confirmation process, it became dramatically evident that there is no one person, nor, indeed, one single voice to speak on behalf of African Americans. Whites often ask blacks what they think of black individuals like New York's controversial Reverend Al Sharpton, or Virginia's more mainstream Governor Douglas Wilder, as if there were a "black view" on these personalities. The truth of the matter is that African Americans are so diverse now that it has become impossible to identify a single black position on any important issue. The diversity of black opinion, which can be viewed as a sign of maturity within the African-American community, has significant political implications. It means that, on the whole, blacks are less

willing than they used to be to take cues from their traditional leadership, even when that leadership is more or less
united.

In the case of the Thomas confirmation, however, the
usual voices of African-American leadership were sharply
divided. Not even their loyal followers could find an
unambiguous signal to which they might respond. After
weeks of soul-searching and hard political debate, the National Association for the Advancement of Colored People
opposed Thomas, the Southern Christian Leadership Conference supported him, and the National Urban League
failed to take a position. In the end, what carried the day
for Clarence Thomas was the support of conservatives for
one of their own, the desire of many African Americans—
and some whites—to have a black face on the Supreme
Court, and lastly, the tendency of African Americans to
rally around wounded black leaders who they feel are
being maligned or attacked unjustly. In what follows I will
argue that serious divisions among traditional black leaders
during the Thomas hearings posed a major dilemma, especially for those Democratic senators who sought first to
determine and later to represent the views of their African-
American constituents.

The Failure of Traditional African-American Leadership
Liberal interest groups have standards of acceptability for
potential Supreme Court justices, a set of criteria by which
they evaluate nominees. African-American groups have
generally agreed that the nominees they support should
embrace affirmative-action programs, be prochoice on
abortion, oppose prayer in school, and endorse the protection of civil liberties and civil rights. That is the main

reason why opposition mobilized so quickly against Robert Bork when President Reagan nominated him in 1987 to replace retiring Justice Lewis F. Powell. Bork failed the litmus test of the liberal interest groups, and black groups joined the others in defeating him. Although Judge Thomas's record clearly indicated that he, too, would fail such a litmus test, black-led organizations hedged on whether or not to oppose him, and in the process they abandoned their traditional liberal allies, especially the women's groups, who had joined them in their fight against past conservative nominees.

Let us consider some of what was known about Thomas's ideological track record. When he was chairman of the Equal Employment Opportunity Commission, he disappointed the liberal groups again and again with his refusal to enforce antidiscrimination laws. Even the conservative assistant attorney general for civil rights, William Bradford Reynolds, once chastised Thomas for not enforcing the law, which is said to have provoked the reply "All I have to do is die and stay black."[1] Under Thomas the number of cases in which the EEOC found cause to suspect discrimination plummeted from 72.5 percent in October 1979 to 43.9 percent by the first half of 1986.[2] Thomas allowed hundreds of age-discrimination cases to lapse without his agency taking any action, which forced Congress to extend the deadline for the resolution of these cases. Thomas publicly opposed affirmative-action programs, something dear to the hearts of the liberal interest groups. In fact, he had gone out of his way to publicize his record in this matter to the conservatives upon whom he depended for support in his career. By the mid-1980s, his views on most civil rights issues had assumed a clear neoconservative cast. In 1985, for instance, Thomas told a reporter:

America should not fall into the trap of blaming all the problems faced by blacks or other minorities on others. We are not beggars or objects of charity. We don't get smarter just because we sit next to white people in class, and we don't progress just because society is ready with handouts.[3]

Similarly, in 1987, he amplified his position on affirmative action:

I firmly insist that the Constitution be interpreted in a colorblind fashion. It is futile to talk of a colorblind society unless this constitutional principle is first established. Hence, I emphasize black self-help, as opposed to racial quotas and other race-conscious legal devices that only further and deepen the original problem.[4]

Maybe in order to score additional points with conservatives, Thomas, who was later to deny ever having discussed the landmark case of *Roe* v. *Wade,* implied that he opposed abortion on the grounds of natural law.[5] In a speech at the conservative Heritage Foundation, Thomas praised as a splendid example of natural-law thinking an antiabortion article written by Lewis E. Lehrman, in which *Roe* v. *Wade* was called a "coup against the Constitution" and abortion described as a "holocaust" against fetuses. Thomas, moreover, reaffirmed many of his conservative views the day after his nomination on July 2, 1991, just before he stopped giving interviews, apparently complying with instructions from the White House:

> I don't believe in quotas. America was founded on a philosophy of individual rights, not group rights. The civil rights movement was at its greatest when it proclaimed the highest principles on which this country was founded— principles such as the Declaration of Independence, which were betrayed in the case of blacks and other minorities. . . . I believe in compensation for actual victims [of discrimination], not for people whose only claim to victimization is that they are members of a historically oppressed group.[6]

As the above statements suggest, when President Bush announced on July 1, 1991, that Clarence Thomas was "the best man on merits" to succeed Justice Thurgood Marshall, liberal organizations had plenty of information with which to rate their man. Following their own established criteria for evaluating the fitness and views of political appointees, the major black-led organizations should have announced immediately a position against the nominee and then tried to mobilize black public opinion in that direction. What ensued, however, was confusion and chaos, because the desire of some African Americans to have a black face on the Court caused their leaders to renege on their commitments to their natural coalition partners. This indecisiveness enabled the pro-Thomas forces to rally and gain momentum. By the time most of the liberal organizations had reached an anti-Thomas opinion, it was too late to stop his confirmation.

The extent of the disarray of the black-advocacy organizations was extraordinary. It took the Congressional Black Caucus (CBC) ten days to reach its decision to oppose the confirmation of Thomas.* Joseph Lowery, the president of the Southern Christian Leadership Conference, is said to have been offended because the Black Caucus had not consulted him: "The CBC set themselves up as the voice of black America. They were rounding third base before the umpire said play ball," said Lowery.[7] His group eventually came out in favor of confirmation. Gradually, over a period of three months, black organizations across the country staked out their positions on the nomination, but a clear voice for or against the confirmation never emerged from African-American leaders, a fact, as I have said, that was particularly troubling to the Democratic senators keen to know the views of the black population.

For African Americans in general, the whole issue surrounding the nomination was confounded by Thomas's race. Some blacks wondered whether or not a black man could actually be a political conservative, and whether he could really believe the things he claimed to espouse. Some grappled with that issue and concluded that perhaps he was merely an opportunist who said these things only to get a lifetime appointment on the nation's highest court. Others, recognizing that the Supreme Court already had a conservative majority and that Bush would only use the rejection of Thomas to appoint a conservative member of some other racial or political group, decided that, given the choice between a black conservative and a white one, they preferred the one who had been called a "nigger."

*Predictably, Gary Franks of Connecticut, the sole Republican member of the Caucus, declined to join the others in attempting to mobilize grass-roots opposition.

There were also many positive views of Thomas. One man undoubtedly summed up many supporters' feelings when he said:

I think that when Thomas is positioned as a jurist, he is actually going to do the right thing. . . . Like me, he has to put food on the table. That experience people do not forget quite as easily as many black people fear he has. I identify with the guy. He won't forget what he went through. And he will have survived a stringent life under a microscope. I don't care what he says publicly. He'll do the right thing as a solid thinker, and not an ideologue, when the time comes.[8]

Throughout the confirmation process, African-American leaders were divided over what type of representation the people most needed—a black face or an advocate and protector of hard-won black gains. To understand their differing views, it is useful to define the concepts of descriptive and substantive representation.[9] People are descriptively represented when certain of their demographic characteristics—race, gender, social class, or ethnicity—coincide with those of their representative. Thus, women, blacks, and Protestants are descriptively represented on the current Supreme Court, but Jews, Hispanics, and Native Americans are not. Substantive representation occurs when a representative actually advances the interests of his or her constituents.

Descriptive representation may or may not coincide with substantive representation. Black faces in political offices in and of themselves do not guarantee that black interests will be served. President Ronald Reagan, for example, advanced descriptive representation when he appointed Linda Chavez (a Hispanic) and Clarence Pendleton (an African American) to the Civil Rights Commission. Since both were conservatives, he did not advance substantive representation of the large numbers of their respective racial groups who favored the liberal civil rights policies that Chavez and Pendleton opposed. Hence, a majority of their group members went unrepresented. Chavez and Pendleton, moreover, were not isolated cases in their time. President Bush sought the same in the nomination of Thomas. Bush knew that for many African Americans, Thomas's race would be the primary consideration, and that black solidarity would take precedence over everything. He also knew that a completely white Senate Judiciary Committee would find it very difficult to interrogate a black man, especially one who had grown up in poverty.

Bush calculated correctly. By the week of September 10, a national poll showed that a strong majority of African Americans (60 percent) supported Thomas's confirmation. There were many reasons for this support. First of all, many African Americans felt that they could relate to Thomas. They saw him as a man with a background more like their own than the background of many of their anointed black leaders. They saw a man from the South, who had risen above poverty and who reportedly still held values that were much closer to their own than those of the black leadership.

Furthermore, it is important to remember that in general, African Americans are not nearly as single-mindedly liberal as they are often portrayed to be. On non-economic issues, in fact, a clear stand of conservatism is evident.

Fewer blacks than whites approve of abortion on demand (28 to 41 percent); fewer blacks than whites approve of married women working (70 to 76 percent), or like the idea of female politicians (65 to 75 percent),[10] and though large percentages of both blacks and whites support school prayer, blacks are generally more supportive of the issue than whites.[11] Moreover, while black-interest groups strongly support preferential treatment of minorities in employment and in college admissions, an opinion poll conducted for the American Enterprise Institute found vast differences between the attitudes of the black public and black-interest-group leaders on this issue: 77 percent of black leaders supported preferential treatment of minorities, yet only 23 percent of the black public did.[12] The same poll revealed similar patterns in the perceptions of the black public with regard to the magnitude of job discrimination (74 percent of the black leaders believed there was substantial discrimination, but only 40 percent of the black public did). The question of whether or not African Americans were improving their economic status was another divisive issue: 39 percent of the leaders said no, while 66 percent of the black public said yes. Thus, 61 percent of the black leaders saw a deterioration in black living standards compared with only 34 percent of the black public.[13] In addition to these issues, on which the black public seems to disagree with the black leadership, there is also an increasingly visible group of black conservatives, including Gary Franks, Shelby Steele, Glenn Loury, and Stephen Carter, who—like Clarence Thomas—often reject the positions of the traditional black leadership and have themselves become leaders of subgroups.[14]

Interestingly enough, however, despite this conservative

trend, African Americans continue to vote for and other-wise support the traditional liberal black leadership. For example, a majority of blacks (between 54 and 56 percent) said that they thought that the NAACP and the Reverend Jesse Jackson, both of whom opposed Thomas, and most civil rights organizations, represented their views and served their interests. On the other hand, black support for the groups that endorsed or failed to take a position on Thomas has traditionally been more limited: Support for the Urban League, which did not take a position, rests around 34 percent, while support for the Southern Christian Leadership Conference, which endorsed Thomas, is only 25 percent.[15] The very fact that so many African Americans still show support for the traditional liberal black leadership groups suggests that if the major groups had acted quickly and unitedly against Thomas, they could have blocked the confirmation. But because much of the traditional black leadership failed to follow their established criteria for evaluating Supreme Court nominees, pollsters were left to find that a majority of African Americans supported Thomas despite the very serious questions that were raised about his qualifications as well as his character. The proclamations of Jesse Jackson and the NAACP alone were not enough to dissuade them from supporting one of their own.

The doubts about Thomas's professional qualifications concerned his lack of experience on the bench as a federal appeals court judge, and the fact that the American Bar Association found him only minimally qualified. This alone could have put an end to his confirmation process long before Professor Anita Hill from the University of Oklahoma came forward with her charges of sexual harassment. As we know, there was a great deal of skepticism about Professor Hill's charges in the Senate and in the country.

For African Americans generally, the issue was not so much whether Hill was credible or not; she was dismissed because many saw her as a person who had violated the code of censorship, which mandates that blacks should not criticize, let alone accuse, each other in front of whites.[16] To many blacks Anita Hill behaved as they might have expected a white woman to behave, pointing her finger and accusing a black man of a sexual offense. Thomas, apparently more aware of the social norms and sense of solidarity than Hill, appealed to the group for protection against a "high-tech lynching" brought about by a "sister" who had violated the code of silence.[17] These reactions have to be seen against the background of events like the drug bust of former District of Columbia mayor Marion Barry and the indictment of Representative Floyd Flake, which was found to be baseless. There was a general sense among African Americans that this was another instance in which a prominent black was unjustly exposed and that Hill's charge was part of some sinister plot to harm a "brother." They therefore rallied to Thomas's defense much as the blacks in Chicago had rallied behind Representative Gus Savage after a black Peace Corps worker had accused him of sexually harassing her.[18] It was in such an atmosphere that the Senate had to act, and after what were essentially two separate proceedings, it voted 52 to 48 to confirm Clarence Thomas with the largest number of negative votes for any successful Supreme Court nominee in history.[19] One newspaper wrote: "Not since Lucius Lamar, an 1888 Supreme Court appointee of President Grover

Cleveland, won by four votes 32–28 has the margin of victory been so close. And there were only 72 senators then, compared to 100 today."[20]

The Senate's Search for Direction

The United States Senate has always been a body dominated by white males. Only three blacks and sixteen women have ever served in that chamber of the bicameral Congress; of these, only four women (Margaret Chase Smith [R-Maine] Barbara Mikulski, [D-Maryland], Nancy Landon Kassebaum [R-Kansas] and Paula Hawkins [R-Florida]), and one black (Edward Brooke [R-Massachusetts]) were directly elected. At present, there are only two females in the Senate: Kassebaum, who supported Thomas, and Mikulski, who opposed him. The Judiciary Committee, created in 1816, has to make recommendations to the full Senate on presidential nominees; the absence of women and African Americans on this committee need not be further pointed out here. This placed the Senate as a whole in a particularly difficult situation, and they eventually managed to alienate two large parts of their constituencies: feminist groups and blacks. I have no doubt that Democratic senators sought to represent the preferences of both groups. Women, however, vote with even less cohesion than blacks. The senators, therefore, looked toward the black civil rights lobby for direction, but, hearing no clear voice there either, many did what was politically expedient—they followed the polls and avoided committing themselves for as long as possible.

As most of us know, unlike the members of the House of Representatives, who serve two-year terms, senators are elected to serve six-year terms, with a third of the Senate up for reelection every two years. Of the thirteen "swing" Democrats, whose votes Republicans needed to confirm Thomas, five are up for reelection in 1992: David Boren (Oklahoma, with a 7 percent black population in his constituency), John Breaux (Louisiana, 31 percent), Alan Dixon (Illinois, 15 percent), John Exon (Nebraska, 4 percent), and Wyche Fowler (Georgia, 27 percent). Four others, who are not up for reelection in 1992, have significant black populations in their states: Ernest Hollings (South Carolina, 30 percent), J. Bennett Johnston (Louisiana, 31 percent), Sam Nunn (Georgia, 27 percent), and Richard Shelby (Alabama, 25 percent). These senators, all southerners, apparently made their decisions on the basis of public-opinion polls that showed popular support for Thomas among blacks. For southern Democrats, African-American voters are far more crucial to their reelection prospects than women's groups.

Splitting along party lines, the two women in the Senate reflected the divisions among women and blacks throughout the rest of the country. Senator Nancy Kassebaum, who voted and spoke in favor of confirmation, nevertheless said that she had no intention of taking part in an "intellectual witch hunt against Professor Hill."[21] Barbara Mikulski, the Senate's other female, commented: "The same people who gave us the worst of racial stereotypes in political campaigns—the Willie Horton ad—have now smeared Anita Hill."[22] Given the fact that female politicians are often more sensitive to issues affecting women than men, we can safely guess that had there been a woman on the Judiciary Committee, there might have been a more vigorous questioning of Thomas. Closer scrutiny of his answers might have been enough to keep him off the court. The fourteen white men on the Senate committee felt too vulnerable to charges of lynching an uppity black man—Senator Edward Kennedy (D-Massachusetts) and Senator Dennis De Concini (D-Arizona) may have had more reason than most to feel vulnerable under the circumstances.* The befuddled white male senators, therefore, took the easy way out of an awkward situation, and they voted to confirm Thomas, while lambasting their institution and decrying the political process that set them up as judges.

Reflections on Thomas and Affirmative Action: A Personal Note

For me the Senate Judiciary Committee proceedings were intensely personal. Over the period that the black leadership could not make up its mind, I went from being neutral toward the nomination to opposing it.

My change occurred before Professor Anita Hill entered the picture. As I reflected on Thomas's bootstrap defense of his suitability for the Supreme Court, I became opposed to his confirmation. I too am an African American from an impoverished background—indeed, one much more impoverished than that of Clarence Thomas. Moreover, I arrived at my present state without the type of assistance that Thomas had from his grandparents and the nuns he credited as his educational mentors. By Thomas's logic my

*Senator Kennedy's reputation as a womanizer is well known to the American public. Similarly, Senator De Concini is one of the Keating Five senators, who were involved in the Savings and Loan scandal of late 1989.

background should qualify me more than his qualifies him for a seat on the Supreme Court. Over the years Thomas has preached self-reliance and denounced self-pitying complainers. Yet as Jesse Jackson so eloquently said, "When the heat was turned up and the pressure applied in the Senate hearings, his first line of defense was not color-blindness, merit or innocence, but race, race, race."[23]

In the ascension of Judge Clarence Thomas to the seat vacated by Justice Thurgood Marshall, I see one of the strongest reasons for *not* having certain types of affirmative-action programs. Affirmative action, as originally envisioned, was to ensure a "fighting chance," not a case for lowering standards. When President George Bush stood before the nation and said this man was the best qualified for the position, where were the black conservatives who knew better? Where were they when Thomas, who had long decried the use of race for political advantage, resorted to the use of racial symbols and racial imagery? Where were the black conservatives, when one of their own resorted to the use of a double standard? Indeed, the poor performance of black leadership groups raises the question as to whether African Americans would not be better off if all elected officials stopped searching for a unanimous black leadership and instead consulted the people themselves, as the senators were forced to do. Major problems arose because the traditional black leadership groups failed to follow their own established criteria for evaluating policies and political appointees that might adversely affect black interests. The double standards of both groups, black conservatives and traditional leaders, led to the debacle. When we do away with double standards for evaluating people, whether in public or elsewhere, we will all be much better off.

NOTES

1. Juan Williams, "A Question of Fairness," *The Atlantic,* vol. 259 (February 1987), p. 70.
2. Ibid.
3. Clarence Thomas, as cited in the *Los Angeles Times,* November 15, 1985.
4. Thomas, letter to the editor, *Wall Street Journal,* February 20, 1987.
5. Thomas, "No Room at the Inn," *Policy Review* (Heritage Foundation), Fall 1991, p. 78.
6. Thomas, as cited in the *Wall Street Journal,* July 2, 1991.
7. Joseph Lowery, as cited in "Caucus Reiterates Thomas Opposition," *Washington Times,* September 13, 1991.
8. "Most Americans Are Undecided on Court Nomination, Poll Finds," *New York Times,* September 10, 1991.
9. Hannah F. Pitkin, *The Concept of Representation* (Berkeley: University of California Press, 1967).
10. Gerald D. Jaynes and Robin M. Williams, Jr., *A Common Destiny: Blacks and American Society* (Washington, D.C.: National Academy Press, 1989), pp. 214–15.
11. *The Gallup Report,* No. 273, July 1988, p. 16.
12. "Some people say that to make up for past discrimination, members of minority groups should be given preferential treatment in getting jobs and places in college. Others say that ability, as determined by test scores, should be the main consideration. Which point of view comes closest to how you feel on this matter?" in Linda S. Lichter, "Who Speaks for Black America?" *Public Opinion,* August-September 1985, p. 43.
13. Ibid., pp. 42–43.
14. "Conservative Blacks Heartened by Thomas," *Chicago Tribune,* November 15, 1991; Fred Barnes, "The Minority Minority," *New Republic,* September 30, 1991; Stephen Macedo, "Dou-

glass to Thomas," *New Republic,* September 30, 1991.

15. Louis Harris Poll of five hundred black adults conducted the week of August 29 to September 2, 1991, reported in "How Blacks View Thomas and Their Leaders," *Business Week,* September 16, 1991.

16. "Hill's Testimony Broke with Afrocentrism," *San Francisco Chronicle,* October 26, 1991.

17. Clarence Thomas's testimony before the Senate Judiciary Committee, *Congressional Quarterly Weekly Report,* October 19, 1991, p. 3070.

18. "Savage: Running on the Edge," *Washington Post,* March 9, 1990; "Savage Attacks 'White Racist Press,' " *Washington Post,* March 22, 1990; "A House Member Is Accused of Sexual Impropriety on Trip," *New York Times,* July 20, 1989; "Black Support for Nominee Rises," *Chicago Tribune,* October 15, 1991.

19. "Questions About Thomas, the Man, Obscured Clues About Thomas, the Jurist," *New York Times,* October 27, 1991.

20. "Racism Accusation Helped Counteract Harassment Charge," *Detroit News,* October 16, 1991.

21. "Excerpts from Senate Debate on Thomas Nomination," *New York Times,* October 16, 1991.

22. Ibid.

23. The Reverend Jesse Jackson, as quoted in "Race Tactic Deplored, but Seen as Effective," *Boston Globe,* October 16, 1991.

HOMI K. BHABHA

A Good Judge of Character:
Men, Metaphors, and the Common Culture

My grandfather used to have a statement. "I can read your letter but I can't read your mind."
> —Judge Clarence Thomas to
> Senator Biden

Even though I grew up in a comfortable, middle-class world, I've always hurt for black America and what white Americans did to blacks. But Clarence taught me to go beyond that—to treat all people the way you wanted to be treated.
> —Virginia Thomas, on husband Clarence,
> *People Weekly,* November 11, 1991

Justice, it is said, must not only be done, it must be seen to be done. In America today, racial justice is too often left undone, and for that very reason the debate around "multiculturalism" must *be seen to be done,* as noisily and publicly

as possible. In various acts of media prestidigitation, as if
seeing is believing, the multicultural magic rolls on: live on
prime time, maximum exposure in the academic journals,
repeatedly regurgitated in that slew of intellectual reviews
that Woody Allen once collectively named "Dissentary."
Sometimes it is done as the "political correctness" debate;
sometimes as "canon" fodder. At times the debate is
located in the university—ethnic studies, gay and lesbian
literatures, popular culture, media studies; at other times it
focuses on the "inner city"—crime, drugs, punishment.
What runs across these very diverse social institutions and
draws them into the same argument is an assumption that
those common values and consensual freedoms that have
defined the "American" way of life, circa Norman Rock-
well or Andrew Wyeth, are now being policed by racial,
sexual, or "ideological" minorities.

In the shadow of the spectacle there exists a profound
emergency in the everyday life of minorities. With some
justification, then, there are those who believe that if the
American dream is now mourned melodramatically as having run aground on the Scylla of culture—the fate of the
humanities—then the American nightmare has long preceded that event, playing out its horror in the Charybdis of
anarchy—social deprivation and racial antagonism. Is this
what is meant by history repeating itself first as tragedy,
then as farce? After the breakup of the USSR, the problematic unification of Germany, the dissolution of the so-
cialist Second World, the rise of racism and neofascism in
western Europe, the demonic divination of David Duke,
the "pacification" of the Caribbean, the conquest of Sad-

dam Hussein, it is George Will's considered opinion published in *Newsweek* that Lynne Cheney's task at the National Endowment for the Humanities is considerably more perilous than that of her husband, Defense Secretary Dick Cheney, because "the foreign adversaries her husband Dick must keep at bay are less dangerous, in the long run, than the domestic forces with which she must deal. These forces are fighting against the conservation of the common culture that is the nation's social cement."[1] Why this hysteria around the humanities? Who are the barbarians storming the gates of the common culture?

Between Scylla and Charybdis, caught between a rock and a whirlpool, the vision of that sceptered isle—the common culture, the nation's cement—suddenly emerges. Like all myths of the nation's "unity," the common culture is a profoundly conflicted ideological strategy. It is a declaration of democratic faith in a plural, diverse society and, at the same time, a defense against the real, subversive demands that the articulation of cultural difference—the empowering of minorities—makes upon democratic pluralism. Simply saying that the "nation's cement" is inherently sexist or racist—because of the underlying logic of late capitalism and its patriarchal overlay—ironically provides the "common culture" argument with the alibi it needs. The vision of a common culture is perceived to be an ethical mission whose value lies in revealing, prophylactically, the imperfections and exclusions of the political system as it exists. The healing grace of a culture of commonality is supposedly the coevality it establishes between social differences—ethnicities, ideologies, sexualities—"an intimation of simultaneity across homogeneous empty time" that welds these different voices into a "unisonance" that is expressive of the "contemporaneous community of the national culture."[2]

The dangers inherent in the concept of a contemporaneous "common" culture are not limited to politically conservative discourses. There is a pervasive, even persuasive, presence of such a paradigm in the popular rhetoric of multiculturalism. A range of "nation-centered" cultural discourses (on a wide axis from right to left) readily intone the mantra of the minorities—race, class, gender. Those who have been historically excised by the process of liberal social democracy, and could be the resources for its most stringent political critique, now become the icons—if only the verbal icons—of its cultural existence. Suddenly, lip service is paid to the representation of the marginalized. A traditional rhetoric of cultural authenticity is produced on behalf of the "common culture" from the very mouths of the minorities. A centralizing, homogeneous mode of social authority is derived from an ever-ready reference to cultural "otherness."

Clarence Thomas's now infamous reference to a "high-tech lynching" at the hands of the (white) senators and the (white) media, is only the most dramatic illustration of this process of regulating and normalizing the politics of difference. Raising the figure of the lynched black man is Thomas's attempt to divert attention from the content or substance of Anita Hill's sexual-harassment charges. But beyond that, Thomas uses the vivid imagery of an antiracist language to silence the feminist discourse on sexual harassment which, in this case, demands a double and displaced articulation of race and gender. The harassment complaint emerges through a play of power that works through subordinate gender relations in the workplace that are not symmetrical with class relations. The signs of ethnic and racial identity are used to create a "cover"—a black mask—that facilitates coercion. The woman's right to the inviolability of her own bodily space, both personal and professional, is abrogated by a "down-home," paternalistic naturalization of the workplace into an extension of the "black" community.

In Thomas's testimony there is a decisive attempt to obscure the reality of sexual politics in the workplace by way of a spurious familial metaphor that creates the illusion of an identity of interests. Refusing to entertain any questions or speculations "about my personal life or my sex life with anybody outside the workplace," Thomas then rhetorically reinvents the workplace as the familial space— "My clerks are my family. They're my friends. . . . I don't know why a son or a daughter or a brother or a sister would write some book that destroys a family. I don't know."[3] This familiarizing, familial discourse associatively picks up the unifying "black" resonance of a common culture that then explicitly disavows the question of sexuality—Sex within the family? God forbid!—and sanitizes the power relations of the workplace by turning them into filial responsibilities.

Sociologist Orlando Patterson's defense of Thomas is centered in the paradigm of the "common culture" and displays, as I've been arguing, the self-defeating use of race and ethnic difference sans feminine sexuality and, consequently, against women's rights. If Thomas disavows the sexual-harassment charges altogether, Patterson turns them into erotic excess, the Rabelaisian, carnivalesque style of a black subculture. According to this tortuous argument, Anita Hill stands condemned not because she lied or fantasized but because she was insensitive to Thomas's "down-home style of courtship" and unappreciative of tribal rites when "Judge Thomas allegedly regaled her with his Rabelaisian humor *(possibly as a way of affirming their common origins)*" (my italics).[4] According to Professor Patterson, Anita Hill is disingenuous because "she has lifted a verbal style that carries only minor sanction in one subcultural context and thrown it in the overheated cultural arena of mainstream, neo-Puritan America." For his part, Judge Thomas would be justified in lying ("denying making the remarks even if he had in fact made them"), "because the deliberate displacement of his remarks made them something else [and] on the utilitarian moral grounds that any admission would have immediately incurred a self-destructive and grossly unfair punishment."

After sweeping claims for cultural particularism, ethnic essentialism, and a touch of down-home *nostalgie de la boue,* Patterson's argument becomes, surprisingly, a plea for the emancipation of African Americans into the free-market world of individualism: "a diverse aggregate of perhaps 30 million *individuals* with all the class differences, subcultural and regional resources, strengths, flaws and ideologies we find in other large populations" (my italics). Is this the melting pot calling the seething kettle black?

The place of Afro-Americans in the maturing of America as a common culture—the common thread of my argument—is now secured by disavowing all forms of systemic, socially structured differences—race, gender, class, sexual minorities, the underclass, youth. These must not merely be seen as conceptual categories for understanding the workings of the hierarchy of power; nor are they simply signs of social differentiation. They are also the affective sites of political discrimination, cultural contestation, social disjunction, and "subaltern" solidarity that have been crucial in forming the historic memories and psychic identities of minority communities. These articulations of cultural difference represent modes of living whose most poignant personal testimonies come from a collective awareness of suffering and a communal struggle toward agency and empowerment. To hold out the soiled promise of "plural" individualism as if it were the Great Black Hope is a debilitating and damning destiny to behold. Listen to the professor preach, one last time: ". . . for what all African Americans won from their [Thomas and Hill's] pain, 'perfected by this deed,' this ritual of inclusion, is the public cultural affirmation of what had already been politically achieved: unambiguous inclusion, unquestioned belonging. The culture of slavery is dead."

Is this Rabelaisian or, in Thomas's words, simply Kafkaesque? Whichever way, it is only a short step away from Thomas's own beliefs expressed by Virginia Thomas, his wife, in the epigraph to this essay. The way to transcend the culture of slavery, the way not to hurt for blacks, is to go beyond "blackness" into the myth and illusion of the common culture: "unambiguous inclusion, unquestioned belonging." Unambiguous for whom? Unquestioned by whom? In dovetailing Patterson's argument with Thomas's position, I am not suggesting that these arguments are identical. I am stressing the power of the idea of a *common* culture to homogenize a diverse range of intellectual and ideological positions, and to transform them into a persuasive political rhetoric of ethical idividualism. This extinguishes the historical agency of "race"—"The culture of slavery is dead!"—and displaces the gendered politics of the workplace into the naturalized discourse of community and "common origins"—Rabelaisian humor, subcultural style, down-home courtship rituals. Cultural commonality, as the necessary condition for the empowerment of minorities, is contained in a supposedly "impersonal" discourse.

A striking illustration of this strategy of "authority" through impersonality is evident in Thomas's appeal to a "neutrality thesis" in the judicial hearings as a way of disavowing his own conservative beliefs and commitments. This is part of Ronald Dworkin's[5] brilliant argument that Thomas conveniently espoused an absolute natural-law perspective—based on the principle of "original intention"—during the nomination hearings, whereas all his previous writings and lectures had argued for a conservative *interpretation* of the Constitution to justify his opposition to abortion and affirmative action.

> But the interpretive claim plainly rejects the ideal of neutral adjudication that Thomas claimed to hold when he spoke in the hearings about stripping down like a runner. . . . Thomas said, in his speeches, that the liberals had been using the interpretive natural law method to support liberal decisions, and he encouraged conservatives to use the same method in a radically different direction . . . against what he called "run-amok judges" but also "run-amok majorities"—majorities who might vote for permissive abortion laws or affirmative action "set-aside" programs or restrictive economic regulation (pp. 44–45).

Once more, opportunistically, Thomas chooses a metaphor to represent himself—"stripping down like a runner"—and it is a metaphor that is quite revealing in the context of the lurid body language that was to come. The stripped-down judge is the perfect double image of "justice" within the common culture. It represents the neutrality and "impersonality" of impartial judicial authority. But the very possibility of "justice" is premised on the naturalized body of the individual, unmarked by the politics of cultural difference—class, race, gender, or power. The representative figure of the Law—whether as lawmaker or lawbreaker—is most commonly recognized to be not the individual as "person" but that body of social, political, and philosophical thought that we associate with varieties of individualism.

It is here, then, that the double image of the stripped judge turns into a strategy of dissembling. For if Thomas concealed his "interpretive" natural-law beliefs by publicly affirming the absolute natural-law position, he did so through a process of disavowal that Dworkin carefully catalogues.* He used the neutrality thesis to conceal his active political interpretations of the law in the conservative cause, continually evading the issue of his political commitments by attributing them to some contingent, circumstantial cause that produced a misunderstanding or a misinterpretation. Bound by the chains of his political ideologies, Thomas showed himself to be a poor escapologist but a consummate obfuscator. As Dworkin reports, when questioned about his endorsement of Lewis Lehr-

---

*My understanding of these legal issues and the illustrations that support them are based on Dworkin's useful essay. The argument I am developing on the basis of Dworkin's information, and the context in which I am placing his insight, are both very different from his own exemplary discussion.

man's article "The Declaration of Independence and the Right to Life," he claimed that he had only used it because he was speaking in the Lehrman Auditorium and, anyway, having only skimmed it, he could hardly be blamed for missing the salient fact that Lehrman illustrates natural-law thinking on the basis of a "right to life" argument. His proclaimed ignorance of *Roe* v. *Wade* is as disingenuous as it is now, quite appropriately, infamous.

My point is not to suggest simply that Thomas is a liar. Such personal proof leads to a form of "individual" retribution that detracts from an understanding of the discourse of disavowal that goes hand in hand with the "common culture" argument. Thomas deals with the investigation into sexual harassment much as he deflects the judicial questioning, by resorting to a strategy of just such disavowal. In both instances what is being disavowed is not just Thomas's record on legal issues or sexual harassment. Disavowal is not simply a strategy for concealing the past; it is a productive discourse that shapes the present political moment in its attempt to institute and authorize a hegemonic, conservative discourse of racial "disadvantage."

What is historically salutary for the politics of multiculturalism is Clarence Thomas's deftly staged reversal of fortune—from alleged sexual harasser to publicly lynched patriot. In the earlier part of his testimony Thomas plays the role of the black-folk apostle of the American dream—honorable Catholic origins, the rise from poverty, the striving for excellence, the leavening of class mobility, then the laurels and libations. Suddenly, once the sexual allegations are tabled, Thomas turns into the avenging angel, the avatar of "race" memory. This strategic, self-serving switch of roles—which has attracted extended comment

and condemnation—is remarkable. But it is not as significant as the collusion of both roles in the creation of a sign
of "racial victimage" within a masculinist mode of cultural
authority. Whether Thomas is the hero of the American
dream or the hanged man of the American racial nightmare, it is the function of this discourse to disallow the
"gendering" of the sign and subject of race.

The common culture promises "individual" emancipation to the likes of Clarence Thomas, black bourgeois, on
the grounds that they become representative *men of color*. I
do not mean to trade gender insults in the tawdry tradition
of the "politics of identity." In fact, I would argue, it
would be perfectly possible for a woman to occupy the role
of a representative man, in the sense I am giving to that
term. For "masculinism" as a position of social authority is
not simply about the power invested in the recognizable
"persons" of men. It is about the subsumption or sublation
of social antagonism; it is about the repression of social
divisions; it is about the power to authorize an "impersonal" holistic or universal discourse on the representation
of the social that naturalizes cultural difference and turns it
into a "second"-nature argument.

The common culture is the ideological purveyor of this
"impersonal" order of things. But its impersonality is un-
gendered only to the extent that its masculinism is so
kneaded into the processes of power that it becomes—in
computer jargon—a "default" mode. It is a sex that need
not speak its name because to do so would be to circum-
scribe its immanent authority. The inscription of masculinity is like the name of the father which, in certain cultures,
cannot be uttered within the family because to do so would

be to turn its awesome, ineffable authority into a representation, mere mimesis. How does this work?

When Thomas turns on the senators with the lynching charge, he is not so much playing on their guilt, as has been suggested, as much as he is attempting to deflect the collective guilt through which a masculinist common culture attempts to contain the articulations of sexual difference. His dramatic attack is a way of disavowing the content of Anita Hill's testimony. More pertinently, it is a disabling strategy aimed at repressing her enunciative mode: the social space from which she speaks as a black woman, outside the collusions of the "common culture." For despite her avowed Republican sympathies, by speaking out against Thomas she refuses to cooperate in the down-home subcultural sexist narrative (*pace* Patterson); and she also refuses to collude in the family-style individualism of collaboration and careerism (the protection and patronage she once sought from Thomas). Breaking with both these taboos—choosing neither race nor individualism in her defense—Anita Hill's testimony reveals nothing less than the systematic and structural abuse of women in the workplace under patriarchal labor and gender relations. Her stance represents a critique of the concept of the "workplace," and indeed the category of women's work.

These are both traditionally defined as parts of the public sphere, participating in the dialectic of class, or the ameliorative discourse of affirmative action, but untouched by the more complex contradictions of gender difference and sexuality. Hill's intervention highlights the "affective" identifications and the psychic investments through which women are both "objectified" in the workplace and live out a range of alienated images of themselves in the wider society. But the social anxiety unleashed by Anita Hill's testimony goes beyond the statement or proof of the sexual exploitation of women.

In removing the fig leaf from the private parts of the public discourse of power and professionalism, Hill makes a historic, objective record of the feelings, the range of affective experiences—conscious, repressed, ambivalent, inconsistent, enraged, dependent—that are an effect of the exploitation of women. The threat of her testimony lies in her ability to speak from a position of relative power with a measure of privilege—without any radical political program—in order to give voice to the silence and guilt that binds most sexually harassed working women in a community of endurance. Catharine MacKinnon has written that "feelings are a material reality of it [sexual harassment]", and what Anita Hill has done by enunciating those feelings—giving them a discursive, institutional reality—is decisive to the discussion.

Hill has exorcised the guilt of silent, self-blaming women who have endured sexual harassment as the price of economic survival, by demonstrating the endemic, systemic nature of harassment: "Because they are economically vulnerable, they are sexually exposed; because they must be sexually accessible, they are always economically at risk. In this perspective, sexual harassment is less 'epidemic' than endemic."[6] But Hill's testimony has done more than illustrate the human or sexual costs of economic exigency. It demonstrates how what is endemic in the economic system may be articulated not at the level of political "rationalities" but at a more complex, affective, psychic level. Politics is as much a process of the ambivalent production of subjects and psychic identifications—sexuality, guilt, dependency—as it is a more "causal" discourse of governmental objects and objectives—alienated labor, wage differentials, affirmative legislative action. Hill's testimony returns the burden of guilt where it belongs: to the collective *unconscious* of a masculinist common culture.

For once Hill has made the link between the "endemic" and the "affective," the issue of sexual harassment is no longer limited to individual versions of the truth and specific cases. We are now in that crepuscular region of social knowledges—child abuse, sexual harassment, blackmail, bribery, domestic violence, date rape, institutionalized racism—which, because they are common knowledge, are usually kept quiet—"scream quietly or the neighbors will hear." But it is precisely the protection of this common guilt that binds a community of abusers in a kind of sadistic solidarity, in a conspiracy of knowing and unknowing that protects and propagates the banality of evil.

Summoning up all the vacuous ferocity of a mock cock-fight, Thomas turns toward the senators and the wider public, using the hanging black body to save his own neck. But beyond that personal fate the metaphor of lynching is a movable feast of the common culture: a way of denying the structural abuse of a woman, like Anita Hill, by substituting the rhetorical figure of a black male victim. Thomas offers up the lynched body as a sacrificial object—a totem meal—shared between the senators and himself to expunge the guilt and anxiety generated by Anita Hill's charges. Within patriarchy, the totem meal reaffirms the "common culture" in the act of expiating the guilt generated by the murder of the totemic figure or the primal father. The ritual slaughter, accompanied by the communal incorporation of the dead body, is an act of affirming and renewing the "male" membership of the community: "the root of all blood covenants by which men made compacts with each other even at a late period of history."[7]

The totem meal sets the stage for drawing together both metaphors of victimage that Thomas elicits in his defense: the racial and the familial. The content of these fantasmatic rituals of martyrdom are less important than the maneuverable, mobile positions that Thomas can occupy as a result of them. So he is the black man lynched by the technologies of state and media spectacle; but he is also the sacrifical object of "his" family of clerks—the father set upon by his children in some mindless act of parricide. In Thomas's own words, "I don't know why family members turn on each other . . . why a son or a daughter would write some book that destroys a family."[8]

Freudian psychoanalysis sees the totem meal as being central to the father complex in the creation of social laws, taboos, and institutions within patriarchal society. The myth is now narrated in terms of the parricidal murder of the tyrannical primal father by his sons, who are in search of unbridled power and women. The murder is essential to the transmission of male lineage and the dominance of masculinist power. For after the father's body is (symbolically) incorporated by the sons, they reinstitute the father's prohibitions (incest, for instance) in an act of retrospective or "deferred obedience." The ensuing "guilt" becomes the basis on which the sons or brothers create a moral code and a social system inevitably founded on crepuscular, anxious, and ambivalent knowledges where "each man is conscious that he is performing an act . . . that is justifiable through the participation of the whole clan," so that, to quote Freud again, "society [is] based on complicity in the common crime; religion [is] based on the sense of guilt and the remorse attaching to it; while morality [is] based partly on the exigencies of this society and partly on the penance demanded by the sense of guilt."

This is a way of regulating the aggressivity that constitutes the social bond—the nation's cement—through forms of knowledge that tacitly acknowledge the violence of its founding moment without consciously avowing it. The guilt generated by the widespread occurrence of sexual harassment in the workplace is normalized in much the same way. It is tacitly acknowledged or silently tolerated as part of the masculinist ethos of the workplace, or it is shrouded in jokes, framed in tortuous laws, defused as rumor or paranoia, frequently lost in the courts as too "personal" a complaint.[9]

It is the "normalization" of shared guilt that Clarence Thomas offers to the senators in the symbolic body of the lynched man. By quite literally changing the subject of the inquiry from sexual harassment to racial victimage, Thomas deploys a dissembling, displaced form of guilt. He evokes a painful memory of ritualized male racial violence to displace the patriarchal "guilt" endemic to gendered relations—sexual harassment—within the workplace. In this metaphoric transference Thomas activates a primal guilt—between men—which can be assuaged by a pious commitment to the myth of the "common culture," and an invitation to join the plural world of "individuals"— both ethical acts easily accomplished in the elevation of Clarence Thomas to the Supreme Court. If the lynched body is black, its real color is its gender. Masked by a history of racial oppression that has become a convenience rather than a conviction, you can hear Thomas say to his interrogators, "I may be accused of sexual harassment, but ain't I a man?"

The anxiety caused by charges of sexual harassment are profoundly complex in both a psychic and a legal sense. For the act of sexual harassment—quite apart from the pornographic projection in this instance—is the misuse of institutional power and status in the pursuit of what is a private fantasy or desire that finds its aphrodisiac in the "public," exhibitionistic context of the encounter. Anita Hill, who was framed stereotypically as a spurned woman, a fantasist, an unreliable witness, gave the clearest enunciation of the bestial imagery and the pornographic imagination to which she had been subjected. Thomas, who wailed at being imprisoned in a "black" sexual stereotype, could only talk of sexual harassment through the proxy of metaphor and the rhetoric of inversion—as if he were not speaking of himself, as if he were unable to address the issue. In that language, too, there is guilt and anxiety. By creating a familial frame for Hill's charges, by substituting the lynched man for the abused woman, Thomas refuses to acknowledge the place from which Hill speaks—sexuality in the workplace—as he addresses himself to the common culture of fathers and brothers.

Yet all along, in his search for the displacing, even duplicitous, metaphor that would disavow Hill's witness and her voice, Thomas is in fact confirming her "truth" even while he is contesting her testimony. In providing a knowledge of sexual harassment as a structural endemic condition that finds its social form as affective, even psychic reality, Hill has subtly complicated the question of "truth." Thomas can no longer just confirm or deny the allegations, because the widening circle of guilt makes that option futile, or purely formalistic. The very system of truth and falsity within which he operates, as part of the common culture, is founded on the evasion of the endemic reality of women's exploitation. And likewise, Anita Hill must be believed not because she was personally speaking the truth, but because her affective language is symptomatic of the collective "sexual" condition of working women.

Thomas's metaphors are entirely self-serving; he is the black totem of the White House. But beyond that, Thomas's move to metaphor as a rhetoric of disavowal—as a way of acknowledging the trauma without accepting the event—is a displaced, perhaps repressed, recognition of the fact that he cannot speak in his defense: he cannot occupy the position of truth. If not in his own words, then by virtue of his metaphors, Clarence Thomas has implicitly, unconsciously, put himself on trial. For his metaphors reveal the impossibility of containing the issue of women's harassment and exploitation within the limits of the legal discourse, or the confines of the workplace, or the space of the family. The empowerment of women is itself like the process of metaphor: a transformative act of the political imagination that makes new connections, breaks boundaries of sense, maps rare sources of sensibility, and embodies other, unsettling regimes of truth.

NOTES

1. Quoted in Louis Menand, "What Are Universities For?" *Harper's,* December 1991, p. 56.
2. Benedict Anderson, *Imagined Communities: Reflections on the Origins and Spread of Nationalism* (London: Verso, 1983), p. 133–34.
3. "The Thomas Nomination," *New York Times,* October 13, 1991.
4. Orlando Patterson, "Race, Gender and Liberal Fallacies," *New York Times,* op-ed page, Sunday, October 20, 1991.
5. Ronald Dworkin, "Justice for Clarence Thomas," *New York Review of Books,* vol. 38, no. 18 (November 7, 1991), pp. 41–45.
6. Catharine A. MacKinnon, *Sexual Harassment of Working Women* (New Haven and London: Yale University Press, 1979), p. 55.
7. Sigmund Freud, *Totem and Taboo* (New York: Norton, 1989), p. 171.
8. Thomas, as reported in "The Thomas Nomination."
9. For an elaboration of the legal implications of the term "personal," see Catharine MacKinnon, *Sexual Harassment,* pp. 83–90: "Personal is the most common descriptive term for the incidents. It is usually used as if it conclusively renders legal remedies unavailable, as if to the extent an occurence can be described as personal the person has no legal rights" (84).

CHRISTINE STANSELL

White Feminists and Black Realities:
The Politics of Authenticity

For historians the Thomas-Hill hearings echoed an old, sad story. The painful division between antiracism and feminism goes back to the days of turmoil and hope after the Civil War. In 1865 the radicals of the Republican Party, the party of black emancipation and women's rights, began to break away from their commitment to universal suffrage to push through the Fifteenth Amendment, which gave the vote to the freed*men*. In abandoning women's suffrage they reasoned that such a radical measure would only compromise any amendment for wider enfranchisement, and that the needs of the freedmen were more urgent. "This hour belongs to the negro," Wendell Phillips admonished the women abolitionists in a phrase that epitomized what would become the conventional equation of Afro-American identity with masculinity. Some leaders of the women's movement—Lucy Stone, for example—followed the Republican leadership, believing that their own demands could wait until the bloody revanche in the South was stilled and the crisis of black male citizenship resolved. Others—most notably Elizabeth Cady Stanton and Susan B. Anthony—broke ranks to form their own uncompromising movement for "woman suffrage," in the process abnegating their commitment to black freedom. In the postwar movement they helped to found, black women would be excluded for decades and black men would long be disdained.

This moment of emancipation, its great promise of justice hedged in from the beginning by compromises and double deals, gave rise to chronic tensions in American politics between universalist aspirations and particularist claims. The demand for women's rights had grown from the movement to abolish slavery; early white feminists had developed their program of full citizenship in concert with a vision of freedom for Afro-Americans, analogizing "the bonds of womanhood" to the bonds of slavery. Slavery's defeat had encouraged hopes for momentous democratic change. "Out of this struggle we must come with higher ideas of liberty, the masses quickened with thought," Elizabeth Stanton had exalted at the end of the war. "I have no misgivings as to the result."

But the shifting alliances of the post–Civil War era shattered those hopes of rights for all. To be sure, the radical Republicans deemed the "negro" to bear an emancipatory promise that would eventually unfold for others, the "women" of "woman suffrage" included, but who, exactly, was the "woman" and who was the "negro"? Was it indeed only realistic and fair for the Republicans to ask white women to put aside their interests to help the more truly oppressed African-American men? In her classic study of the rupture during Reconstruction, Ellen Dubois reminds us how different the alignments would have been had feminists campaigned for the vote for women white *and* black. Their failure to do so, along with the Republicans' abandonment of their cause, gave birth to an enduring syllogism of American political understanding: if the "negro" was male, then the "woman" was white.[1]

For many years now, feminists have carried on a searching examination of racism in the contemporary women's movement. Afro-American feminist scholars—Hazel Carby, Paula Giddings, bell hooks, Barbara Christian, among others—have insisted that as long as black women are absent from feminist considerations, we cannot reconcile a commitment to women's liberation with an allegiance to black freedom. For the most part, white feminists have embraced this insight, but in the process, a touch of wishful thinking has crept in: as if heeding black women would bring about some automatic reconciliation between black men and enlightened white women, as if all—or most—forms of black politics could accommodate most—or all—forms of feminism, as if black women's political role was somehow to harmonize the interests of white feminists and the Afro-American community.

These critiques and self-critiques have without question opened up the intellectual milieu of feminism to enlivening new debates and questions. But the political division of labor whereby black feminists come to serve as go-betweens between their white counterparts and other black people also reproduces the old distinction between the politics of race and the politics of women. Present modes of feminist antiracism encourage confrontations and self-castigation as white feminists look at themselves, but also allow a lack of interest in and active ignorance about the complexity of current Afro-American politics to flourish, disguised as reverence toward an undifferentiated Afro-American experience.[2] In this intellectual climate, which eschews politics for identity, Clarence Thomas could pass himself off as a representative man of his race.

I

Shortly before Anita Hill first made her story public, *Tikkun* magazine published the proceedings of a roundtable discussion of a group of legal theorists and scholar-activists who had met under the journal's auspices to discuss the nomination of Clarence Thomas to the Supreme Court. Viewed retrospectively, the discussion was fraught with ironies, veins of ambiguity and dissension that would, upon Hill's revelations, crack open. The participants spent most of their time on a workaday debate about the merits of affirmative action, but when the conversation took a feminist turn, the exchanges generated some heat. What was Thomas's relationship to a broader African-American life? The legal scholar Kimberlé Crenshaw and the philosopher Cornel West gave a feminist spin to their answers, stressing the dangers of ignoring Thomas's roots in a conservative, patriarchal tradition. Certainly, West noted, Thomas "represents a historical strand of African-American culture, but it's a deeply reactionary—I would even say authoritarian—strand." Crenshaw, resounding in her absolute opposition to the nomination, emphasized the racism and misogyny that lay intertwined at its very heart. The right had succeeded in paralyzing a liberal opposition which, because Thomas was black, shied away from discussing what Thomas really represented. And that was, in Crenshaw's prescient view, "a very specific ideology about Black women—an ideology of put-down that is a growing phenomenon within the Black community."[3]

Before Anita Hill appeared, however, Crenshaw's comprehension of the centrality of sexual politics to the nomination was not widespread. Catharine MacKinnon, the sole white woman in the *Tikkun* discussion, has made her career as a radical feminist, not a liberal; indeed, she was recently featured in a cover story in the *New York Times Magazine* as the apogee of feminist militance, at least in legal circles. Her remarks nonetheless vividly illustrated Crenshaw's point about the blind spots of the left opposition.

MacKinnon began her reflections on Thomas ambivalently enough but quickly turned to pleasant observations about the candidate's credentials. It was Thomas's background—the "reality" and "life experiences" of his southern past—that swayed her toward a comfortable view of the nomination. In contrast to the critics who saw Thomas's use of autobiography in the hearings as an opportunistic evasion, MacKinnon saw the centrality of personal narrative, what she termed Thomas's "reality," as an emblem of political and intellectual potential. Never a woman to pass lightly over male failings, MacKinnon nonetheless warmed to Thomas as a man closer to "reality" than others of his sex. "I sense that he is connected with reality," she mused, "that he approaches issues from an actual experiential base rather than the kind of abstracted-from-life categories of legal analysis. . . . When he talks, he seems to start off with life experiences." As she waxed on about the virtues of Thomas's reality, MacKinnon fancied how she might share it, discursively, with the judge. "Liberals don't speak to the reality of people like Judge Thomas," she asserted, but she, the radical feminist, could: "I feel that I can talk to this man. My test is: will reality get in?" She then criticized women's groups for being too narrow-minded in opposing Thomas for his conservatism and what it implied about his position on abortion; his proximity to reality, she maintained, was far more salient.

"Reality" was of course Thomas's hardscrabble background, the biography of disentitlement that would, presumably, lead him to distrust—like MacKinnon herself—the legal fictions of abstract rights for all. Interestingly, in the face of Thomas's story of African-American manhood besieged and triumphant, this leading feminist found Thomas's studied detachment from the abortion issue to be unimportant. Surely all the women who carry unwanted pregnancies, including poor women from Georgia, have their own "reality," which might have entered into MacKinnon's assessment of Thomas. But then—and this is my point—some people's realities seem more real, more redolent of sentiment, more authentic than others'.

On one level, MacKinnon's remarks reveal only her own bad judgment and a flirtation with conservatives that goes back to the days she captained the antipornography movement in the mid-1980s. On another, they show how easily snookered even a sophisticated and militant feminist can be when the issue is racial identity. And on yet another, they embody a long romance of American radicals with some imagined folk authenticity, a form of left-wing condescension that looks for ideas from the privileged and "life experiences" from the poor. MacKinnon unwittingly drew upon a sensibility that since the turn of the century has attracted liberal and radical intellectuals to autobiographies of the working poor—especially those of men—as templates for a political progressivism comparable with their own. It would have been one matter for MacKinnon to make a case for Thomas on principled grounds, an analysis based on evidence from his publications and speeches, but this was the kind of reasoning she rejected from women's groups. It was, rather, autobiography that captivated her, and autobiography which she cited as evidence of Thomas's latent capacity for empathy for the socially and legally disadvantaged.

Missing in these meditations was any attention—even speculative or theoretical—to the patriarchalist elements of the autobiography that Crenshaw and West had highlighted. Absent was any sense that Thomas's experiences might make him antipathetic rather than sympathetic to those suffering from lack of privilege. There was not even a dash of intellectual caution about the uses of "reality"—a lapse striking in a thinker who has spent her career as a lawyer showing how self-serving and hollow are the versions of "reality" that men—sexual harassers, for example—can invoke to shore up their privileges. So Thomas emerged from MacKinnon's analysis as an incipient man of the people, one with his quirks, to be sure, but ultimately a person much closer to the authentic stuff of oppression and injustice than liberals with all their abstract gabbling about "rights."

II

What was this autobiographical "reality" that a leading feminist found so resonant with the promise of social justice? "Affecting, even inspiring," the *New York Times* called Thomas's story, a judgment echoed throughout the national media. In truth, Thomas's tale was a more or less conventional narrative of growing up black and male in the American South at mid-century, told not especially skillfully or eloquently. As many commentators observed, the story of growing up black was structured as a rags-to-riches tale of rising from obscure and humble origins to high places by dint of application and hard work. Less noticed was the story of growing up male, linked to the theme of uplift through the figure of Thomas's grandfather, a hard and determined, even authoritarian man whose fervent ambition and economic success against great odds inspired the young boy. Indeed, reading the story through a feminist lens, you notice that it turns upon the moment Thomas left his downtrodden mother to live with his grandfather. The breakup of his nuclear family released him and his brother from the downward pull of his mother's poverty and his tiny little Georgia town and propelled him into the orbit of his grandfather's high expectations and hard-edged racial pride. Fortified by a mission and a sense of self-esteem instilled by the older man, the autobiographical Thomas began his trudge upward from one modest achievement to another.

To give Thomas his due, his use of autobiography in the hearings was limited to a short sketch of his boyhood in the Georgia countryside, the hard days with his mother in a Savannah tenement after his father left them, and the happy times he spent with his grandparents and with the nuns in parochial school. He tried to balance his Algeresque claims to providential fortune by acknowledging the collective generosity from which he benefited along his way, the bred-in-the-bone altruism of the black people who helped to raise him and the lessons they taught him about the importance of helping others. But as the hearings proceeded, and Thomas refused continually to engage with questions about his legal, political, and philosophic positions, this restrained account expanded to fill the void and eventually came to dominate popular discussions of the nominee.

Thomas's rendering of his coming-of-age story cloaked the tropes of manhood in favor of those of a triumphant racial identity—the "uppity" black he would later invoke as the target of a conspiracy involving Anita Hill. But however buried Thomas's story of leaving women behind for an inspiriting masculine presence, that sublimated tale resonated with other male narratives, lending an otherwise shopworn "reality" emotional interest and credibility.

While political commentators raised questions about the inordinate role that Thomas's life story was playing in the debate over his confirmation, the opposition generally stayed clear of the story itself, leaving only a handful of black dissidents to express skepticism about the precise nature of his account. Law professor Patricia A. King, in testimony before the Judiciary Committee, sought to pry apart the conflation of reality, autobiography, and character by putting the narrative in the context of a broader Afro-American experience. "Virtually all of us over the age of forty have at least one exceptional grandparent who has been injured and severely humiliated by racism in America," she reminded the senators. King touched upon her own childhood in the segregated South, but stressed that she was reluctant to discuss her story in public—not because she was ashamed but because she refused to identify her family history with her "capacity to function effectively as an adult, or professionally as a lawyer and legal educator." Similarly, in *Time* magazine, editor Jack E. White gently criticized the ways in which Thomas was capitalizing upon experiences common to thousands of black Americans, including his own. He too had a heroic grandfather, who "despite poverty and racial oppression so harsh it seems almost unimaginable today" educated sixteen children. But "proud as I am of my family's achievements," White contended, "I know there is nothing unique—even uncommon—about the strides we've made."

Except for scattered voices, however, opponents treated Thomas's autobiography gingerly. Among feminists, who tend to look balefully upon male self-aggrandizement in any form, Thomas's invocation of racial oppression virtually immunized him to public interrogation about the gendered elements of his self-presentation. How much we had yet to learn from the women whose absences had been folded into the story!

III

From a feminist point of view, Thomas's rendition of the life of his sister Emma Mae Martin constitutes a minor scandal. In 1980, on the eve of Reagan's first inauguration, Thomas, then just a congressional aide, attracted the notice of nationally prominent ideologues with a speech before black conservatives in which he excoriated the effects of welfare on poor African Americans. To animate his generalities, he recounted the toll that government handouts had taken on his own family. "She gets mad when the mailman is late with her welfare check," he declared of his only sister. "That's how dependent she is. What's worse is that now her kids feel entitled to the check, too. They have no motivation for doing better or for getting out of that situation." Thomas was already learning to profit from presenting himself as a witness to a conservative public from the world of "real" Afro-Americans.

Martin's story, a journalist for the *Los Angeles Times* was to show, was quite different.[4] Martin had only been dependent on public assistance once in her life, during a severe family crisis. In 1955, after their house burned down, their mother sent Thomas and his brother to live with their grandfather and her daughter Emma Mae to live with an aunt in Pin Point. As Thomas began his upward climb through the educational system, Martin was still back in Pin Point, finishing high school, marrying, bearing three children, and raising them alone after her husband left her. While Thomas was attending Yale, she was working two minimum-wage jobs to support the family. When the aunt who had raised her suffered a stroke, Martin quit her paid jobs to take care of her and went on welfare. The four and a half years she lived on public assistance, caring for a disabled relative and her own children, were a brief interruption in a life otherwise spent keeping clear of welfare dependency in a town where black women pick crabmeat, or, as Martin does at present, cook on the night shift at the hospital. This was the woman whom Thomas implied was queening it about on handouts from the state.

Thomas's use of his sister's story in 1980 was more than accidental. He drew upon widespread hostilities toward women that conservatives were finding it easy to drum up, *especially* when the women were poor and even more so when they were black. The New Right's attack on social entitlements had gained momentum even before Reagan took office. As the feminist scholar Rosalind Petchesky observed astutely in 1981, the conservatives were mobilizing public support for their depredations of social programs by moving "in two interrelated directions: against social welfare and the poor, and against feminism and women."[5] The ghosts of supposedly lazy, parasitical black mothers floated about antiwelfare rhetoric; fantasies of willful and lascivious black teenage girls presided over cuts in public funding for abortion. It's essential to understand that while Thomas's public views on the equality of women were (and remain) prudently veiled and moderate, he launched his career in the national spotlight by exploiting an image of his own sister that was unabashedly racist and misogynist.

Kimberlé Crenshaw, in the *Tikkun* discussion, was one of the few feminists who fully comprehended the import of the Martin episode. Crenshaw fiercely drove home her case for the magnitude of Thomas's sexism. The Martin story, she argued, was meant "to capitalize upon existing beliefs about the poor, about Blacks, and about women— all of which come together in the image of the Black welfare queen whose plight is solely rooted in her dependence on the state." Crenshaw briefly and efficiently showed how different Thomas's life experiences looked when placed against his sister's: "the real story of the difference between Thomas and his sister is a story of gender and class. Namely, he was sent to school to be educated. She wasn't. She took care of people. He didn't. She probably took care of him, too." Indeed, Martin continued through the nomination procedure to honor family loyalties and her brother's well-being: she refused to respond to journalists seeking to muckrake the Thomas family history, and, in a show of solidarity, appeared in Washington to sit behind her brother at the hearings. Crenshaw stressed how Thomas's story of upward mobility was intimately related to—dependent upon—Martin's life of immobility.

Unfortunately, this aggressive feminist reinterpretation went unnoticed, at least in Washington; when the Judiciary Committee came to consider whether or not Thomas was lying about Anita Hill, no one thought to ask if he had lied about his sister. But by that time, the public was considering Thomas's relationship to women rather than to race issues, and Martin, the poor black woman, did not altogether register on public consciousness as a "woman." Rather, as a figure in a discussion of welfare policy, she was subsumed in a language of race, and there forgotten.

IV

In contrast to debates over welfare, the discourse of sexual harassment calls up the figure of a victim who is only a woman, nothing else. Anita Hill, who would be derided as a liar, schemer, and sociopath, was easily and properly recognizable as a victim of sexism. If contemporary feminism could not see Thomas's representation of his sister as absolutely critical to his qualifications, Anita Hill was, in contrast, instantly recognizable to us—despite her conservative politics—as a subject with whom we might empathize.

Hill's story, we now know, was immediately familiar to thousands of women. Her "experiential base"—to return to a phrase of MacKinnon's—was a realist narrative thick with details: a workingwoman's tale of insults small and large, of swallowing pride and shrugging off discomfort in the anticipation of career advancement, of feeling discomfort turn to humiliation and humiliation to mortification, and of vainly, chronically hoping it would all go away. It was a single woman's story of parrying sexual advances and interpreting sexual codes. If the polls showed that only a third of the nation believed Hill's accusations, that one-third was nonetheless mobilized, partisan, angry, and utterly solid in their support. Hill's situation was readily identifiable, her choices entirely plausible, and her dilemmas were well known to feminist scholarship and contemporary women's writing.

Hill recounted the details and characters of a working-woman's life—a roommate, a boyfriend, a backhanded flirtation with a neighborhood jogger (the dismal Doggett), a broken stereo. Thomas and his supporters, in contrast, conjured up a grand drama of male victimization that swept back and forth between ancient misogynist themes—the scorned woman, the woman as pawn—to Thomas's irresponsible and confused representations of Afro-American history, featuring himself as a martyred lynch victim. Thomas's testimony never dwelt on what he did but on who he was—a return to the autobiographical strategy: a loyal supporter of women, the benign patriarch of an extended workplace family, a colleague betrayed, a proud black man hounded and hunted down. Employing a language of manly defiance, Thomas drew himself as a victim of Hill's lies and the plots of her left-wing manipulators.

Incredibly, many people found this convincing. Hill's tempered, reasoned, and calm recital of places, names, dates and incidents—the entire context she created—came to be seen, against Thomas's oratory of wounded pride, as so fantastic as to constitute an episode of mental delusion. Contempt for women took an interesting turn away from pretraditional imagery of feminine duplicity to draw upon the terms of psychiatric modernism: Hill was a "sociopath," and perhaps we can be grateful that the Republicans threatened her only with perjury charges and not with commitment to a mental institution. Ironically, with Hill's "fantasies," we are back to "reality"—that essence with which Anita Hill, the sociopathic woman, lost touch but which grounded Clarence Thomas in the rich stuff of authentic and racialized masculinity from beginning to end. Thomas had set up his claim to racial reality long before, and although the narrative jump from affirmative-action kid to lynching victim outraged historians, it moved all those who had already seen him in their imaginations as a poor black boy catching minnows back in Georgia.

V

Feminists, of course, were unanimous in their ardent championship of Hill. Even the wavering Catharine Mac-Kinnon shifted gears without, as far as I know, so much as a mention of her brief rhetorical romance with Thomas and his life experience, and became a suitably severe network commentator on sexual-harassment law. Certainly, the great surge of feminist anger was heartening and the coming together of white and black women on this issue a cause for gratitude. The fact that Anita Hill testified at all, and that her accusations had such a stunning impact on national politics, testifies to the continuing power of the American women's movement, however diffused it may be; in Europe, where feminism is immeasurably weaker, mystified commentators could only sneer and chortle at the American "puritanism" about sex that fueled the controversy.

But certainly, too, the outcome was bitter, a dismaying revelation of the calamitous uses to which the right can turn the opposition between "blacks" and "women." How does a black woman who speaks of sexual oppression by a black man come to be seen as a white man's pawn? How does the black man whom she implicates come to represent oppressed African-American men? How did Thomas's autobiographical penumbra protect him from the suspicions that would easily light on a similarly bluffing, swaggering, belligerent man in any traffic court?

As Kimberlé Crenshaw so brilliantly put it in the early fall of 1991, this man climbed his way up over black women's bodies. His contempt for his sister came clothed as a conservative denunciation of poverty programs; veiled by the symbols of race and class, his misogyny went largely unremarked by feminists. His contempt for Anita Hill came clothed as a black man's brave stand against racism; veiled by the symbols of race and masculinity, his misogyny went uncontested among many black people. We are back at the divide of Reconstruction.

This time, however, white feminists have the immeasurable advantage of the fellowship—albeit tentative—which African-American feminists have offered. The interventions of a theorist like Crenshaw remind us how much more sharply and intelligently feminists black and white need to think about "race," not solely as an issue of the racist proclivities of white identity but as a paramount issue for women in our time. The shell game of identity politics—moving people from the "black" box to the "woman" one, and from the "woman" box to the "white" one—may protect white feminists from the uncomfortable business of learning and thinking aloud about male privilege in black politics. But unless we grow more skillful in our thinking and our tactics, as we learned, we have little to counter the conservatives' sleight-of-hand.

NOTES

1. Ellen Carol Dubois, *Feminism and Suffrage: The Emergence of an Independent Women's Movement in America, 1848–1869* (Ithaca: Cornell University Press, 1978). See especially, pp. 68–70.
2. These attributes, diffuse and half-conscious, are seldom spelled out but tinge the prevailing earnest tone in discussions of race. One effect, especially striking among literary critics, is to confine the understanding of the continuing complications of black politics and of Afro-American communities, both contemporary and historical, to an abstract and reified category—"race" —and then to inquire as to the extent to which white feminist work embraces this linguistic sign. For an example of this kind of earnest bad faith, see literary critic Jane Gallop's invocation of "race"—and her idealizations of African-American feminist critics—as the abstract powers that will free her from an intellectual romance with French postmodernism. It is striking that a white woman, in the name of antiracism, can talk unabashedly about black people as fantasy figures. (Jane Gallop, Marianne Hirsch, Nancy K. Miller, "Criticizing Feminist Criticism," in Marianne Hirsch and Evelyn Fox Keller, *Conflicts in Feminism* [New York: Routledge, 1990], pp. 363–64.)
3. All references to *Tikkun* come from the September-October 1991 issue: "Roundtable: Doubting Thomas," pp. 23–30.
4. Nicole Plett's research for me has located the story by Karen Tumulty in the *Los Angeles Times,* July 5, 1991, as the origin of subsequent discussion of Emma Mae Martin.
5. Rosalind Pollack Petchesky, "Antiabortion, Antifeminism, and the Rise of the New Right," *Feminist Studies,* summer 1981, p. 222.

NELLIE Y. MCKAY

Remembering Anita Hill and Clarence Thomas:
What Really Happened When One Black Woman Spoke Out

It was over in a few days, coming like a hurricane that whipped across the landscape of our lives, leaving a trail of wreckage and a less immediately apparent rainbow in its wake. On the surface of our busy days, the obscene spectacle ended, the shouting died down, newspaper editorial writers and op-ed–page columnists found more pressing subjects to pursue, and the almost unbridled fury that exploded from the nominee during the latter part of the Clarence Thomas Supreme Court confirmation hearings, in response to Anita Hill's allegations of sexual harassment against him, subsided into calm. In what appeared a return to business as usual, over the protests of many (though not the majority of the country), on November 3 a not unblemished Clarence Thomas was sworn into office and now serves on the nation's highest court. Given his present age and life expectancy, he may well hold that seat for almost twice as long as a large proportion of today's fif-teen-to-twenty-five-year-old American black men will live. How could a man whose character and fitness for the job raised so many serious doubts on the part of so many thoughtful, serious people (aside from the political interests involved) during the confirmation process still go on to be given so much power? Is it just politics, we ask, or once again a reminder that women's lives and words do not count for very much?

Her ordeal over, Anita Hill returned to Norman, Okla-homa, her supporters hope, to put the events of her har-rowing days in the glare of Washington, D.C.'s savage political arena behind her, and to resume the regular rhythms of her life. The faces, voices, and the ugly recrimi-nations that from our television screens, radio speakers, and daily papers bombarded our senses during those eventful October days receded, and the bitter, open quarrel be-tween these two well-matched, upwardly mobile, middle-class black people was no longer the focus of the entire country's attention. But some asked: could this really be the end?

For a brief span of time the eyes and ears of the nation and the world had focused on the unrehearsed, riveting drama of two intelligent, successful African Americans locked in an acrimonious public struggle over their good names and the measure of their characters. Nor was this a simple difference of opinion. Few issues could have been more explosive; there were no possible loopholes to claim misunderstandings of the past they shared: one, we know, told the truth; the other lied; and the stakes in their con-frontation seemed almost as high for both. By that time in the hearings, for Thomas, the results seemed likely to determine his defeat or success for the prize that represented the ultimate pinnacle of his career; for Hill, the outcome would be crucial to her ability to continue to build her own personal and professional future. Or we can reasonably assume that at least one of the principals saw it that way, and so did most onlookers.

Over the years, white Americans have grown accustomed to (and have even taken for granted) the appalling statistics on black-on-black crime among the least privileged of the group; never before had they had the chance to observe such a violent verbal disagreement of such personal dimensions between so articulate a woman and a man from among the privileged of the black race. Nor was this a private altercation inadvertently brought into public view, for in recent times sexual harassment in the workplace, regardless of the race or class or ages of the accusers or those accused, has become the single most crucial issue at the center of conflicts arising between women and men in every workplace in the country. When information on Anita Hill's allegations against Thomas and his denials first reached the media, she made clear that she would testify and openly reveal to the Senate and the nation the full nature of those allegations to "clear her name" of any suspicion that underhand motives prompted her to fabricate such awful charges against a man she knew, and on some levels, admired. So sure was she of her just position that she voluntarily took a polygraph test to prove her point. He, with a great display of arrogance, scorned the idea of submitting himself to such a test while he thundered and roared his denials, daring the white men chosen to decide on his fitness for the Court to deny him access to that seat.

Once an employee of Clarence Thomas's, and now a tenured professor of law, called to testify before the Senate Judiciary Committee, Hill recollected (in male locker-room language so vivid it must have sometimes embarrassed the roomful of white men to whom she spoke) the lurid details of her claims of Thomas's breach of professional conduct and his abuse of her in the early 1980s. Even at the time of the hearings Hill was not a willing witness, and on her own would not have come forward with the charges. When the abuses occurred, she had coped with them privately as best she could, and then let them rest. That she agreed to make the allegations public when she did was testimony to her understanding of her civic duty in conjunction with her religious training and her sense of moral responsibility. Called upon as she had, even against her will, she could do no less than tell the truth of her experiences as she knew them, as sordid as that was, and as difficult as she must have found the telling. And when the public aspect of this trial by fire was over for her, to some, Anita Hill was a traitor to her race; or a liar; or at best a pawn of left-wing political activists with interests opposed to President George Bush's; to others she had struck the most powerful blow yet, after two decades of feminist struggle, against the sexual harassment of women in the workplace. The end could not be in the Senate hearing room in Washington, D.C.

While Europeans, much more accustomed to sexual scandals in their politics than we are, generally wondered what the fuss was all about, throughout the hearings the fever of American interest in the case and in its outcome ran extremely high. Reasons for this interest were varied. On one end, there were those who enjoyed the prurient

titillation of the revelations—the legendary prowess of the
black male, his out-of-control sexual appetite that for generations gave white mobs license to perpetrate enormous
sufferings on the black community in the name of the
"protection" of white womanhood from the "beast"; on
the other end, there was a cross section of women in
particular with deep concerns about the long-term effects
of the exposé on Hill, and on the future of women's safety
from sexual harassment in the places where they work.
Many of these women, black and white, even felt that
future prospects of women's willingness to speak out
against this particular abuse—a recent phenomenon in
which the few who speak are extremely reticent—rested
on the outcome of Anita Hill's testimony.

Between those poles of interest some blacks who supported the importance of Anita Hill's testimony in the
hearings nevertheless worried about its implications. For
example, there were concerns for the possible polarization
effects such allegations could have on relationships between young black women and men, especially on those in
the professional middle class. Other people expressed genuine anxieties about the social costs of such public "washing" of the race's "dirty linen." But the larger majority of
African Americans, consisting mainly of the "folk" and
working classes, but including intellectuals and profession-
als as well, oblivious to or rejecting the social significance
of the racial-sexual politics in the drama they had witnessed, even believed that Hill's allegations were extrane-
ous to the single goal they admitted: the confirmation of
Clarence Thomas for a seat on the Supreme Court. In their
minds Thomas's rise from the humblest of black beginnings to the nominee for the post made him deserving of

that honor. In his favor some argued that in spite of his record to the contrary, once secure on the Court, he would remember his origins and support an agenda to benefit the least socially privileged. Early on, moderate and radical white feminists joined those who gave Hill their support, some unaware of the complexities embedded in a black woman's speaking out as she did against a black man. Nor, from the time that Hill spoke, were many people, white or black, women or men, neutral in their feelings on the merits of the opponents' positions: one either believed Anita Hill's clear and explicit accounts, or Clarence Thomas's passionate, boisterous denials of them. Those who supported Hill had not forgotten or counted for nothing that Thomas had been untruthful earlier in the hearings.

But even now the calm that followed that storm is hardly a settling of the events of those charged days in October 1991. For who can forget the image of an articulate, impressively calm, self-possessed, courageous Anita Hill before the Senate committee, one who must have known that in order to save his nominee, the president would stop at nothing short of attempting to ruin her reputation; or the treatment she received at the hands of the white men she faced in the Senate hearing room; or that the majority of those who heard her testimony either did not believe or willed themselves not to believe her story; or when they acceded her belief, negated her courage and integrity by feeling that notwithstanding the nature of the circumstances, Clarence Thomas deserved to be confirmed. These aspects of the events cannot easily be put to rest. By the end, too, it was clear that Anita Hill, youngest daughter of a poor but loving family, a well-respected law professor, would never be the same as she had been before she went to Washington that fateful week. Never again, even in Norman, Oklahoma, will she be able to retreat from the larger-than-life public person she was that day in Washington into the anonymity of a small-town law professor. Having disturbed the routine dealings of the political power brokers in the nation's capital, and having achieved more than thousands (maybe millions) of feminist and feminist supporters have in twenty years of campaigns to raise the consciousness of all Americans on the issue of sexual harassment, her life will never again be as it was before she raised those allegations against Clarence Thomas. But, then, never again will she have to contemplate, in private rage or shame, the secret that she held within herself (revealing it partially only to her closest friends) for a decade of her life. She had recovered for herself the power that Clarence Thomas once tried to take from her, and even the Senate's contemptible treatment of her had not scarred her quiet dignity.

Remembering Anita Hill and Clarence Thomas and those hearings now, one sees differently the winnings and the losses of those days than they appeared in late October 1991. And while on neither side was there a neat closure to the unfortunate events, and while for some there are still public doubts about who spoke the truth and who did not, nobody's world collapsed. For those who believed Hill, it is now much clearer that while she may have lost the battle of keeping Clarence Thomas from the Court (which was more her supporters' deep desire than her own), and while undoubtedly she will encounter unpleasant incidents and even career obstructions as a result of having spoken out, the larger war she may not have meant to raise is far from over. Most likely, she will leave the field of this struggle, at least as so public a player, but others will carry on, with renewed vigor, to press the case for women's right to safety from sexual harassment in the workplace, and their struggle will be easier because of what she did for six hours on one day in October 1991. For the first time since the struggle for women's rights began, it is now possible to be assured that all America's consciousness has been raised on this issue. On the other hand, in spite of his seeming victory, Clarence Thomas's "good" name, in spite of the support he received from the White House and his loud disclaimers of wrongdoing, is irrevocably tarnished. Until his death, ghostly shadows of Anita Hill's allegations will haunt his steps and more often than he may ever know cast doubts upon his public words. Anita Hill's case against Clarence Thomas did not close when the hearings were over; it rested.

At the same time, in spite of the powerful politically backed efforts to ruin her reputation (how many black women have so directly adversely affected a presidential choice and themselves been such direct targets of the president's anger and will to destroy them?), with the exception of those with motives to discredit her, it was difficult for many of us who saw and heard Anita Hill before the Senate Judiciary Committee during those grueling hours to find her testimony other than convincing and sincere. She was impressive; and in appearance and demeanor she confirmed the words of others who knew her well and later spoke on her behalf. Politically conservative, deeply religious, by temperament repelled by the nature of the allegations she made, but a woman of strength and integrity willing to stand behind those allegations, however painful that stance was for her, she would have needed years of drama lessons to perfect her act that day had she been other than what she appeared to be.

When she agreed to testify, Anita Hill was a woman confronted with the difficult choice of telling or not telling the dirty details of what millions of women in this country suffer daily and are too afraid to dare tell. And in her telling, millions of women identified with her, and understood perfectly well (even if some senators pretended they never did) the power relations that kept her from pressing charges against her harasser-employer at the time, and caused her to promote an amicable relationship with him long after she left his staff. During and after her testimony millions of American women of all races dredged up long-buried memories of similar harassments in their pasts and felt in Anita Hill's allegations the chance to finally exorcise uneasy ghosts they attempted to bury long ago. And other women, perhaps afraid to face compromises made with themselves for survival when they did, denied themselves and her the truth of the women's reality of which she spoke. But perhaps the greatest beneficiaries (besides herself) of Anita Hill's publicly uttering her allegations of sexual harassment against Clarence Thomas, a black man (one with influence and power), are the millions of black women for whom her action represented a further breaking of the bonds of generations of black women's silence on and denial of their differences with black men, because of gender issues, and their right to be full human beings despite the conflicts of race and sex. For in all of their lives in America, whatever the issue, black women have felt torn between the loyalties that bind them to race on one hand, and sex on the other. Choosing one or the other, of course,

means taking sides against the self, yet they have almost
always chosen race over the other: a sacrifice of their self-
hood as women and of full humanity, in favor of the race.

At the same time, shrouded in centuries of white and
black women's silence, and until recently perhaps spoken
only softly behind closed doors in the company of sympathetic women, women's allegations of sexual harassment
against men, a behavior that had no name until the 1980s,
are probably as old as our civilization. That the world never
heard those powerless voices makes them no less real or
anguished. As feminist studies of patriarchy confirm, male
domination of women over time was achieved through
various means, including the use of force against women's
sexuality. Recent scholarship also tells us that sexual crimes
against women, verbal or physical, are directly connected
to the exercise of power over and violence against them to
achieve the subordination of women. The history of black
women in America is the case study in how this will to
power, violence, and women's subordination coalese at the
intersection of race and sex. The story begins with the rape
of African slave women by white men across the Middle
Passage and on the plantations of the South, connects with
the black men who, during the Civil Rights Movement
boasted of practicing that assault on black women before
attempting it on white women, and joins itself to the white
and black men who even now, as the treatment of Anita
Hill by Clarence Thomas and the Senate Committee
demonstrated, continue to assault them with impunity.
Hill's testimony represented a strong rejection of that
racial-sexual oppression and the denial of the gendered self
that perpetuates black and white male power over black
women. For, as the group has discovered over almost four

hundred years in America, there is such a thing as racial-sexual oppression that is neither wholly racial nor wholly sexual, but as inseparable as the racial-sexual self. Individually and collectively, black women's struggle against their oppression occurs at the intersection where the sexual and racial sources of this oppression come together.

It was inevitable that race and politics should join together to be the most prominent factor in the Thomas nomination for the Supreme Court. Thomas, the second black person ever to be proposed for a seat on the bench, was preceded only by recently retired Justice Thurgood Marshall, the lone liberal voice on that body in recent years. Marshall's appointment, a racial-political choice made by President Johnson at the height of the civil rights era, was part of Johnson's far-reaching plans to reform the infrastructure of America's racially segregated and racially oppressive society. When the aged and ailing justice announced his retirement in the spring of 1991, after almost twenty-five years of service in the position, most people anticipated, correctly, President Bush's selection of a conservative Republican (black) man to replace the retiree.

But from the beginning the nomination created controversy. Predictably, many voices rose in opposition to the president's unabashed stacking of the Supreme Court with conservative justices, observing that Thomas would bring to the Court an entirely opposite philosophy on civil rights and women's issues, among others things, from Justice Marshall's. The more liberal Court on which Marshall served for many years had done much to promote the human and legal rights of blacks, women, gay men, lesbians, people with physical handicaps, poor people, the elderly indigent, and others who felt themselves deprived of their rights as human beings. In the opposition to Thomas the general sentiment was that in Marshall's work prior to and during his tenure on that body, over a period of almost fifty years, he had helped to shape some of the most important legal policies affecting the lives of people in those groups. Given Thomas's record, critics had good reason to feel that on the Court he would help to undo Marshall's achievements in areas like *Roe* v. *Wade* and affirmative action, although the latter initiative had enabled him (Thomas) to break out of his humble background to gain his social and career goals. In short, Thomas's appointment, the critics held, would insure a homogeneity of conservative political and philosophical consensus among the justices.

On the other hand, also in the national preconfirmation debate, a number of critics opposed the nomination on the basis of what they considered Judge Thomas's inadequate qualifications for a seat on the highest court of the land. Subsequently, the American Bar Association's very low rating of him seemed to confirm the negative estimation. In this regard, for many black intellectuals, liberals and conservatives, the president's assertion that his nominee was the "most qualified [black] person" for that seat was an insult to the African-American community (in which legal experts had suggested names of more qualified black conservative Republicans) and a gesture that undermined the bona fide intentions of affirmative action. Those who opposed him were further disheartened by Thomas's early appearance before the Senate Judiciary Committee: his evasion of questions pertaining to his positions on crucial issues to come before the Court in the near future, and his evident lack of truthfulness on the issue of *Roe* v. *Wade* were especially troubling. But the Senate committee was divided, and by the time of the official hearings, confirmation seemed likely. Without a doubt, the late news item of Anita Hill's allegations against the nominee gave the opposition hope for the nomination's defeat.

Like the president, but for far less devious political reasons and with purer motives than his actions suggested, the majority of black people who supported Clarence Thomas's nomination (before and after Anita Hill's allegations became public) did so because of his race, which for them far outweighed other considerations. Although Thomas had spent most of his forty-three years distancing himself from his lowly background, they identified with him on that basis. As the nominee for the Court, to them he symbolized the ultimate in black triumph over hundreds of years of racial oppression. For decades to come, his name will be held up as a model of achievement for countless young black boys and girls in his native Georgia and in places far and wide across this country. This identification with and support for Thomas is not difficult to understand, for it comes directly out of the long history of the racial oppression of Africans and African Americans in this country, beginning with slavery, passing through the postbellum years of legal segregation and other race-restricting social codes, and continuing in the present forms of discrimination that still deny millions of black people equal access to the promise of America. Buried deep in the collective black psyche, but never outside of easy recollection, is the knowledge that underlying racial oppression in this country are long-held white theories of the inherent inferiority of people of African descent. For numbers of black people, every major success by any black person puts a nail in the coffin of those theories and further advances the group. The Thomas nomination to the Court was, for them, another success for the race.

Consequently, for many black people, Anita Hill's speaking out against Clarence Thomas as she did, even in telling the truth, was an act of much larger dimensions than possibly undermining the credibility and fitness of the then-judge for the job to which he aspired. In the first place, any allegations she could make that cast doubt on the wisdom or rightness of the nomination of Judge Thomas to the Supreme Court would violate the racial taboo of revealing "family affairs" to the white world. But more serious than what might be ascertained an "inappropriate airing of dirty linen," in exposing a situation that called into question the sexual conduct of a black man, to those minds, Anita Hill committed treason against the race. This was the most serious infraction she could make against the understood inviolability of race loyalty. This loyalty espouses that the oppression that black men have suffered and continue to suffer at the hands of the white world entitles them to the unqualified support of black women, even to their self-denial. Interestingly, there are no circumstances that require such a sacrifice of black men.

In this light, for most African Americans the stand-off between Anita Hill and Clarence Thomas was a matter of grave concern that had deep roots in the troubled history of the group. In fact, black men have long contended that black women often work against the best interests of the race, and of its men in particular, in their relationships with white liberal men and feminists especially. While it is true that the women have been more mobile than the men, achieve social successes in larger numbers, and have more stable records of employment (although they have lower-status jobs and earn less than black men), that has partly been true because black women have more single-mindedly—not only for themselves but for all black people—pursued survival, and always were willing to do necessary work, however menial—work that white women and men have not wanted to do—to keep themselves and others alive. For example, seldom, no matter how difficult the circumstances of their lives, do black women leave their children to the mercy of the world; the absent father is both stereotype and, too often, reality in the black community. In addition, black women never spend the psychic energy doubting their womanhood that black men do in struggling to recover their manhood lost to slavery and to more contemporary black oppressions.

Yet even during slavery, when black men were unable to protect their womenfolk from either the whip or the master's sexual abuse, black men accused their women of cooperating with the white master against them. Since Emancipation, large numbers of black men, to say nothing of millions of black children, have survived because black women scrubbed floors, cooked thousands of meals, took care of children and the sick and/or aged, tolerated abuses of all kinds, and generally worked themselves into illnesses and early deaths in the houses of white people. And even as they took the benefits of these women's meager earnings, and in their shame abused the women too, black men accused these women of collaborating with the "enemy" to perpetuate the continued oppression of the men. From this perspective, one that had some of her supporters concerned for the effects of her testimony on the relationships of young women and men within the African-American community, Hill's allegations were another demonstration of black women's knowing efforts to destroy the upward social climb that black men find so difficult to accomplish.

And this was exactly the element that Clarence Thomas chose to exploit in making his vicious attack against Anita Hill in his rebuttal of her allegations. He pointed his finger, raised a thunderous voice to the Senate committee, and challenged the fourteen white men in that chamber to use Anita Hill's testimony to deny his confirmation. In calling the proceedings a "high-tech lynching," a vulgar display of temper or loss of self-control, he provoked and shocked his listeners, even some of his supporters. If the committee did not recommend his confirmation, regardless of sentiments entertained prior to the latter portion of the hearings, he would hold Anita Hill's testimony and white male racial discrimination responsible for his defeat. Thus, Clarence Thomas pointedly accused his former aide of that old bugaboo: black women's complicity with white men against black men. At the same time, since lynching is always (although erroneously) associated with race and sex, Thomas's evocation of the single most emotional issue at the heart of the black and white community's relationship further inscribed his determined use of racial-sexual politics to gain his ends. In this configuration, Thomas's abuse of Anita Hill in the Senate chamber was no less contemptible than his actions toward her a decade earlier. Many who listened to his tirade were angered by the travesty of Thomas reaching backward so easily to don the robes of a black past he spent all his life avoiding, only to trivialize the horrors of the lynching of thousands of innocent victims, women and men, by comparing his situation to theirs. And all in an effort to reach his goal of personal power.

But the bitterest irony of all was embedded in the figure of Clarence Thomas on the witness stand, defending himself against the allegations of a black woman, whose female forebears for many generations, when the dangers of torture and death for the innocent were imminent, protected their black men—fathers, brothers, sons, husbands, friends, and lovers—as best they could, from the ropes and fires his blasphemous claims profaned. As many have commented since those awful three days in Washington, what Thomas conveniently failed to remember about his history was that the lynching of black men always occurred as a function of terror aimed at the powerless and never at the president's handpicked men. Besides, no man, white or black, has ever faced death for the sexual abuse of a black woman.

In like manner Anita Hill met with open racial and sexual abuse at the hands of the white men on the Senate committee. Many who heard and watched her testify found it difficult to believe the venom in the compulsive need on the part of some of her interrogators to transform her character. Because Anita Hill is black and a woman, but fits none of the stereotypes of black women to which most white people are accustomed (the mammy, the slut, the virago, etc.) these men could find no reference point for her, and therefore she had no believability for them. That is why some had to make her over for themselves, imposing on her other images more comfortable for them. Consequently, in the deadly game of make-believe these men played, the intelligent, articulate, conservative, ambitious young black woman who faced the extraordinarily trying circumstances of the Senate hearing with dignity and calm became the delusionary opportunist who bided her time while she planned the destruction of Thomas for imaginary wrongs he did to her, the calculating, frustrated spinster whose amatory intentions toward her ambitious, aspiring superior had been rebuffed, and the woman rejected because of her insane sexual drive. Once vested with these images, these men could recognize her and find a place to fit her into their concepts of black women. Then they treated her as such. And so, by the end of the testimony against her, in the eyes of some, Anita Hill was no longer the brave young woman who captured the admiration of millions who saw her on their television screens. By then she seemed transformed into the dupe of left-wing political activists or white feminists, a vengeful lesbian feminist herself, or just an evil person bent on unwarranted revenge to ruin her former employer. Here was the triumph of the politics of race and sex at the highest levels of the government of the United States of America. A black woman had dared to speak out, had dared to claim her right to be heard as undivided "black" and "woman." And that was what happened when one black woman spoke out: attempted character assasination of a brave young black woman while a black man, under the shadow of doubts about his character and his qualifications for the job, was confirmed to the nation's highest court of law. It was the ugly game of power politics that confirmed how little value white and black men place on black women's lives.

But was that all that really happened? Absolutely not. In fact, Anita Hill was not transformed into something she was not. At no time during the proceedings did she give up the power in herself to those who tried to take it from her. In the Senate room her head was high and she was not daunted by efforts to intimidate her. And although it was clear that her testimony would have no effect on the vote from that exclusive aging white male club, when Anita Hill stepped from her plane back onto her home soil and greeted her well-wishers, the African queens from whose loins she sprung must have beamed on each other in great approval. In her quiet dignity, in the way she held her head, in her simple statement of determination to resume her rightful life and put the other behind her, and in the splendor of her own radiance, she was an unconquered African-American queen. Anita Hill was not destroyed by Clarence Thomas, neither in the early 1980s nor in the early 1990s. Nor was she destroyed by the senators who did their best to accomplish that, nor by the women and men who testified against her to that same end, nor even by the president of these United States of America. A proud great-granddaughter, she had nobly upheld the heritage of her regal African great-grandmothers and her slave-survivor grandmothers.

And now there is an account set up for the good of the nation from the proceeds of the legacy of Anita Hill's testimony at the confirmation hearings, which though it will continuously be spent will never be depleted. For years to come, at every level of American life, her role in the drama of Clarence Thomas's nomination to the Supreme Court will be a vigorous and controversial topic of debate. And while many Americans still do not understand its meaning, many more do now than did only a few short months ago, and there are none who have not now heard of sexual harassment or that there are laws to protect women from its abuse. Warriors against its evils are better armed than ever before.

And yet Anita Hill was not the first black woman to speak out in America. Contrary to what many others believe, black women in this country have never been silent, it is simply that often, in a racist-sexist disregard and even denigration of them, others do not listen, and therefore almost never hear their voices. From the poet Phillis Wheatley in the eighteenth century, to Maria Stewart, Frances Harper, Harriet Jacobs, Anna Julia Cooper, and dozens of others—writers, teachers, preachers, and women bent on social reform in the nineteenth century, to Ida B. Wells, Pauli Murray, and hundreds of twentieth-century women from all walks of life and members of all professions—black women have always spoken loud and clear. Anita Hill comes from a venerable tradition of women speaking out.

For example, in the nineteenth century a few people listened to and heard a black woman named Sojourner Truth, a former slave, religious mystic, radical abolitionist, and campaigner for women's rights speak out eloquently on the rights of all human beings regardless of race or sex. But Sojourner Truth was an unlettered woman whose words survive only because some who heard her wrote them down. Sojourner was never afraid to speak the truth, not even when at least one man charged that she was not a woman. A granddaughter of Sojourner Truth, like her forebear baring her breasts to prove her sex to disbelieving men, Anita Hill was not afraid to bare the sordid words that proved to white men in the Senate the assault that she claimed. This time they were forced to listen, but they did not hear, for what they thought they saw and heard was unrecognizable as the truth of what she spoke.

But in the aftermath of what occurred in Washington, we know that others heard, and will *bear witness*. Among them were thousands of outraged African-American women who closed ranks and spoke out in one voice against the seating of Clarence Thomas on the Supreme Court, and pledged to defend themselves and each other against the abuse such as Anita Hill received from Clarence Thomas, the United States Senate, and the office of the president. From now on they will protest loudly the racial-sexual politics that wantonly dismisses African-American women's experiences, or slanders their collective character. Neither Sojourner Truth, nor Anita Hill, nor any other African-American woman will ever be forced again to stand alone to speak while the power politics of race and sex are used against her in that way. And the coming together of these thousands of enraged black women in "defense of ourselves" after almost four hundred years of sacrifice for others was another and even more important thing that happened when one vulnerable and afraid, but brave and dignified, black woman named Anita Hill spoke out in Washington, D.C.—before the nation and the world—in October 1991. Anita Hill's case against Clarence Thomas, not closed, but wide open, is now the cause of thousands of African-American women united in opposition to the destructive power of racial-sexual politics. Borrowing from the words of Sojourner Truth, they seem to be saying: if one lone woman named Eve could turn the world upside down, then thousands of angry black women might certainly be able to turn it right side up this time.

MARGARET A. BURNHAM

The Supreme Court Appointment Process and the Politics of Race and Sex

When, on July 1, President Bush announced his nomination of Clarence Thomas for the Supreme Court, he stretched credulity by declaring that his pick was the "best man for the job on the merits." In the very next breath, as if to make his meaning crystal clear, the president went on to say that his choice of Thomas had nothing to do with "quotas," and that the nominee's life stood as an example of achievement that "speaks eloquently for itself."[1]

Although he could hardly have predicted the roller-coaster ride from July 1 until the nomination was approved in October, events were ultimately to prove the correctness of the president's hunch that in Thomas he had made a near-perfect pick. Even if his experience was sparse and his scholarship weak, Thomas fit the political bill like a glove. Indeed, at the end of it all, Bush had accomplished

more than he could ever have hoped for when he introduced Thomas to the country from Kennebunkport.

He had solidified the Rehnquist-Scalia block on the
court; had thrown to the black community a crumb it
could neither digest nor spit out; had given wedge politics,
which he hopes will keep him in the White House four
more years, a dry run; had thrown into national prominence a small but vocal band of black conservatives; and
painted the Democrats as a bunch of inept, braying jack-
asses who could not bring order to their own House, much
less a nation. From the beginning, Thomas was a gamble
for the Republicans, for they knew that it would be more
difficult to get him through the Senate than had been the
case with either of the two previous nominees, Justices
Anthony Kennedy and David Souter. But it was a gamble
that paid off royally. As one GOP strategist crowed after
the final Senate vote, "We won our nominee. We hurt the
Democrats. Everything beyond that is pure political
gravy."[2]

What was different about the political context of this
nomination fight that led to its success whereas the fight to
win a seat on the Court for Judge Robert H. Bork in 1987
had failed? How can we begin to untangle the powerful
and complex web of race and gender politics underlying
the Thomas appointment proceedings?

Prior to the Thomas appointment, the Bork campaign
was the defining point of departure, both for those engaged
in the struggle over the ideological balance in the federal
courts, as well as for those seeking to understand the seesaw
relationship among the three branches of national government. Judge Bork was by no means the first presidential

choice to be rejected—although none before him had suffered such a wide margin of defeat (58–42)—nor was he the first nominee over whom a battle royal was fought. The historic dimensions of the Bork struggle are to be found in the fact that, for the first time, the forces who favored and opposed the nominee launched large-scale, national campaigns. These campaigns triggered intense attention to the nominee by the Senate, including a wide-ranging examination of the judge by the Judiciary Committee that served simultaneously to engage the public in a national discussion about the Supreme Court and its work and to reveal the views of the committee members themselves about the Court.

The circumstances of the Bork defeat have been usefully detailed in a broad range of books and articles by observers and participants in the events. Herman Schwartz, in *Packing the Courts: The Conservative Campaign to Rewrite the Constitution,* suggests that Bork aroused and united hitherto disparate constituencies for whom the campaign was a forum to organize resistance to Reagan's largely successful effort to load the lower federal courts with young, white male conservatives of kindred ideology. Another account, *The People Rising: The Campaign Against the Bork Nomination,* by Michael Pertschuk and Wendy Schaetzel, provides a day-by-day view of the campaign, detailing how the coalition was held together, the relationship between national strategists and local activists, and the scope of an unprecedented presidential-candidate-style media campaign. Activists from the conservative side have written as well, most notably *Ninth Justice: The Fight for Bork,* by Patrick McGuigan and Dawn Weyrich. McGuigan, with Daniel Casey, head of the American Conservative Union, coordinated the fight for the nomination. His book, an inside story chock-full of deals and betrayals within the conservative camp, lays much of the blame for the defeat at the steps of the White House, which, it claims, failed to defend Bork aggressively.[3]

If conventional wisdom is any guide, President Reagan faced an uphill battle with Bork from Day One. Here was a president nearing the end of a long and contentious tenure, one hallmark of which had been his promise to rope in a federal judiciary that he viewed as too prone to legislate. In the nomination-confirmation waltz, his dance partner was a Senate led by the other party. These are just the sort of circumstances that have given rise to bitter confirmation fights in the past. Moreover, the nominee's famous paper trail provided much ammunition for his opponents and his haughty, abrasive personality cooled the enthusiasm of some of his would-be allies.

It appears that, in nominating Bork, the Reagan White House failed to evaluate these factors accurately when sizing up the likely opposition. This was not only a costly but unnecessary mistake, for the administration's experience in several earlier campaigns against its judicial appointments should have put it on notice that insisting on someone from the far right like Bork would invite havoc. The anti-Bork forces did not start from scratch in 1987, but rather had garnered experience in successfully opposing Jefferson Sessions's nomination to a federal district judgeship and unsuccessfully opposing Daniel Manion's to be a Seventh Circuit judge, as well as Rehnquist's promotion to the position of chief justice. The civil rights organizations had led these efforts; significantly, women's organizations and other groups had played a less central role.

Something else was in the Bork mix that augured ill for the president. Judge Bork was nominated to replace retiring Justice Powell, who had served as a swing vote between the liberal and conservative wings of the court. True, neither Rehnquist nor Antonin Scalia had been entirely acceptable to civil rights groups and their allies in the Senate when their nominations were considered in 1986. Rehnquist had been challenged for, among other things, his harassment of minority voters as a poll watcher in Phoenix, Arizona, and, in opposing him, Senator Kennedy had declared him to be "too extreme on race, too extreme on women's rights, too extreme on freedom of speech, too extreme on separation of church and state, too extreme to be Chief Justice." Although the committee vote on Rehnquist split thirteen to five, Antonin Scalia, whose name went up to the Senate at the same time, won unanimous committee approval even though, like Justice O'Connor before him, he refused to answer most questions, including one about his views on the seminal case of *Marbury* v. *Madison*.[4]

But it was apparent that Rehnquist's promotion and Scalia's appointment would not threaten the fundamental balance on the Court. Bork, on the other hand, especially now in synergistic combination with Rehnquist and Scalia, would surely mean a new court majority that might vigorously reach out to erase the Warren court's legacy and perhaps overturn *Roe* v. *Wade*. Thus his nomination struck a raw nerve among rights groups that were already alarmed about the aggressive reconstitution of the lower federal courts.

These groups were poised to act when Reagan named Bork. Their skills had been sharpened at the time of the

Rehnquist and Scalia nominations, which, as Ralph Neas of the Leadership Conference on Civil Rights remarked, "served as educational opportunities and laid a foundation for future battles." Kate Michelman of the National Abortion Rights Action League promised that if Bork were nominated there would be "an all-out frontal assault like you've never seen before." Bork's opponents knew that they had to gain the advantage quickly, bestir the senators' constituencies back home, and pull in a diversity of interests. Senator Kennedy, in declaring that "Bork's America is a land in which women would be forced into back-alley abortions and blacks would sit at segregated lunch counters" threw down the gauntlet on the very day of the nomination, giving pause to colleagues who might otherwise have announced themselves in favor too early. Black opposition was critical to the coalition, otherwise southern Democrats might yield to pressure from conservative factions in their states. Two key groups, the Leadership Conference and the Alliance for Justice, hired professional organizers for the first time to direct the mass campaign. Employing focus groups and polling techniques, media consultants helped pluck out themes that could most effectively carry the message that Bork's views were, in essence, un-American.[5]

But the coalition did more than shape the sound bite. Individual groups exhaustively researched Bork's record, and the results of that research were widely disseminated in appeal letters, press statements, and issue briefs. In the black community, radio talk-show hosts picked their way through law-review verbiage to remind their listeners that Bork had opposed the Public Accommodations Act when it was first proposed in 1964 and that he had criticized cases striking down the poll tax, restrictive voting requirements, and restrictive covenants in housing. The academic community added its voice, with almost 40 percent of all law teachers in the country on record in opposition to the nomination. Ultimately, hundreds of groups that had never before participated in a judicial nomination campaign—including, for the second time in its history, the ACLU—mobilized their memberships.[6]

In contrast, the campaign launched by the White House was late in starting and lazily focused. Apparently relying on the conventional wisdom that notwithstanding some opposition, Bork would be confirmed, Reagan did virtually nothing to show support for his nominee over the summer. Distracted by the Iran-Contra scandal and seemingly oblivious to the firestorm gathering around the corner, the president made one speech in late July in support of the candidate. To the despair of conservatives on the right, he compared Bork to Justice Felix Frankfurter, and the White House sought to cast their man as a Powell moderate. By the time the hearings had commenced, the polls showed Bork's initial support falling off, and the president responded by calling a few senators, but it was too late to recapture the initiative. The view of the authors of *Ninth Justice* is that the White House intentionally soft-pedaled Bork's views and discouraged conservative groups from aggressively defending him because it thought such support would backfire by giving credence to the opposition's claims that Bork was the intellectual guru of the hard right. Whatever the strategic reason, White House support was too little too late.

In his testimony before the Judiciary Committee Bork provided generous explanations of his views, but failed to allay the concerns of the members that his appointment would threaten the hard-won but yet unstable national consensus about the Supreme Court's role in protecting civil rights, privacy, and First Amendment rights. Of particular concern were Bork's views decrying as inappropriate the Court's leadership in civil rights. While restating his opposition to precedents dating back more than twenty years, he told Senator Kennedy that the poll tax was no big deal because it was "just a $1.50."[7]

Echoing the explanations many senators gave as to why they could not support Bork, Senator Lawton Chiles (D-Florida) noted that "I thought the question of [the] poll tax [was] a settled issue."

Senator Bill Bradley (D-New Jersey) put it this way:

> Above all, white America must assure black America that the legal basis for black advancement remains unchallengeable and the determination to enforce the law remains unquestioned. The Supreme Court is the ultimate guarantor of that assurance. We must have a Supreme Court that understands the need to make opportunity a reality for minorities who historically have been excluded from jobs, from schools, from full participation in society.[8]

Senator Alan Cranston (D-California) worried that appointing Bork "would reopen heated debates over civil rights, abortion, and a host of other issues that could tear our Nation apart."[9]

By all accounts, the overwhelming opposition of blacks to Bork was the engine driving the campaign against him. The Democrats owed their control of the Senate to newly elected southerners whom black voters had helped elect.

After Bork's testimony, polls showed that his support dropped significantly in the south; the day following the close of the hearings, ten senators, many of them southern Democrats, announced their opposition to Bork, and the next day, a majority of the Senate were lined up in the nay column. When the final vote was taken, every southern Democrat except one voted against Bork, and most pronounced that they cast their votes because of Bork's hostility to the Court's role in protecting civil rights. Interestingly, President Reagan decried the defeat of Judge Bork as the dirty deed of a "lynch mob" and he bemoaned the use of "sophisticated modern technology to distort a distinguished man's public and private views."[10]

Four years to the day after Reagan presented Judge Bork to the American people, President Bush introduced Clarence Thomas. In selecting Thomas, and then in securing his confirmation, the White House demonstrated that it had thoroughly absorbed the hard lessons of the Bork defeat. Again, southern Democrats and their black constituents were the key, but this time, with a pleasant, conservative black nominee, the White House was sure it could win them over.

Black support, it was hoped, would cancel out opposition from prochoice forces. That a wedge could be driven right down the middle of the old anti-Bork coalition was evident from what was now known about the conflicts confronted by those who helped construct that coalition— conflicts that echoed long-standing tensions among rights supporters. Black groups organizing against Bork had been reluctant from the beginning to work with abortion rights groups. Dissension within its ranks had compromised the role of the Leadership Conference. With this nomination the White House could exploit these rifts to good purpose.

The strategy showed promise the very day after Thomas's nomination was announced. On July 2, relying on his EEOC record and his Heritage Foundation speech praising Lewis Lehrman's antiabortion article, Kate Michelman pronounced the nominee unfit, while Douglas Wilder, not yet a Democratic presidential candidate but close to it—and who was himself seen as the well-behaved black who could save the Democrats from Jesse Jackson—endorsed him. Senators Kennedy and Patrick Leahy (D-Vermont) took a wait-and-see tack, as did People for the American Way and the Alliance for Justice. When the NAACP held its national convention in early July, it reserved judgment on the nominee, and, at its annual meeting, the more conservative Urban League declined to take a position. Even though his views were fairly well known from his two previous confirmation hearings, instead of launching right into a grass-roots campaign as had been done with Bork, Thomas's potential opposition undertook a review of his record during the summer months and essentially bided time until the hearings.[11]

In the meantime, in contrast to Reagan's disorganized approach in the early life of the Bork campaign, the Bush White House wasted no time in packaging their nominee. Media strategists double-voiced the famous Pin Point story to show, on the one hand, the strength of the nominee's character, and on the other, the verity of GOP claims that even the poorest American can make it to the top without government help. The story ultimately came to assume the mythic dimensions of other character-trait sagas about American political figures—Lincoln's log cabin, George Washington Carver's peanuts. Thomas was the "young man from the provinces" who started on the farm, went to the city to face life, and ended up on the top of the Hill. The story tapped into the American faith in the virtues of small-town life and in the character-building qualities of the migration experience. Photographed with an elderly Pin Point neighbor who had traveled by bus to Washington, Thomas's message was that "I have left Pin Point, but Pin Point has not left me." Early in the process the whole country thus became invested in Thomas's success and transformed into a cheering squad for their "local black boy made good"—if he can, anyone can, and if he can't, none of us can.

Under the guidance of Kenneth Duberstein, a former Reagan aide, and Fred McClure, a black Bush strategist, Thomas, again in contrast to Bork, made all the right moves on the Hill before the hearings. In visits to more than fifty senators, he presented himself as humble, deferential if not obsequious, an ordinary guy with an extraordinary story, the kind of black man a white senator—especially one from the South—could feel comfortable with. The counterpoint to Thomas's good character portrait was a virulent TV ad attacking the personal ethics of Democrats Kennedy, Cranston, and Biden— from which, after it had done its damage, the White House disassociated itself.

In the meantime, the sidebar to the Thomas stories was the news that black conservatives were the new voice to be reckoned with in the public-policy debate. The nomination represented the ascendency of a political force that hitherto had been "squelched" by the so-called civil rights orthodoxy. That these "new arrivals"—black Republicans—had been around for years without making any significant political inroads among African Americans—Bush got just 10 percent of the black vote in 1988—was conveniently ignored. Thomas, Dinesh D'Souza, Glenn Loury—these people were now being touted as the cutting edge of black political expression—the black antidote to the purveyors of the "politically correct."

By the time the hearings began, the conventional wisdom was that the momentum was with the nominee. No one expected that his testimony would be informative as to his constitutional views. Largely because Court nominees Souter and Kennedy had been allowed to deflect the tough questions that were on every senator's mind, Thomas, too, would be permitted to obfuscate. It was Justice Kennedy who, following on the heels of Bork's "tell all" approach, had shown that success in the hearings involved side-stepping the abortion question while supporting settled civil rights jurisprudence, the general right of privacy, and general principles of stare decisis.

When Thomas finally testified, Pin Point became a cloak wrapped around his shoulders, shielding him from the senators' softball missiles aimed at exposing his civil rights record. In his opening statement he reminded his listeners once again that "as kids [in Pin Point my brother and I] . . . caught minnows in the creeks, fiddler crabs in the marshes; we played with plovers and skipped shells across the water." He had attended segregated schools and, as a college student, majored in English literature, because, he said, he found it "painfully difficult" to speak correct English. Who in that caucus room could challenge him on his commitment to black rights.[12]

For their part, the Democrats on the committee appeared not to have a strategy for approaching the nominee.

The irony here was that Thomas was more vulnerable than any previous nominee—at least since Rehnquist—on civil rights matters, because, unlike the previous nominees, he had made his career as a civil rights basher. His Heritage Foundation speech lauding Lerhman's views and the statements he had made about natural law merely hinted at the nominee's abortion position, but his record on civil rights was ample and unambiguous.

But, apparently intimidated by the Pin Point story, the senators barely asked Thomas about the policies he followed at the EEOC, where he had been Reagan's hatchet man. He had sat by while his agency's budget was chopped in half and its caseload jettisoned. From 1980 to 1987 the EEOC's caseload was cut back 300 percent. A General Accounting Office study found that by 1987 the agency's district and state offices were closing 40 to 80 percent of their cases without proper investigation. Moreover, Thomas had led the ideological charge against affirmative action. But when he was questioned by senators about his views and his record, he silenced them by reminding them that "it should be clear from my biography that I understand that racism exists."[13]

Preferring instead to explore his thoughts on natural law—a subject not easily translatable into talk-show jargon—the senators missed an opportunity to expose fully the nominee's role as a prime civil rights backlasher. Accordingly, black public opinion was not as sharply mobilized by the hearings as it could have been.

Women, on the other hand, did not see Thomas as the threat Bork had been on abortion. On gender equality, the aim of the White House was to defuse women's concerns by casting questions about Thomas's civil rights record as an ideological dispute about the politics of how to achieve equal justice—i.e., should minorities benefit from quotas—rather than as a substantive debate about whether his actions in, for example, abandoning pay discrimination cases on behalf of women constituted a calculated disregard for the laws he was supposed to be enforcing. EEOC Vice Chairman Rosalie Gaull Silberman dismissed complaints that Thomas had dumped thousands of sex- and age-discrimination cases as "amount[ing] to nothing but politics." His opponents didn't like Thomas, she said, not because of anything he had done to harm the interests of women but because he was "not politically correct."[14]

By soft-pedaling Thomas's role in the Reagan-Bush assault on civil rights, the Democrats committed a double foul. In the first place, rather than exploit the opportunity to reveal the cruel cynicism of Bush's opposition at that time to the new Civil Rights bill (which would have embarrassed the bill's chief Republican sponsor and Thomas mentor, Senator Danforth), the Democrats virtually conceded the success of the Republican effort to unravel public support for civil rights progress by waving the "quotas" flag. Secondly, their gentleman's approach to the nominee's civil rights record took moderate Republicans who proclaimed themselves to be pro–civil rights, like Pennsylvania's Arlen Specter, a swing vote on the committee, off the hook. Specter told some of the witnesses against Thomas, "I would suggest his character is shown more by his roots than his writings. Why not rely on his character?"[15]

In view of the fact that the polls had held for Thomas throughout the hearings, and that when they started, Senator Howell Heflin and perhaps committee chairman Joseph

Biden seemed prepared to vote with the nominee, the committee's split vote came as something of a surprise. Early in the hearings, Heflin had said he was generally satisfied with Thomas and would probably vote for him. But in the end, he voted against him along with six other Democrats, explaining that he had to vote his "conscience" and that Thomas's disavowal of his previous views troubled him. Other committee Democrats cited similar reasons for their opposition—his refusal to explain his judicial philosophy, and his disavowal of his past stands harshly criticizing affirmative action, mocking the congressional process, and suggesting opposition to abortion. Senator Kennedy complained about the "vanishing views of Judge Thomas." More than a rejection of Thomas because he was anti–civil rights, the Democrats' vote appeared to speak to their frustration with a process that discouraged meaningful dialogue on the nominee's views.[16]

But again the committee Democrats might well have been in a stronger position to influence their southern colleagues had they stated plainly that Thomas was unacceptable not because he appeared to be a prevaricator but because his record showed him to be anti–civil rights. As it was, the confused Democratic message provided little guidance either to the public or to the rest of the Senate. It was, for example, difficult to follow the logic of Senator Heflin's argument. He had initially supported Thomas, knowing full well what his record was. But he voted against him because Thomas moderated his views at the hearing. What if Thomas had stuck with his earlier positions? Where would that have left the senator? The judge was saying, in effect, "I'm not the ogre my opponents have made me out to be. I'm really a nice guy." And Heflin's response, in effect, was, "I think you really are an ogre and you're lying when you claim you're not. If you had just stuck to the truth, I would have voted for you."

We now know, of course, that when they voted, the committee members had Professor Anita Hill's report in hand. One wonders whether this inside information, and the fear that it might not remain confidential, may have led some senators like Heflin, who would otherwise have voted for Thomas, to be more cautious.

In any event, even after the committee failed to recommend him, it appeared Thomas had the votes he needed in the Senate. By September 27, the day of the committee vote, nine Democrats had announced their intention to vote with the forty-three Republican senators, and in the days before the Hill allegations became public, four others declared they would vote to confirm. But everything changed once Hill's charges became a page-one story. Ironically, Thomas would probably not have been able to hold on to these thirteen Democrats had the Senate voted as scheduled on October 8—two days after the Hill allegations became public. But after the hearings, ten of the thirteen—including seven southern Democrats—voted for Thomas. None of the three Democrats who withdrew their support after the hearings were from the South.

When Thomas finally squeaked by the Senate with a vote of 52 to 48, many in the media pointed to women's groups and the traditional civil rights leadership as the big losers. After Thomas's testimony the president gushed about the strength of black support for his nominee, and, in the postmortems after the vote, in almost euphoric prose, the media reported that the gender gap had all but disappeared, with both women and men strongly supporting Thomas. What exactly did the polls reveal, and what is the political significance of what happened to the nomination after Professor Hill made her charges?

An opinion poll conducted for ABC News and the *Washington Post* showed a pronounced shift in the views of both men and women from the time Hill's charges became public on October 6 until the time of the Senate vote. Initially, women's support for Thomas dropped significantly more than did that of men, but ultimately both groups concluded he should be confirmed. Before anything was known about Hill, a four-point difference separated the sexes; 65 percent of the men and 61 percent of the women thought Thomas should be confirmed. But shortly after Hill's charges were aired, women's support dropped to 43 percent and there was a gap of eight points between men and women. That gap increased to a whopping sixteen points after Hill's testimony, with 43 percent of the women and 59 percent of the men believing he should be confirmed. But on the day after the hearings closed, the gap had returned to just four points, with 61 percent of men and 57 percent of women agreeing that Thomas should be confirmed. On the question of whether they believed Thomas or Hill, both men and women believed Thomas over Hill two to one, with, again, a negligible four-point spread between the sexes.[17]

The polls showed little difference between the views of married and unmarried women, or between women who work outside the home and those who do not.[18]

That women initially opposed confirmation after the Hill charges became public but then, even after Professor Hill's persuasive and highly credible testimony, came around to support the judge, suggests that the calculated White House strategy of smearing Hill struck its mark.

More significant than the gender gap was the gulf between whites and blacks. In the first place, black support for the nominee, which was well over 50 percent, jumped five points in the aftermath of the hearings, while white support, on the other hand actually dropped about five points from September to the end of the hearings. Among blacks, over one-third thought the judge should be confirmed even if the charges were true, while only one-fifth of whites felt that way. When asked whether Thomas had been the victim of racism in the hearings, more than twice as many blacks as whites—43 percent to 20 percent—said they thought he had been. Along the same lines, when a different pollster inquired whether the respondent thought the charges were "an orchestrated campaign to discredit the nominee's character," three out of every five black respondents answered yes, while whites divided more narrowly, with a 49 to 41 percent plurality assessing the charge as part of an orchestrated strategy.[19]

There is reason to suggest that the "believe Thomas" numbers may in fact not have accurately reflected the true feelings of those polled, but rather signaled a peculiar case of cognitive dissonance. These figures for blacks and whites as well as for women and men may have been somewhat inflated as some respondents perhaps grappled with the discomforting realization that although they doubted Thomas's testimony, they felt that he nevertheless should be confirmed.

Certainly, a significant number of blacks believed that even though guilty as charged, the man should not be denied a Supreme Court seat. It is difficult to say whether these African Americans supported Thomas because they did not consider sexual harassment to be disqualifying conduct, or because they believed that Thomas, even if he had done what he was charged with, should not be victimized by what they perceived to be racism on the part of the Senate committee, or whether they felt that as a black man, Thomas deserved confirmation no matter what the circumstances.

Coupled with the poll data, the anecdotal evidence generated by man-in-the-street interviews and the like suggests that Thomas triggered intense feelings of racial solidarity among blacks who were, first of all, embarrassed in a "let's not wash our dirty linen in public" sort of way by the hearings; secondly, on guard against what they perceived to be white political machinations targeting a black public figure; and thirdly, gratified to see a black man picked for the Supreme Court. That Thomas's ratings went up among blacks after the Hill hearings, while he experienced a slight erosion of support among whites, suggests that black support did not represent an endorsement of Thomas's politics as much as it did sympathy for a black man being undressed in front of white people. How else to explain why he was more favorably viewed *after* being accused of such horrible conduct than *before,* especially when one-third of the blacks who supported his confirmation thought he was guilty of the charge.

Now to the question of "dirty linen." For many African Americans, the Thomas-Hill dispute was *not* about how men treat women, but about how black men and women relate to one another—a long-debated subject about which strong feelings run deep. Within African-

American political and cultural life the question of how to accommodate gender tensions has always been linked to black perspectives on white racism and how best to struggle against it. Although it is now generally accepted that male chauvinism hinders the efforts of black men and women to build strong relationships, there is a fairly widespread view that nothing is to be gained from public discussion of the black male-female conflict because, first of all, whites will intentionally exploit these gender tensions to sow disharmony within the race at a time when racial unity is needed, and secondly, white opinion of blacks will be negatively affected by what they learn about their gender and sexual conflicts. These views were advanced by critics of Alice Walker when the film *The Color Purple* was released and by those who felt Ntozake Shange's *For Colored Girls Who Have Considered Suicide When the Rainbow Is Enuf* exposed too much about the anguish black women feel about their relationships with men. When Michelle Wallace's *Black Macho and the Myth of the Superwoman* was published in 1979, she, too, was attacked for similar reasons. As one commentator, Julia Hare, publisher of the journal *Black Male/Female Relationships,* wrote:

There is no question now that more black women are angrier than before. Some of us have never hesitated in recent times to hawk our misplaced rage in the white man/woman's marketplace—"For Colored Girls . . ." "The Black Macho . . ." "Sistuhs . . ." *ad infinitum;* and there will be more of the same in this new wave of what Tony Brown so aptly calls the "marketing of black male inferiority."[20]

Even if her charges were true, then, Anita Hill should not have exposed Thomas before 200 million white folk, but rather the dispute should have been kept within the family, the argument goes. (It bears mentioning here that typically the "washing dirty linen" taboo seems to strike complaining black women—as opposed to black men—with particular force. Few have criticized Spike Lee's *She's Gotta Have It,* or, more recently, *Jungle Fever,* for letting the white world in on black gender problems; perhaps the exemption for this artist—who has taken to new heights the commercialization of black sexual interaction in all its complexity—is related to the fact that his work is not about women seeking to unloosen themselves from the constraints of traditional notions of sexuality, as was that of Walker and others.)

African Americans were more prone to accept Thomas's defense that it was he who was the victim than were whites. When, after the hearings, Bush spokesman Marlin Fitzwater was asked what Thomas meant by a "high-tech lynching," he suggested the reference was to Senate Democrats and civil rights leaders, and went on to say that "blacks are going to question whether these [Democrats] have the right to tell them how to think." But more likely than not, blacks who bought into Thomas's "lynching" defense did not specifically have the committee's liberal Democrats and the civil rights leadership in mind. The backdrop, rather, was a bitter history of public attacks on black male public figures—assaults that often, indeed, were conspiratorial in nature and, too, that often involved charges of sexual misconduct. King the womanizer; Adam Clayton Powell the Bimini beach bum; Malcolm the criminal. And more recently, William Gray, at the time chairman of the Democratic National Committee, maligned by a Justice Department leak. The great majority of blacks only focused in on Thomas closely in the wake of Anita Hill's charges. For these observers the abject cynicism of the "lynch" accusation would have been difficult to discern without the political context of Thomas's anti–black rights record. They would more likely have seen the conflict as yet another attempt to reduce a powerful black man to his genitals, and thereby ruin him.[21]

The conspiracy theory takes on yet another layer here when one considers the nature of the charge against Thomas. Because sexual harassment is seen as a plank in the white-feminist program, the views of many blacks about white feminists kicked in to shape their feelings about Hill and Thomas. *Jet* magazine, covering Thomas's Rose Garden swearing-in, reported that one Thomas supporter who was in the Senate hearing room said of the hearings, "The only folk the senators noticed were the White women opposing Thomas and the Black people rallying for him."[22]

For some, then, the contest was between a black man and his allies and white women (read "feminists"). Longstanding black resentment and impatience with feminism undoubtedly rendered some more receptive to the not-so-veiled GOP charge that those "orchestrating" the charges were women's groups angry with Thomas because of his suspected views.

Not only have blacks been influenced by the last decade's antifeminist backlash, carefully detailed in Susan Faludi's recent work *Backlash,* but contemporary antifeminist ideology piles on top of fairly widespread and longtime black antifeminist thought, the basic tenets of which are (1) that white women are competitors for jobs that

312 / RACE-ING JUSTICE, EN-GENDERING POWER

might otherwise go to blacks, and that, because of the potency of racism, the women are better positioned to get those jobs; (2) that the complaints of white feminists are less compelling than those of racial minorities, or, put another way, what right does Anita Hill, a well-educated lawyer, have to complain about harassment on the job when more black men are in prison than in college; and (3) that feminism has driven a wedge between black women and men and thereby crippled blacks' ability to fight racism.[23]

The misogynist epithets that were hurled at Anita Hill were no doubt absorbed by many African Americans both in the context of these hostile views of white feminists and through the murky lens of black male-female interaction. Was she the spurned woman? For some blacks, the real proof of this lay in the fact that Thomas had married a white woman, therefore—in this view—rejecting Anita Hill in a particularly painful way. Was she the treacherous betrayer? Indeed, yes, bringing down the black man in the same manner as, for example, Marion Barry's ex-girlfriend cum FBI collaborator. Did she act out of ambition, and was she stridently aggressive? (As one pro-Thomas witness exclaimed to the senators, "The Anita Hill I knew was nobody's victim.") Indeed, yes again: she was yet another example of a black woman seeking to advance at the expense of a black man, just as white feminists advocated.[24]

Was she being used? In a political world in which groups "rank-order" priorities, many blacks heard in Hill's voice not the anguish of a black woman who had been abused, but the soundtrack of a white-feminist agenda. Some feminist commentators who were featured in the media perhaps unwittingly fed into this sense that it was feminists against blacks. When, for example, Tom Brokaw asked Catharine

MacKinnon whether sexual harassers tend to be repeat offenders, she answered, "Well, I hate to put it this way but he's not dead yet." She clearly was not thinking about how that might sound to a black woman in small-town Georgia—the constituency that mattered here more than any other. Blacks hearing white feminists speak that way about the nominee were more likely to credit the GOP claim that Anita Hill was being used; Hill, an intelligent black woman, would not, of her own volition, seek to kill or "lynch" a black man. She therefore had to be a pawn.

Undoubtedly, the failure of traditional civil rights groups to effectively defend Anita Hill contributed to the perception among blacks that this was not their issue. Most civil rights opinion-makers were ambivalent about the Hill charges. Even after her persuasive testimony few could be heard condemning Thomas's alleged conduct or even taking the tack that many of the politicians assumed—sexual harassment is abominable, but it may not have been proved here. Into this vacuum stormed the White House, with its suggestion that Anita Hill was the instrument of a lynching orchestrated by feminists to further their own agenda.

Black views of feminism are as much shaped by unthinking adherence to stereotypes about the role of women as by genuine concerns about the plight of African-American men. At a time when even the national media have taken to referring to black men as an "endangered species," many blacks felt it unseemly to attack a self-made man like Thomas.

Some who study black life and sexuality have articulated the view that black males whose masculinity is beseiged by American racism may compensate by sexually aggressive behavior. But this perspective lends support to ancient myths about black men's sexual prowess. The challenge for blacks who consider these issues is to locate an approach that acknowledges the complicated reality that has been created by a racism that seeks at once to confine black masculinity and to manipulate white fears of the black male sexual aggressor. The Thomas conflict landed in the middle of that discourse.

Thomas used these contradictions to his advantage when, with evident frustration, he told the senators that although he had faced many barriers in his life and overcome them, he could not overcome "this process." And he was appealing directly to black men when he said "this [charge] plays into the most bigoted, racist stereotypes that any black man will face. If someone wanted to block me because of my views on the Constitution, that's fine. . . . But to destroy me [by this caricature]. I would have preferred an assassin's bullet." Although many whites could not comprehend his meaning in as much as his accuser was herself black, African Americans understood him to be saying that, once again, a black man had been stripped of his humanity, his capacity to think, dream, lead, and love, and reduced to an erect penis.[25]

Finally, Thomas understood how to manipulate class divisions to generate support among blacks. Pin Point is the story of millions of African Americans who, in Thomas, saw the possibilities for their own success enlarge. The buttons worn by Thomas's Georgia neighbors who lined the halls outside the caucus room read, IF CLARENCE CAN, I CAN TOO! Even as they comprehend the tremendous obstacles created by racism, blacks want fervently to believe that they can live out the American dream—that hard work and prayer will land you on top. Civil rights groups criticized Thomas as unworthy of Thurgood Marshall's seat because of the nominee's record. But some blacks saw another message in the comparison. Marshall was not of the grass roots; he was part of the "civil rights establishment." Thomas's reference in the hearings to skin color as perhaps a factor in the conspiracy against him was a subtle appeal to blacks who feel left out of an elite middle class. *Jet* magazine reported the comment of a GOP historian that Thomas's victory represented a "victory of the Black men over the yellow men. . . . Light-skinned Blacks down through history have dominated the scene. During slavery, the Blacks were the field hands. Then came the age of mulattos. Now the mantle of self-imposed color limitation has been lifted. We don't have to rely only on Black people who are light skinned."[26]

If Thomas and his strategists skillfully pushed all the right buttons to win the black grass roots, they also knew how to create a groundswell of sympathy among whites. White Americans seek tangible proof that our social institutions and political systems are fair and rational. Like blacks, they want to believe that hard work will be rewarded, no matter how humble a person's beginnings. Clarence Thomas was, for them, living proof that racism is not as bad as some have claimed. His life represented, finally, a reconciling of American ideals of just rewards and the American reality of racial prejudice. In faulting "the process" that he had not been able to overcome, in calling it Kafkaesque and McCarthy-like, Thomas tapped into the way Americans express their sense of decency. Was it fair that he should be stymied when he was so close to his dream by a ten-year-old charge of using offensive language? Most Americans felt not.

Given the dense complexity of these crosscurrents of race, gender, and class attitudes, could the Democrats have done anything to try to affect a different result? Whether the result would have been different, of course, one cannot say with certainty, but surely the Democrats misstepped at a number of critical turns in the proceedings. The mistakes made in the initial handling of Anita Hill's complaint were fully ventilated at the time of the hearings. But there are a number of other areas that have not received the attention they deserve.

In the first place, by failing, during the first hearings, to hold Thomas responsible for his abominable civil rights record, the Democrats missed an opportunity to shore up black opposition to the nominee. As it was, when the Hill charges were aired, most blacks still knew little about the nominee except that he had had it tough coming up. Likewise, women were not mobilized because of Thomas's anti-women's-rights record so far as civil rights is concerned; rather, abortion became the central issue of women's rights organizations, and the senators followed suit.

In the second place, by refusing to state clearly the substantive grounds for their opposition, Democratic committee members like Heflin abdicated their responsibility to provide leadership to other Democratic senators. Southern Democrats and black constituents alike would perhaps have responded differently if Heflin had said that he was voting against Thomas because his civil rights record was unacceptable.

Thirdly, once the second hearings began, the committee

leadership did a tremendous disservice by announcing that the burden of proof was on the accuser, and that Clarence Thomas was entitled to the benefit of the doubt. Senator Biden, a lawyer, was just plain wrong in analogizing this procedure to a criminal trial. The burden of proof is a method by which the law allocates the risk of a wrong decision between two contesting parties. In a criminal case, where the defendant stands to lose his freedom, the law assigns the risk of a wrong decision to the state, which must prove guilt beyond a reasonable doubt. In a civil case, the risk of a wrong decision is shared by the parties.

Prior to Professor Hill's charges, it was quite clear that Thomas bore the burden of proving to the Senate his fitness to serve on the Supreme Court. That was as it should be. Anita Hill's charges were clearly relevant to the question of Thomas's fitness, and should have been considered on the same basis as all the other material that came before the committee. That is to say, Thomas should have been required to show that, notwithstanding the allegation, he was a fit nominee. Senator Kennedy had it right when he said that "in a case of this vast magnitude, where so much is riding on our decision, the benefit of the doubt should go to the Supreme Court and the American people."[27]

The consequences of this error on the part of Senator Biden were quite grave. The polls showed that not many of those watching the hearings were unequivocally sure whom to believe. In one poll over 60 percent of those surveyed could not say that the allegations were more "probably" true or false. A firm majority of those questioned felt it was unlikely the charges would definitely be proven true or false. In these circumstances, where the burden of proof had been placed on Anita Hill, a viewer whose mind was in equipoise would likely be of the opinion that Thomas should be confirmed. Since the polls were a heavy influence on the votes cast by the senators, the improper allocation of the burden of proof and the consequent distortion of the polls was a serious matter. Moreover, by telling Thomas that he enjoyed the benefit of the doubt, the committee opened the door for him to, in effect, decline fully to participate by claiming he hadn't heard Professor Hill's testimony.[28]

Finally, getting the burden of proof wrong from the beginning provided a convenient fig leaf for those senators who, when it came time to vote, wanted to have it both ways. Many took the floor to denounce sexual harassment out of one side of their mouths while claiming they had to vote for Judge Thomas because he was entitled to the benefit of the doubt. Senator Boren's comment was typical: "In my mind, Judge Thomas has not been proven guilty. When the hearings began, the presumption was with Judge Thomas because he was the accused, and the presumption remains with him today because the hearings were inconclusive in my mind and to many Americans." Senator Larry Pressler (R-South Dakota) issued a press release with the headline "Pressler Votes for Thomas, Praises Hill." Senator Larry Craig (R-Idaho) announced a new office policy to protect women from sexual harassment in the course of his Thomas endorsement speech.[29]

Notwithstanding the much-ballyhooed changed national consciousness on the question of sexual harassment in particular and gender relations in general in the wake of the Thomas nomination, rights advocates lost ground in the ideological battle over issues of race and gender equality. In a political sleight of hand that has served them well elsewhere, the right appears to have succeeded in co-opting the issue of sexual harassment while damning the very feminists who first brought it to the American public. After the vote Bush attacked Thomas's opponents as "women activist feminist groups" seeking to derail the nomination for their own purposes. "We saw some people that wanted to bring this man down for reasons having nothing to do with sexual harassment, but we also saw the prevailing wisdom of the American people."[30] And in Clarence Thomas the right has a powerful symbol to perpetuate their view of America as a fair place full of opportunity for all who work hard.[30]

Above all, what this nomination process taught is that black progress and progress for women are inextricably linked in contemporary American politics, and that each group suffers when it fails to grasp the dimensions of the other's struggle. It will take careful strategies and strong coalitions to reverse these setbacks.

NOTES

1. "Bush Announces the Nomination of Thomas to Supreme Court," *Congressional Quarterly Weekly Report,* vol. 49 (199), p. 1851.

2. Quoted in Tom Wicker, "Waltz of the Democrats," *New York Times,* October 20, 1991.

3. Herman Schwartz, *Packing the Courts: The Conservative Campaign to Rewrite the Constitution,* (New York: Scribners, 1988); Michael Pertschuk and Wendy Schaetzel, *The People Rising: The Campaign Against the Bork Nomination,* New York: Thunder's Mouth, 1989; Patrick McGuigan and Dawn M. Weyrich, *Ninth Justice: The Fight for Bork* (Washington, D.C.: Free Congress Research and Education Foundation, 1990).

4. Nomination of Justice William Hubbs Rehnquist, Hearings Before the Senate Committee on the Judiciary, 99th Cong., 2nd sess., 1986, pp. 15–16.

5. *"served as educational opportunities":* Cohodas, "Reagan Leaving Conservative Mark on Courts," *Cong. Q. Weekly Rep.,* vol. 44 (1986), p. 2729; *"all-out frontal assault":* Cannon and Kurtz, "Senate Leaders Give List of 10 Possible Nominees," *Washington Post,* July 1, 1987; *"Bork's America":* Congressional Record, vol. 133, S9188 (daily ed., July 1, 1987).

6. Nomination of Robert H. Bork to be Associate Justice of the Supreme Court of the United States, Hearings Before the Senate Committee on the Judiciary, 100th Cong., 1st sess., (1987), pt. 3 of 3, p. 1899 (statement of Senator Biden) (hereinafter Bork Hearings).

7. Bork Hearings, pt. 1 of 3, p. 129.

8. *"poll tax a settled issue":* Cong. Rec., vol. 133, S14,981 (daily ed., October 23, 1987); *"above all, white America must assure":* Cong. Rec., vol. 133, S12,984 (daily ed., September 29, 1987).

9. *Cong. Rec.,* vol. 133, S13,119 (daily ed., Sept. 30, 1987).

10. Informal Exchange with Reporters, *Weekly Comp. Res. Doc.,* October 12, 1987, p. 1143.

11. "Group Opposes Thomas," *Boston Globe,* July 3, 1991.

12. "Thomas Spars with Committee over Natural Law, Abortion," *Cong. Q. Weekly Rep.,* vol. 49 (1991), p. 2643.

13. *He had sat by while:* "Critics Renew Charge Thomas Flouted Law at EEOC, *Boston Globe,* July 3, 1991; "EEOC and State Agencies Did Not Fully Investigate Discrimination Carges," U.S. General Accounting Office, October 1988, Report on the EEOC by the House Education and Labor Committee, 1986; *"It should be clear from my biography":* "Deflecting Tough Questions, Thomas Stumps Senators," *Cong. Q. Weekly Rep.* Vol. 49 (1991); p. 2623.

14. "Critics Renew Charge," *Boston Globe,* July 3, 1991.

15. "Thomas Hearings Illustrate Politics of the Process," *Cong. Q. Weekly Rep.,* vol. 49 (1991), p. 2692.

16. "With a Split Vote over Thomas, Panel Sends Bush a Message," *Cong. Q. Weekly Rep.,* vol. 49 (1991), p. 2787; *"vanishing views":* ibid., p. 2688.

17. The polling data comes from the *New York Times,* October 15, 1991; *USA Today,* October 14, 1991, October 16, 1991; *Washington Times,* October 16, 1991, October 20, 1991; "Political Fallout from Thomas Vote," *Cong. Q. Weekly Rep.,* vol. 49, p. 3028 (citing the Washington Post/ABC News Poll).

18. "Public Tends to Believe Thomas by 48% to 35%," *Los Angeles Times,* October 14, 1991.

19. *black support up 5 points:* ibid.; *more than twice as many blacks: USA Today,* October 14; "an orchestrated campaign": *Los Angeles Times,* see note 18.

20. Julia Hare, *"What Next, Black Women," Black Male/Female Relationships,* November–December 1979, p. 4.

21. "Bush Hopes for Gains with Blacks," *USA Today,* October 16, 1991.

22. Clarence Thomas, "I Give God Thanks that The Senate Approved Me," *Jet,* November 4, 1991, p. 5.

23. Susan Faludi, *Backlash: The Undeclared War Against American Women* (New York: Crown), 1991.

24. "Woman with Guts Puts a Scare into America," *Los Angeles Times,* October 17, 1991.

25. "For the Record," *Cong. Q. Weekly Rep.,* vol. 49, p. 3071.

26. *Jet,* November 4, 1991, p. 6.

27. "With Thomas Edge Steady, Senators' Vote Due Today," *New York Times,* October 15, 1991.

28. *Los Angeles Times;* see note 17.

29. *Boren:* "With Thomas Edge Steady, Senators' Vote Due Today," *New York Times,* October 15, 1991; *Pressler and Craig:* "Sex, Race, TV: 'Explosive' Mix," *USA Today,* October 16, 1991.

30. "Bush Says He Would Have Favored Closed Sessions," *New York Times,* October 18, 1991.

WAHNEEMA LUBIANO

Black Ladies, Welfare Queens, and State Minstrels:
Ideological War by Narrative Means*

Let's face it. I am a marked woman, but not everybody knows my name. . . . "Sapphire" . . . or "Black Woman at the Podium": I describe a locus of confounded identities, a meeting ground of investments and privations in the national treasury of rhetorical wealth. My country needs me, and if I were not here, I would have to be invented.

—Hortense Spillers

A society is possible in the last analysis because the individuals in it carry around in their heads some sort of picture of that society.

—Karl Mannheim

*I believe Anita Hill's account. This reading of the discourse around Hill's allegations, however, is not dependent upon believing her. I am deconstructing here the ways that meanings are constructed and/or influenced by power in the debate that went on as a result of her charges, the ways that public discourse is influenced by activating salient and preexisting

There are pictures that function as *cover stories* in and of themselves; they (both the pictures and cover stories) simultaneously mask and reveal political power and its manipulations. Cover stories cover or mask what they make invisible with an alternative presence; a presence that redirects our attention, that covers or makes absent what has to remain unseen if the *seen* is to function as the *scene* for a different drama. One story provides a cover that allows another story (or stories) to slink out of sight. Like the "covers" of secret agents, cover stories are faces for other texts, different texts. They are pretexts that obscure context, fade out subtexts, and, in the case of the Clarence Thomas hearings, protect the texts of the powerful.

On the twelfth and thirteenth of October, the *New York Times* juxtaposed photographs of Anita Hill and Clarence Thomas. The chronology and context of these juxtapositions were important. They articulated a particular ideo-

---

narratives. My essay turns textual analysis into a lens focusing on the overlap of political, economic, and cultural issues. One does not have to believe Hill, or to see her as a feminist, a worker-saint, or another Rosa Parks in order to think about, recognize, or map the workings of power, or to examine the ways in which the engine of the United States' political economy runs, as I argue here, on the fuel of certain cultural politics. Hill did not choose to quit her job and wait tables, to be a word processor, or to do anything else that might have made her a more politically sympathetic, "attractive," or "authentic" victim. That she didn't does not preclude our attending to the operations of power in this historical moment, or our examining how narratives of race and gender undergird the political economy of the United States; how those narratives appeared during and in the hearings; and how they continue to allow the political status quo to resist change. Clarence Thomas's position and repositionings were the manifestation of a sophisticated set of power deployments. Notwithstanding Hill's much-discussed "ambition" and notwithstanding what might be her complicity in the Reagan and Bush administrations' hamstringing of the EEOC, in this historical moment Anita Hill is not the articulation of state power. Clarence Thomas is.

logical salience, not the least because of the subliminal effect of the placements—occurring at the particular points in the hearing when they did—as narrative shorthand for, first, pretense of thematic balance, and then, reassertion of business as usual:

1. October 12, when the outcome of the second hearings seemed undecided, at least in the media's explicit discussions, photographs of the two ran side by side. Identically posed, Hill and Thomas were pictured with their right hands raised for the swearing-in. The placement of the photographs suggested their equality before the sight of those watching this spectacle taking place before some bar of justice, in front of an oversight committee.

The side-by-side visual equality of representation obscured the dramatic disparity of power hidden by the juxta-position: Thomas, head of the EEOC, judge, and friend of powerful men, chosen for his position and admired by our head of state, beneficiary of the apparatuses of state power—and a man who would be among the most power-ful if confirmed by the Senate, next to a woman professor of law, holding a faculty position at a state university, and whose photograph was reproduced in the newspaper be-cause of Thomas's alleged transgressions. This insistence on foregrounding the *individual* nature of accusation and re-sponse—regardless of where one lays the blame—was characteristic of much of the media's discussion of these proceedings.*

2. Twenty-four hours later, pictures of Hill and Thomas were again juxtaposed, only by then much had changed. Thomas had declared himself to be the victim of a "high-tech lynching" and the two photographs ran after calls responding to the televised hearings had begun to come into CNN, other television stations, and various radio talk shows around the country. This time the photographs were placed on the page next to the headline "Theater of Pain." Discussion, at least as the corporate and/or main-stream press was recording it, seemed to be cohering around the idea of Thomas as the central figure in that "theater." In this photographic arrangement, the mission-ary position is assumed, or resumed, male on top, female on bottom. *This* placement, a representation of gendered

---

*I use "individual" perjoratively here because I am examining the prob-lem of discussions of this moment that insisted on seeing individuals outside of political power. Individuals are always wrapped in larger world narrative contexts. The problem with constructions of mythic individualism is that their ties to power go unnoted.

power relations, was the visual harbinger of the newly, if only implicitly, established discovery of a new "American" hero: Clarence Thomas, man under siege and warrior for the reassertion of order and the law.

These pictures, through their timing and their spatial arrangement, were signposts for a successful set of narrative constructions, activations, and deployments by the state* —including what people are reminded of when certain categories, phrases, and abstract figures with political resonance are evoked. State power did its work by virtue of its invisibility and because it is embedded in the public's understanding of everyday occurrences and beliefs. Photographs, such as those I discuss here, and other salient narratives, are the means by which sense is made in and of the world; they also provide the means by which those who hold power (or influence the maintenance of power)

---

*By "state," I mean both the system of formal governmental and economically influential entities of executive mandate, legislation, policy-making, and regulation—the president, his Cabinet, administration—and economically and politically powerful legislators, as well as the "common ideological and cultural construct" that "occurs not merely as a subjective belief, incorporated in the thinking and action of individuals [but] represented and reproduced in visible everyday forms" (Timothy Mitchell, "The Limits of the State: Beyond Statist Approaches and Their Critics," *American Political Science Review,* vol. 85, no. 1 [March 1991], p. 81). Among those "everyday forms" I include things like the constantly evoked concerns over categories of thought like "threats to national well-being" or "American-ness," or, clichéd and (often conservative) commonsense understandings about gender and race.

In other words, when I speak of state power in regard to Thomas's position in the confirmation hearings, I'm bringing together, for example, the actual workings of the executive branch of the government—concretized here in my use of "President Bush" or "the state"—on behalf of Thomas; the various connections that Thomas's career has had to powerful and influential government and economic entities and individuals; *and* the ways that the national public reproduced state concerns and interests in their understandings of and responses to the Thomas-Hill events.

make or attempt to make sense of the world *for others*. Such narratives are so naturalized, so pushed by the momentum of their ubiquity, that they seem to be reality.[1] That dynamic is the work of ideology.

As a result of the "work" done by such narratives, Thomas's own power was masked; that power and the state power that supported him throughout the debate were naturalized as his "dignity," "character," and "integrity."* Those three words, used as descriptions of his basic essence, were divorced from any sustained attention to the history of his behavior, career record, or written philosophy. His "integrity"—which seemed to be based largely on some historical integrity accorded his grandfather's occupation as sharecropper, for example—was simply and unquestionningly accepted. Because the interrogation of his actually existing judicial and political record was muted, no mechanism existed that would have supported a challenge to this integrity.

Newspapers, radio programs, and television networks, stations, and programs, need not deliberately contrive to make absent certain narratives by presenting others; it is unnecessary that the work of (or on behalf of) power go on via conspiratorial agreement or arrangement. Such work goes on because the media, along with other public and private entities (including institutions, churches, schools, families, and civic organizations, among others), constantly

*There were honorable exceptions to this general silence on Thomas's history; much of the alternative, noncorporate (and nondaily) press and their writers (e.g., *The Nation, The Village Voice, The Progressive, In These Times, Extra, Lies of Our Times,* and *Z Magazine*) were consistent in their depth, comprehensive and insightful in their analysis and their reportage. Additionally, at least one electronic network, the Activists Mailing List, was active in disseminating information about Thomas and his background.

make available particular narratives and not others. In turn, such consistently reinforced presences reproduce the world in particular ways: what we see becomes what we "get," what we believe. The photographs I refer to above represent visually, first, the seemingly equal position of accuser and accused, and then, the reassertion of the customary dominance of male and institutional authority back in its rightful place: order in the court, here comes the judge. Thomas was the cover text and the pretext. Here the subtext—the disappeared, the absent—was the narrative of power. Those photographs, however, are only the surface manifestation of narrative ideological battle.

A particular set of narratives did battle for this confirmation. A specifically nuanced "blackness"* was constructed and strengthened by narratives preexisting in the national historical memory around two figures, the "black lady" and the "welfare mother" or "queen" in such a way as to do battle on behalf of power.[2] Categories like "black woman," "black women," or particular subsets of those categories, like "welfare mother/queen," are not simply social taxonomies, they are also recognized by the national public as stories that describe the world in particular and politically loaded ways—and that is exactly why they are constructed, reconstructed, manipulated, and contested. They are, like so many other social narratives and taxo-

---

*Here, by "blackness," I mean conscious awareness by an individual of being part of a group—Negroes, black Americans, Afro- or African Americans—with a particular place in history and a political relationship to other groups within the geopolitical site of the United States. Blackness is also a way of referring to the existence, as a socially constructed fact, of that group.

nomic social categories, part of the building blocks of "reality" for many people; they suggest something about the world; they provide simple, uncomplicated, and often wildly (and politically damaging) inaccurate information about what is "wrong" with some people, with the political economy of the United States. They even stand for threats to ideas about what the relationship of the family to the state ought to be.* Welfare queen and black lady were and are cover stories that shielded the text of power—by being extravagantly displayed narratives already in circulation and engaging our attention—before, during, and since the Thomas hearings. And against that backdrop, Thomas functioned as a minstrel—not as an unwitting or ignorant dupe but as a power figure who drew on and articulated— from behind his black skin surface—white state power.

I argue that the narrative, or the cathected set of narratives signaled by the category "black women," or represented by the place of individual black women as they are figured in the arena of cultural politics, is what made it possible to mobilize wider support for Thomas. More, I suggest that those narratives can work and did work as a form of shorthand, functioning effectively even when their content was and is not explicitly spelled out. As is the case with words such as "woman," "character," "merit," or "decline in the American way of life," these particular

---

*Kimberlé Crenshaw also notes that the plight of the welfare queen is "solely rooted in her dependence on the state" ("Round-table: Doubting Thomas," *Tikkun,* vol. 6, no. 5 [September-October 1991], p. 27.) But my intention here is to map the ways in which mere economic dependence gets figured in narrative terms as an allegorical cover story of moral or character failing and draws our attention away from the political economy to a different "spectacle" altogether.

narratives' contents have been constructed over time and transformed to fit the requirements of maintaining the present terms of the U.S. political economy.

Because of their historical and political salience, the welfare queen and the black lady are two figures who exist as narratives guaranteed to mobilize support for Thomas's confirmation from almost every sector of U.S. society. Those figures constitute a constellation of ideas about women, family, economics, and cultural well-being; and their narrative deployments in the interests of maintaining the status quo dissolve the line between "real" and "cultural" politics. The most immediately recognizable figure, the welfare queen, is omnipresent in the media—even when (and perhaps especially when) she is not explicitly named. Given a couple of centuries (and, in the corporate and/or mainstream press, an especially intense couple of decades) of seeing and hearing the behaviors and economic position of poor African Americans laid at the door of their "problematic" family structure and/or culture, given the various ways in which every large urban newspaper and most small-town newspapers remind us of the "blight" (political, social, and economic) of the cities, and given the ubiquity of political and community figures whose commentary focuses on attributing the "decline of the nation" to the urban poor and the inappropriateness or inadequacy (take your choice) of state intervention against those problems, the welfare queen is omnipresent in discussions about "America's" present or future even when unnamed. All of those things are constantly in the news (not that welfare queens were ever much out of the news)—urban crime, the public schools, the crack trade, teenage pregnancy are

WAHNEEMA LUBIANO / 333

all narratives in which "welfare queen" is writ large.*
(Recently the *Moynihan Report* is itself back in the news.)

It is difficult to conceive of a "normal," an unprob-
lematic, space in our historical moment for black women
outside of the demonic-narrative economy of the welfare
queen or the betrayal-narrative economy of the black-
lady overachiever—both figures about which Moynihan
warns. And deploying the two narratives does double
duty for the machinations of the powerful. What comes
out of and is supported by the *Moynihan Report* is alarm at
the existence of two problems: the single black female
parent (more explicitly central as a policy problem) and
the (less central and, thus, meriting less *explicit* attention)
black female overachiever. The two figures' pernicious
hold on the national imagination constantly springs to
devastating life in the service of ideology. What seems to
"threaten" the individual Clarence Thomas? What is
used, finally, to discredit both Anita Hill and Emma Mae
Martin as individuals? Their existence as social narratives.
How do the two function as narratives? What constantly
invigorates them? Those narratives work not simply by
virtue of what is said within the narratives themselves,
but by what is called on that is connected to them. What,
then, are we being asked to remember? In the economy
of the Thomas-Hill discourse, a set of tropes were mobilized on Thomas's behalf, among them the culture-of-
poverty discourse. How might those tropes have been

*In other words, "welfare queen" and "black lady" are socially con-
structed categories, similar to those that Spillers describes as "markers so
loaded with mythical prepossession that there is no easy way for the agents
buried beneath them to come clean" (p. 65).

tacked onto Hill and Martin, the other, less-discussed woman?

The ways in which narratives that mark those figures were embedded in the debates around Hill and Thomas are complex. For many people, Thomas occupied almost mythic ground in this discourse; he articulated and seemed to embody the Horatio Alger success myth, the ultimate American individual—and lest we forgot that he embodied the myth, countless media commentators reminded us that he did. His story moved along three equally salient axes: (1) he was proof that anyone, any individual, can succeed who tries hard enough; (2) he was just an individual with a right to privacy like anyone else; and (3) he represented, in fact embodied, an entire history of black men oppressed by a more powerful group. Against that background, Thomas's much less visible, and certainly unarticulated (in most forums), connections with powerful people, and the differences between Thomas's treatment within his family and that of his sister, were "disappeared."

Thomas and his grandfather became, within the economy of those myths, the bringers of order, of law—against chaos, against anarchy—the male figures so desperately needed in (and missing from) Moynihan's "black family." Thomas's mention of his grandfather functioned to invoke nostalgia for a golden age when black men were real men (and present in their families), a nostalgia that could find its desired object in Thomas himself, the present-day embodiment of that age. Thomas made of himself not a "man" but an empty mythical vessel into which the state could pour what it needed and then attempt to make all of us consume it as blackness, an ineffable "blackness," in order to draw attention away from what we were actually consuming: yet another narrative of state power.

The lesson implied by the *Moynihan Report* (as well as the vicious "common sense" of certain policy-makers and social commentators), in many ways the Ur-text for the simplistic "culture of poverty" discussions as they are represented in the media,[3] is that the welfare-dependent single mother is finally the synecdoche, the shortest possible shorthand, for the pathology of poor, urban, black culture. Responsible for creating and maintaining a family that can only be perceived as pathological compared to the normative (and thus allegedly "healthy") family structure in the larger society, the welfare mother is the root of greater black pathology. But the flip side of the pathological welfare queen, as Moynihan's own language tells us, is the other kind of black woman—the black lady, the one whose disproportionate overachievement stands for black cultural strangeness and who ensures the underachievement of "the black male" in the lower classes because "ours [the U.S.] is a society which presumes male leadership in private and public affairs."[4] And because the culture of African Americans seems not to fit into this pattern, Moynihan tells us, it "is placed at distinct disadvantage."[5] There we have it. Whether by virtue of *not achieving* and thus passing on bad culture as welfare mothers, or by virtue of *managing to achieve* middle-class success via education, career, and/or economic successes (and thus, I suppose, passing on genes for autonomous female success?), black women are responsible for the disadvantaged status of African Americans.

Make no mistake about it: in the grip of a recession, with political figures outdoing each other to shift the blame away from the structural inadequacies of the political economy and its effect on all of the poor, most of the working class, and an increasingly larger share of the middle class, the lines between real and cultural politics disappear in the creation of all-purpose scapegoats. Before, during, and since the Thomas hearings, the decline of "America" has been linked somehow to the popularly despised vision of its being or threatening to become a "welfare state." With that specter constantly before U.S. citizens, the adjective "welfare" demonizes anything that follows it, something that David Duke—only the most extreme and dramatic articulator of a narrative that we can read in any newspaper almost any day of the week—learned and recently manipulated in Louisiana very well (even if he was ultimately unsuccessful in getting himself elected). What welfare mothers/queens and black ladies—as cover stories that draw our attention away from the abuses and failures of our political-economic structure—also do is to undermine the notion of family (actually existing families as well as normative ideas about the family) as entirely private, individual, and not connected to the state or the collective public.

Between the specters of Emma Mae Martin—denounced by Thomas as an example of "welfare dependency" (read: welfare queen)—on the one hand, and Anita Hill—embodiment of black-lady status—on the other hand, the confirmation of Thomas could be viewed as necessary to help save the life of the nation, which might otherwise go down the tubes trying to fight the pathology of the urban black poor dragging at its heels. Here, as in other times, black women function as the narrative means by which the country can make up its mind yet again about a whole set of issues. Of course, that Hill was single (as well as middle-class) helped; in that way she could be painted as the ultimate threatening outlaw—a loose cannon, out to subvert the "family," the "American" family. What Thomas's confirmation process needed was just that kind of "outlaw" to make an appearance so that the "hero" could emerge. To many African Americans, Thomas's distortion of his less fortunate sister's situation was a mean-spirited and unheroic action; thus, without Hill's outlawness, Thomas could not have become a hero.* Her appearance, and especially the thematic use made of her by Thomas's supporters and the state, made his confirmation much more certain.

Within the terms specifically of, or influenced by, the *Moynihan Report* and generally of the discourse on the "culture of poverty," "welfare queen" is a phrase that describes economic dependency—the lack of a job and/or income (which equals degeneracy in the Calvinist United States); the presence of a child or children with no father

---

*On the other hand, both Lisa Jones (*Village Voice,* November 12, 1991, pp. 27–28) and Crenshaw wrote about the *lack* of critical response to Thomas's distortions about his sister by many African Americans. Crenshaw argues that Thomas's misrepresentations did *not* constitute a stumbling block for their support, that "Thomas reflects a very specific ideology about Black women—an ideology of put-down that is a growing phenomenon within the Black community" (p. 27). While I don't completely disagree with Jones and Crenshaw, still, I think, given the letters in newspapers around the country, and the calls from African Americans to radio talk shows, that enough African Americans (even though a minority) were troubled by his distortions that their (and others') disapproval was a factor that made a counternarrative necessary.

and/or husband (moral deviance); and, finally, a charge on the collective U.S. treasury—a human debit. The cumulative totality, circulation, and effect of these meanings in a time of scarce resources among the working class and the lower middle class is devastatingly intense. The welfare queen represents moral aberration and an economic drain, but the figure's problematic status becomes all the more threatening once responsibility for the destruction of the "American way of life" is attributed to it. Demonic is not too strong a word to describe the politics of that narrative. Emma Mae Martin embodied that narrative; she, as Thomas described her,[6] was one of those drawing the nation down into the depths of despair. This narrative is not new: not only was it useful to Duke, it has been explicitly reinvigorated by the *New York Times*'s recent attempts to breathe new life into Moynihan and his report, and by the governors, state legislatures, and presidential candidates who have declared war on the welfare poor, epitomized as welfare mothers and AFDC (Aid to Families with Dependent Children) families, *not,* for example, as government-subdized corporations or upper-class individuals and families subsidized by tax cuts and credits.*

Read the newspapers, watch television, or simply listen to people talk: among other things, welfare queens are held

---

*The *Report* has more lives than a cat and it continues to heavily influence discussions in the corporate and mainstream media about the urban poor. The theme of the destructive "underclass" has a place in our collective memory that is being dusted off for yet more work as various states cut welfare benefits and newspapers print additional descriptions of the depreciations of the poor—welfare recipients prominent among them, as always—on "attractive welfare states" like California. Politicians gain credibility for themselves by coming out against the notion of the United States as a welfare state.

responsible for the crack trade and crack babies. And they combine that with moral degeneracy within their families—for example, they trade sex for crack in front of their children. (Within the economy of this narrative the crack dealer is also demonized, but he is the creation of his pathological "nurturer" because it is she who reproduces the culture.) Behind the bland and leaden policy language that paints her as simply incapable is something more vicious, which finds its outlet in other ugly images and language. She is the agent of destruction, the creator of the pathological, black, urban, poor family from which all ills flow; a monster creating crack dealers, addicts, muggers, and rapists—men who become those things because of being immersed in *her* culture of poverty.

Such women are totally unlike Thomas, whose story about his grandfather resonates so thoroughly across a public imagination accustomed to myths about heroic male individuals that his mother's history and that of any other women in his family—and their own particularity—are erased. His grand*father* was the proper nurturer—the stand-in for the law's order at home. Unlike Thomas's sister.

Hill, about whom I will say more below, is the narrative constituted by the other Moynihan trope—the black female overachiever and betrayer of a possible black patriarchy—but whose existence is noted at least as far back as the eighteenth century in David Walker's *Appeal . . . to the Coloured Citizens of the World.'*[7] Both she and Martin can be seen as exemplifying the pathology of the category "black women." And the attacks on the two women were exercises of state power by means of invoking racist and sexist stereotypes passing themselves off as social-science-supported policy.

What is a welfare state, finally, but a government that assumes responsibility for its citizens' well-being; theoretically, at least, it takes care of those who cannot take care of themselves: children, for example. And according to narratives about welfare queens, what is the reason such children need care? The misbehavior of their mothers, who either never had or cannot keep their husbands. So what is going to destroy America? Black welfare queens in particular and black female misbehavior in general. And it does not matter that all such children needing state care are not black, or that poverty and unemployment are reasons that they need state care; what matters, what resonates in the national mind's eye, is the constant media-reinforced picture of the welfare queen—always black. Within the terms of this narrative, however, Thomas not only neutralizes his sister early by caricaturing her, or by reminding his listening and watching audience of her existence as a caricature, he triumphs over her. But after that, who almost destroys the state's standard-bearer in these hearings? An overachieving black lady. The flip side of the pathology coin, the welfare queen's more articulate sister.

The two of them—threatening to bring down further destruction on all normal Americans (as J. C. Alvarez so loved saying)—have to be contained. The attack that focuses on them comes together in particular kinds of ways. When Hill, already aberrant by virtue of her class status, is referred to as a lunatic—someone who fantasizes; when she's referred to as a lesbian—someone whom we are to see as unnatural in a heterosexual family romance, or as someone telling a story that ought to be kept away from children; when her very "ladylike" (another word for "middle-class") behavior is read as an aberration because a black lady is either an oxymoron, or yet another indication of the pathology of African-American culture; then she's as demonized (although differently so) as the welfare queen.

Hill is a threat either because she's *not* a real lady (not "ladylike")—she's a debater, she holds her own aggressively in an argument, and she's ambitious—or because she *is* a real lady—by virtue of her class standing. In either case she is dangerous. In a way, she is even more of a threat to male dominance than Thomas's sister—the welfare queen—because the national public "recognizes" his sister but does not know as easily and as consciously how to recognize the lady. We're accustomed to thinking of the welfare queen as pathological because we've "learned" the story of the culture of underdevelopment; Hill is demonized because we don't *know* who she is.* And her quiet, direct, and tearless (read: unfeminine) delivery worked against her.

Class position and status came into play to marginalize Hill at the same time that the class position of the powerful male (Thomas) was ignored. According to the statement of J. C. Alvarez, a self-described "real American,"† Hill's education and career trajectory discredited her because, for Alvarez, an educated Yale Law School graduate has no

---

*Recently, Susan Douglas noted that Hill looked and acted prim, even prudish (*In These Times,* November 6–12, 1991, p. 18), behavior seen as deviant because it wasn't exuberant, earthy, physically expressive. It went against the grain of media, especially television, portraits of black women. This is a media criticism, of course, that countless African-American feminists and cultural commentators have made for decades.

†Ironically, the self-described "John Q. Public" and "ordinary American" J. C. Alvarez is herself a Princeton University graduate (class of '77). Howard Taylor, Princeton University, brought this information to my attention.

victim "authenticity," no right to fears about her relationship to a powerful man or to the marketplace.[8] Alvarez's
assessment of Hill's inauthenticity as a victim was echoed
by numerous callers to CNN and radio talk shows who
indicated that they didn't believe Hill because, unlike an
uneducated person—a factory worker, for example—Hill
had options; she could get another job. The upward mobility demonstrated by Thomas's career—and celebrated in
the media and on the Senate floor—became in Hill's case
simply more reason for distrust of her. The suspicious
anti-Hill callers, aware of Hill's class position and relative
labor flexibility, were completely blind to Thomas's class
position and power.

The logic of narratives that demonized Hill didn't seem
to require rational defense whether or not such narratives
were vulnerable to rational critique. Think of the casual
linkages—so beloved of Orrin Hatch, Strom Thurmond,
and Alan Simpson: lesbian, spurned woman. It doesn't
matter that no one was ever lynched on behalf of a lesbian,
or that being a woman spurned by a man implies hetero-
sexuality. That lesbian and spurned woman cannot be rationally linked together simply means that a debased
discourse doesn't care whether the terms of "othering" are
logical or not. Any demonic narrative will do in a pinch,
even two or three, it simply depends upon what demon is
most effective in making the sense of the world that power
requires.

The final, most devastating subtext, however, of the
black-lady narrative is affirmative action—everybody's
football. And there were code words that linked Hill with
affirmative action: J. C. Alvarez's remarks about corporations looking for "women like [Hill]," for example, a

possible corporate search that provided reason for Alvarez
and the general public to doubt Hill's credibility. How did
affirmative action and Hill function together as demonic
narratives that worked on behalf of Thomas's confirmation? Regardless of whatever arguments could be and have
been made on behalf of affirmative action, whether or not
Hill went to school as an affirmative-action student,
whether or not she got any of her positions as a result of
affirmative action or equal-opportunity programs, she's
tarred with the affirmative-action brush by virtue of the
salience of affirmative action in the news and the political
game-playing that went on around the civil rights bill.
Affirmative action then became another powerful (and
largely unspoken) reason that the public could not trust
Anita Hill's story—because affirmative action is the reason
that the national public thinks it *knows* she could have
gotten another job and therefore should have left the one
she had. Thus, the public was given yet another sin to lay
at the feet of affirmative action: Anita Hill. And such is the
horrible double edge of that particular blade, that another
sin was laid (simultaneously) at *Hill's* feet: her potential
employment attractiveness in affirmative-action terms.

Affirmative action created the monster Hill, who then
came forward to do battle against the white knight (or the
black knight on behalf of white state power), Clarence
Thomas, who intended to do away with the dragon of
affirmative action. Despite the *fact* of his affirmative-action-
aided education, he proudly articulated antiaffirmative-
action credentials and experience. And for those looking
for additional reasons to support Thomas, Hill's performance before the Senate committee made it clear why affirmative action is a bad idea: affirmative action means that

U.S. children will have to hear educated African Americans talk about pubic hair, long dongs, big breasts, and bestiality in Senate chambers!

Affirmative action, welfare state, and welfare queen have become a mantra, evoked as single (albeit complicated) signs for and of everything wrong with the United States; those words do yeoman duty, especially in a debased discourse that seeks to undermine the need for state assistance: i.e., people don't need jobs to prosper—never mind that the industrial basis for most African-American (and other working-class) conventionally male employment has fled the country to farther-flung and cheaper sites—people only need the right kind of moral nurturing and socialization to succeed. And if they don't get the right kind of moral training, then of course the country will go to the dogs. Within the terms of the convergent narratives of the Thomas hearings, the message was clear: at the end of history, with the smoking gun in her hand, stands a two-faced figure: Ms. Black Professional/the welfare queen. Only Thomas's confirmation could avert the end of civilization as we know it.

Within the economy of that simplistic narrative, how could the state not win? And Thomas was its linchpin.

In this debate "Anita Hill" and "Emma Mae Martin" were not actually existing individuals as much as they were narrative stand-ins for certain properties of the mythic black-lady and welfare-queen categories. The names of the two actually existing women became increasing unimportant as the "names" for their "types" took over the discourse. The existence of those names—black lady and welfare queen, even unspoken—saved Thomas's name and his *nomination,* or his *naming,* to the Supreme Court. Given the fact that some people were paying attention to criticism of Thomas's EEOC record, his connection to lobbyists for South Africa, his improper behavior in overturning a $10.4 million damage award against Ralston Purina, and his attacks on his sister, the state might not have managed to pull off his confirmation or to make it as publicly popular as it turned out to be.

The particular confluence of these narratives (and the political work they did) demanded that Thomas (as Alisa Solomon also notes in the *Village Voice*)⁹ *become* "black," have a public racial "conversion experience," but I would add that the conversion experience was even more necessary in order for the *state* to "pass" as black. Blackness, as an abstraction, did battle for Thomas because few people actually belonging to the group "black" or "African-American"* would have gone to war on behalf of Thomas the corrupt judge, Thomas the bigot, Thomas the incompetent and inadequate head of EEOC. But for Thomas the black male victim of "Sapphire"—black female emasculator and betrayer of black men and carrier of black family pathology—well, the African-American legions would and did rise to battle against her. Out of the ooze of his past record climbed Thomas, the *real* black thing.

As necessary as it was to the state, however, that the African-American community be seen to support this nomination, such support was not in and of itself sufficient

*While I make no claims about racial biology, given the political reality of twentieth-century U.S. life and more than three hundred years of history, here I refer to the idea of "blackness" as a social fact if not a biological reality.

to secure Thomas's confirmation. The whole country had to be engaged in the making and marking of Thomas as hero, especially given the media attention to critiques of, and pressure brought to bear by, feminists of various races and ethnicities; thus the need for the welfare queen/black lady narratives.

Nonetheless, what of blackness?* Under what conditions? In our attention to the history of racism in the United States, African Americans have learned to keep in our memory the unrelenting attacks on our existence as a group regardless of whatever else might be at stake. But blackness is simply too large and unelaborated a category to carry the weight of analysis in this case. Thomas has class allegiances and alliances that are inimical to the interests of most of the group in this country. He has made a political career arguing against racism as a constitutive element of material existence for black people, and working against the interests of black people of both genders and women of all races. Nonetheless, Thomas's conservatism disappeared, covered over by the soothing balm of black common sense.

What are we to make of many African Americans' insistence on seeing Thomas simply as a black person being attacked by white people? Both Thomas's and the right's abilities to buffer him by taking advantage of black rage and white-liberal guilt depended on the construction of a mythic blackness as a category emptied of history and female gendering. In such discussions "woman"—as in a woman scorned or spurned, a vicious liar or deluded

---

*Here I refer to both the social construction and political consciousness senses of blackness as defined in the footnote on p. 330.

psychotic—is timeless and colorless. Such a dynamic ensures the rhetorical slippage embodied in the travesty of his use of lynching as metaphor; its historical baggage is elided in the hysteria of the moment.*

This means that certain kinds of black individuals were constituted as needing protection from other members of the group: "Any black person who goes against what people think black people should do or think becomes the object of attack," according to the testimony of Dr. Nancy Fitch (formerly of Thomas's staff). Her assertion, which wrongly and ahistorically insists that criticism within the group has the power to silence dissent, echoes the right's assertions that only black conservatives are the *real* dissenters, the real rugged individuals and, as such, are objects of black "political correctness." Within the terms of this narrative economy Thomas becomes like black lynching victims of old—a black threat to be neutralized by, well, by whom, really? To whom does Thomas pose a threat? Certainly *not* to white and powerful men, not to the state.

Further, if lynching, like the lash of the whip or scars on the slave's back, is the most concrete enactment of race oppression, then the narratives of "grandfather, the sharecropper," lynching, and endangered black manhood all came together in a devastating way. Against this scenario,

*Some metaphorical uses of lynching and abuses of its historical specificity were arrogantly transparent in their deployment. Peggy Noonan wrote (in an op-ed piece in the October 15, 1991, *New York Times*) that "regular Americans" did think Thomas was being lynched, "not because he's a black man—*they saw Robert Bork swinging from the same tree*—but because he's a conservative" (my emphasis). If Thomas's evocation of lynching as a defense against the Senate committee's feeble interrogation of his past behaviors was cynical, then Noonan's attempt to wrap lynching, with its specific and racist history, around Bork was obscene.

a critique of a black conservative is transformed into a threat to individualism, becomes un–American, and it does so despite the fact that Hill is conservative (although less so than Thomas), that most of the people supporting her on the committee floor were identifiable as conservatives. Hill's conservatism disappears also, but not in the way that Thomas's does—hers disappears without the balm of blackness. Instead, she becomes the embodiment of black female betrayal or "white" (by fiat) feminist cat's-paw.

The efficacy of the lynching metaphor is due to problematic recourse to black common sense that reasons thusly: they (whites) are out to get us. Such common sense, of course, has much past and present evidence to buttress it. Unfortunately, impelled by the strength and general historical accuracy of that common sense, African Americans who moved uncritically over to (or were always on) Thomas's side protected "white" state power and upper-class privilege in the name of blackness and out of concern for black manhood. Such was the metaphysical dilemma posed by regarding the social fact of blackness and its political and cultural significance from too crude a common-sense vantage point.* And because when the chips were down, and blackness from this common–sense perspective equals only black *man*hood, Hill's race became both hypervisible and invisible at the same time. That it "disap-

---

*One recurrent form of patriarchal idiocy that relied on knee-jerk allegiance to blackness as masculine terrain was articulated in the language of Ishmael Reed: "White feminists will go to any means to advance *their* cause, Thomas is right about being lynched" (my emphasis; *In These Times,* October 23–29, 1991, quoted by Salim Muwakkil). With this stunningly reductionist insight, Reed erased Hill's own agenda, her conservatism, and the vitality of black feminism, while allying himself with the mouthpiece of white state power.

peared" and "reappeared" is important, but more important is how it disappeared and reappeared at the same time. With no check on Thomas's evocation of his blackness, with no real check by Democrats or the mainstream press, Hill got whiter.

Blackness as a mobilizing rhetorical resource for Thomas was enhanced for African Americans by narrative presentation of a "Sapphire" figure. Nonetheless, as I asserted earlier, while mobilizing blackness was necessary to turn Thomas (the racial conservative who does not believe in or exhibit racial solidarity) into a black hero for African Americans, doing so was insufficient to guarantee popular acceptance of his confirmation among the larger population. It was the political work done by the tainted presence of the black lady—with her class privilege so consistently recognized, evoked, and articulated—and the equally but differently tainted and powerfully present figure, the welfare queen, that constituted the vehicle by which Thomas could ride both from and into history as the black hero fighting the forces of U.S. entropy and bad women.*

---

*Various journalists, political analysts, and cultural critics have delineated ways in which we can understand the moment of these hearings and the discourse surrounding them in ways that allow us to see genuine gendered and racialized challenges to the successful and multifaceted operations of power. And those of us who opposed Thomas did what we could with the evidence available about Thomas and his record—in scattered spaces in the media, in groups that lobbied the Senate and the committee, in networks that provided information to the Senate committee, and under unenviable circumstances. But while we challenged the workings of conservative narratives of race and gender, we were unable to interrupt the workings of such ideas as they took flesh in a particular moment. Specific cultural politics did the work of stabilizing the U.S. political economy in this moment as it has in the past.

The slogan "Men have to listen to women" (something people said over and over again when they wrote in the newspaper or talked on television)

Further, this narratively constructed pathology of black women reasserted *America's* health in the minds of much of its citizenry. State power is patriarchal power whether it is externally imposed or produced and reproduced within the individual, private, and domestic realms of black communities. The state's manipulation of narratives like the poverty-produced "welfare queen" and the affirmative-action-produced "black lady" not only perpetuate racism and sexism but guarantee the continued unequal distribution of economic resources. And that is precisely what I mean by ideological war by narrative means. Understanding those operations is how we can recognize the blurring of the line between real and cultural politics. These narratives masked the general but more elusive operations of power. They forced our attention away from power, from the selection of political elites, from the failures of the U.S. political economy, and toward a particular individual drama. At the same time that the second set of Thomas confirmation hearings were going on: (1) President Bush vetoed legislation that would have added more weeks of

---

used as a political imperative was a very good place to begin, but the complications inherent in the constitutive elements of that phrase surfaced quickly. What women? The question arose because women who were supporters of a very powerful man (who will be even more powerful) came forward to do battle on behalf of the continued operation of uncritiqued power. Women like J. C. Alvarez, who defined "real" womanhood and told us what a "real" victim of sexual harassment would do, seized the category "woman" in order to make it impossible for other women, or at least one woman in particular, to be heard.

And of course some men did listen to women. In fact, they rushed to listen to particular women: Senator Simpson, who found it impossible to believe anything Hill and her supporters had to say, found that he could listen to the string of women defending Thomas and attacking Hill; he listened and begged for more.

unemployment benefits to people out of work more than six months; (2) Bush "worried" (at least according to the *New York Times*) about banks, their loans, and a sluggish economy—he "approved" some "measures" and spoke of taking "more steps" to help "stabilize" the economy; and (3) at the same time, Haitian demonstrators marched at different locations in the country in support of Haiti's deposed President Aristide.

In those moments the state withheld bread and put on a media "circus" instead of alleviating any of the abuses of its economy. Meanwhile, news of yet another geopolitical site where the relation between raw events of power and ideological contestation, in a part of the hemisphere in which U.S. economic and political policy and interests are heavily involved, was being written in the margins of newsprint framing the "spectacle" being played out on CNN. The political economy of the United States was being reconstructed in narrative terms that placed discussion of poor unemployed people, banks, and Haiti on the margins of the newspaper pages—*outside* the frame of the Thomas-Hill controversy. The spectacle around Hill's charges covered over the overlap between what seem to be private matters and the public abuse of male power and obscured the ways in which the realm of the private is permeated with real or public politics. None of this was new. Approval for the Persian Gulf War, for example, was sustained in considerable part by the consistent demonic spectacle of Saddam Hussein, alternately cast as a madman, a rapist, and/or a homosexual via T-shirts, novelties, radio shows, television, and the print media. Visually, textually, politically, the operation of a powerful state exercised and maintained its power by any means available to it, with the connivance of much of the press, the broadcast media, and the national public. And those places where power was least visible might well be where it was most present.

Photographic placement was not the only means by which power was hidden: textual examples abounded. One of the most egregious was written by R. W. Apple, Jr., in the *New York Times:*[10] "The Senators who must vote on Tuesday were left with only two options: Either she was telling the truth or she is a sociopath; either these horrifying events took place or she, for some reason invented them." One would have to look long and hard for a better example of a syntax mugging on behalf of the more powerful figure in these hearings: Thomas as agent is absent from this sentence. On the other hand, Hill, as syntax agent, makes three appearances: (1) possible truth-teller, (2) sociopath, or (3) inventor of events. But there is no Thomas agency even where, in term of syntactic parallelism, one might most expect to see him (or it) as in "horrifying events took place."* No Thomas there; even if the events *happened,* they did so passively, they took place without his doing. To see more clearly how this piece of a sentence protects the more powerful figure, consider how else the reporter *could have* written this part of the sentence: "Either he is a liar, or she is a sociopath; either he is guilty of horrifying abuses of power or she is guilty of inventing them."

Further into the same article, Apple's protection of power was extended from Thomas in particular to cover, generally, those powerful institutional sites that are, appar-

---

*This distortion of language belongs up there with another hall of fame example of passive political "guiltspeak": "Mistakes were made."

ently for him, never contaminated with abusive language and/or behaviors: "Either he said these wretched things to her—things that one associates with the seamiest of criminal cases or the raunchiest of locker rooms, not with the *Senate* or *Supreme Court*—or he did not" (my emphasis).

Thomas is the state incubus returning as the masque* of blackness within the sanctity of the Senate. The spectacle of the Thomas hearings did not just mask the operation of state power in the political economy; it did the work. In so far as the state-assisted Thomas was able to "make" himself and to be made the mythological black patriarchal male figure—and thereby marginalize Martin and Hill both as real people and as the categories they represent—then the political economy was made flesh. Thomas's elevation through the second hearings to his place as exemplar of solid American heroism and virtuous blackness laundered the state's relationship to racism, to the economic and political abuse of poor people generally, poor black people specifically, and to black women of whatever economic level. His elevation put a black face on patriarchal and oligarchic business as usual. But state power does not act on its own—the narratives deployed here were effective precisely because they circulate, with the considerable help of the corporate and/or mainstream media, through the culture.

---

*I use "masque" here in the Renaissance sense: "An entertainment in which a procession of masqued or otherwise disguised figures represented a highly imaginative action . . . the spectacle was of the greatest importance to the presentation of the mythological or similarly fantastic subjects" (taken from Alex Preminger, ed., *The Princeton Handbook of Poetic Terms* [Princeton: Princeton University Press, 1986]). In short, my reference to Thomas and his confirmation process as a masque means that his spectacle of blackness was a disguised display of power.

Across history, and certainly in this moment, one of the most reliable all-purpose scapegoats has been the black woman. In this moment both the "welfare queen" and the "black lady" are pathologies created by an erring state: welfare queens are poor and pathologically dependent because of state welfare handouts, and black ladies are pathologically independent because state-influenced or -assisted affirmative-action programs keep such ladies from what they might otherwise become: the spousal appendages of successful black patriarchs. Thomas, on the other hand, was constructed as the quintessential self-made man. If he could be seen as essentially self-made (i.e., without the help of the state), then Hill and Martin could be seen to represent the bad results of state intervention. The state thus makes its own interventions (however inadequate and attenuated) on behalf of poor and middle-class black women look like mistakes it needs to rectify. (Tougher times ahead for the disadvantaged for their own good!) With Thomas's ascension to the Supreme Court, it disavows its bad progeny— the two women—and claims its good progeny—the self-made, as opposed to state-made, man.

By confirming Thomas, by affirming the black father, the stand-in for state power, not only did the state and Senate do business as usual, but the black-female threat to what "America" means was wrestled to the ground. No wimps here: the black-female "troubles" are over for now; America is back and standing tall. Bush is in control again, standing firmly on the nation-threatening black-female "thing." The imaginary demons were contained while the latest embodiment of the eternal "undead" of state power (or the *real thing*) moved on to his seat in Washington, D.C.

. . .

The first pair of pictures I described at the beginning of this essay "hid" real power inequities by flaunting visual egalitarianism; the second pair simply used spatial placement to reassert unarticulated hierarchy. Consider three other pictures given prominent place in the *New York Times*.

1. On October 11, a front-page photograph of Thomas striding across his lawn was placed directly above an article about Hill entitled "A Private Person in a Storm." Perhaps the *Times* (perversely?) thought that Hill was so very private that a photograph of her adversary could stand in for her, or perhaps the newspaper was simply hedging its bets, or—even more frighteningly—the editor never noticed that a picture of Thomas was marginalizing yet another narrative about Hill. Whatever. Still, Thomas (and his privacy) were clearly on view and on top. And Hill (and her privacy) were disappeared, or were at least subordinated to Thomas—on the bottom.

2. On October 10 a picture of Thomas and Bush sitting together somewhere in the White House ran on the front page. The two men are seated together; Thomas is smiling and looking at Bush; Bush is looking solemnly toward the camera. The "great white father" embodies—in his presence in that picture and by his proximity to Thomas—the presence of state power and determination. Seeming to lean slightly closer to the camera, Bush is out front in every sense of the phrase. This picture ran before the second hearing began, when state power was more obviously making itself explicit; before the push began to represent Thomas as an individual about to be attacked by the big

bad Senate committee. It was the last time during these hearings that the photographic spotlight (in the *Times*) was on Bush.

3. On October 13, the same day as the "Theater of Pain" picture I referred to earlier, a photograph of Thomas and Senator Danforth ran inside the *Times*. Thomas is gazing down at the floor following the end of the hearing after his "I would have preferred an assassin's bullet" speech. Danforth, his friend and advisor, is touching Thomas's shoulder with his hand. Again, Thomas is in the presence of power and being comforted by it. This picture reinforced the narrative of a hurt and suffering Thomas. In fact, by then, "he has suffered enough" was the common

and constant refrain. Compared to all those he harmed as head of EEOC, or those who sought and did not receive help through the EEOC? Compared to those who might be in a position to be harmed by his elevation to the Supreme Court bench?

Coda

There are questions that this essay has tried to address: What does it mean to see or hear power so constantly elided or treated as if separable from gender or racial dynamics? What is a black politics—absent class and/or gender specificity? What is being coerced when "woman" is used in specific ways—especially when categories like

"black woman" are not explicitly articulated but are, nonetheless, overwhelmingly present? Where are women in relation to class and/or power? What of specific women (powerless in and of themselves) acting as articulators of power positions? How did pro-Thomas voices mobilize "history" onto their side and why did it work? What are the drawbacks for civic debate and political process when historical themes are used as a shorthand to dramatize crises and manipulate or motivate sympathies—a kind of persuasion by evocation and recognition of congruence?[11]

Because of the relative success of the state in this moment, I have written an alarmist critique. But in the end I stave off despair by remembering some expressions of skepticism that undermined the process against which this essay warns. Some cut through this ugliness by contesting the narratives in circulation throughout this hearing: the alternative press generally, and specific writers in the corporate and mainstream press; and various people who called into CNN and radio talk shows around the country who articulated their suspicion about the absence of discussion about President Bush's work in all of this, or who spoke of their anger over the ways in which race was being deployed, or who wondered out loud about what this spectacle meant in the middle of a recession. Some made use of the media to question the workings of power—for example, Democratic Representative Craig Washington, speaking for the Congressional Black Caucus, responded to telephone callers during a segment on CNN and shed heavily Texas-inflected light on the darkness.

One finds hope where one can and sometimes in unexpected places. *People* magazine ran stories on Anita Hill and on Clarence and Virginia Thomas. In the short (two-page) article (October 28, 1991) on Anita Hill, they seemed to adhere to their customary human-interest structure. But that article was written apparently without her participation; there were no new pictures of Hill with her family— all the photographs used were pictures from her past, of her parents at the hearing, and of their home. There was no interview with her, no new quotes from her; in short, it was human interest without the presence of the private or "human" Hill. However, surprisingly (for me at least), the article was appended with five pages of women's narratives (complete with pictures), all of whose experiences supported the credibility, at least, of Hill's reasons for not coming forward at the time of the harassment. *People* followed those five pages with separate boxes on Catharine MacKinnon and Deborah Tannen talking about sexual harassment.

The second article (November 11, 1991) was a long interview with Virginia Thomas. The article ran multiple photographs of both of the Thomases, including one picture of the two reading a Bible on the couch. What a cover story, I thought. How could it not work, especially in conjunction with the "wife," the legitimate woman, narrating her story? I assumed that its effect would be a replay of the two panels of women who supported Thomas in the second hearings, that the picture of Virginia Thomas sitting so comfortably in (and so much of) the domestic sphere with her husband—and holding on to one of the most widely circulated texts in the nation—would speak so loudly against Hill's "outlaw" position that Hill's own narrative would vanish from view. I was certain that support for the Thomases would explode all over the letters-to-the-editor page of a later issue. In the issue (three weeks later) that carried the responses, however, while *People* indicated that "Virginia Thomas's account . . . brought more letters than any other story this year," most of the mail was *negative,* many of the letters printed (from people who might well be Christians but were clearly not taken in by the picture—and yet another cover story—of Bible-holding domesticity) were cogently contemptuous; to wit:

It would appear from Virginia Thomas's story that Justice Clarence Thomas should have been nominated for sainthood instead of the Supreme Court.

When I was a kid, taking the Lord's name in vain meant swearing or cursing. These days I'm inclined to think it means tossing around the name of God to protect or promote one's public image. I still believe Anita Hill. *(People,* December 2, 1991)

These examples, appearing in such a forum, made it a little easier for me to believe something that is a necessary tenet of faith for those engaged in criticizing and fighting undemocratic operations of power: power is never completely successful.

NOTES

1. "[T]he narrative takes on its own impetus as it were, so that one begins to see reality as non-narrated. One begins to say that it's not a narrative, it's the way things are." From Gayatri Chakravorty Spivak, *The Post-Colonial Critic: Interviews, Strategies, Dialogues* [New York: Routledge, 1990: p. 19].

2. My mapping of the ways that the black-lady and welfare-queen figures did ideological "work" in this historical moment was informed by Hortense Spillers's "Mama's Baby, Papa's Maybe: An American Grammar Book," *Diacritics,* vol. 17, no. 2 (Summer 1987), pp. 65–81, from which the epigraph that begins this essay is drawn—an analysis of the *Moynihan Report* (Daniel Moynihan, *The Moynihan Report and the Politics of Controversy: A Transaction Social Science and Public Policy Report,* eds. Lee Rainwater and W. L. Yancey, Cambridge: MIT Press, 1967).

3. The television special produced by Bill Moyer, "The Vanishing Family: Crisis in Black American" (CBS Special Report, 1986), is a case in point. It was based on Daniel Moynihan's *Negro Family: The Case for National Action* (Washington, D.C.: Department of Labor, Office of Policy, Planning & Research, 1965).

4. *The Moynihan Report,* 75.

5. Ibid.

6. Thomas's comments were reported, for example, in the *New York Times* of July 7, 1991: "She gets mad when the mailman is late with her welfare check. That's how dependent she is . . . What's worse is that now her kids feel entitled to the check, too. They have no motivation for doing better or getting out of the situation." In short, as Avery Gordon (University of California, Santa Barbara) said in response to my argument above, Thomas's remarks paint a picture of Martin as a woman "addicted to" welfare who passes on that addiction to her

children; she is the mother of addiction. "Mothering addiction" underwrites the logic of the culture of poverty, a logic that isn't a cultural thesis at all, but a sociobiological thesis (private conversation, January 13, 1992).

7. David Walker, *Appeal, in Four Articles; Together with a Preamble, to the Coloured Citizens of the World* . . . (1829), reprinted in Herbert Aptheker, *One Continual Cry,* (New York: Humanities Press, 1965).

8. Avery Gordon extended my argument thusly: "We could not know—since 'we don't know who she is'—that she could really be a woman sexually hararssed. Whatever other ideological work the attack on a 'black lady' has to do, it has to ensure that no woman in her position could be seen as sexually harassable; which was why the concept of reasonable doubt had to be deployed in irrational phantasmatic terms. It was easier to suggest that there are no 'knowable' women in her position" (private conversation, January 13, 1992).

9. *Village Voice,* October 22, 1991, p. 25.

10. *New York Times,* October 12, 1991.

11. "Persuasion by congruence" is Raphael Allen's phrase (private conversation, Princeton University, December 29, 1991).

KENDALL THOMAS

Strange Fruit

"Myth," writes Roland Barthes, "deprives the object of which it speaks of all History."[1] This line from *Mythologies* appears in Barthes's famous analysis of the *Paris Match* cover photograph of a black soldier saluting the French flag. Barthes observes that like all myth, this photograph plays a "game of hide-and-seek" between meaning and form. At the level of denotative meaning, argues Barthes, the photograph is simply that of a black man in a military uniform, his eyes uplifted, saluting the French flag.* It is a "linguistic sign." At the level of connotative form, the photograph is

---

*In fact, as Eve Tavor-Bannet has noted, there is no French flag in the photograph. (Eve Tavor-Bannet, *Structuralism and the Logic of Dissent* [Urbana: University of Illinois, 1989], p. 54.) The presence of the flag is inferred, or more precisely, imagined. At one level, then, Barthes's reading of the *Paris Match* cover reflects the force of the very ideological myth he aims critically to expose.

a "mythic signifier," a powerful icon and conductor of French nationalist ideology. In Barthes's reading, the mythic signification of the photograph is "that France is a great Empire, that all her sons, without any colour discrimination, faithfully serve under her flag, and that there is no better answer to the detractors of an alleged colonialism than the zeal shown by this Negro in serving his so-called oppressors."[2]

Lost in all this, of course, is the history of the pain, suffering, and death France inflicted on its darker sons and daughters. This bloody, brutal story of domination and degradation is utterly erased from the image of the soldier whose patriotic pose is captured in the photograph. For Barthes the *Paris Match* cover represents a mythic "deformation" by which the ideology of French imperialism "deprives" the Negro in the photograph of his history, "half-amputates" him, changes him into a "speaking corpse," relegates him "to the confines of humanity," renders him nothing more than a "gesture" or an "image-at-one's disposal."[3] I want to take Barthes's suggestive formulation of the semiotic mechanisms by which myth "distorts"[4] (etymologically, "twists apart") history as a frame of reference for discussing the deformations of African-American history that took place during the Senate Judiciary Committee hearings on the allegations of sexual harassment leveled by Professor Anita Hill against then Supreme Court nominee Judge Clarence Thomas.

The chief rhetorical conductor through which the representation of African-American history was channeled in the Thomas-Hill hearings came in the form of the now notorious "lynching" metaphor. This trope made its first appearance late Friday evening, when Thomas returned to respond to the testimony Hill had offered earlier in the day. During his opening remarks Thomas described himself as the victim of a "high-tech lynching." The judge depicted the proceedings as an effort to "destroy" him, an attempt to "assassinate" him set in motion when Professor Hill's "sensitive allegations" were "selectively leaked" in a "distorted way" to the national press. For Thomas the meaning of the "dark days" that followed the revelation of the charges leveled against him was clear:

> [From] my standpoint as a black American, as far as I'm concerned, it is a high-tech lynching for uppity blacks who in any way deign to think for themselves, to do for themselves, to have different ideas, and it is a message that unless you kowtow to an old order, this is what will happen to you. You will be lynched, destroyed, caricatured by a committee of the U.S. Senate rather than hung from a tree.*

The language of death had already figured in the rhetorical politics surrounding the Thomas confirmation. A month before, John Danforth, Thomas's former boss and most visible congressional patron, had spoken on the Senate floor of the nominee's ordeal on "murderers' row," the five days of meetings during which Thomas had been prepped for the hearings before the Judiciary Committee. In his testimony Judge Thomas invested this metaphoric of death with a much more sinister, and decidedly racial,

*As of the writing of this essay, no official transcript of the Thomas confirmation hearings has been released. Quotations from the hearings in this essay are taken from published excerpts of testimony before the Senate Judiciary Committee.

meaning. "I will not provide the rope for my own lynching or for further humiliation."

No African American listening or watching Judge Thomas could mistake his meaning or miss the depth of his feeling. Most of us can recall being told stories about the horrors of lynching. I will never forget the sad and angry voice of my grandfather as he told me of a lynching that took place in 1955, one year after the Supreme Court's famous *Brown* decision, and two years before I was born. During a visit with relatives in Mississippi, a fourteen-year-old Chicago boy named Emmett "Bobo" Till allegedly whistled at a young white woman who worked in a drug-store where he had gone to buy some chewing gum. Till did not know that he had just transgressed the South's deepest racial taboo.

During the night that followed, two white men, one of them the white woman's husband, appeared with a gun at the shack where Till was staying. Over the protests of Till's uncle, the two men took the boy away for "questioning." Two days later Till's naked body was found floating in the Tallahatchie River. Till had been bludgeoned and shot in the head. His murderers had then used barbed wire to tie a 125-pound cotton-gin blower around his neck and had thrown his corpse in the river. Some weeks later, an all-white Tallahatchie County jury acquitted Till's accused murderers.[5]

In one painful metaphor Thomas's testimony invoked this scandalous history of the ritual torture, mutilation, and murder of thousands of black Americans at the hands of white American mobs. Thomas could not have chosen more vivid language to convey his conviction that, but for the color of his skin, he would never have been asked to answer these questions about the content of his character. The metaphor, however, was misplaced.

It may be true, as Judge Thomas said, that the revelation of Professor Hill's allegations in the media and the spectacle of the Judiciary Committee hearings left an "indelible mark" on him. It may be too that in the minds of many, the charges leveled against Judge Thomas resurrected damaging and denigrating sexual stereotypes about African-American men. Nonetheless, Thomas's denomination of the controversy as a "lynching" did a disservice to the memory of the suffering and death inflicted on the black Americans with whom he compared his confirmation ordeal.

The differences between the tragedy of lynching and the spectacle in Washington were simply too stark to ignore. To see why this is so, we might begin by looking at the most sustained exchange regarding the history of lynching and its contemporary resonance that occurred during Thomas's testimony before the Judiciary Committee. The judge repeatedly insisted that Professor Hill's allegations of sexual misconduct had tainted him with long-held stereotypes about black male sexuality. During his colloquy with Thomas, Senator Orrin Hatch posed a series of rather friendly questions that allowed the judge to amplify his views regarding the "intriguing" assertions (to use the senator's word) regarding the sexual mythology ascribed to black men:

SENATOR HATCH: When you talk in terms of stereotypes, what are you saying here? I mean, I want to understand this. . . . You said some of this language is stereotyped language? What does that mean? I don't understand.

JUDGE THOMAS: Senator, language throughout the history of this country, and certainly throughout my life, language about the sexual prowess of black men, language about the sex organs of black men and the sizes, etc. That kind of language has been used about black men as long as I've been on the face of this earth, and these are charges that play into racist, bigoted stereotypes, and these are the kind of charges that are impossible to wash off. And these are the stereotypes that I have in my tenure in Government, and conduct of my affairs, attempted to move away from and to convince people that we should conduct ourselves in a way that defies these stereotypes. But when you play into a stereotype, it's as though you're skiing downhill. There is no way to stop it. And this plays into the most bigoted, racist stereotypes that any black man will face.

SENATOR HATCH: I saw—I didn't understand the television program, but there were two black men—I may have it wrong, but as I recall, there were two black men talking about this matter, and one of them said, she's trying to demonize us. I didn't understand it at the time. Do you understand that?

JUDGE THOMAS: Well, I understand that, and any black man in this country—Senator, in the 1970's, I became very interested in the issue of lynching. And if you want to track through this country in the 19th and 20th century the lynchings of black men, you will see that there is invariably, or in many instances, a relationship with sex, and an accusation that that person cannot shake off. That is the point that I'm trying to make, and that is the point that I was making last night, that this is high tech lynching. I cannot shake off these accusations, because they play to the worst stereotypes we have about black men in this country.

We may leave aside the obvious distinction between the blood justice of the rope and faggot and the expansive legal process afforded Thomas. We may ignore as well Thomas's concession under further questioning that the details of Hill's charges did not in fact play on the "racist, bigoted stereotypes" (to use the judge's term) ascribed to black men that so outraged him. More pertinent in this context is what the judge did not say about the mythology of black male sexuality around which the practice of lynching revolved. As a self-styled historian of lynching, Thomas must surely know that the logic of lynching entailed a charge much more specific than the abstract "relationship with sex" to which he refers. Throughout its history the central and constantly recurring rationale for the torture and murder of lynch mob victims who were African-American men was that they were in fact sexual criminals. The "archetypal crime" for which lynching served as a punishment was "having a black man rape (touch, approach, look at, be imagined to have looked at, talk back to, etc.)" a white woman.[6]

Moreover, no African-American man was ever lynched on the word of an aggrieved black woman. This was because black women had no honor that a white lynch mob felt bound to respect. Indeed, the historical record of victims of racial violence in America must include the names of many African-American women. In addition to suffering rape and other forms of sexual terror, a number of black females lost their lives at the hands of lynch parties. In some instances these women were the "collateral" victims of violence aimed against black men. In other cases African-American women were the principal targets of lynch mobs. These murders were as inflected by white sexual racism as were those of black men. In his *Rope and Faggot,* Walter White recounts the story of a black woman in Georgia who allegedly threatened to seek the prosecution of a group of white men who had lynched her sharecropper husband.

> [T]hey bound her ankles together and, by them, hanged her to a tree. Gasoline and motor oil were thrown upon her dangling clothes; a match wrapped her in sudden flames. Mocking ribald laughter from her tormentors answered the helpless woman's screams of pain and terror. The clothes burned from her crisply toasted body, in which, unfortunately, life still lingered; a man stepped towards the woman and, with his knife, ripped open the abdomen in a crude Caesarian operation. Out tumbled the prematurely born child. Two feeble cries it gave—and received for answer the heel of a stalwart man, as life was ground out of the tiny form.[7]

This story of the black women who were caught up in the violent whirlwind of lynching has largely been hidden from history, and remains unknown even to African Americans. In my view the symbolic violence done to these forgotten women in the Thomas-Hill hearings was every bit as real as the harm the judge decried, and in which Thomas made himself complicit by omitting it from the history seminar he offered the American public. In using the lynching metaphor, Judge Thomas pulled the scab off one of the ugliest wounds in the history of this nation. His silence regarding the relevance of the language of lynching in the experience of black women may well have inflicted another.

I have drawn attention to the gendered genealogy of
racist violence in America. I do so to underscore the simple
fact that notwithstanding his resort to the language of
lynching, the parallel Thomas sought to draw between the
committee hearings and the horror of racist violence distorts the historical record, and must thus be deemed an
instance of myth in the sense in which Barthes uses the
term. This is not to say that I completely concur in the
belief that Thomas's misplaced metaphor was an "Academy award-winning" display of "cynicism and opportunism" by a man "who has distanced himself from his race in
the past."[8] Nor do I fully subscribe to the redemptive
reading of Thomas's words as evidence that he had reached
the painful recognition that the historical ties that bind him
to the African-American community could not be broken.[9] Both of these interpretations may be granted a local
validity. However, neither of them seems to me to capture
the larger significance of the nominee's condemnation of
the committee hearings as a reenactment of the primal
lynching scene. In my view Thomas's reliance on the
language of lynching, and his significant omission of its uses
against black women, must be understood in terms of
another, equally tragic theme in the history of race in
America, which is also inscribed in the transcript of the
hearings.

The key moment in the unfolding of this second theme
came toward the end of Thomas's testimony before the
Judiciary Committee, in the answer Thomas offered in
response to a query from Senator Arlen Specter. Specter
asked Judge Thomas to recall a conversation between the
two of them that took place shortly after the FBI report was
submitted to the members of the Judiciary Committee.

The subject of that conversation was the question of Professor Hill's motivation, a matter about which Judge Thomas had earlier testified he had been "eating his insides out":

SENATOR SPECTER: Judge Thomas, when I met with you on the morning of September twenty-seventh before the Judiciary Committee voted, I had asked you at that time about these charges, having seen the FBI report the night before. And I was asking you about the question of motivation and you made some comments to me at that time, although somewhat sensitive I think are worth exploring for just a moment now. And that was the comment you made about a possible concern that Professor Hill might have had regarding your dating a woman who was of a lighter complexion. Would you amplify what had happened and respond, testify as to what had happened in that regard?

JUDGE THOMAS: Senator, I think it is sensitive and, uh, I think enough sensitive matters have been discussed here. I, uh, would reluctantly, uh, uh, discuss it but, uh, I was merely speculating and groping around for some rationale. And the point that I was making to you is that there seemed to be some tension, uh, between, uh, uh, as a result of the complexion of the woman I dated and the woman whom I chose, uh, to be my chief of staff, uh, or my executive assistant and some reaction, as I recall it, to my preferring individuals of the lighter complexion.

SENATOR SPECTER: Did Professor Hill not get a position that she was working for within your staff?

JUDGE THOMAS: Uh, again, I can't remember the exact details of it but I think she wanted to have that position, the executive assistant position. But that's again, Senator, that is speculation as to what the motivation would be, and I hesitate to even mention it.

This is a remarkable colloquy, not least because Thomas's remarks regarding his professional and personal "preference" for "individuals of the lighter complexion" must be read as an oblique reference to what remains America's ultimate taboo: sex that actually or symbolically crosses the color line. Only a few weeks before the Thomas nomination was announced, Spike Lee's film *Jungle Fever* had brought the question of interracial sex and marriage into the public eye (*Newsweek* published a cover story on the film, under the caption "Tackling a Taboo"). And yet, as the politics of the Thomas nomination unfolded, a tacit consensus very quickly emerged that the public discourse would say as little as possible about the obvious fact that the judge's wife was a woman, to use her husband's phrase, of "the lighter complexion." Those who watched the hearings on television could not fail to note that the nominee's clear discomfort as he "reluctantly" repeated publicly what he had privately told Senator Specter was mirrored in the tense look on Virginia Thomas's face.

Stated bluntly, the judge's "hesitation" with respect to this "sensitive" matter was not surprising. In 1967, the year Clarence Thomas graduated from the St. John Vianney Minor Seminary in Savannah, and twenty years before his marriage to Virginia Thomas, the Court on which he now sits was asked to consider the constitutionality of Virginia's Racial Integrity Act of 1924. This law prohibited marriage between blacks and whites. At the time, Virginia was one of sixteen states that proscribed and punished such marriages. In *Loving* v. *Virginia,* the Supreme Court held that the Virginia law violated the equal-protection and due-process clauses of the Fourteenth Amendment.[10] Chief Justice Warren's opinion also condemned the statute on ideological grounds. The Virginia law, in the Court's eyes, was a blatant attempt "to maintain White Supremacy."[11]

When set against the backdrop of his earlier accusations that he was the victim of a "high-tech lynching," the irony of Thomas's revelations regarding his "preference" for "individuals of the lighter complexion" could not have been lost on students of American constitutional history. As Judge Leon Higginbotham noted in an open letter to Justice Thomas, but for the decision in *Loving* v. *Virginia,* Clarence and Virginia Thomas would be felons in the state where they currently reside, and subject to prosecution, conviction, and imprisonment.[12] In an editorial regarding the Thomas-Hill affair published in the *New York Times,* sociologist Orlando Patterson argued that the hearings definitively demonstrated that the "culture of slavery" is dead, that the state of African Americans is now one of "unambiguous inclusion [and] unquestioned belonging."[13] In my view this contention can be sustained only if one holds a narrowly instrumental view of the politics of race in America. Like many Americans, Patterson mistakenly construes racism as a predominantly "dominative" phenomenon (to use Joel Kovel's term), which is present only when one can point to the "open flame of race hatred."[14] Against this view, Kovel argues that in modern America racism takes a primarily "aversive" form. The characteristic gesture of aversive racism is not violence, but avoidance. As Kovel puts it, the aversive racist simply "tries to ignore the existence of black people, tries to avoid contact with them, and at most to be polite, correct and cold in what-ever dealings are necessary between the races."[15] The per-sistence of aversive racism in contemporary America forces the recognition that the history of slavery, as I have noted elsewhere, is far from finished.[16] Nowhere is this aversion more profoundly felt than with respect to interracial sex and marriage.

Thus, I would contend that close attention to the terms of the nominee's response to Specter's question warrants a very different interpretation of the politics of race in the Thomas-Hill hearings than Patterson invites, an interpreta-tion that casts the lynching metaphor, and the rest of Thomas's testimony, in a more sinister light. In short, the rhetorical politics of the judge's "speculations" regarding Anita Hill's motives ultimately tell us much more about the personality of Clarence Thomas than they do about the purported "pigment envy" of the woman who accused him of sexual harassment.

To see why this is so, we must consider the tissue of tropes in which the lynching metaphor and Thomas's testi-mony as a whole was inscribed. One of the recurrent rhetorical figures to which Thomas resorted in order to discredit the allegations of sexual harassment was the idea-image of dirt. As I argue presently, this language provides a revealing glimpse into the ideological world of the new justice. Thomas spared no effort to hammer home his views about the character of Hill's charges:

I think that this is disgusting. I think that this hearing should never occur in America. This is a case in which this sleaze, this dirt, was searched for by staffers of members of this committee, was then leaked to the media, and this committee and this body validated it and displayed it at prime time over our entire nation. How would any member on this committee, any person in this room, or any person in this country, would like sleaze said about him or her in this fashion? Or this dirt dredged up and this gossip and these lies displayed in this matter. . . .

At another point in his testimony, Thomas challenged the members of the Judiciary Committee to "parade every single one" of the women with whom he had worked "and ask them in their relationships with me whether or not any of this nonsense, this garbage, trash that you've siphoned out of the sewers against me, whether any of it is true." Thomas condemned the Judiciary Committee for allowing the U.S. Senate to "be used by interest groups and hate mongers and people who are interested in digging up dirt to destroy other people." Thomas was particularly critical of the Senate staffers who made "[c]alls all over the country specifically requesting dirt" about him. "They went around this country looking for dirt, not information on Clarence Thomas, dirt. Anybody with dirt. Anything. Late night calls. Calls at work. Calls at home. Badgering. Anything. Give us some dirt."

Most discussions of the rhetorical politics of the Thomas-Hill hearings have accorded pride of place to the role played by the language of lynching. Less attention has been paid to the metaphorics of dirt. However, a reading of the transcript of the hearings indicates that it was the idea of dirt and associated figures of pollution, contamination, and defilement that Thomas used most often to characterize the charges against him. Anthropologist Mary Douglas has noted that dirt and the constellation of practices that revolve around it have historically functioned as a symbolic matrix for notions and norms of order and its opposite.[17] Our ideas about dirt serve as cultural flashpoints for the elaboration and enforcement of dominant social conventions.

What is the meaning of Thomas's references to "dirt," "sleaze," "garbage," and the like? There is no easy answer to this question, because the most salient feature of this language is its indeterminacy. The discourse of defilement may be interpreted in a number of ways, which I can only sketch here. One might read Thomas's remarks to mean that the allegations of sexual harassment lodged against him are "dirty" because they are untrue. Thus, Thomas dares the committee to "parade" before it the women with whom he worked. Thomas implies that, unlike Anita Hill, these women will reveal the truth, by attesting to the "purity" of his workplace relations. Alternatively, one might take the discourse of defilement as a "due-process" claim: the charges are "dirt" because they have been made public, or because they have contaminated the propriety of Senate confirmation hearings. Thomas suggested more than once that the appropriate forum for such grave charges as those leveled by Hill was not a Senate committee but a court of law. Thomas's point seemed to be that there was a method by which these matters might have been more properly or (to play on the French word *propre*) cleanly considered. A third reading of Thomas's pollution imagery would take us into the substance of the charges against him. From this perspective the allegations of sexual harassment are "dirty" because genital sexuality (as in the references to penis sizes, pubic hair, etc.) and dirt are somehow linked,[18] at least outside the "private life" or "sanctity" (to use Thomas's words) of the bedroom.

Another possible interpretation of the metaphors of dirt and defilement to which Thomas resorted in his testimony forces us to focus on their decidedly racialist cast. A starting point for such a reading is Mary Douglas's contention that pollution ideas for which dirt is a marker serve as the figural infrastructure of a broader structure of thought, whose "key-stone, boundaries, margins and internal lines are held in relation by rituals of separation."[19] The Thomas-Hill hearings may thus be said to have represented the unexpected second act in what was to have been a short but significant national ritual of separation. What I have in mind here is not only the adversarial separation of the Senate along partisan lines (as in the allusion by its members to the Republican and Democratic "sides"), or the atavistic image of the "battle of the sexes" of which the hearings were taken to be an episode (as when the delegation of female members from the House of Representatives presented themselves at the door of the Senate chambers). I am thinking as well of the ritual of separation that set Clarence Thomas apart from the great masses of African Americans.

Though obvious once acknowledged, the separative dimensions of the Thomas confirmation hearings are easily overlooked. From the moment his nomination was announced, the politicians and the popular press went out of their way to present an image of a man who was unique and at the same time exemplary. Judge Thomas was heralded (in the words of *Newsweek* magazine) as a "Black Horatio Alger," who had raised himself up from the poverty of Pin Point to a position of power and prominence. This was the Clarence Thomas who was a living embodiment of the American dream, and at the same time, a man who had not forgotten from whence he came. It was in the light of this image that Senator Specter spoke on the Senate floor of Thomas's "looking out of his judicial chamber's window and seeing young African Americans being brought for criminal trials. 'And there,' he said, 'but for the grace of God go I.' " In a more aggressive spirit Senator Danforth defied his colleagues to name one member of the Senate "who knows disadvantage as Clarence Thomas knows disadvantage":

> I consider him to be a great American because he has come further in his life than anyone I have ever known. . . . Nobody here was born black in the segregated South. Nobody here was raised in a shack for 7 years without plumbing, in a broken home. Nobody knows that. Nobody has experienced that. Clarence Thomas has.

Alongside this autobiographical picture stood a second, more ideological image of Thomas's exemplary uniqueness, which had to do with his politics. In this vision, what made Thomas exceptional was the fact that he had defied the national civil rights establishment and its liberal white patrons, dared to "be his own man" and chosen, as he put it, "the loneliness of the black conservative." In the floor debates after the first stage of the Thomas hearings, Senator Hatch and others described the nominee as a "man of fierce independence" whom opponents wanted to "sacrifice . . . on the twin altars of preferences and reverse discrimination." When he appeared before the Judiciary

Committee in response to the charges of sexual harassment, Thomas himself insisted that the hearings regarding
Hill's allegations were proof positive of what would happen to "uppity blacks who in any way deign to think for
themselves, to do for themselves, to have different ideas";
he was being punished, as he saw it, for refusing to "kowtow to an old order." This view was echoed in a recent
article in *Commentary* magazine written by Arch Puddington. The author depicts Thomas as one of a small coterie
of black "iconoclasts," an emergent vanguard whose ideas
represent a challenge to the "established racial leadership."
In Puddington's argument, Thomas has courageously "di-
verge[d] from what the current crop of black leaders defines as the truth," and charted a course that has unfairly
"earned [him] the racial elites' scorn and opprobrium."[20]

The insistent focus on the ideology and ideological
uniqueness of Clarence Thomas suggests that his nomination to the Supreme Court was intended to be what
constitutional theorist Bruce Ackerman has called a "transformative" judicial appointment. Ackerman coined the
term to capture what he took to be the central lesson of the
confirmation hearings on Robert Bork. Ackerman argues
that had Bork been successfully named to the Supreme
Court, his appointment would have marked an effective,
albeit informal, constitutional amendment, because Robert
Bork possessed both the talent and temperament to force
the Court "to spearhead a radical judicial break with the
past."[21]

Although the terms of Ackerman's analysis take us some
way toward an understanding of the meaning of the
Thomas appointment, they do not go far enough. A successful account of the Thomas nomination must come to

grips with the specificity and significance of race as an independent factor in the politics of Supreme Court appointments. From this vantage point the Senate's confirmation of Clarence Thomas must be understood as a decisive repudiation of that part of our constitutional past during which the Supreme Court was thought to be one of the few institutional arenas in this country in which African Americans and other people of color could successfully wage their struggle for racial justice. With the retirement of Thurgood Marshall, President Bush's decision to nominate Thomas to the Court confirmed what many of those who follow the politics of the Supreme Court had been saying for some time: people of color should no longer look to the Supreme Court of the United States to protect their constitutional rights. Clarence Thomas's nomination made it emphatically clear that the Bush administration was not content simply to close off the Supreme Court as an avenue for progressive social change. That objective had already been achieved through previous appointments to the Court. Nor was it enough to cripple the civil rights community by forcing its legal advocates to fight to defend the gains that had been won. In symbolic terms the Thomas nomination was a wholesale rejection of the moral legacy of the Civil Rights Movement, and the memory of the suffering and struggle that the story of that movement has come to represent in American political culture. For this reason I believe that the Thomas confirmation hearings were not "transformative" at all. To the contrary. I would submit that the appointment of Clarence Thomas to the Supreme Court is more correctly characterized as a "deformative" moment in the history of American constitutional politics. In my view it is only the strength of his deformative credentials that explain the Bush administration's decision to replace Thurgood Marshall with a man who has shown himself both able and eager to castigate black leaders who "bitch, bitch, bitch, moan and whine"; to condemn his predecessor's mildly critical remarks during the bicentennial of the constitution as a near-treasonous "assault" on the document itself; and to deny that there was any "moral basis for racial policies" intended to "make up for a history of deprivation."

Taking these observations as a point of reference, we are now in a position to consider more precisely why the discourse of dirt and defilement formed the central motif in Thomas's testimony during the second stage of his confirmation hearings. For my part I cannot help but read these figures as the semiotic scars of a damaged and deformed life. One need look no further than the tone and texture of his language to see the degree to which the second African American to sit on the Supreme Court must be deemed not only a functionary, but the first fruit, of racist ideology in the new constitutional order.

How is this claim to be understood? In his article "Clarence Thomas and the Blacks," Arch Puddington reserves some of his most acerbic commentary for Derrick Bell, Bruce Wright, Charles Rangel, Alvin Poussaint, and other African Americans who, as Puddington sees it, would "deny the nominee the right to call himself black."[22] Puddington argues that Thomas in fact "seems pessimistic about the prospects for a society free of racism," and offers as evidence of Thomas's "strong conviction" in this regard remarks made in the course of an interview with Juan Williams: "There is nothing you can do to get past black skin. I don't care how educated you are, how good you are at what you do—you'll never have the same contacts or opportunities, you'll never be seen as equal to whites." Puddington conveniently fails to mention other comments Thomas has made, which indicate that Thomas is decidedly more ambivalent about this state of affairs than Puddington would have us believe. For example, on at least one occasion Thomas has shared his bitter recollection of his childhood in Savannah, where he was nicknamed "ABC," an acronym for "America's Blackest Child," and "ridiculed not only for his extremely dark complexion but also his hair—they called it 'nigger naps'—and thick lips."[23] Thomas himself has said that these and similar experiences produced a sense of self in which "you hate yourself for being part of a group that's gotten the hell kicked out of them." Elsewhere, he has described himself as part of a "mixed-up generation": "I don't fit in with whites and I don't fit in with blacks."

In the confirmation hearings Thomas complained that he felt "as though something has been lodged against me and painted on me and will leave an indelible mark on me." At another point during his testimony Thomas described the "racist, bigoted stereotypes" that had been "pinned" on him as "the kind of charges that are impossible to wash off." If one situates these remarks in the context of his metaphorical description of Hill's allegations, it would seem that the problem with the doubts articulated by some about Thomas's spiritual and emotional connection to the black experience in America to which Puddington refers lies not so much in the fact that they are implausible but that they are simply underdocumented.

The analysis of Joel Kovel is helpful here. In his *White*

Racism: A Psychohistory, Kovel notes that few people "have suffered the appellation of filthiness so much as Negroes."[24] This nominative fate may be traced primarily to the fact that "the blackness of black skin (even if it is really brown)"[25] has been fused with the idea of dirt, and more generally, with the image of anything that can pass out of the body, such as feces. In Kovel's view, the notion that blacks are "an essentially dirty and smelly people"[26] is the generative substrate of the racial fantasies that provide the psychosymbolic framework of white racism. Kovel's argument is too complex to treat here in any detail. What bears remarking here is his claim that the "nuclear experience" of white racism "is a sense of disgust about the body of the black person based upon a very primitive fantasy: that it contains an essence—dirt—that smells and may rub off onto the body of the racist."[27]

What Kovel does not explore is the degree to which the primal fantasy of white racism insinuates itself into the psychic structure of those against whom it is directed and becomes inscribed in the "mind [and] very skin"[28] of its victims. Frantz Fanon captures the psychosocial movement by which this process of reverse projection takes place when he writes that "the black man [must not only] be black; he must be black in relation to the white man."[29] Fanon maintains that the construction of the black self in a racist society is the work of "the other, the white man, who had woven me out of a thousand details, anecdotes, stories."[30] Indeed, for Fanon, "what is often called the black soul is a white man's artifact."[31]

These are hard sayings, but the rhetorical politics of the Thomas confirmation forces the recognition that they hold a certain horrific truth. I have suggested that the Thomas confirmation hearings may be understood in symbolic terms as a ritual of separation. Among the things from which Thomas was symbolically separated was the fact of his blackness. Although his proponents did not hesitate to make much of his racial roots, Thomas was chiefly represented, in the words of Iowa Senator Charles Grassley, as a "Republican judicial conservative who opposes quotas, and also happens to be black." This insistence on the essentially contingent character of Thomas's race provided a field for the practice of a rhetorical politics in which the nominee was figuratively sundered into the "two Clarence Thomases" whom his opponents could never quite pin down. On the one hand, Thomas was a "black Horatio Alger." This Clarence Thomas embraced, indeed, celebrated his filiative origins, from a safe distance, and in the knowledge that he was undeniably different from the black masses from whom he had come. On the other hand, Thomas was a "Republican judicial conservative." The identity of this latter Clarence Thomas was constituted first and foremost by the force of his ideological affiliations, which were constantly validated by his Republican patrons in the White House and Senate, who effectively accorded him a kind of "honorary whiteness." Any doubts regarding Thomas's suitability for this elevation in status were resolved publicly by Republican Senator Danforth, and privately (in terms that were perforce unspoken) by Thomas's equally conservative wife.

During the first stage of the confirmation hearings Thomas was able to negotiate successfully between these two separate selves. His ability to do so may be laid to the fact that both of these identities were mythic selves or "performances" for which Thomas had been carefully prepared during his five days on "murderers' row." The public revelation of Anita Hill's charges against Thomas abruptly interrupted the carefully orchestrated separative ritual of the confirmation hearings. Forced to improvise from the materials at hand, Thomas deftly deployed the lynching metaphor, and thus assumed the identity of the innocent black victim, the very role he had in the past so vocally and visibly eschewed. Even here, however, the judge managed to distort the actual record, and thus prevent a fall from myth into the history of race in America. Thomas's use of the rhetoric of lynching was an act of what Barthes calls "language-robbery," in which the memory of the torture and murder of thousands of African Americans was appropriated for the sake of a "brief act" of linguistic "larceny."[32] By all accounts, Clarence Thomas seems to have succeeded. One can only hope that future generations will not forget the millions whom Thomas has condemned to harvest this strange and bitter crop.

NOTES

1. Roland Barthes, *Mythologies,* trans. Annette Lavers (New York: Hill & Wang, 1972), p. 151.
2. Barthes, *Mythologies,* p. 150.
3. Ibid., pp. 122, 133, 152, 146.
4. Ibid., pp. 121–22.
5. For a history of the Emmett Till case, see Stephen Whitfield, *A Death in the Delta: The Story of Emmett Till* (New York: Free Press, 1988).
6. Joel Kovel, *White Racism* (New York: Columbia University Press, 1984), p. 67.
7. Walter White, *Rope and Faggot* (New York: Arno Press, 1969), pp. 27–29.
8. "Black Skin, White Mask," *Amsterdam News* (New York), October 19, 1991.
9. This was the spirit of the "hope" expressed by Maya Angelou in an article written before the revelation of the sexual harassment charge. Maya Angelou, "I Dare to Hope," *New York Times,* August 25, 1991.
10. *Loving* v. *Virginia,* U.S., vol. 388 (1967), p. 1.
11. Ibid., p. 11.
12. A. Leon Higginbotham, "An Open Letter to Justice Clarence Thomas from a Federal Judicial Colleague," *University of Pennsylvania Law Review,* vol. 140 (1992), pp. 1005, 1024–25.
13. Orlando Patterson, "Race, Gender and Liberal Fallacies," *New York Times,* October 20, 1991.
14. Kovel, *White Racism,* p. 54.
15. Ibid.
16. Kendall Thomas, "A House Divided Against Itself: A Comment on 'Mastery, Slavery, and Emancipation," *Cardozo Law Review,* vol. 10 (1989), pp. 1481, 1500.
17. Mary Douglas, *Purity and Danger: An Analysis of Concepts of*

Pollution and Taboo (New York: Routledge, 1991).

18. Klaus Theweleit, *Male Fantasies*, vol. 1, *Women, Floods, Bodies, History*, trans. Stephen Conway (Minneapolis: University of Minnesota Press, 1987).

19. Douglas, *Purity and Danger*, p. 41.

20. Arch Puddington, "Clarence Thomas and the Blacks," *Commentary*, February 1992, p. 28.

21. Bruce Ackerman, "Transformative Appointments," *Harvard Law Review*, vol. 101 (1988), pp. 1164, 1168.

22. Puddington, "Clarence Thomas," p. 29.

23. Nat Hentoff, "America's Blackest Child," *Village Voice*, September 10, 1991.

24. Kovel, *White Racism*, p. 82.

25. Ibid., pp. 82–83.

26. Ibid., p. 83.

27. Ibid., p. 84.

28. Calvin Hernton, *Sex and Racism in America* (Garden City, N.Y.: Doubleday, 1965), p. 65.

29. Frantz Fanon, *Black Skin, White Masks*, trans. C. L. Markmann (New York: Grove Press, 1967), p. 110.

30. Ibid., p. 111.

31. Ibid., p. 14.

32. Barthes, *Mythologies*, pp. 131, 125.

CORNEL WEST

Black Leadership and the Pitfalls of Racial Reasoning

The most depressing feature of the Clarence Thomas/Anita Hill hearings was neither the mean-spirited attacks of the Republicans nor the spineless silences of the Democrats—both reveal the predictable inability of most white politicians to talk candidly about race and gender. Rather, what most disturbed me was the low level of political discussion in black America about these hearings—a crude discourse about race and gender that bespeaks a failure of nerve of black leadership.

This failure of nerve was already manifest in the selection and confirmation process of Clarence Thomas. Bush's choice of Thomas caught most black leaders off guard. Few had the courage to say publicly that this was an act of cynical tokenism concealed by outright lies about Thomas being the most qualified candidate regardless of race. The fact that Thomas was simply unqualified for the Court—a claim warranted by his undistinguished record as a student (mere graduation from Yale Law School does not qualify one for the Supreme Court!); his turbulent eight years at the EEOC, where he left thirteen thousand age-discrimination cases dying on the vine for lack of investigation; and his mediocre performance during a short fifteen months as an appellate court judge—was not even mentioned. The very fact that no black leader could utter publicly that a black appointee for the Supreme Court was *unqualified* shows how captive they are to white-racist stereotypes about black intellectual talent. The point here is not simply that if Thomas were white they would have no trouble uttering this fact from the rooftops, but also that their silence reveals that they may entertain the possibility that the racist stereotype is true. Hence their attempt to cover Thomas's mediocrity with silence. Of course, some privately admit his mediocrity then point out the mediocrity of Judge Souter and other Court judges—as if white mediocrity is a justification for black mediocrity. No double standards here, this argument goes, if a black man is unqualified, one can defend and excuse him by appealing to other unqualified white judges. This chimes well with a cynical tokenism of the lowest common denominator— with little concern about shattering the racist stereotype or furthering the public interest in the nation. It also renders invisible highly qualified black judges who deserve serious consideration for selection to the Court.

How did much of black leadership get in this bind? Why did so many of them capitulate to Bush's cynical strategy? Three reasons loom large. First, Thomas's claim to racial authenticity—his birth in Jim Crow Georgia, his childhood spent as the grandson of a black sharecropper, his undeniably black phenotype degraded by racist ideals of beauty, and his gallant black struggle for achievement in racist America. Second, the complex relation of this claim to racial authenticity to the increasing closing-ranks mentality in black America. Escalating black-nationalist sentiments—the notion that America's will to racial justice is weak and therefore black people must close ranks for survival in a hostile country—rests principally upon claims to racial authenticity. Third, the way in which black-nationalist sentiments promote and encourage black cultural conservatism, especially black patriarchal (and homophobic) power. The idea of black people closing ranks against hostile white Americans reinforces black male power exercised over black women (e.g., to protect, regulate, subordinate, and hence usually, though not always, use and abuse women) in order to preserve black social order under circumstances of white-literal attack and symbolic assault.

Most black leaders got lost in this thicket of reasoning and thus got caught in a vulgar form of racial reasoning: *black authenticity—black closing-ranks mentality—black male subordination of black women in the interests of the black community in a hostile white-racist country*. This line of racial reasoning leads to such questions as "Is Thomas really black?"; "Is he black enough to be defended?"; "Is he just black on the outside?" et al. In fact, these kinds of questions were asked, debated, and answered throughout black America in barber shops, beauty salons, living rooms, churches, mosques, and schoolrooms.

Unfortunately, the very framework of this line of racial reasoning was not called into question. Yet as long as racial reasoning regulates black thought and action, Clarence Thomases will continue to haunt black America—as Bush and his ilk sit back, watch, and prosper. How does one undermine the framework of racial reasoning? By dismantling each pillar slowly and systematically. The fundamental aim of this undermining and dismantling is to replace racial reasoning with moral reasoning, to understand the black-freedom struggle not as an affair of skin pigmentation and racial phenotype but rather as a matter of ethical principles and wise politics, and to combat black-nationalist views of subordinating the issues and interests of black women by linking mature black self-love and self-respect to egalitarian relations within and outside black communities. The failure of nerve of black leadership is to refuse to undermine and dismantle the framework of racial reasoning.

Let us begin with the claim to racial authenticity—a claim Bush made about Thomas, Thomas made about himself in the hearings, and black nationalists make about themselves. What is black authenticity? Who is really black? First, blackness has no meaning outside of a system of race-conscious people and practices. After centuries of racist degradation, exploitation, and oppression in America, blackness means being minimally subject to white supremacist abuse and being part of a rich culture and community that has struggled against such abuse. All people with black skin and African phenotype are subject to potential white-supremacist abuse. Hence, all black Americans have some interest in resisting racism—even if their interest is confined solely to themselves as individuals rather than to larger black communities. Yet how this "interest" is defined and how individuals and communities are understood vary. So any claim to black authenticity— beyond being the potential object of racist abuse and heir to a grand tradition of black struggle—is contingent on one's political definition of black interest and one's ethical understanding of how this interest relates to individuals and communities in and outside black America. In short, blackness is a political and ethical construct. Appeals to black authenticity ignore this fact; such appeals hide and conceal the political and ethical dimension of blackness. This is why claims to racial authenticity trump political and ethical argument—and why racial reasoning discourages moral reasoning. Every claim to racial authenticity presupposes elaborate conceptions of political and ethical relations of interests, individuals, and communities. Racial reasoning conceals these presuppositions behind a deceptive cloak of racial consensus—yet racial reasoning is seductive because it invokes an undeniable history of racial abuse and racial struggle. This is why Bush's claims to Thomas's black authenticity, Thomas's claims about his own black authenticity, and black-nationalist claims about black authenticity all highlight histories of black abuse and black struggle.

But if claims to black authenticity are political and ethical conceptions of the relation of black interests, individuals, and communities, then any attempt to confine black authenticity to black-nationalist politics or black male interests warrants suspicion. For example, black leaders failed to highlight the problematic claims Clarence Thomas made about his sister, Emma Mae, regarding her experience with the welfare system. In front of a conservative audience in San Francisco, Thomas made her out to be a welfare scrounger dependent on state support. Yet, like most black women in American history, Emma Mae is a hardworking person, sensitive enough to take care of her sick aunt, and she was unable to work for a short period of time. After she got off welfare, she worked two jobs—until three in the morning! This episode reveals not only a lack of integrity and character on Thomas's part; failure to highlight it by black leaders discloses a conception of black authenticity confined to black male interests, individuals, and communities. In short, the refusal to give weight to the interests of black women by most black leaders was already apparent before Anita Hill appeared on the scene.

The claims to black authenticity that feed on the closing-ranks mentality of black people are dangerous precisely because this closing of ranks is usually done at the expense of black women. It also tends to ignore the divisions of class and sexual orientation in black America—divisions that require attention if *all* black interests, individuals, and communities are to be taken into consideration. Thomas's conservative Republican politics does not promote a closing-ranks mentality; instead, his claim to black authenticity is for the purpose of self-promotion, to gain power and prestige. All his professional life he has championed individual achievement and race-free standards. Yet when he saw his ship sinking, he played the racial card of black victimization and black solidarity at the expense of Anita Hill. Like his sister Emma Mae, Anita Hill could be used and abused for his own self-interested conception of black authenticity and racial solidarity.

Thomas played this racial card with success—first with appeals to his victimization in Jim Crow Georgia and later to his victimization by a "high-tech lynching"—primarily because of the deep cultural conservatism in white and black America. In white America this cultural conservatism takes the form of a chronic racism, sexism, and homophobia. Hence, only certain kinds of black people deserve high positions, that is, those who accept the rules of the game played by white America. In black America, this cultural conservatism takes the form of an inchoate xenophobia (e.g., against whites, Jews, and Asian Americans), systemic sexism, and homophobia. Like all conservatisms rooted in a quest for order, the pervasive disorder in white and, especially, black America fans and fuels the channeling of rage toward the most vulnerable and degraded members of the community. For white America this means primarily scapegoating black people, women, gays, and lesbians. For black America the targets are principally black women and black gays and lesbians. In this way black-nationalist and black-male-centered claims to black authenticity reinforce black cultural conservatism. The support of Louis Farrakhan's Nation of Islam for Clarence Thomas—despite Farrakhan's critique of Republican Party racist and conservative policies—highlights this fact. It also shows how racial reasoning leads disparate viewpoints in black America to the same dead end—with substantive ethical principles and savvy, wise politics left out.

The undermining and dismantling of the framework of racial reasoning—especially the basic notions of black authenticity, the closing-ranks mentality, and black cultural conservatism—leads toward a new framework for black thought and method. This new framework should be a *prophetic* one of moral reasoning, with its fundamental ideas of a mature black identity, coalition strategy, and black cultural democracy. Instead of cathartic appeals to black authenticity, a prophetic viewpoint bases mature black self-love and self-respect on the moral quality of black responses to undeniable racist degradation in the American past and present. These responses assume neither a black essence that all black people share nor one black perspective to which all black people should adhere. Rather, a prophetic framework encourages *moral* assessment of the variety of perspectives held by black people and selects those views based on black dignity and decency that eschew putting any group of people or culture on a pedestal or in the gutter. Instead, blackness is understood to be either the perennial possibility of white-supremacist abuse or the distinct styles and dominant modes of expression found in black cultures and communities. These styles and modes are diverse—yet they do stand apart from those of other groups (even as they are shaped by and shape those of other groups). And all such styles and modes stand in need of ethical evaluation. Mature black identity results from an acknowledgment of the specific black responses to white-supremacist abuses and a moral assessment of these responses such that the humanity of black people does not rest on deifying or demonizing others.

Instead of a closing-ranks mentality, a prophetic framework encourages a coalition strategy that solicits genuine solidarity with those deeply committed to antiracist struggle. This strategy is neither naive nor opportunistic; black suspicion of whites, Latinos, Jews, and Asian Americans runs deep for historical reasons. Yet there are slight though significant antiracist traditions among whites, Asian Americans, and especially Latinos, Jews, and indigenous people that must not be cast aside. Such coalitions are important precisely because they not only enhance the plight of black people but also because they enrich the quality of life in the country.

Lastly, a prophetic framework replaces black cultural conservatism with black cultural democracy. Instead of authoritarian sensibilities that subordinate women or degrade gays and lesbians, black cultural democracy promotes the equality of black women and men and the humanity of black gays and lesbians. In short, black cultural democracy rejects the pervasive patriarchy and homophobia in black American life.

If most black leaders had adopted a prophetic framework of moral reasoning rather than a narrow framework of racial reasoning, the debate over the Thomas-Hill hearings would have proceeded in a quite different manner in black America. For example, both Thomas and Hill would be viewed as two black conservative supporters of some of the most vicious policies to besiege black working and poor communities since Jim and Jane Crow segregation. Both Thomas and Hill supported an unprecedented redistribution of wealth from working people to well-to-do people in the form of regressive taxation, deregulation policies, cutbacks and slowdowns in public service programs, takebacks at the negotiation table between workers and management, and military buildups at the Pentagon. Both Thomas and Hill supported the unleashing of unbridled capitalist market forces on a level never witnessed before in this country that have devastated black working and poor communities. These market forces took the form principally of unregulated corporative and financial expansion and intense entrepreneurial activity. This tremendous ferment in big and small businesses—including enormous bonanzas in speculation, leveraged buy-outs and mergers, as well as high levels of corruption and graft—contributed to a new kind of culture of consumption in white and black America. Never before has the seductive market way of life held such sway in nearly every sphere of American life.

This market way of life promotes addictions to stimulation and obsessions with comfort and convenience. These addictions and obsessions—centered primarily around bodily pleasures and status rankings—constitute market moralities of various sorts. The common denominator is a rugged and ragged individualism and rapacious hedonism in quest of a perennial "high" in body and mind.

In the hearings Clarence Thomas emerged as the exemplary hedonist, addicted to pornography and captive to a stereotypical self-image of the powerful black man who revels in sexual prowess in a racist society. Anita Hill appears as the exemplary careerist addicted to job promotion and captive to the stereotypical self-image of the sacrificial black woman who suffers silently and alone. There should be little doubt that Thomas's claims are suspect—those about his sister, his eighteen-year silence about *Roe* v. *Wade,* his intentions in the Heritage Foundation speech praising the antiabortion essay by Lewis Lehrman, and the contours of his conservative political philosophy. Furthermore, his obdurate stonewalling in regard to his private life was symptomatic of all addicts—passionate denial and irrational cover-up. There also should be little doubt that Anita Hill's truth-telling was a break from her careerist ambitions. On the one hand, she strikes me as a person of integrity and honesty. On the other hand, she indeed put a premium on job advancement—even at painful personal cost. Yet her speaking out disrupted this pattern of behavior and she found herself supported only by people who opposed the very conservative policies she otherwise championed, namely, progressive feminists, liberals, and some black folk. How strange she must feel being a hero to her former foes. One wonders whether Judge Bork supported her as fervently as she did him a few years ago.

A prophetic framework of moral reasoning would have liberated black leaders from the racial guilt of opposing a black man for the highest court in the land and feeling as if one had to choose between a black woman and a black man. Like the Congressional Black Caucus (minus one?), black people could simply oppose Thomas based on qualifications and principle. And one could choose between two black conservatives based on their sworn testimonies in light of the patterns of their behavior in the recent past. Similarly, black leaders could avoid being duped by Thomas's desperate and vulgar appeals to racial victimization by a white male Senate committee who handled him gently (no questions about his private life, no queries about his problematic claims). Like Senator Hollings, who knows racial intimidation when he sees it (given his past experiences with it), black leaders could see through this rhetorical charade and call a moral spade a moral spade.

Unfortunately, most of black leadership remained caught in a framework of racial reasoning—even when they opposed Thomas and/or supported Hill. Rarely did we have a black leader highlight the moral content of a mature black identity, accent the crucial role of coalition strategy in the struggle for justice, or promote the ideal of black cultural democracy. Instead, the debate evolved around glib formulations of a black "role model" based on mere pigmentation, an atavistic defense of blackness that mirrors the increasing xenophobia in American life and a silence about the ugly authoritarian practices in black America that range from sexual harassment to indescribable violence against women. Hence, a grand opportunity for substantive discussion and struggle over race and gender was missed in black America and the larger society. And black leadership must share some of the blame. As long as black leaders remain caught in a framework of racial reasoning, they will not rise above the manipulative language of Bush and Thomas—just as the state of siege (the death, disease, and destruction) raging in much of black America creates more wastelands and combat zones. Where there is no vision, the people perish; where there is no framework of moral reasoning, the people close ranks in a war of all against all. The growing gangsterization of America results in part from a market-driven racial reasoning prevalent from the White House to the projects. In this sense, George Bush, David Duke, and gangster rap artists speak the same language from different social locations—only racial reasoning can save us. Yet I hear a cloud of witnesses from afar—Sojourner Truth, Wendell Phillips, Emma Goldman, A. Philip Randolph, Ella Baker, Fannie Lou Hamer, Michael Harrington, Abraham Joshua Heschel, Tom Hayden, Harvey Milk, Robert Moses, Barbara Ehrenreich, Martin Luther King, Jr., and many anonymous others—who championed the struggle for freedom and justice in a prophetic framework of moral reasoning. They understood that the pitfalls of racial reasoning are too costly in mind, body, and soul—especially for a downtrodden and despised people like black Americans. The best of our leadership have recognized this valuable truth—and more must do so in the future if America is to survive with any moral sense.

KIMBERLÉ CRENSHAW

Whose Story Is It, Anyway?
Feminist and Antiracist Appropriations of Anita Hill

As television, the Clarence Thomas/Anita Hill hearings played beautifully as an episode right out of "The Twilight Zone." Stunned by the drama's mystifying images, its misplaced pairings, and its baffling contradictions, viewers found themselves in a parallel universe where political allegiances barely imaginable a moment earlier sprang to life: an administration that won an election through the shameless exploitation of the mythic black rapist took the offensive against stereotypes about black male sexuality; a political party that had been the refuge of white resentment won the support, however momentary, of the majority of African Americans; a black neoconservative individualist whose upward mobility was fueled by his unbounded willingness to stymie the advancement of other African Americans was embraced under the wings of racial solidarity; and a black woman, herself a victim of racism, was symbolically transformed into the role of a would-be white woman whose unwarranted finger-pointing whetted the appetites of a racist lynch mob.

But it was no "Twilight Zone" that America discovered when Anita Hill came forward. America simply stumbled into the place where African-American women live, a political vacuum of erasure and contradiction maintained by the almost routine polarization of "blacks and women" into separate and competing political camps. Existing within the overlapping margins of race and gender discourse and in the empty spaces between, it is a location whose very nature resists telling. This location contributes to black women's ideological disempowerment in a way that tipped the scales against Anita Hill from the very start. While there are surely many dimensions of the Thomas-Hill episode that contributed to the way it played out, my focus on the ideological plane is based on the idea that at least one important way social power is mediated in American society is through the contestation between the many narrative structures through which reality might be perceived and talked about. By this I mean to focus on the intense interpretive conflicts that ultimately bear on the particular ways that realities are socially constructed. Ideology, seen in the form of the narrative tropes available for representing our experience, was a factor of social power to the extent that Anita Hill's inability to be heard outside the rhetorical structures within which cultural power has been organized hampered her ability to achieve recognition and support. Thus, Anita Hill's status as a black female—at the crossroads of gender and race hierarchies— was a central feature in the manner in which she was (mis)perceived. Because she was situated within two fundamental hierarchies of social power, the central disadvantage that Hill faced was the lack of available and widely comprehended narratives to communicate the reality of her experience as a black woman to the world.

The particular experience of black women in the dominant cultural ideology of American society can be conceptualized as intersectional. Intersectionality captures the way in which the particular location of black women in dominant American social relations is unique and in some senses unassimilable into the discursive paradigms of gender and race domination. One commonly noted aspect of this location is that black women are in a sense doubly burdened, subject in some ways to the dominating practices of both a sexual hierarchy and a racial one. In addition to this added dimension, intersectionality also refers to the ways that black women's marginalization within dominant discourses of resistance limits the means available to relate and conceptualize our experiences as black women.

In legal doctrine this idea has been explored in terms of doctrinal exclusion, that is, the ways in which the specific forms of domination to which black females are subject sometimes fall between the existing legal categories for recognizing injury.[1] Underlying the legal parameters of racial discrimination are numerous narratives reflecting discrimination as it is experienced by black men, while the underlying imagery of gender discrimination incorporates the experiences of white women. The particularities of black female subordination are suppressed as the terms of racial and gender discrimination law require that we mold our experience into that of either white women or black men in order to be legally recognized.

The marginalization of black women in antidiscrimination law is replicated in the realm of oppositional politics; black women are marginalized in feminist politics as a consequence of race, and they are marginalized in antiracist politics as a consequence of their gender. The consequences of this multiple marginality are fairly predictable— there is simply silence of and about black women. Yet black women do not share the burdens of these elisions alone. When feminism does not explicitly oppose racism, and when antiracism does not incorporate opposition to patriarchy, race and gender politics often end up being antagonistic to each other and both interests lose. The Thomas/Hill controversy presents a stark illustration of the problem as evidenced by the opposition between narratives of rape and of lynching. These tropes have come to symbolize the mutually exclusive claims that have been generated within both antiracist and feminist discourses about the centrality of sexuality to both race and gender domination. In feminist contexts, sexuality represents a central site of the oppression of women; rape and the rape trial are its dominant narrative trope. In antiracist discourses, sexuality is also a central site upon which the repression of blacks has been premised; the lynching narrative is embodied as its trope. (Neither narrative tends to acknowledge the legitimacy of the other; the reality of rape tends to be disregarded within the lynching narrative; the impact of racism is frequently marginalized within rape narratives.) Both these tropes figured prominently in this controversy, and it was in this sense that the debacle constituted a classic showdown between antiracism and feminism. The tropes, whether explicitly invoked, as lynching, or implicitly referenced, as rape, served to communicate in shorthand competing narratives about the hearings and about what "really" happened between Clarence Thomas and Anita Hill. Anita Hill was of course cast in both narratives, but because one told a tale of sexism and the other told an opposing tale of racism, the simultaneity of Hill's race and gender identity was essentially denied. In this sense, both feminist and antiracist told tales on Anita Hill, tales in which she was appropriated to tell everybody's story but her own.

These competing appropriations of Anita Hill within feminist and antiracist discourses represent a persistent dilemma that confronts black women within prevailing constructions of identity politics: dominant conceptions of racism and sexism render it virtually impossible to represent our situation in ways that fully articulate our subject position as black women. While Thomas was able to invoke narratives that linked his situation to the sexual oppression of black men and thus have his story understood as relevant to the entire black community, Hill remained unable to represent even herself, much less other similarly situated black women.

In this essay I want to elaborate how the cultural dynamics surrounding the Thomas-Hill conflict are better understood in terms of Hill's intersectional disempowerment. My argument proceeds as follows. Addressing first the dominant paradigm for understanding the exercise of gender power, the narrative trope of the raped (white) woman, I discuss how Hill's experience in fact partly fit this rhetorical structure, and how her lack of power can be understood in part through the ways that white feminists have articulated gender domination. Second, however, I highlight Hill's intersectional identity by likewise showing the ways that the rape-trial analogy didn't fit, and how the limitations of traditional feminist discourse worked to suppress the more nuanced experience that Hill was communicating. In the second part of the essay I turn to race discourse and discuss how Hill's experience was partially explicable in terms of the dominant discourse of racial liberation. But this same discourse, embodied in the image of the lynched black man, also worked to disempower Hill in relation to Clarence Thomas.

I. Anita Hill as a Victim of Sexual Domination—The Rape Trope

Anita Hill was primarily presented to the American public as simply a woman complaining about sexual harassment. Her plausibility in that role was dependent upon the degree to which she could be fit within the dominant images of sexual victimization. Those images, in turn, have been heavily critiqued in the feminist articulation of gender politics. My argument here is that one consequence of the feminist movement's tendency to think about gender power and dynamics in terms of what we might call a universalist or essentialist form is that it depicts the structural forms that gender power plays in the white community as representing gender pure and simple. While many elements of the dominant feminist discourse about gender power and sexuality clearly did apply to Anita Hill—for example, the tradition of impugning charges of sexual aggression with baseless allegations of psychic delusions or vengeful spite—the grounding of the critique on white women meant that, in a sense, Hill (and Thomas) had to be deraced, so that they could be represented as actors in a recognizable story of sexual harassment. While white feminists were in general the most consistent and vocal supporters of Hill, the fact remains that both her lack of fit into the dominant imagery of the violated madonna and, more specifically, the feminist movement's inability to develop alternative narratives comprehending the ways that women of color experience gender power, led to the particular dynamics that many of her supporters themselves were unable to understand, dynamics that included the rejection of Hill by the majority of black women as well as white women.

Feminist legal scholars have frequently used rape as a framework to capture both the way women experience sexual harassment and the way the law shapes the claims of the few courageous women who come forward. Feminist scholars and activists have long criticized the way the adjudication of sexual aggression is animated by myths about women, about assumptions regarding their veracity and their integrity, and by doubts about their grasp on reality. In both rape and sexual-harassment cases the inquiry tends to focus more on the woman's conduct and character rather than on the conduct and character of the defendant. As a consequence, rape law does less to protect the sexual autonomy of women than it does to reinforce established codes of female sexual conduct.

Part of the regulation of sexuality through rape law occurs in the perception of the complaining witness at the rape trial. Building on the idea that reality is socially constructed in part through ideologically informed images of "men" and "women," feminist legal work has emphasized the ways that perceptions of the credibility of witnesses, for example, are mediated by dominant narratives about the ways that men and women "are." Within this framework, the vast disparity between male and female characterizations reflects a gendered zero-sum equation of credibility and power. The routine focus on the victim's sexual history functions to cast the complainant in one of several roles, including the whore, the tease, the vengeful liar, the mentally or emotionally unstable, or, in a few instances, the madonna. Once these ideologically informed character assignments are made, "the story" tells itself, usually supplanting the woman's account of what transpired between the complainant and the accused with a fiction of villainous female intentionality that misleads and entraps the "innocent" or unsuspecting male in his performance of prescribed sexual behavior. Such displacing narratives are overwhelmingly directed toward interrogating and discrediting the woman's character on behalf of maintaining a considerable range of sexual prerogatives for men. Even the legal definitions of the crime of rape itself are inscribed with male visions of the sexual sphere—the focus on penetration, the definitions of consent (with the once-conventional requirement of "utmost resistance"),[2] the images of female provocation and spiteful false accusation, and the links between desirability, purity, chastity, and value.[3]

The feminist narrative of the rape trial did in many ways account for the dynamics that Anita Hill put into play. For example, a good deal of the hearings was allegedly devoted to determining the credibility of the parties. Anita Hill's subordination through the notion of credibility is revealed in the relatively wide range of narratives that Thomas's defenders could invoke by simply describing events and impressions that had little to do with what transpired between Hill and Thomas in private. For example, the conversation that Anita Hill allegedly had with John Doggett was deemed relevant within a narrative that presented Hill as an undesirable woman who constructed relationships with men who rejected her. Testimony that she was aloof, ambitious, and hard to get along with was relevant within a narrative that presented her as calculating and careerist. The continuous focus on failure to resign after the harassment began fit into a narrative that presented her as a woman who did not meet the utmost-resistance standard because she was apparently unwilling to exchange her career for her "honor"; she was thus unworthy to make the claim.

Yet there were many narratives that could have been told about Thomas that bore on his credibility. For example, his quite startling shift in philosophy during the eighties and his subsequent "confirmation conversion" could have been understood as bearing on his reputation for truthfulness;[4] his derogatory public references to his sister could be seen as further evidence of his willingness to bend the truth;[5] his participation in an administrative position paper recommending reduced enforcement of sexual harassment could have been interpreted as suggesting a dismissive attitude toward the problem of sexual harassment. Moreover, the testimony of Angela Wright and two other corroborating witnesses could have been used to suggest that there was in fact a pattern of harassment,[6] and most obviously, evidence relating to his consumption of pornography could have been used to suggest a source for the elusive Long Dong Silver. That none of these narratives were seriously pursued while countless narratives about Anita Hill were—though they were arguably less relevant—demonstrates how the interpretive structures we use to reconstruct events are thoroughly shaped by gender power.

II. Race and Chastity: The Limitations of the Feminist Paradigm

Feminist discourse speaks to the particular way in which Anita Hill was disempowered through the very structuring of the inquiry, yet it could account for only part of the context within which Anita Hill acted. The particular intersectional identity of Hill, as both a woman and an African American, lent dimensions to her ideological placement in the economy of American culture that could not be translated through the dominant feminist analysis.[7] Again using the parallel between rape and sexual harassment, these race-specific aspects of black women's experiences are accessible.

Rape and other sexual abuses in the work context, now termed sexual harassment, have been a condition of black women's work life for centuries. Forced sexual access to black women was of course institutionalized in slavery and was central to its reproduction. During the period when the domination of white women was justified and reinforced by the nineteenth-century separate-spheres ideology, the few privileges of separate spheres were not available to black women at all. Instead, the subordination of African-American women recognized few boundaries between public and private life. Rape and other sexual abuses were justified by myths that black women were sexually voracious, that they were sexually indiscriminate, and that they readily copulated with animals, most frequently imagined to be apes and monkeys. Indeed, their very anatomy was objectified. Patricia Hill Collins notes that the abuse and mutilation that these myths inspired are memorialized to this day in a Paris museum where the buttocks and genitalia of Sara Bartmann, the so-called Hottentot Venus, remain on display.[8]

The stereotypes and myths that justified the sexual abuse of black women in slavery continue to be played out in current society. They are apparent in the experiences of women who are abused on their jobs and in the experiences of black women elsewhere in society. For example, in many of the sexual-harassment cases involving African-American women, the incidents they report often represent a merging of racist myths with the victims' vulnerability as women. Black female plaintiffs tell stories of insults and slurs that often go to the core of black women's sexual construction. While black women share with white women the experience of being objectified as "cunts" "beavers," or "pieces," for them those insults are many times prefaced with "black" or "nigger" or "jungle." Perhaps this racialization of sexual harassment explains why black women are disproportionately represented in sexual-harassment cases. Racism may well provide the clarity to see that sexual harassment is neither a flattering gesture nor a misguided social overture but an act of intentional discrimination that is insulting, threatening, and debilitating.

Pervasive myths and stereotypes about black women not only shape the kinds of harassment that black women experience but also influence whether black women's stories are likely to be believed. Historically, a black woman's word was not taken as truth; our own legal system once drew a connection—as a matter of law—between lack of chastity and lack of veracity. In other words, a woman who was likely to have sex could not be trusted to tell the truth. Because black women were not expected to be chaste, they were likewise considered less likely to tell the truth. Thus, judges were known to instruct juries to take a black woman's word with a grain of salt. One judge admonished jurors not to apply the ordinary presumption of chastity to black women, for if they were to do so, they "would be blinding themselves to actual conditions."[9] In 1971 a judge was quoted as saying, "Within the Negro community, you really have to redefine rape. You never know about them." Lest it be believed that such doubts have been banished to the past, a very recent study of jurors in rape trials revealed that black women's integrity is still very deeply questioned by many people in society. One juror, explaining why a black rape victim was discredited by the jury, stated, "You can't believe everything they say. They're known to exaggerate the truth."[10]

Even where the facts of our stories are believed, myths and stereotypes about black women also influence whether the insult and injury we have experienced is relevant or important. One study concluded, for example, that men who assault black women are the least likely to receive jail time; when they do, the average sentence given to black women's assailants is two years; the average for white women's assailants is ten years. Again, attitudes of jurors seem to reflect a common belief that black women are different from white women and that sexual aggression directed toward them is less objectionable. In a case involving the rape of a black preteen, one juror argued for acquittal on the grounds that a girl her age from "that neighborhood . . . probably wasn't a virgin anyway."

These responses are not exceptional, as illustrated by the societal response to the victimization of Carol Stuart, the Boston woman whose husband murdered her and then fingered a black male. It would strain credibility to say that the Boston police would have undertaken a door-to-door search of any community had Carol Stuart and her fetus been black, or, on a similar note, that Donald Trump would have taken out a full-page ad in the *New York Times* calling for the reinstatement of the death penalty had that investment banker raped in Central Park been a black service worker. Surely the black woman who was gang-raped during that same week, whose pelvis and ankles were shattered when she was thrown down an elevator shaft and left to die, along with the twenty-eight other women who were raped that week and received no outpouring of public concern, would find it impossible to deny that society views the victimization of some women as being less important than that of others.

Black women experience much of the sexual aggression that the feminist movement has articulated but in a form that represents simultaneously their subordinate racial status. While the fallen-woman imagery that white feminists identify does represent much of black women's experience of gender domination, given their race, black women have in a sense always been within the fallen-woman category. For black women the issue is not the precariousness of holding on to the protection that the madonna image provides or the manner in which the madonna image works to regulate and thereby constrain black women's sexuality. Instead, it is the denial of the presumption of "madonna-hood" that shapes responses to black women's sexual victimization.

White feminists have been reluctant to incorporate race into their narratives about gender, sex, and power. Their unwillingness to speak to the race-specific dimensions of black women's sexual disempowerment was compounded by their simultaneous failure to understand the ways that race may have contributed to Anita Hill's silence. Their attempt to explain why she remained silent spoke primarily to her career interests. Yet the other reasons why many black women have been reluctant to reveal experiences of sexual abuse—particularly by African-American men—remained unexamined. In fact, many black women fear that their stories might be used to reinforce stereotypes of black men as sexually threatening. Others who may not share this particular concern may nevertheless remain silent fearing ostracism from those who do. Black women face these kinds of dilemmas throughout their lives; efforts to tell these stories may have shaped perceptions of Anita Hill differently among black women, perhaps providing some impetus for breaking through the race-versus-gender dichotomy. Content to rest their case on a raceless tale of gender subordination, white feminists missed an opportunity to span the chasm between feminism and antiracism. Indeed, feminists actually helped maintain the chasm by endorsing the framing of the event as a race versus a gender issue. In the absence of narratives linking race and gender, the prevailing narrative structures continued to organize the Hill and Thomas controversy as either a story about the harassment of a white woman or a story of the harassment of a black man. Identification by race or gender seemed to be an either/or proposition, and when it is experienced in that manner, black people, both men and women, have traditionally chosen race solidarity. Indeed, white feminist acquiescence to the either/or frame worked directly to Thomas's advantage: with Hill thus cast as simply a de-raced—that is, white—woman, Thomas was positioned to claim that he was the victim of racial discrimination with Hill as the perpetrator. However, that many black people associated Hill more than Thomas with the white world is not solely based on the manner in which feminist discourse is perceived as white. As discussed below, the widespread embrace of Thomas is also attributable to the patriarchal way that racial solidarity has been defined within the black community.

III. Anita Hill as Villian: The Lynching Trope

One of the most stunning moments in the history of American cultural drama occurred when Clarence Thomas angrily denounced the hearings as a "high-tech lynching." Thomas's move to drape himself in a history of black male repression was particularly effective in the all-white male Senate, whose members could not muster the moral authority to challenge Thomas's sensationalist characterization. Not only was Thomas suddenly transformed into a victim of racial discrimination, but Anita Hill was further erased as a black woman. Her racial identity became irrelevant in explaining or understanding her position, while Thomas's play on the lynching metaphor racially empowered him. Of course, the success of this particular reading was not inevitable; there are several competing narratives that could conceivably have countered Thomas's move. Chief among them was the possibility of pointing out that allegations relating to the sexual abuse of black women have had nothing to do with the history of lynching, a tradition based upon white hysteria regarding black male access to white women. Black women's relationship to the lynch mob was not as a perpetrator but as one of its victims, either through their own lynching or the lynching of loved ones. Moreover, one might have plausibly predicted that, given Thomas's persistent denunciation of any effort to link the history of racism to ongoing racial inequalities, the American public would have scornfully characterized this play as a last-ditch effort to pull his troubled nomination out of the fire. African Americans in particular might have easily rejected Thomas's bid for racial solidarity by concluding that a man who has adamantly insisted that blacks be judged on the content of their character rather than the color of their skin should not be supported when he deploys the color of his skin as a defense to judgments of his character. Yet the race play was amazingly successful; Thomas's approval ratings in the black community skyrocketed from 54 percent to nearly 80 percent immediately following his performance. Indeed, it was probably his solid support in the black community, particularly in the South, that clinched the seat on the Court. Implicit in this response was a rejection, at times frighteningly explicit, of Anita Hill.

The deification of Thomas and the vilification of Anita Hill were prefigured by practices within the black community that have long subordinated gender domination to the struggle against racism. In the process the particular experiences of black men have often come to represent the racial domination of the entire community, as is demonstrated by the symbolic currency of the lynching metaphor and the marginalization of representations of black female domination. Cases involving sexual accusations against black men have stood as hallmarks of racial injustice; Emmett Till, the Scottsboro boys, and others wrongly accused are powerful symbolic figures in our struggle for racial equality. Black women have also experienced sexualized racial violence; the frequent and unpunished rape and mutilation of black women by white men is a manifestation of racial domination. Yet the names and faces of black women whose bodies also bore the scars of racial oppression are lost to history. To the limited extent that sexual victimization of black women is symbolically represented within our collective memory, it is as tragic characters whose vulnerability illustrates the racist emasculation of black men. The marginalization of black female narratives of racism and sexuality thus worked directly to Thomas's advantage by providing him with the ready means to galvanize the black community on his behalf. Thomas's angry denunciations of Hill's allegations as a "high-tech lynching" invoked powerful images linking him to a concrete history that resonated deeply within most African Americans. Hill, had she been so inclined, could have invoked only vague and hazy recollections in the African-American memory, half-digested experiences of black female sexual abuse that could not withstand the totalizing power of the lynching metaphor.

The discourse of racial liberation, traditionally built around the claim of unequal treatment of black and white people, is of course relevant to the Thomas-Hill conflict, but only partially. In one sense the racial narrative of differential treatment based on race partly comprehends the situation that Hill was in. It seems relatively clear that had Hill been white she would have been read differently by most Americans; as a black female, she had to overcome not only the burdens that feminists have so well articulated in the rape-trial trope but the additional obstacles of race. But, like the dominant feminist narrative, it is again only partial; the abstract description of differential subordination based on skin color is crystallized into narrative tropes that

translate racial inequality into the terms of inequality between men.

The relative potency of male-centered images of sexual
racism over female-centered ones is manifested in the contemporary marginalization of black female sexual abuse
within black political discourse. Dominant narratives
representing the intersections of racism and sexual violence
continue to focus on the way that black men accused of
raping white women are disproportionately punished relative to black-on-black or white-on-white rape. Within
traditional antiracist formulations, this disproportionality
has been characterized as racial discrimination against black
men. Yet the pattern of punishing black men accused of
raping white women more harshly than those accused of
raping black women is just as surely an illustration of discrimination against black women. Indeed, some studies
suggest that the race of the victim rather than the race of
the defendant is the most salient factor determining the
disposition of men convicted of rape. Clearly, black
women are victims of a racial hierarchy that subordinates
their experiences of sexual abuse to those of white women.
Yet this intersectional oppression is rarely addressed in
antiracist discourses in part because traditional readings of
racism continue to center on power differentials between
men. Consequently, there is relatively little emphasis on
how racism contributes to the victimization of black
women both inside and outside the criminal-justice system. The rape of black women has sometimes found its
way to the center of antiracist politics, particularly when
the rapist is white. But the more common experience of
intraracial rape is often disregarded within antiracist politi-

cal discourses, perhaps as a consequence of the view that politicizing such rapes conflicts on some level with efforts to eradicate the prevailing stereotype of the black male rapist. While racism may help explain why white victims are more likely to see their assailants punished than are black victims, one must look to gender power within the black community in order to understand why this persistent devaluation of black women is marginalized within the prevailing conceptions of racism.

Intraracial rape and other abusive practices have not been fully addressed within the African-American community in part because African Americans have been reluctant to expose any internal conflict that might reflect negatively on the black community. Although abiding by this "code of silence" is experienced by African Americans as a self-imposed gesture of racial solidarity, the maintenance of silence also has coercive dimensions. Coercion becomes most visible when someone—male or female— breaks the code of silence. Elements of this coercive dimension of gender silence is illustrated in part by the coverage of the hearings in the black press. In many such accounts Hill was portrayed as a traitor for coming forward with her story. Many commentators were less interested in exploring whether the allegations were true than in speculating why Hill would compromise the upward mobility of a black man and embarrass the African-American community. Anger and resentment toward Hill was reflected in opinions of commentators traversing the political spectrum within black political discourses. Liberal, centrist, and conservative opinion seemed to accept a view of Hill as disloyal and even treasonous.[11] One columnist, a teacher, reported—without criticism—that one of her third-grade students advocated that Hill be taken out and shot. The theme of treachery was also apparent in a column authored by psychologists Nathan and Julia Hare. In an article titled "The Many Faces of Anita Faye Hill," they linked Hill to other black women who had in some way violated the code by linking gender issues to black women. Along with the almost routine vilification of Alice Walker, Ntozake Shange, and Michelle Wallace was also criticism of Congresswoman Maxine Waters and Faye Wattleton for their prochoice activities and of Margaret Bush Wilson, chair of the NAACP, for opposing Thomas's nomination on the basis of his antiaffirmative-action stand despite the fact that "white women benefit more from affirmative action than Blacks." The Hares ended their piece with a remarkably candid warning to other "Anita Hills" in the making: "We'll be watching you."

The rhetorical deployment of race-based themes to ostracize Anita Hill as an outlaw in the black community received an unexpected boost from noted Harvard sociologist Orlando Patterson in a widely circulated opinion piece that appeared in the *New York Times*.[13] While many critics who lambasted Hill for voicing her complaints shied away from offering a direct defense of the behavior of which she complained, Patterson deployed race to normatively embrace such behavior and to ostracize Anita Hill for having been offended by it at all. Themes of treachery and betrayal, so central in Hill's indictment for breaking the code of silence, reemerged as disingenuity and inauthenticity under Patterson's indictment of Hill for acting white. Setting forth what the preconversion Thomas might have pejoratively labeled an affirmative-action defense to sexual harassment, Patterson argued that Thomas's sexual taunting of Professor Hill was defensible as a "down-home style of courting," one that black women are accustomed to and apparently flattered by. According to Patterson, even if Thomas did say the things Anita Hill claimed he said, not only must Thomas's behavior be weighed against a different racial standard, but Thomas's identity as a black man must be taken into account in determining whether he was justified in perjuring himself. Patterson concludes that in this case perjury was a justifiable means toward winning a seat on the highest court of the land because white America could never understand that such sexual repartee was in fact common among black men and women.

Patterson's text warrants extensive analysis because it articulates and exemplifies the underlying ways in which certain notions of race and culture function to maintain patriarchy and deny or legitimize gender practices that subordinate the interests of black women. Patterson's argument basically functions as a cultural defense of the harassment Hill complained about. Similar defenses have been articulated in various forms to justify other misogynistic or patriarchal practices perpetuated by some black men. Indeed, were the thesis not so readily available in the rhetorical discourse within the black community, one might follow Senator Hatch's allegation that Hill found Long Dong Silver in a court case and wonder whether Patterson's defense of Thomas was found in the case of *California* v. *Jacinto Rhines*.[14] Mr. Rhines, a black man, appealed his conviction for raping two black women, arguing that his conviction should be overturned because the trial court failed to take into account cultural differences between blacks and whites. This failure, he claimed, transformed an ordinary consensual encounter into an actionable rape.

According to Rhines, the victim implicitly consented to having intercourse with him when she agreed to accompany him to his apartment. Rhines also argued that the victim was unreasonable in feeling threatened and coerced by his behavior. Black people are often quite animated and talk loudly to each other all the time, he contended. Because the social meaning of the event in the black community differed dramatically from the way whites would read the event, Rhines concluded that he was wrongly convicted. This "cultural defense," trading on familiar stereotypes of black women as hardier than white women, and more accustomed to aggressive, gritty, even violent sex, essentially amounted to a claim that the complainant was not really a rape victim because she was black.

What caused the downfall of Rhines's argument was that he was unable to explain why the "victims" were apparently unaware of these cultural codes. Whether unreasonable or not, if the women were frightened, the sexual intercourse that occurred was coerced. The court was not only unconvinced that race had any bearing on a woman's reaction to coercion; it also deemed Rhino's argument an "inexcusable slur" designed to "excuse his own conduct by demeaning females of the Black race."

For Rhines's argument to have worked, he would have had to convince the court that the cultural practice he identified was so pervasive that the victim's claims of fear and nonconsent were implausible. In effect, Rhines had to convince the court that the black woman should be held to a different standard of victimhood because she was black. Patterson's argument picks up where Rhines's argument failed. Through labeling Hill's reaction to Thomas's "flirtations" disingenuous, Patterson implies that either

Hill was not, in fact, emotionally injured by Thomas's barrage of sexual innuendo or that if she was, she was influenced to reinterpret her experience through the lens of middle-class white feminism. Indeed, he suggests that the harassment may have actually served to affirm their common origins. This pattern of "bonding" is apparently so readily acceptable that any black woman who is offended or injured by it must be acting on a white feminist impulse rather than a culturally grounded black female sensibility.

Patterson has subsequently defended his argument as an attempt to counter the failure of white feminists to comprehend the many ways that gender issues differ across race and class lines.[15] There should be, of course, little question that sexism often manifests itself in varying ways within racial contexts. The complexities of racism present black women with many issues that are unfamiliar to white feminists. Yet one of the thorniest issues that black women must confront is represented by Patterson's own descent into cultural relativism. Patterson subtly transformed the quite perceptive claim that black women often have different issues with black men than white women do with white men into a claim that sexual harassment as described in the testimony of Anita Hill is not one of them. He seemed to ground this assertion on a claim that black women have played along with and apparently enjoyed this "sexual repartee." Thus, like Rhines, he argued that attempts to sanction this behavior as abusive or offensive to black women are grounded in a white feminist misreading of black cultural practices.

There are a number of reasons why Patterson's analysis is off the mark in explaining the particularities of black women's sexual subordination, yet it succeeds wonderfully as a discursive illustration of it. Patterson's argument initially rests on a failure to draw any distinction between sexual practices that occur privately and those that occur within the work environment. More fundamentally, the argument reflects a failure to understand the power dynamics that shape those sexual practices in the first place. His argument thus amounts to an uncritical acceptance of sexual practices that he observes in some social settings, an assumption that these practices are characteristic of the whole, and a use of these practices as a normative base to discredit black women who claim to be offended and injured by them.

Patterson's misunderstanding of the nature of sexual harassment is exemplified by his failure to take into account the particular consequences of sexualizing relationships in a highly stratified work environment. In defending Thomas's alleged banter by claiming that such behavior is typical among black men and black women, Patterson constructs the relationship between black men and women as essentially personal and self-contained, no matter what the context. Thus, the rules that prevail in the private social world dictate the terms and conditions of interaction in the more public work world. Setting aside for the moment the power dynamics that shape sexual repartee elsewhere, Patterson overlooks the fact that the highly stratified workplace so thoroughly raises the stakes for black women that engaging in this sexual competition, however skilled at or familiar with the "game" they might be, is a dangerously risky proposition. In a work context, black women are not dealing with a man who, when rebuffed or bested by a woman, will simply move on. Often they are dealing with a supervisor who can wield his superior institutional power over them either to impose sanctions for their response or to pressure them to compromise their sexual autonomy. Patterson's failure to understand these workplace consequences of sexual harassment is actually consistent with the responses of federal judges who initially refused to see sexual harassment as anything other than private sexual banter that routinely occurs between men and women. Because these practices are quite common throughout society, judges saw them as normative and indeed essential to relations between men and women. Women plaintiffs, however, eventually succeeded in forcing courts to recognize that regardless of the currency of sexual game-playing elsewhere, the perpetuation of these practices in the workplace significantly contributes to women's subordination in the work force.

Black and white women thus share the burden of overcoming assumptions that sexual harassment in the workplace is essentially a "private" issue. Yet race does shape the problem somewhat differently for black women. The racial specificity is grounded in the fact that there is a certain connection between black men and black women born from a common social history of racial exclusion. Often there is a sense of camaraderie between African Americans, a "we're in this together" sensibility. I call this a zone of familiarity, one that creates expectations of support and mutuality that are essential to survival in a work world that is in some ways alien. In fact, this camaraderie is based on a belief that ultimately came to bear on Thomas's behalf—a belief that the interests of African Americans as a whole are advanced by efforts to increase the number of successful and well-placed blacks. However, this zone of familiarity can sometimes be seen as one of privileged sexual access as well. Consequently, one of the workplace dilemmas faced by black women is trying to negotiate between overlapping expectations in this zone, to maintain much-needed relationships but to avoid unwanted intimacy. This camaraderie and the notions of a shared fate make many black women reluctant to complain about or even to decisively reject the harasser. No doubt this silence contributes to some degree of confusion as to exactly where the boundaries between desired camaraderie and unwanted intimacy exist. This confusion, however, does not render sexual harassment a nonissue. Quite the contrary: claims similar to those made by Patterson contribute to the problem by reinforcing attitudes that feminist critiques of sexuality and power are inapplicable to the sexual dynamic between black men and women. This failure to confront and debate the terms of sex and power allows men to continually dismiss the possibility that their actions or advances might be unwelcome.

Even if we acknowledge that confusion about boundaries might sometimes contribute to harassment, this possibility does little to account for occasions when black men intentionally use and abuse power over black women. Indeed, it was this misuse of power that was consistently misinterpreted or intentionally mischaracterized during the hearings. Ironically, Patterson's characterization of Thomas's alleged behavior as "down-home courting" recalls Hatch's disbelief that any man who wanted to date a women would use such an offensive approach. Although Patterson, of course, seems to be saying "Yes, he would, if they were black" while Hatch maintains that such a man would be a pervert, they are actually in agreement that sexual harassment is really about a miscommunicated negotiation over dating. Yet the kind of sexual harassment that women find threatening and harmful is seldom about dating but is, instead, often an expression of hostility or an attempt to control. All women have probably experienced abusive, sexually degrading comments that are almost routinely hurled our way when we initially decline or ignore a solicitation from strangers. Sexual harassment is often no different, particularly in contexts where the harasser believes for whatever reason that the woman needs to be "loosened up," "brought down to size," or "taught a lesson."

Patterson's defense of the kind of behavior Hill described remains troubling even outside a formally stratified work context. Patterson's argument takes as a given the sexual repartee that he believes is simply endemic to the black community "down home." Since he has observed black women responding to such sexual verbal gestures by putting men in their place, he contends that it was somehow "out-of-character" and consequently disingenuous for a black woman to claim that she was repulsed and injured by it. Moreover, such verbal gestures are not only typical but somewhat desirable as down-home courting. Of course, Patterson's failure to specify where "down home" is (it later turns out to be working-class Jamaica) gives uninformed readers the impression that all African Americans are familiar with, participate in, and enjoy this "Rabelaisian humor." The fact that many black people—African-American and Afro-Caribbean alike—do not participate in this "down-home" style is actually beside the point. The more troubling issue is how his attempt to defend this mode of sexual repartee by focusing on black women's participation in it so completely overlooks the way in which this sexual discourse reflects a differential power relationship between men and women.

Patterson assumes that simply because black women have responded to such behavior by displacing aggressive sexual overtures onto a plane of humor and wit, they are neither offended nor threatened by it, and that somehow this "style" is defensible as cultural. Yet merely because black women have developed this particular style of self-defense does not mean that they are not defending themselves against unwanted sexual gestures. A description of the particular way in which women participate and respond to this sexual repartee does not suffice as an analysis of its power dimensions or as a reasonable defense of its subordinating characteristics. Patterson's claims do succeed in centering white women's patterns of interactions by implying that since black women respond differently to verbal aggression, then what they experience is not sexual harassment. Yet women of all races, classes, and cultures no doubt respond in different ways, ways that probably reflect to some degree their particular sociocultural position. White middle-class women have a repertoire of responses to deflect verbal aggression as do working-class black women and middle-class black women, and these responses are likely to differ. The humor or verbal competition that typifies the way some black women react to harassment probably results from the dearth of options available to nonelite black women within a society that has demonstrated manifest disregard for their sexual integrity. After all, to what authority can women who have been consistently represented as sexually available appeal? Since they have little access to any rhetorical or social power from which to create a sphere of sexual autonomy, it is not surprising that some women have learned to displace the aggression onto a humorous, discursive plane. The paradox of Patterson's position is that, given the greater exposure of black women to various forms of sexual aggression, many have developed defense mechanisms that Patterson then points to, in effect to confirm the racist stereotypes that black women are tougher than white women and thus not injured by the same practices that would injure white women. Black women's historical lack of protection becomes a basis for saying no protection is necessary.

Finally, it may be that Patterson's argument, while intellectually and politically indefensible, might in fact provide a clue into how someone like Clarence Thomas might differentiate between women. The plausibility of the *People* magazine image of Thomas and his wife together reading the Bible in their home as a counterimage to Hill's charges made sense for a public that would assume that he would in fact treat all women the same.[16] In other words, sexual harassment is read as only implicating a deraced notion of gender power. But like many men, black and white, Patterson perpetuates images that give a ready rationale for different treatment of black and white women. White women could be pure, madonna-like figures needing vigilant protection, but black women can take care of themselves—indeed, they even implicitly consent to aggression by participating in a cultural repartee.

The overall strategy of Patterson's defense seems to rest on an assumption that merely identifying the culturally specific dimensions of some practice or dynamic constitutes a normative shield against any criticism of it. But mere descriptions of the practices do little to engage the conditions of power that created them. This point is not unfamiliar to African-American scholars and activists. Indeed, there was a time when "cultural defense" arguments were made against those who opposed the racial caste system that prevailed in the South. Many white community leaders argued that patterns of interaction between blacks and whites were maintained by mutual consent and that local blacks were content in their subordinate roles. Having portrayed blacks as willing participants in the racial regime, defenders of the southern way of life were able to claim that demands for equality were imposed from without by northern agitators who did not share the cultural mores of the South.

African Americans as a group refused to allow these arguments to deter their quest for equality. Focusing on the coercive conditions under which consent had been maintained and enforced, critics revealed the way that white supremacy was manifest in relationships not only between dominant whites and subordinate blacks but among blacks as well. Most important, critics exposed the role of coercion in creating these "voluntary" racial practices. This critique included a full accounting of the way that dissent and other counterhegemonic practices were suppressed.

Drawing on this history, the deployment of the cultural defense where gender subordination is alleged requires that we examine not only the way that cultural practices among African-American men and women are an expression of particular power arrangements but also the different means by which these practices are maintained and legitimated. A critical dimension of this examination involves acknowledging the ways that African-American women have contributed to the maintenance of sexist and debilitating gender practices. For example, the Anita Hill controversy and the commentary it has spawned have shed light on how women's own participation in this conspiracy of silence has legitimated sexism within our community. Our failure to break ranks on the issue of misogyny permits writers like Patterson to argue not only that these behaviors are harmless but that they function to affirm our cultural affinity. Our historical silence functions in much the same way that Hill's silence did: we have played along all this time; thus it is far too late in the game for black women to voice offense.

Of course, not all black women have silently acquiesced in sexism and misogyny within the African-American community. Indeed, many writers, activists, and other women have voiced their opposition and paid the price: they have been ostracized and branded as either man-haters or pawns of white feminists, two of the more predictable modes of disciplining and discrediting black feminists. Patterson's argument is of course a model illustration of the latter mode.

In the ongoing debates over black feminism, some critics argue that their objective is not to suppress discussions of gender power within the black community but to stem the tide of negative black stereotypes. Yet even this principle, when examined, reveals a pattern of criticism that seems to suggest that the concern over black male stereotypes functions in a specifically gendered way. For example, the black community has sometimes been embroiled in a debate over political and literary representations of black women's experiences of sexism and misogyny.[17] Yet there is a remarkable willingness to accept, virtually without debate, similar images of black men when these images are valorized and sometimes politicized. Ranging from political tracts such as Eldridge Cleaver's *Soul on Ice* to movies such as *Boyz 'N the Hood* to rap lyrics such as those of NWA, the Geto Boys, and 2 Live Crew, black men have been depicted in sexist and often violently misogynistic terms. In these "scripts" black women serve simply as the objects of masculine rage or sexuality. Yet when the objects take on the voice and the same male images are re-presented through the eyes of the newly empowered subjects, accusations fly. This suggests that it is not the perpetuation of the images themselves that enrages these writers' harshest critics but rather the implicit critique and complaint that is being lodged against patriarchy in the black community. Take, for example, the aforementioned and highly acclaimed movie *Boyz 'N the Hood*. Had the story been told through the perspective of any of the women in the movie, *Boyz* probably would have been picketed as yet another example of black feminist male-bashing.

The framing of these conflicts, along with Patterson's defense of Clarence Thomas, reveals how politics and culture are frequently deployed to suppress or justify many of the troubling manifestations of patriarchial power within the black community. Of course, cultural integrity and political solidarity are important values in the black community. Yet the ways in which these values have functioned to reinscribe gender power must constantly be interrogated. That black people across a political and class spectrum were willing to condemn Anita Hill for breaking ranks is a telling testament to how deep gender conflicts are tightly contained by the expectation of racial solidarity. But more specifically it is a testament to the greater degree to which differences over gender are suppressed as compared

with other political differences. The vilification of Anita
Hill and the embracing of Clarence Thomas reveal that a
black woman breaking ranks to complain of sexual harassment is seen by many African-Americans as a much greater
threat to our group interests than a black man who breaks
ranks over race policy. This double standard is apparent in
Patterson's rush to defend Thomas's behavior and to assail
Professor Hill. Stumbling over the central contradiction in
his own argument, Patterson cites as a benefit of the hearings the fact that African Americans don't all think alike
and are instead a diverse aggregate of thirty million people
"with class differences, subcultural and regional resources,
strengths, flaws and ideologies." Unfortunately, Patterson
cannot see that African-American women might also differ
in their willingness to tolerate a particular "sexual style,"
that class and subcultural differences might as readily explain why Professor Hill and other black women might
take offense at this "down-home courting style" just as
these same differences might explain why Thomas and
many of his associates reject affirmative action. Yet, in
Patterson's world, Anita Hill and other black women are
no longer black, while Thomas and other critics of group-
based race policies are simply diverse. At the very least,
Professor Patterson's celebration of diversity should be extended to allow women like Anita Hill the same independence and integrity that he so enthusiastically grants to
neoconservatives like Clarence Thomas.

IV. Political Implications

Now, over a year after one of the most extraordinary
public spectacles involving race and gender in this country's history, we are left asking what have we learned.

Among the most painful of the lessons to be drawn from the Thomas-Hill affair is that feminism must be recast in order to reach women who do not see gender as relevant to an understanding of their own disempowerment. In an attempt to recast the face of feminism, women organizers have to begin to apply gender analysis to problems that might initially appear to be shaped primarily by exclusively racial or class factors. Nonwhite and working-class women, if they are ever to identify with the organized women's movement, must see their own diverse experiences reflected in the practice and policy statements of these predominantly white middle-class groups.

The confirmation of Clarence Thomas, one of the most conservative voices to be added to the Court in recent memory, carries a sobering message for the African-American community as well. As he begins to make his mark upon the lives of African Americans, we must acknowledge that his successful nomination is due in no small measure to the support he received from black Americans.[18] On this account, it is clear that we still operate under a reflexive vision of racial solidarity that is problematic on two fronts. First, our failure to readily criticize African Americans, based on a belief that our interests are served whenever a black rises through the ranks of power, will increasingly be used to undermine and dismantle policies that have been responsible for the moderate successes that group politics have brought about. Already, African-American individuals have played key roles in attacking minority scholarships, cutting back on available remedies for civil rights injuries, and lifting sanctions against South Africa. While group-based notions of solidarity insulate these people from serious criticism and scrutiny, it is precisely their willingness to pursue a ruthlessly individualist agenda that renders this strategy effective and ultimately profitable. Yet the Thomas-Hill story is about more than the political ways that racial solidarity must be critically examined. It is also about the way that our failure to address gender power within our community created the conditions under which an ultimately self-destructive political reaction took place. If we are not to continue to be victimized by such understandable but still counterproductive responses, we must achieve a more mature and purposeful vision of the complex ways in which power is allocated and withheld in contemporary American politics. In particular, we must acknowledge the central role that black women's stories play in our coming to grips with how public power is manipulated. If black women continue to be silenced and their stories ignored, we are doomed to have but a limited grasp of the full range of problems we currently face. The empowerment of black women constitutes therefore the empowerment of our entire community.

1. See Crenshaw, "Demarginalizing the Intersection of Race and Gender in Antidiscrimination Law, Feminist Theory, and Antiracist Politics," 1989 *Chicago Legal Forum* 139.

2. As recently as 1978, Wigmore's Treatise on Evidence, Section 62, provided that where the nonconsent of a rape complainant is a material element in a rape case, "the character of a woman for chastity is of considerable probative value in judging of the likelihood of that consent." Wigmore went on to say that "the same doctrine should apply . . . in a charge of mere assault with intent to commit rape or of indecent assault, or the like, not because it is logically relevant where consent is not in issues, but because a certain type of feminine character predisposes to imaginary or false charges of this sort." Some states continue to admit such evidence in certain instances.

3. Historically, a woman was required to fight off her attacker until her resistance was overcome. If a woman failed to struggle, or if she gave in before she was subdued, the conclusion drawn was that she was not raped. See Susan Estrich, "Real Rape," 95 *Yale Law Journal* 1087, 1122 (1986): "in effect, the 'utmost resistance' rule required both that the woman resist to the 'utmost' and that such resistance must not have abated during the struggle."

4. See "An Analysis of the Views of Judge Clarence Thomas," NAACP Legal Defense and Education Fund, Inc., August 13, 1991, pointing out the contradiction between Thomas's pre-1986 speeches and writings and the speeches and writings he produced starting in late 1986. His earlier statements explicitly condemned only three Supreme Court decisions—*Dred Scott, Plessy v. Ferguson,* and a conservative decision. In contrast, the later statements contained "an outburst of denunciations of both the Supreme Court and its civil rights decisions." The

Legal Defense Fund position paper also points out Thomas's shift from praising Justices Black, Douglas, Frankfurter, and Warren to praising Scalia and Bork.

5. Thomas's criticism of his sister as a welfare dependent created an image that contrasted starkly with her actual work history, which included both work-force participation and caring for family members. See Joel Handler, "The Judge and His Sister: Growing Up Black," *New York Times,* July 23, 1991.

6. Wright, a former employee of the Equal Employment Opportunity Commission during Thomas's tenure with the commission, is quoted as saying that Judge Thomas pressured her for dates, asked her breast size, and showed up at her apartment uninvited. Peter Applebom, "Common Threads Between the Two Accusing Thomas of Sexual Improprieties," *New York Times,* October 12, 1990.

7. I do not mean to suggest that race is only relevant in the sexual domination of black women. Race is clearly a factor—though a hidden one—in white women's experiences, just as gender also figures in the experiences of black men. However, because white is the default race in feminism and male is the default gender in antiracism, these identity characteristics usually remain unarticulated.

8. Patricia Hill Collins, "The Sexual Politics of Black Womanhood," *Black Feminist Thought: Knowledge, Consciousness, and the Politics of Empowerment* (New York: Unwin Hyman, 1990), p. 168.

9. See Jennifer Wriggins, "Race, Racism and the Law," 6 *Harvard Women's Law Journal* 103 (1983).

10. See Gary LaFree, *Rape and Criminal Justice: The Social Construction of Sexual Assault,* (Belmont, Calif.: Wadsworth Publishing, 1991).

11. Hamil R. Harris, "Hill Is Lying, Says EEOC Staffer," *Washington Afro-American,* October 12, 1991, quoting Armstrong Williams, who called Hill "an outrageous liar"; "Betrayal of Friendship," *Bay State Banner,* October 17, 1991, attacking Anita Hill's credibility and stating that the case "demonstrates the vulnerability of all men in important positions to bogus

sexual harassment charges as a power play by ambitious women." And in the white press, many of the black women interviewed expressed little or no sympathy for Hill, ignoring the reality of their own experiences with gender-based abuses of power, and placing the responsibility for avoiding harassment squarely on the shoulders of the victim. See Felicity Barringer, "The Drama as Viewed by Women," *New York Times,* October 18, 1991, A12, documenting women's adverse reactions to Hill: "It's unbelievable that a woman couldn't stop something like that at its inception," said one. Another asked, "Wouldn't you haul off and poke a guy in the mouth if he spoke in that manner?" And still another said had this to say: "You have to make sure you get across that you're a professional. If someone isn't willing to accept that, you make sure you're not in a room alone with him."

12. See Nathan Hare and Julia Hare, "The Many Faces of Anita Hill," in *The Final Call,* the newspaper published by The Nation of Islam under Minister Louis Farrakhan. The headline on the paper in which the Hares' article appeared read "Thomas Survives High-Tech Lynching."

13. Orlando Patterson's "Race, Gender, and Liberal Fallacies" appeared in the *New York Times* on October 20, 1991, the Sunday following Thomas's confirmation.

14. *People v. Jacinto Aniello Rhines,* 131 Cal. App. 3d. 498, May 6, 1982.

15. See "Roundtable: Sexuality in America After Thomas/Hill," *Tikkun,* January/February 1992, p. 25.

16. Virginia Lamp Thomas, "Breaking Silence," *People,* November 11, 1991, p. 111. Virginia Hill tells how she and her husband invited two couples to their home to pray for two to three hours each day. "They brought over prayer tapes, and we would read parts of the Bible," she stated.

17. Mel Watkins, "Sexism, Racism, and Black Women Writers," *New York Times,* June 15, 1986; Donna Britt, "What About the Sisters? With All the Focus on Black Men, Somebody's Getting Left Out," *Washington Post,* February 2, 1992, citing black male objections to Alice Walker's and Ntozake Shange's work, and

questioning where those black male voices are when black male violence is being condoned . . . glamorized, ignored; Susan Howard, "Beware of 'Blacklash,' " *Newsday,* February 12, 1992, arguing that there is a blacklash against black women, and citing the communities' unwillingness to forgive Alice Walker and Ntozake Shange for writing *The Color Purple* and *For Colored Girls Who Have Considered Suicide When the Rainbow Is Enuf* to support this proposition.

18. "In Other Words," *USA Today,* March 7, 1992: "Rookie Justice Clarence Thomas already is leaving his mark on America's legal system. Based on the dissent he wrote in a recent case, it's not just a mark—it's more like a welt. Fortunately, all but one other justice on the high court viewed the actions of a Louisiana prison guard—who shackled and beat a prisoner—as the kind of cruel and unusual punishment that the Eighth Amendment forbids. . . . Those who harbored hopes that Justice Thomas might feel a shred of concern for society's victims got a firm sock in the kisser." In another of his more notable contributions, in *Presley v. Etowah County Commission,* Thomas paid tribute to his southern roots by denying the voting-rights claims of a newly elected black official who was deprived of decision-making authority. Even the Bush administration agreed that the actions violated the Voting Rights Act.

PAULA GIDDINGS

The Last Taboo

The agonizing ordeal of the Clarence Thomas nomination should have taught us a valuable lesson: racial solidarity is not always the same as racial loyalty. This is especially true, it seems to me, in a postsegregation era in which solidarity so often requires suppressing information about any African American of standing regardless of their political views or character flaws. Anita Hill's intervention in the proceedings should have told us that when those views or flaws are also sexist, such solidarity can be especially destructive to the community.

As the messenger for this relatively new idea, Anita Hill earned the antipathy of large segments of the African-American community. More at issue than her truthfulness—or Clarence Thomas's character or politics—was whether she *should* have testified against another black person, especially a black man, who was just a hairsbreadth away from the Supreme Court. Of course, Anita Hill was not the only black person who testified against the nomination of Clarence Thomas, nor even the only woman to do so. But the nature of her complaint went further. It forced a mandate on gender: "the cultural definition of behavior defined as appropriate to the sexes in a given society at a given time," to borrow historian Gerda Lerner's definition. For many, what was *inappropriate* was that a black woman's commitment to a gender issue superseded what was largely perceived as racial solidarity. Still others, I think, reacted to an even greater taboo, perhaps the last and most deeply set one. This was to disclose not only a gender but a sexual discourse, unmediated by the question of racism. What Hill reported to the world was a black-on-black sexual crime involving a man of influence in the mainstream community.

The issues of gender and sexuality have been made so painful to us in our history that we have largely hidden them from ourselves, much less the glaring eye of the television camera. Consequently, they remain largely unresolved. I am convinced that Anita Hill, by introducing the issues in a way that could not be ignored, offered the possibility of a modern discourse on these issues that have tremendous, even lifesaving import for us.

I.

It is our historical experience that has shaped or, perhaps more accurately, misshaped the sex/gender issues and discourse in our community. That history was broached by Clarence Thomas himself when he used the most remembered phrase of the hearings: "high-tech lynching." Thus, he evoked the image of the sexually laden nineteenth-century lynching—often announced several days in advance to assure a crowd—after which the body was hung, often burned, mutilated, and body parts, including genitals, were fought over for souvenirs. These were low-tech lynchings. Interestingly, it was almost exactly a century ago, in 1892, when the number of African Americans being lynched, 241, reached a peak after steadily escalating since the decade before. Then the epidemic of mob murder against blacks continued with impunity because of the perception that black men, no longer constrained by the "civilizing influence" of slavery, had regressed to a primitive state and were routinely raping white women. At that time "rape, and the rumors of rape [were] a kind of acceptable folk pornography in the Bible Belt," observed historian Jacquelyn Dowd Hall.

Although Thomas's application of this phenomenon to his own situation was highly questionable, even ironic, in one way he was substantially correct. Now, as a century ago, white men, regardless of their own moral standing, still exercise the power to judge blacks on the basis of their perceived sexuality. However, what many failed to take into account with Thomas's evocation was that it was a black woman, Ida B. Wells, who initiated the nation's first antilynching campaign. For lynching was also a woman's issue: it had as much to do with ideas of gender as it had with race.

Often overlooked is the fact that black men were thought capable of these sexual crimes *because* of the lascivious character of the women of the race in a time when women were considered the foundation of a group's morality. Black men raped, it was widely believed, because black men's mothers, wives, sisters, and daughters were seen as "morally obtuse," "openly licentious," and had "no immorality in doing what nature prompts," as Harvard-educated Phillip A. Bruce, brother-in-law of writer Thomas Nelson Page, observed in his influential *Plantation Negro as Freeman* (1889). As one offer of proof, the author noted that black women never complained about being raped by black men. Other observers such as the following southern female writer to the popular periodical *The Independent* confirmed:

> Degeneracy is apt to show most in the weaker individuals of any race; so negro women evidence more nearly the popular idea of total depravity than the men do. They are so nearly lacking in virtue that the color of a negro woman's skin is generally taken (and quite correctly) as a guarantee of her immorality. . . . And they are evidently the chief instruments of the degradation of the men of their race. . . . I sometimes read of a virtuous negro woman, hear of them, but the idea is absolutely inconceivable to me. . . . I cannot imagine such a creation as a virtuous black woman.

The status of black women had been dramatically etched into the annals of science earlier in the century. It was in fact personified in the figure of a single South African woman by the name of Sara Bartmann, aka the "Hottentot Venus." In 1810, when England was in the throes of debate about the slave trade, Ms. Bartmann was first exhibited in London "to the public in a manner offensive to decency," according to observers at the time. (Gilman, 1985)

What made Ms. Bartmann such a subject of interest was

the extraordinary size and shape of her buttocks, which
served as a displacement of the fascination with female
genitalia at the time. Sara Bartmann was displayed for five
years, until she died, in Paris, at the age of twenty-five. Her
degradation by what was defined as science and civilization
did not end there. An autopsy was performed, preparing
her genitalia "in such a way as to allow one to see the
nature of the labia." Her organs were studied and reported
upon by Dr. George Cuvier in 1817, coolly comparing
Ms. Bartmann's genitalia with that of orangutans. Her sexual organs were then given to the Musée de l'Homme in
Paris—where they are still on display.

Sara Bartmann's sexual parts, her genitalia and her buttocks, serve as the central image for the black female
throughout the nineteenth century, concludes Gilman. It
was also the image, he notes, that served as an icon for
black sexuality throughout the century.

It is no coincidence that Sara Bartmann became a spectacle in a period when the British were debating the prohibition of slavery. As historian Barbara Fields and others
have pointed out, there, as in North America, race took on
a new significance when questions arose about the entitle-
ment of nonenslaved blacks to partake of the fruits of
Western liberty and citizenship. In North America, Euro-
Americans had to resolve the contradictions between their
own struggle for political freedom and that of the black
men and women they still enslaved. This contradiction was
resolved (by both pro- and antislavery whites) by racialism:
ascribing certain inherited characteristics to blacks, characteristics that made them unworthy of the benefits of first-
class citizenship. At the core of those characteristics was the
projection of the dark side of sexuality, now literally em-

bodied by black females. The use of a broad racial tarbrush, in turn, meant looking at race through the veneer of ideology: an institutionalized set of beliefs through which one interprets social reality. By the nineteenth century, then, race had become an ideology, and a basis of that ideology had become sexual difference. If there was a need for racialism in the late eighteenth century, it became an absolute necessity by the late nineteenth century, when lynching reached its peak. For after the Civil War, the Thirteenth, Fourteenth and Fifteenth amendments granted freedmen suffrage and black men and women many of the privileges of citizenship. In a state like Mississippi, which had some of the strongest black political organizations of any state, this translated into the kind of empowerment that saw, in the 1870s, two black men serve as U.S. senators, and blacks as secretaries of state and education, among other high offices. Throughout the South, especially, there was also dramatic evidence of African Americans gaining an economic foothold as the numbers of black-owned businesses and black landowners increased.

Additionally, unprecedented numbers of African American men and women were attending both predominantly white and predominantly black colleges, and aspiring to professional positions deemed out of reach just a generation before. This was even true of black women. By the 1880s the first black women were passing state bar exams to become attorneys, and were the first women of any race to practice medicine in the South. By the turn of the century, Booker T. Washington's National Business League reported that there were "160 Black female physicians, seven dentists, ten lawyers, 164 ministers, assorted journalists, writers, artists, 1,185 musicians and teachers of

music and 13,525 school instructors." The period saw a
virtual renaissance among black women artists and writers.
The Philadelphia-born sculptor Meta Warwick Fuller was
under the tutelage of Auguste Rodin; Frances Ellen Harper
and Pauline Hopkins published two of the earliest novels
by black women; Oberlin-educated Anna Julia Cooper
published *A Voice from the South* (1892), a treatise on race
and feminism that anticipated much of the later work of
W. E. B. Du Bois; and journalist Ida B. Wells, in 1889, was
elected as the first woman secretary of the Afro-American
Press Association.

Ironically, such achievements within a generation of
slavery did not inspire an ideology of racial equality but
one of racial difference, the latter being required to maintain white supremacy. That difference would be largely
based on perceptions of sexual difference, and as noted
before, the foundation of sexual difference lay in attitudes
about black women.

II.

By the late nineteenth century, however, difference would
be characterized at its most dualistic: as binary opposition—not just in terms of race and sexuality but of gender
and class as well. Such oppositions were effective means of
social control at a time when the country was losing its
sociosexual mooring in the face of radical and fundamental
changes driven (like now) by a technological revolution.
For if the late twentieth century was shaped by advances
like the computer, the late nineteenth was adjusting itself
around innovations such as the typewriter, the gasoline-
driven car, the internal-combustion airplane, the sewing
machine, the incandescent light, the phonograph, and the

radio. Such innovations bring on new systems of marketing and financing them, and thus new possibilities of wealth, as the late nineteenth-century emergence of the Rockefellers, Morgans, Du Ponts, and Carnegies attest. In addition, new corporate cultures increased urbanization, made sex outside of the family more possible and contributed to the increased commodification of sex in forms of pornography and brothels, as it became more associated with pleasure rather than merely reproduction. At the same time, money and the labor-saving devices allowed middle-class women to spend less time doing domestic housework and more time seeking education and reform outside of the home. Add to this growing numbers of immigrants from eastern and southern Europe, the increasing disparity between the haves and the have-nots (by 1890, the poorest one-half of families received one-fifth of all wages and salaries), labor unrest and unemployment that reached 30 percent in some years during the decade, and the need for control becomes obvious. That control was effectively handled through creating categories of difference through binary opposition. For example, maleness was defined by its opposition to femaleness; whiteness by its opposition to blackness. The same dualism applied to the concepts of civilization and primitivity, purity and pollutedness, goodness and evil, public and private. The nineteenth-century paradigm regarding sexuality tied all of these oppositions together, which operated to the detriment of blacks and women in general, and black women in particular.

For example, in the late nineteenth century, men were believed to have a particularly rapacious sexual drive that had to be controlled. The last thing needed at home was a woman who had the same sexual drive that men had; what was needed was in binary opposition to perceived male sexuality. What was needed was a woman who did not tempt, and was thus synonymous with "good." And so, although in another period women were thought to have strong, even the more ungovernable, sexual drives, by the late nineteenth century, they were thought to have hardly any libido at all. Furthermore, female sexuality was now considered pathological. (Gilman, 1985) That meant, of course, that good women did not have erotic feelings, and those who might have had inappropriate urges were recommended to see physicians like J. Marion Sims or Robert Battey, who employed radical gynecological surgery, including clitorectomies, to "correct" masturbation and other forms of sexual passion. (D'Emilio, Freedman, 1988) Such severe methods were necessary to sustain diametrically opposed identities to "bad" women: lower-class women, and especially black women.

Economically lower-class women fell under the "bad" column by virtue of the fact that they worked outside the home and thus were uninsulated from the sexual aggression of the society. Certainly, it was the former group of women who made up the growing numbers of prostitutes, a label that could fall even on women more drawn to casual sex than to remuneration, and were of great interest to scientists as well as white middle-class female reformers and repressed men. With Sara Bartmann as a model and basis of comparison, their sexual organs were studied, codified, and preserved in jars. Anthropologists such as Cesare Lombrosco, coauthor of the major study of prostitution in the late nineteenth century, *The Prostitute and the Normal Woman* (1893), wrote that the source of their passion and pathology lay in the labia, which reflected a more primitive structure than their upper-class counterparts. One of Lombrosco's students, Abele de Blasio, focused on the buttocks. His specialty was steatopygia (excessive fat on the buttocks), which was also deemed to be a special characteristic of whores—and, of course, black women. They would represent the very root of female eroticism, immorality, and disease.

In the medical metaphors of the day, the sexual organs of sexual women were not only hotbeds of moral pathology, but of disease. In the nineteenth century the great fear was of a sexually transmitted disease that was spreading among the population, was incurable, and after invading the body, disfigured and decomposed it in stages. The name of the disease was syphilis and it was the era's metaphor for the retribution of sexual sin. Despite evidence to the contrary, it was seen as a disease that affected not only persons but groups perceived as both licentious and deviant. Prostitutes of course fell into this category, but it did not seem to affect business. Science even abandoned long-held views to accommodate the paradigm. Formerly, it was believed that Christopher Columbus's sailors had introduced the disease to Europe. Now the new wisdom traced it to a form of leprosy that had long been present in Africa and had spread into Europe during the Middle Ages. At the wellspring of this plague were the genital organs of black women. (Gilman, 1985)

As the epitome of the immorality, pathology, and impurity of the age, black women were seen in dualistic opposition to their upper-class, pure, and passionless white sisters. It was this binary opposition of women (black men's sex drives were not seen as inherently different than those of white men, only less controlled) that was the linchpin of race, class, and even gender difference. It was this opposition, furthermore, that also led to lynching. For it was the white women's qualities, so profoundly missing in black women, that made black men find white women irresistible, and "strangely alluring and seductive," in the words of Phillip Bruce.

III.

Categorizing women through binary opposition had a devastating impact. Even the relatively privileged middle-class white women were subjected to the sexual tyrannies of the age. The opposition of public, a male sphere, and private, a female one, led to conclusions that imprisoned women in the home. The eminent Harvard-trained physician Dr. Edward Clarke, for example, wrote in his influential book *Sex in Education* (1873) that education could ruin a woman's sexual organs. Ideas about male sexual irrepressibility in opposition to women's passionlessness were largely responsible for the fact that "rape in marriage was no crime, nor even generally disapproved," "wife-beating was only marginally criminal," and "incest was common enough to require skepticism that it was tabooed," according to historians Linda Gordon and Ellen Carol DuBois (1983). Women would have to untangle and rework paradigms in order to protect themselves and, as DuBois and Gordon note, exercise their right to enjoy the pleasure of sex. Toward this end, white feminists began challenging the oppositional frameworks concerning the sexuality of men and women. For example, Dr. Elizabeth Blackwell, a physician, offered the startling counteropinion that men and women had equal sexual urges, thus providing a rationale for consensual sex in marriage—and for "free lovers" outside of marriage as well. They also regulated the torrent of male sexuality by insisting that women should only be required to have sex when they wanted to get pregnant. Called "voluntary motherhood," it was a "brilliant" tactic, says Gordon, for it "insinuated a rejection of male sexual domination into a politics of defending and improving motherhood." And at a time when they still had little power or even identity outside of the home, women disdained abortion and contraception, insisting—in a world of depersonalized sex—on maintaining the link between sexual intercourse and reproduction. Consequently, say the authors, the principle of marital mutuality and women's right to say no was established among white middle-class couples in the late nineteenth century. This is perhaps evidenced by the fact that although birth-control methods were not widely approved, the birthrate among white native-born women declined by 1900 to an average of 3.54—50 percent below the level of the previous century!

Despite their enlightened views on such issues as a single standard of sexuality for men and women, as well as others, white feminists fell short on issues like nonmarital rape, probably because of its interracial implications. Although they could bring themselves to counter gender oppositions, those which involved race, and to a lesser extent class, seemed to be beyond their reach. This would be left to black feminists like Ida B. Wells and others who constantly challenged the dualism between good and bad, black and white, and its implications especially as it affected African-American women.

Ida Wells simply turned this paradigm on its head, with her own empirical evidence gathered from her investigation of the circumstances of 728 lynchings that had taken place over the previous decade. Her meticulously documented findings would not only challenge the assumption of rape—which also exonerated black women to a significant extent—but also included findings about the lynching of black women as well as their sexual exploitation at the hands of whites. It was black women who needed protection, Wells insisted, as "the rape of helpless Negro girls and women, which began in slavery days, still continued without reproof from church, state, or press," thus changing their representation to that of victims. Her most dramatic challenge to the paradigm, of course, was her questioning of the passionless purity of southern white women. There *were* interracial liaisons between black men and white women, Wells published in her findings, but they were consensual and often initiated by white women. In May of 1892, Wells would publish the editorial that got her exiled from the South: "If Southern white men are not careful . . . ," she challenged, "a conclusion will be reached which will be damaging to the moral reputation of their women." (Wells, *On Lynchings* [New York: Arno Press, 1969]) Wells, perhaps the first leader to broach the subject of black sexual oppression after slavery, had now completely challenged the period's assumptions. Black men weren't rapists, white men were; black women weren't doing what "nature prompted," white women were; Wells's framework actually rescued both black and white women from their dehumanized objectification.

When, in reaction to Wells's ideas, the president of the Missouri Press Association, John Jacks, wrote a letter calling all black women "prostitutes, thieves and liars," it was the proverbial straw for nascent regional clubs to come together under a national umbrella in 1896. "Read the letter carefully, and use it discriminately" (it was "too indecent for publication"), challenged Boston activist and editor Josephine St. Pierre Ruffin, and "decide if it be not the time to stand before the world and declare ourselves and our principles." Formed as the National Association for Colored Women (NACW), with a membership that would reach 50,000 by 1916, it would act not only as a means to realize suffrage, education, and community development, but the vessel through which black women challenged, in public, the beliefs that were getting black men lynched and black women raped and exploited. Sexual exploitation was so pervasive that it drove black women north in search of safer climes. "It is a significant and shameful fact that I am constantly in receipt of letters from still unprotected women in the South," complained the nineteenth-century Chicago activist Fannie Barrier Williams, "begging me to find employment for their daughters . . . to save them from going into the homes of the South as servants as there is nothing to save them from dishonor and degradation." In 1893, before the predominantly white Congress of Representative Women, Williams challenged that black women shouldn't be disparaged but protected, adding that "I do not want to disturb the serenity of this conference by suggesting why this protection is needed and the kind of man against whom it is needed."

IV.

Nevertheless, despite their extraordinary boldness in bringing this issue before the white public, black women activists were precluded from presenting another kind of

critique, one which was also important. The brutal concept
of binary opposition prevented them from a frank public
discourse concerning intraracial gender relations and sexuality, with which white feminists had been relatively successful. This void was a potentially life-threatening one in
a time of adjustment to nonslavery; a time when gender
roles, altered first by slavery and then by rapid social and
economic changes, were in chaos; a time when the sexuality of both black men and women had to have been twisted
by sexism and racism, and now by numbing poverty.
Ghettos were congealing, families were in disarray, domestic violence was on the increase, cocaine and alcohol were
being abused, and venereal diseases were increasing at an
alarming rate. But in this social Darwinistic environment,
where blacks were judged harshly, even murderously, by
their perceived difference from the white middle-class
ideal, where it was believed that the poor deserved to be
poor because of moral and character flaws, where a man,
as Wells reported, could be lynched under the pretense of
beating his wife, how could there be a public discourse
about such things? How was one going to explain the
higher rates of venereal disease such as syphilis among
blacks? And how was one to explain before a hostile white
public that the higher rates of infant mortality were largely
due to children inheriting "enfeebled constitutions and
congenital diseases, inherited from parents suffering from
the effects of sexual immorality and debauchery" (p. 25),
as an 1897 report, *Proceedings of the Second Conference for the
Study of Problems Concerning Negro City Life,* under the
general direction of W. E. B. Du Bois, then at Atlanta
University, stated?

Publicly voicing such concerns in a society defined by

binary opposition could leave blacks in general and black women in particular vulnerable to the violent whims of whites. It is no wonder that the issues of intraracial sexuality and gender have long been tabooed in public discourse. At the same time, not voicing these concerns have left the community, especially women, bereft of the help and protection so needed. As an anonymous black woman writer, one of the few who dared break the silence of intraracial sexuality, wrote to the *Independent* in 1904, "We poor colored wage-earners of the South are fighting a terrible battle, on the one hand, we are assailed by white men, and on the other hand, we are assailed by Black men who should be our natural protectors." There are sexist backlashes within our community, too.

For black women, the accumulated effects of assault and the inability to "eradicate negative social and sexual images of their womanhood" had "powerful ideological consequences," concludes historian Darlene Hine. To protect themselves, she observes, black women created what she calls "a culture of dissemblance." Hine defines this as "the behavior and attitudes of Black women that created the appearance of openness and disclosure but actually shielded the truth of their inner lives and selves from their oppressors" (p. 292)—and I would add, even from ourselves. This is the reason, I think, why we have not forced such sex/gender discourses, seen primarily as disclosures, in our community. It is why feminist issues, though not women's rights issues, are more problematic for us. Not only is feminism specifically associated with our historic binary opposites—middle-class white women—it demands an analysis of sexual issues. This is why to break through the silence and traditional sense of racial solidarity is such a controversial act for us. This, in turn, largely accounts for the vitriol earned by those who indicate a public discourse on sexuality in their work, such as Alice Walker in *The Color Purple* or Ntozake Shange in *For Colored Girls*. . . . I think these traditional notions are also the reason why Anita Hill's appearance was so controversial in the black community. Those who publicly supported her, namely black scholars and the National Coalition of 100 Black Women—formed in 1970 when the women's movement was making an impact—were those in touch with gender issues and their role in the needed transformation of our institutions and communities. This is the window black women writers have pointed toward but that Anita Hill, in her first-person, clear, unswervingly direct testimony before the public, has actually opened. It was an act of great inner courage and conviction, to turn back the veil of our Du Boisian double consciousness. It was an act that provided clarity about our new status in the late twentieth century.

V.

There would be some that would argue that that status is no more empowered than it was a hundred years ago, thus requiring that we use the same strategies of solidarity. There is no question that, in some ways, the essential aspects of racism and sexism still affect us. This was evident in the statement "African-American Women in Defense of Ourselves," first appearing in the *New York Times* as a paid ad on November 17, signed by 1,603 black women, most of them scholars, in response to the treatment of Anita Hill during the hearings. Insisting that the "malicious defamation of Professor Hill insulted all women of African-American descent," it concluded that "throughout U.S. history, Black women have been stereotyped as immoral, insatiable, perverse; the initiators in all sexual contacts—abusive or otherwise. . . . As Anita Hill's experience demonstrates, Black women who speak of these matters are not likely to be believed. . . ." The words sound very much like those that led women to organize the NACW almost exactly a century ago, and in fact, the similar conditions that previously made us want to wrap ourselves in that protective skin have come back around with a vengeance. Certainly, the late twentieth century, with its dislocating technological revolution, rapacious moneymaking, excesses of sex, guilt and consumption, and incurable diseases viewed as Old Testament warnings should give us pause. For when such a confluence occurs, there are cultural reflexes to create categories of difference, including sexual difference, with all of its murderous Willie Horton, Bensonhurst, David Duke, and Central Park gang-rape implications. And although we may have passed the era that could take a Hottentot Venus seriously, we cannot rest assured that advances in science will save us from such folly. That respectable journals would make connections between green monkeys and African women, for example, or trace the origin of AIDS to African prostitutes—the polluted sexual organs of black women—reveals our continued vulnerability to racist ideology. It tells us that concepts of racial difference (in this situation, sexual practices) can still be used as weapons of degradation, and that the idea of difference turns on sexuality, and sexuality, in this culture, is loaded with concepts of race, gender, and class. This explains in part why the backlashes against women, black and nonblack, as well as race, carry a virulence that goes beyond the fear of competition or the sharing of power once so handily monopolized by others.

On the other hand, there have been some fundamental dramatic changes, largely realized by our own struggle for equality and empowerment, that allow us, in fact demand, a new strategy. For although racism still exists, our situation has changed since the sixties in spite of it. It has changed because of two interrelated developments: the sexual revolution and de jure desegregation. They are interrelated because sex was the principle around which wholesale segregation and discrimination was organized with the ultimate objective of preventing intermarriage. (D'Emilo, Freedman, 1988) The sexual revolution, however, separated sexuality from reproduction, and so diluted the ideas about purity—moral, racial, and physical.

Both desegregation and the sexual revolution make dissemblance and suppression in the name of racial solidarity anachronistic, for they were prescribed to divert perceptions of difference, based on sexual difference between black women and white. Despite the tenacity about ideas of difference, recent sociopolitical developments—further codified by feminist theory as well as black studies—make binary opposition as a sole indicator of meaning passé.

In the meantime, increasing sexual aggression, including date rape on college campuses that tend to be underreported by black women; the number of "children having children," the plague of domestic violence, the breakup of families, and the spread of fatal venereal disease among African Americans at a time when we have more "rights" than ever before, tells us that gender issues are just as important—if not more so—in the black community as racial issues have always been. More than ever before it is essential that we advance a discourse on sexuality that is liberating for those who engage in it and truncating to the souls of those who don't. As Naima Major, former director of the National Black Women's Health Project (NBWHP)—one of the few black institutions that regularly engages in sexuality issues—said to me, most of the black women she sees "seem to cut themselves off at the waist," even when they are coming to talk specifically about sexuality.

This is particularly alarming in view of the fact that we are in a sexually aggressive era, one where sex is commodified and often depersonalized, especially for young women. Their worlds were the subject of a study of adolescents aged fifteen to seventeen, conducted by Pat McPherson and Michelle Fine, and their observations were disturbing. From the stories of these young women, the authors surmised that their generation is more likely to "be aware of, witness to, and victim of" male sexual abuse among both peers and family. Their sexual experiences with peers are not characterized by learning the meaning or enjoyment of sex, or even making choices about engaging in it, but in protecting themselves from what is viewed (as in the past) as the irrepressible sexual drives of the men in their lives. A black adolescent in this interracial group spoke about not her own sexual preferences but the need to satisfy, indeed mollify, men quickly through cunnilingus so that the evening could end early, and hassle-free. And the authors noted that female adolescents also protect themselves by suppressing signs of their gender: by becoming "one of the boys" through not only dress, but through even misogynist behavior and attitudes. These are issues that were addressed a century ago, under similar sociosexual conditions, but the solutions have not been passed on through families or social institutions. We must begin to do it.

The analysis of how sex/gender systems apply to us in the 1990s becomes urgent when we see that *58 percent* of black women beyond the age of eighteen *never* use any form of birth control, according to a 1991 study conducted by the National Council of Negro Women (NCNW). Yet only 1 percent of those women said that they wanted to get pregnant, and only 2 percent said that they did not know how to use birth control. Does this finding indicate ambivalence about separating sexuality from reproduction despite not wanting a child? Does it indicate the desire, however sublimated, to become pregnant? Or, as I suspect, is the finding a reflection of the fact that their male partners look down on birth control?

One thing we know, there seems to be what one might call a cult of motherhood in our community. How else might one interpret the finding of journalist Leon Dash in his book *When Children Want Children* (1988), that nearly a fourth of all unmarried teenage mothers intentionally become pregnant? What does motherhood mean to these youngsters? The ability to exercise maternal authority in lieu of other avenues of self-esteem and empowerment; rebellion against the depersonalization of sex; or perhaps, as a century ago, does this finding represent the effort to control male sexuality? The answers to these questions are important, as the babies of teenagers are more apt to be underweight and thus have learning and other physical disabilities. There is also tragedy in another statistic: 48

percent of the teenagers who intentionally got pregnant later regretted their decision.

Even college students, according to a report by the Black Women's Health Project, indicated a conflict about delaying childbearing in the face of "women's traditional and proper role as mother"—"indeed as a respected 'matriarch' in a community beset by failing family structures." Of course, there is also male pressure insinuated in some of these findings. The college students said that they felt intense pressure from male partners who wanted to be fathers—one of the few avenues toward manhood?—as well as from cultural and religious leaders not to have abortions. Although one has to respect religious and/or moral views about this, you have to wonder if young women are making rational, informed decisions about these things—lives depend on it.

Another issue not engaged adequately is one that Leon Dash discovered after hours of interviews with teenagers over the course of an entire year—the time it takes to get beyond their personal dissemblance strategies. Many of the motives behind sexual decisions—for better sometimes, but often for worse—were shaped by the fact that their families had a tremendous amount of sexual abuse within them, sometimes traced through two, three, or more generations. Ironically, Dash's decision to publicly reveal such information caused more consternation among self-conscious middle-class blacks than the dire implications of the information itself.

If all of this sounds very nineteenth century, there is a reason for it. Black men and women have not had their own sexual revolution—the one we couldn't have before. We need a discourse that will help us understand modern ideas about gender and sex/gender systems, about male privilege, and about power relations; about the oppressive implications of pornography—something even at least one Harvard professor seems not to understand.

In our considerations of Anita Hill, it is important to understand that she spoke not of a physical transgression on the part of Clarence Thomas, but a verbal one masked in pornographic language. Pornography, "a fantasy salvation that inspires non-fantasy acts of punishment for uppity females," as one historian put it, speaks specifically to power relations between men and women. For African Americans these relations remain unanalyzed in the light of the empowerment of black male elites like those represented by Thomas, who, since the seventies, have emerged as gatekeepers for the upward mobility of all blacks in the newly accessible corporate, political, academic and business spheres of influence. It is men, not women, who control the sociosexual and professional relationships in the black community. Among other notions that must be dispensed with is the weak male/strong female patriarchal paradigm that clouds so much of our thinking about ourselves.

Implicit in Hill's testimony is the challenge to transcend a past that once protected, but now twists, the deepest sense of ourselves and our identities. The silences and dissemblance in the name of a misguided solidarity must end. A modern and transformative discourse must begin. Anita Hill has broken through. Let us follow.

NOTES

In this essay, Gerda Lerner's definition of gender can be found in *The Creation of Patriarchy* (New York: Oxford University Press, 1987). Secondary sources regarding Phillip A. Bruce can be found in *The Black Family in Slavery and Freedom, 1750–1925* by Herbert G. Gutman (New York: Pantheon, 1976); and Jacquelyn Dowd Hall explores lynching and rape in *Revolt Against Chivalry: Jessie Daniel Ames and the Women's Campaign Against Lynching* (New York: Columbia University Press, 1971). The issue of the *Independent* referred to is dated March 17, 1904; and explications of Sara Bartmann, the Hottentot Venus, can be found in Sander L. Gilman's essay "Black Bodies, White Bodies: Toward an Iconography of Female Sexuality in Late Nineteenth-Century Art, Medicine and Literature," published in Henry Louis Gates, ed., *"Race," Writing and Difference* (Chicago: University of Chicago Press, 1985, 1986). Analysis of sexuality during different periods in American history can be found in John D'Emilio and Estelle Freedman, *Intimate Matters: The History of Sexuality in America* (New York: Harper & Row, 1988). Discussions of the National Association of Colored Women, black women's status in the nineteenth century and Fannie B. Williams's and Ida B. Wells's antilynching campaign can be found in *When and Where I Enter: The Impact of Black Women on Race and Sex in America* (New York: Morrow, 1984). The article by Barbara Fields is entitled "Ideology and Race in American History" and is found in J. Kousser and James M. McPherson, eds., *Race, Region and Reconstruction* (New York: Oxford University Press, 1982). The references to Gordon and DuBois are found in Ellen DuBois and Linda Gordon, "Seeking Ecstasy on the Battlefield: Danger and Pleasure in Nineteenth Century Feminist Sexual Thought," in *Feminist Studies,* vol. 9., no. 1 (Spring) 1983. The quote by Anna Julia Cooper is in her *Voice from the South* (1893), reprinted by Negro Universities Press (New York) in 1969, pp.

68–69. The report cited under the direction of W. E. B. Du Bois, about blacks' health and sexuality in the late nineteenth century, is entitled *Proceedings of the Second Conference for the Study of Problems Concerning Negro City Life,* originally published by Atlanta University Publications. See vol. I, reprinted by Octagon Books, 1968. The explanation of the culture of dissemblance is found in Darlene Clark Hine, "Rape and the Inner Lives of Black Women in the Middle West: Preliminary Thoughts on the Culture of Dissemblance," in Ellen Carol DuBois and Vicki L. Ruiz, eds., *Unequal Sisters: A Multicultural Reader in U.S. Women's History* (New York: Routledge, 1990). The study on contemporary adolescents is "Hungry for an Us: Our Girl Group Talks About Sexual and Racial Identities," by Pat Macpherson and Michelle Fine. It will be published in Janice M. Irvine, ed., *Sexual Cultures: Adolescence, Community and the Construction of Identity* (Philadelphia: Temple University Press, 1993). The women-of-color study was underwritten by the National Council of Negro Women with the Communications Consortium Media Center and is entitled "Women of Color Reproductive Health Poll," August 29, 1991. The book in which Leon Dash published his findings on pregnant teenagers is entitled *When Children Want Children: The Urban Crisis of Teenage Childbearing* (New York: Morrow, 1989). The report issued in 1991 by the National Black Women's Health Project is entitled "Report: Reproductive Health Program of the National Black Women's Health Project."

A. Leon Higginbotham, Jr., is Chief Judge Emeritus of the United States Court of Appeals for the Third Circuit, and a Senior Fellow at the University of Pennsylvania Law School. He was appointed a district court judge in 1964 and a court of appeals judge in 1977. A graduate of Antioch College and Yale Law School, he has taught as an adjunct professor at the law schools of Harvard, University of Michigan, New York University, University of Pennsylvania, Stanford, and Yale. His book, *In the Matter of Color: Race and the American Legal Process,* has received several national and international awards, and he is the author of more than forty published articles. He is at work on *Shades of Freedom: Race and the American Legal Process* to be published by Oxford University Press in 1993, and an autobiography to be published by Knopf in 1994.

Andrew Ross teaches English at Princeton University. He is the author of *Strange Weather: Culture, Science and Technology in the Age of Limits* (1991) and *No Respect: Intellectuals and Popular Culture* (1989). In addition, he is the editor of *Universal Abandon?: The Politics of Postmodernism* (1988) and a coeditor of *Technoculture* (1991).

Manning Marable is a professor of history and political science, University of Colorado, Boulder. His most recent books are *Race, Reform and Rebellion: The Second Reconstruction, 1945–1990* (1991) and *The Crisis of Color and Democracy* (1992). He is currently completing a political biography of Malcolm X.

Michael Thelwell, author of the novel *The Harder They Come,* is a member of the W. E. B. Du Bois Department of Afro-American Studies at the University of Massachusetts, Amherst. He is working on a novel about the Civil Rights Movement.

Claudia Brodsky Lacour teaches literature and theory at Princeton. She is the author of *The Imposition of Form* (1987), a study of Kant and narrative representation, and is currently working on books on the Enlightenment and Romanticism in Germany, France, and England, and on architectonics in literature and philosophy.

Patricia J. Williams is a professor of law at the University of Wisconsin, Madison. She is the author of *The Alchemy of Race and Rights* (1991) and the forthcoming *The Rooster's Egg*.

Gayle Pemberton is associate director of Afro-American studies at Princeton University, where she also teaches American and Afro-American Studies. Her latest book, *The Hottest Water in Chicago: Family, Race, Time and American Culture,* was published by Faber & Faber.

Nell Irvin Painter is the Edwards Professor of American History at Princeton University, where she teaches the history of the United States South. A Fellow of the National Endowment for the Humanities in 1992–93, she is writing a biography of the black feminist abolitionist Sojourner Truth.

Carol M. Swain is an assistant professor of politics and public affairs at Princeton University's Woodrow Wilson School. She has recently completed a book, *Black Faces, Black Interests: The Representation of African Americans in Congress* (Harvard University Press, forthcoming). Her primary teaching and research interests are congressional politics, campaigns and elections, and public opinion. She has had grants and fellowships from the National Science Foundation and the Ford Foundation, and fellowships from the American Association of University Women.

Homi K. Bhabha works on questions of cultural theory, nationalism, colonialism, and literary criticism. He teaches in the Department of English at Sussex University, England, and was a Humanities Council Senior Fellow and Visiting Professor in the English Department at Princeton University. He is the editor of *Nation and Narration* (1990) and author of *The Location of Culture: Collected Essays* (1992).

Christine Stansell teaches American history and women's studies at Princeton University. She has written widely on sexuality and the politics of gender, including the book *City of Women: Sex and Class in New York, 1789–1860* (1986) and the collection edited with Ann Snitow and Sharon Thompson, *Powers of Desire: the Politics of Sexuality* (1983).

Nellie Y. McKay teaches American and Afro-American literature at the University of Wisconsin, Madison. She writes about American autobiography, black women and men, and on issues in feminism and multicultural education.

Margaret A. Burnham teaches law in the Political Science Department at the Massachusetts Institute of Technology and maintains a private law practice in Boston at Burnham, Hines & Dilday, the first firm of African-American women lawyers in New England. She was the first black woman to serve as a judge in Massachusetts. Her recent publications include "An Impossible Marriage: Slave Law and Family Law" (*Law & Inequality*, 1987); forthcoming in 1992 is *Black Women, Their Families and the Law,* a collection of essays in family history and law.

Wahneema Lubiano teaches in the Department of English and the Afro-American Studies Program at Princeton University, and is presently completing work on a book, *Messing with the Machine: Considerations of Modernism and Postmodernism in African-American Fiction.*

Kendall Thomas is a graduate of Yale College and Yale Law School. He is an associate professor of law at Columbia University, where he teaches constitutional law, and law and sexuality. His most recent work appears in the *Columbia Law Review* and the *University of Southern California Law Review.* Thomas is a coauthor (with Guyora Binder and Jonathan Bush) of a forthcoming book, *Recognizing Freedom: On Slavery and Emancipation After Hegel* (Praeger Press).

Cornel West has taught at Yale University, Union Theological Seminary, and Princeton University, as well as at Harvard University and the University of Paris. He is the author of *Prophecy Deliverance! An Afro-American Revolutionary Christianity* (1982), *Prophetic Fragments* (1988), *The American Evasion of Philosophy* (1989), *The Ethical Dimensions of Marxist Thought* (1991), *Breaking Bread: Insurgent Black Intellectual Life* (1991), and coeditor of *Post-Analytic Philosophy* (1985) and *Out There: Marginalization and Contemporary Cultures* (1990)

Kimberlé Crenshaw is a professor of law at the UCLA Law School. She is a founding member of the Critical Race Theory Workshop. Her articles on race and gender have appeared in the *Harvard Law Review,* the *Stanford Law Review,* and the *University of Chicago Law Review.* She assisted the legal team representing Anita Hill and is currently working on a book on black feminist theory.

Paula Giddings is the author of *When and Where I Enter: The Impact of Black Women on Race and Sex in America* (1984), and *In Search of Sisterhood: Delta Sigma Theta and the Challenge of the Black Sorority Movement* (1988). She is currently a Visiting Professor in the Afro-American Studies Program at Princeton University.